Prevention of
Treatment
Failure

Prevention of
Treatment
Failure

The Use of Measuring,
Monitoring, and Feedback in
Clinical Practice

MICHAEL J. LAMBERT

American Psychological Association • Washington, DC

Published by
American Psychological Association
750 First Street, NE
Washington, DC 20002
www.apa.org

To order
APA Order Department
P.O. Box 92984
Washington, DC 20090-2984
Tel: (800) 374-2721; Direct: (202) 336-5510
Fax: (202) 336-5502; TDD/TTY: (202) 336-6123
Online: www.apa.org/books/
E-mail: order@apa.org

In the U.K., Europe, Africa, and the Middle East, copies may be ordered from
American Psychological Association
3 Henrietta Street
Covent Garden, London
WC2E 8LU England

Typeset in Goudy by Circle Graphics, Inc., Columbia, MD

Printer: Edwards Brothers, Ann Arbor, MI
Cover Designer: Naylor Design, Washington, DC

The opinions and statements published are the responsibility of the authors, and such opinions and statements do not necessarily represent the policies of the American Psychological Association.

Library of Congress Cataloging-in-Publication Data

Lambert, Michael J.
  Prevention of treatment failure : the use of measuring, monitoring, and feedback in clinical practice / Michael J. Lambert. — 1st ed.
    p. cm.
  Includes bibliographical references and index.
  ISBN-13: 978-1-4338-0782-4 (print)
  ISBN-10: 1-4338-0782-3 (print)
  ISBN-13: 978-1-4338-0783-1 (electronic)
  ISBN-10: 1-4338-0783-1 (electronic)
  1. Psychotherapy—Evaluation. 2. Mental illness—Treatment—Evaluation. I. Title.

  RC480.5.L338 2010
  616.89'140072—dc22
                                    2009049228

British Library Cataloguing-in-Publication Data

A CIP record is available from the British Library.

Printed in the United States of America
First Edition

Dedicated to Maddie, Spencer, Zippy, Wytie, Pickle, Ethan, Owen, Ryan, Luke, Noah, Tenzin, and Sonam.

CONTENTS

PREFACE

In this book I summarize a program of research aimed at improving the effects of psychotherapy on mental health. More specifically, I focus on reducing treatment failures by identifying persons at risk of deterioration and providing timely feedback to clinicians so that they may take effective action. Addressing the problems of treatment failure and deterioration requires those in clinical practice to regularly monitor patient response, know when it is problematic, and then take the necessary steps to adjust treatment, if possible. The underlying assumption of this book is that this task can be done most effectively by formally measuring a client's mental health and using changes in mental health functioning to predict the final outcomes of treatment. In this book I document the fact that a significant portion of patients who seek and receive professional services do not find relief, and some even worsen during treatment. In addition, I provide reasons to believe that in routine care, practitioners are overly optimistic about the effects treatment is having and fail to recognize impending poor final outcome. The material presented also makes clear that treatment failure can be substantially reduced if systems of care and clinicians monitor the effects of ongoing treatments.

The book should be especially relevant to those who are training mental health professionals because it offers innovations in practice that are particularly relevant to clinical trainees who are just establishing practice patterns. Practicing professionals will probably find the material presented particularly challenging because it suggests that delivering clinical services in the absence of formally monitoring patient treatment response produces inferior outcomes. In addition, it calls into question therapists' clinical assessment of client treatment response and proposes supplementing clinical judgment with standardized methods. It calls for changes in routine practice. The book is also highly relevant to mental health administrators who are charged with overseeing the delivery of services and maximizing benefits to clients. In addition to enabling timely feedback to clinicians about their clients' treatment progress, administrators will quickly see that the information collected can be used to understand and manage clinical services for the benefit of clients.

The procedures and findings presented here are the result of my long-standing interest in psychotherapy and its effects as well as the contributions of many individuals who have participated with me in developing the methods that are presented. In terms of interests, I began practicing psychotherapy in 1971, working with a variety of clinical populations as a full-time practitioner, and today I have a small private practice. My academic career has been devoted in large measure to understanding and integrating research on the processes and outcomes of psychotherapy, culminating in editing the fifth edition of *Bergin and Garfield's Handbook of Psychotherapy and Behavior Change* (a Science Citation Classic).

I also focused on the important topic of measuring change, realizing that what therapists know empirically about treatment effects is largely dependent on how they operationalize and measure change. At the foundation of a scientific understanding of natural phenomenon is effective measurement. This led me to publish an edited volume with Steven DeJulio and Edwin Christensen: *The Assessment of Psychotherapy Outcome* (1983). Other edited volumes on this topic that appeared around this time attest to the tremendous scientific energy devoted to this area in the 1980s.

In 1991, I had an opportunity to put my scholarship to practical use because of the emergence of managed behavior health care and pressure for quality control and accountability for the consequences of delivered services. I was invited to consult with Human Affairs International, a managed care organization providing coverage for a population base of about 5 million individuals living across the United States. The organization was planning to implement outcome measurement within its private sector business and sought my advice about the measures it had decided to use. On the basis of the kinds of information presented in Chapter 2, the organization had made wise choices of scales, but the battery as a whole was impractical. Because the assessments were to be frequently administered over the entire course of treatment, clients would spend nearly as much time reporting their mental health status as they would receiving treatment. This and other practical matters led Human Affairs International to ask me to develop a self-report outcome measure. During the next year, I took a sabbatical leave from Brigham Young University to make outcome assessment a practical reality within this managed behavior health care company. The task was to develop a self-report measure for adults that could measure important content areas in about 5 minutes and that would be suitable for clients suffering from a wide variety of psychological disorders.

During this time, Gary M. Burlingame, also from Brigham Young University, joined me in test development. In this work, we examined how people responded to items, what happened if they repeatedly took the measure, and the like. We also studied the test versions with factor analysis, reliability estimates, interitem correlations, and similar psychometric studies. These investigations and commentary about problems encountered with various versions of the test were collected from providers and patients and used to modify items and procedures. Thus, a measure with a specific purpose was born.

In the context of managed care it was possible to bring my scholarship to bear on the practical matters of measuring change, predicting deterioration and reducing its rate, and improving mental health outcomes in a large system of care. The service delivery climate at the time emphasized reducing health care costs while trying to maintain the quality of care offered to patients. In addition, there was considerable interest in providing standardized empirically supported treatments and best practices. My personal belief about effective psychotherapy is that psychotherapy, at its best, has a large and important interpersonal aspect that is even more significant than the interventions that are used. The patient forms an intersubjective connection with the therapist, and these individuals work together to find solutions and compromises.

With my interest in improving psychotherapy outcomes, the stage was set for developing measures of treatment response, methods of alerting therapists when patients were not responding sufficiently, and empirical studies to examine the extent to which these new methods were helpful. Readers can judge whether they find the methods, procedures, research findings, and interpretation of these findings, as presented here, persuasive enough to inspire them to make changes in routine clinical practice. In this regard, I hope others will be able both to learn from what I and my colleagues have done and to add to it, because much work remains.

I wish to thank those who have been influential to this work. First are the thousands of individuals who allowed us to monitor their mental health through our measures. Without their sacrifice on behalf of themselves and others, none of this would have been possible. Brigham Young University was very supportive of our work, both in terms of providing a facilitating atmosphere and needed finances. In addition, the professionals at Brigham Young University's Counseling and Career Center made many contributions. The clinicians in the center are perhaps the most studied clinicians in the world, and their courage allowing examination of their clients' outcomes and themselves has been an inspiration.

Several members of the university research team have been pivotal in this program of research. David W. Smart was consistently supportive and somehow able to balance all the conflicting needs of all the individuals on the team, the administration, and therapists. He made things happen despite the difficulties. S. Lars Nielsen also deserves recognition. He was a driving force in every way, and without his commitment to measuring treatment outcomes and using the information to affect services we would have never gotten off the ground. His ability to ask important questions, analyze and interpret data, and be open to findings made him invaluable. What a pleasure to work with someone who is so bright, energetic, and dedicated.

In the beginning of the work, Jeb Brown, Wayne Neff, and Jonathan Huefner, of Human Affairs International shared and expanded a vision of what could be done for patients. When Jeb left Human Affairs International and joined Edward Jones, at PacifiCare Behavioral Health, both carried on this work, and both seemed rather visionary in their sense of how to deliver treatment response feedback for the purpose of maximizing treatment outcome on a very large scale. They devoted themselves to managing care in relation to client benefit rather than imagining that the use of best practices would be enough to exercise their responsibility as service delivery specialists.

In addition, I would like to acknowledge my colleague, Gary Burlingame, also a professor in the Department of Psychology at Brigham Young University. Gary is a multitalented person and friend who has made many contributions to this work, especially in regard to the measurement of child outcomes and outcomes with seriously impaired individuals in the public mental health sector. He remains a valued partner and capable advocate of methods for enhancing patient outcome. His organizational and advocacy skills go well beyond the ordinary. He has been central in this work since its inception and continues to help integrate this work into routine care so that thousands of patients in both the public and private clinical settings have seen a benefit.

Many graduate students helped with the research and continue to be dear friends and colleagues. Among them I am especially grateful to the clinical psychology graduate students who completed highly ambitious doctoral dissertations that contributed greatly to this work. David Vermeersch used innovative methods to examine the degree to which each item in our outcome measures was sensitive to the effects of interventions, thereby maximizing our ability to track patient change. Arthur Finch was the first to use statistical modeling for prediction of treatment failure within this research program, improving on the earlier methods. John Okiishi examined the contribution to outcome of the therapist, helping our research group to understand the amount of variability attributable to therapists.

Jason Whipple created a problem-solving procedure and then conducted the first clinical trial on the problem-solving tools. He also played a central role in the first two clinical trials of feedback. Eric Hawkins conducted our fourth clinical trial and tested the effects of providing clients with direct feedback on their progress. He struggled with the tricky business of gracefully telling patients who were depressed that their progress was insufficient for recovery while encouraging them to remain hopeful that solutions could be found. Cory Harmon conducted our fifth clinical trial, a complex study including many experimental groups. Her ability to design and conduct such a study is a testament to what a doctoral dissertation can be when a talented student is given opportunity and support. Karstin Slade replicated the Harmon study but also examined the speed of feedback and its relation to outcome, another highly demanding project. Russ Bailey examined methods of delivering problem-solving feedback. Each of these studies took more than a year of daily data collection. I am deeply in debt to these exceptional students.

Many other professionals and faculty members also were actively involved in many aspects of this work. It has been a pleasure to associate with so many bright and talented individuals who have played a central role in bringing this work forward.

The following individuals made significant contributions to various aspects of the research reported in this summary. Without their help the findings reported here would never have emerged. In addition to benefiting from their intellectual contributions and tireless efforts, I have been lucky enough to have enjoyed their company and emotional support. I am sure they take pleasure in knowing that in the end their work has affected and is affecting the lives of many individuals. Those who helped include

Ed Anderson	Nathan Hansen	Stevan Nielsen
Steffi Bauer	Cory Harmon	Ben Ogles
Joel Beckstead	Quinten Harvey	John Okiishi
Matthew Bishop	Arlin Hatch	Robert Percevic
Taige Bybee	Derek Hatfield	Bernd Puschner
Kara Cattani-Thompson	Eric Hawkins	Matthias Richard
Davey Erekson	Scott Kadera	Dave Sigmon
Arthur Finch	Kevin Kimball	Kärstin Slade
Ann Gregerson	Hans Kordy	David Smart
Eric Haas	Wade Lueck	Glen Spielmans
Corinne Hannan	Wolfgang Lutz	Joanna Thomas
Wolfgang Hannover	Kevin Masters	Richard Tingey

Crystal Ulibarri   Jarred Warren   Dan Williams
Val Umphress   Kit Westbrook   Bob Wong
David Vermeersch   Jason Whipple
Rome Walter   Brady Wiggins

I hope that readers of this book will be able to use the information presented to augment their work with patients and that this book will stimulate and guide further examination of the scientific foundations and consequences of psychotherapeutic practice.

Prevention of
Treatment
Failure

INTRODUCTION

In this book, I present effective methods of increasing positive client outcomes and reducing negative outcomes. These methods rely on systematically monitoring client *mental health vital signs* (i.e., client treatment response), much as is done in medical practice to manage physical disease. Changes in mental health vital signs and especially deviations from an expected course of recovery can then be fed back to clinicians, supervisors, and clients, along with problem-solving tools—decision support prompts for poorly responding clients. In essence, formal assessment-based practice is advocated as an add-on to clinical practice in routine care for the purpose of maximizing client benefit. These methods are seen as a way of merging good science and good practice, thereby making both a priority.

The contents of this book represent the cumulative efforts my colleagues and I have made to change routine clinical practice to make it more effective. Rather than narrowly presenting the methods, they are placed in the broader context of psychotherapy services, psychotherapy outcome, outcome assessment, and trends in psychotherapy practice, research, and policy. The book is divided into four parts.

PART I. FOUNDATIONS AND CONTEXTS FOR A NEW PARADIGM

Chapters 1 and 2 examine historical and conceptual underpinnings of the science and practice of psychotherapy and the measurement of psychotherapy outcome. Together they provide a context for the procedures and recommendations that follow in the remainder of the book. Chapter 1 orients the reader to historical trends in the practice of psychotherapy, training, research, and health care policy. It provides observations on the history of psychotherapy practice and psychotherapy research and its chaotic state as well as thoughts about the problem of relying on evidence-based *treatments* as a primary solution for maximizing patient benefit. Chapter 1 presents the argument that the form of treatment (e.g., evidence based or not) and cost considerations ought to be of secondary importance in patient care, not the primary forces. There is a better, albeit complimentary, way of integrating science and practice for the good of the patient, and it emphasizes measuring and tracking patient treatment response to facilitate cost-effective care.

It would be difficult for the reader to understand what is being advocated with regard to tracking changes in mental health functioning without a clear understanding of what is meant by *mental health* and *change in mental health* (outcome) in the context of historical and contemporary practices. Chapter 1 provides some of this context.

Chapter 2 begins with a brief history of and salient principles for measuring client mental health functioning and ends with guidelines that were used in developing the measures that are presented in Chapter 3. Chapter 2 focuses on the measurement of patient change as it has been and is currently conducted in highly controlled studies and provides a sense of the scientific philosophy and prevailing paradigms regarding outcomes and outcome-based measurement in mental health care. I hope that this chapter will be helpful in illuminating the importance of past efforts and their influence on this program of research. The measurement of change has been a topic of interest, debate, and controversy since psychological treatments have been provided. This is illustrated by documenting that there are thousands of unique assessment devices and that there are important consequences of selecting measures. Improving client outcome through use of the methods advocated in this book (patient-focused research) is contrasted with standard practices. By presenting this material I hope that the reader will understand what has been done formerly and what is usually done in the context of measuring treatment outcome, why new specific measures were developed for tracking client change, and what limitations naturally arise from the practices advocated in this book.

The important (but neglected) topic of the degree to which measures of patient functioning are sensitive to capturing changes that occur when treatments are offered is discussed. Without change sensitive measures, the enterprise of outcome assessment is doomed to failure.

In addition, Chapter 2 introduces the concept of clinically significant change and its central place in evaluating changes made by individual clients. Clinically significant change is a central and essential component of outcomes management and is highly related to the task of selecting change sensitive measures and reporting mental health vital signs to therapist and patient.

At the end of Part I, I hope that readers will understand the importance of measuring the emerging outcomes of treatment, as they occur—an appropriate reaction to the state of psychotherapy practice at this time. It will also be apparent that using vital sign feedback requires measures that capture a number of important client characteristics, quantify meaningful change, are change sensitive, and can be used across a wide variety of treatment settings (clients), theoretical orientations, and professions.

PART II. MEASURING AND PREDICTING
TREATMENT OUTCOME

Chapters 3 and 4 take the reader into specific measurement tools and predictive methods (scientific underpinnings) that are at the basis of providing feedback to providers and patients. Chapter 3 presents specific measures along with a detailed explanation of their purposes and psychometric characteristics. In Chapter 3, normal functioning and clinically significant change are defined and discussed with regard to these measures. Technical properties of tests, although highly important to some, can be deadly boring to other readers who may want to simply skim this material or trust others' evaluations. Administrators of clinical services and policymakers may also find the material presented too detailed and nuanced to spend much time on the characteristics of particular measures. Such material is nonetheless very important because the methods advocated in this book rely heavily on the psychometric characteristics of the various measures that are presented. Although much of this material can be found in technical manuals and published research studies, some of the most important material is provided in detail here because the measures that are discussed form the scientific and empirical foundation for tracking and reporting client outcome.

Chapter 4 presents the scientific foundation for changing routine clinical practice by arguing that clinicians can easily modify routine practice through inclusion of assessment and prediction. First it is shown that when patient mental health is examined over the course of treatment, patterns of change can be seen and that these have profound practical implications. Psychotherapy's effects can be seen on a session-by-session basis and compared with similar patients' treatment response. Chapter 4 introduces the reader to methods that are used to know if a specific client who is being treated appears to be responding to treatment in a typical manner (the way similarly disturbed clients do) or if the client is deviating so much from what is expected to be at risk of treatment failure.

Part II lays the foundation for understanding the experimental evidence presented in Part III of this book. What, then, are the consequences of measuring patient mental health, tracking changes in psychological functioning over sessions of treatment, comparing the changes made by the individual client with similar clients, and providing this information to therapists (and clients)?

PART III. THE EVIDENCE BASE

Chapter 5 presents evidence from three controlled studies that addressed the following questions: Are treatment effects enhanced when therapists receive progress feedback compared with practicing as usual? How large are these effects? The evidence suggests that under certain specified conditions, progress feedback in routine care can substantially reduce deterioration rates and bolster the number of patients who have a positive outcome.

Chapter 6 summarizes methods and findings from three additional studies aimed at further enhancing outcomes for the subset of clients whose mental health vital signs showed an especially problematic change while in treatment. The development of methods of problem solving (i.e., *clinical support tools*) used to enhance outcome for these patients is described. Because the methods evolved over time as a consequence of studying their effects and clinician reactions to using them, their modification is highlighted. The evidence shows that providing therapists with problem-solving tools further reduces deterioration and bolsters recovery.

At the end of Part III the reader will have a grasp of the level of evidence supporting the methods and procedures advocated in this book. The emphasis so far has been on the advantages of progress feedback and decision support for enhancing the outcome of the individual patient who is currently in treatment. The attentive reader will be able to see that the focus of the recommended treatment methods advocated in this book go well beyond measuring outcome for the purposes of accountability. Nevertheless, monitoring patient treatment response on a session-by-session basis results in the accumulation of outcome data on groups of patients and allows agencies and systems of care, such as insurance companies, to examine outcomes from a traditional program evaluation perspective.

PART IV. ILLUSTRATIONS OF PRACTICE-BASED EVIDENCE FOR OUTCOMES MANAGEMENT AT THE SYSTEM LEVEL

Part IV examines some important questions from the point of view of policymakers. Many questions about the general effects of agencies, clinics, therapists, and treatment programs on patient well-being are asked on a daily basis and internal reports generated. Part IV focuses on some important questions of practical concern that have been published and that have implications for effective practice. Chapter 7 takes a look at accumulated evidence on the effects of individual therapists on their clients. The research evidence shows little variability in patient outcome as a function of which school of therapy (e.g., cognitive behavior therapy, psychodynamic therapy) a therapist has allegiance to, while nonetheless documenting considerable variability in outcome across individual providers. The implications of such research are clear. Administrators might be able to enhance outcomes within agencies, across managed care provider networks, and the like, by making referrals to the most effective therapists. Clinical training programs as well as clinics can become more aware of students or providers whose effects on clients are unusually poor and target training efforts to such individuals.

Chapter 8 focuses attention on additional variables that can affect the general outcomes of mental health care. Topics include the relationship between client satisfaction and client treatment outcome, outcome across ethnic minorities, the treatment outcome for individuals treated as couples or individuals, and the consequences of having intake interviews. These studies illustrate the practical value of archival data for managing services within a particular setting of care and perhaps for practice in general.

SUMMARY AND FUTURE DIRECTIONS

Chapter 9 provides a brief summary of the most important points made in the book and suggests future directions for research and practice. It introduces a number of limitations to the methods that were offered and some implementation issues that must be addressed by those who attempt to put into practice current methods of providing mental health vital sign feedback.

This book is dedicated to bringing some of the accumulated research findings supporting the value of these methods to practitioners, graduate students, administrators, and researchers, with the hope that the integration of research, theory, and practice will bring out the best that can be offered to those who seek and expect effective psychological treatment.

I

FOUNDATIONS
AND CONTEXTS FOR
A NEW PARADIGM

1

SETTING THE STAGE FOR FORMALLY TRACKING CLIENT CHANGE: THE CONTEXT OF CARE

Psychotherapy of various orientations and formats has been found to be effective across a variety of adult patient disorders. The extent and richness of this finding extend over decades of research, thousands of treated individuals, hundreds of settings, and multiple cultures. Psychotherapists should be encouraged by the mass and breadth of empirical results that clearly demonstrate that the treatments they provide reduce distressing symptoms, resolve interpersonal problems, restore work performance, and improve life quality for the majority of those who seek treatment (Lambert & Ogles, 2004).

Specific estimates of the percentage of patients who experience a return to normal functioning or reliably improve vary as a function of the degree of initial impairment, diagnosis, personality functioning, and similar client characteristics as well as treatment characteristics. In a review of outcomes reported in a cross sampling of clinical trials investigating the effects of treating a variety of specific adult disorders (2,109 patients) with a variety of specific treatments (89 different treatment conditions) the rate of recovery was 58%, with an additional 9% of patients reliably improved (Hansen, Lambert, & Forman, 2003). In general, researchers can say that about two thirds of adults who enter treatment in these selective studies have a positive outcome in about 14 sessions, but about one third either show no benefit or worsen.

These same authors examined outcome in *routine practice settings* ranging from employee assistance programs to community mental health centers. Outcomes for these unselected naturalistic samples totaling more than 6,000 patients are presented in Table 1.1. As can be seen, the clients did not fare nearly as well as those in clinical trials, with only about one third showing improvement or recovery. The situation for child outcome in routine care is even more sobering. The small body of outcome studies in community-based usual care settings has yielded an overall mean effect size near zero (Weiss, Catron, Harris, & Phung, 1999; Weisz, 2004; Weisz, Donenberg, Han, & Weiss, 1995), yet millions of youth are served each year in these systems of care (National Institute of Mental Health, National Advisory Mental Health Council, 2001; Ringel & Sturm, 2001). Furthermore, although the broader research base that considers controlled studies with children and adolescents is more impressive, significant concerns exist regarding the applicability and generalizability of these studies to usual clinical care (Garland, Hurlburt, & Hawley, 2006; Weisz, 2004; Weisz et al., 1995).

It is apparent from these data and general reviews of the literature that psychotherapy can be quite positive but that improvements are needed, especially in routine care. This is especially the case for that 5% to 10% of adult patients whose decline in functioning is not prevented (or who find treatment iatrogenic; Lambert & Ogles, 2004). In a comparison of children being treated in community mental health ($N = 936$) or through managed care ($N = 3,075$), estimates of deterioration are even higher (24% and 14%, respectively; Warren, Nelson, Baldwin, Mondragon, & Burlingame, 2009). Just as positive therapy outcomes depend largely on patient characteristics, so too do the negative changes that occur in patients who are undergoing psychological treatments. Even so, positive as well as negative patient change can be affected by therapist actions and inactions. The good news is that psychological treatments can be positive, but the bad news is that this is not inevitable; ways must be found to improve patient outcomes, especially in routine care.

PSYCHOTHERAPY IN CONTEXT

Even so, psychotherapy has come a long way from its humble beginnings as a "new movement" at the beginning of the 20th century and continues to be a field characterized by changing emphases, new developments, and considerable vitality (Freedheim, 1992). It is highly regarded in many parts of the world as an indispensable form of treatment for a variety of mental health problems and personal crises, and it remains a popular endeavor in which a

TABLE 1.1
Number of Patients, by Site, Who Demonstrated Reliable Negative Change (Deteriorated), Did Not Demonstrate Reliable Change (No Change), Demonstrated Reliable Positive Change (Improved), and Demonstrated Reliable Change into the Functional Range (Recovered) and Treatment Dosage

Site	Average treatment length		Deteriorated		No change		Improved		Recovered	
	Sessions	SD	n	%	n	%	n	%	n	%
EAP	3.6	2.0	216	6.6	1,911	58.5	645	19.7	497	15.2
UCC	5.8	5.4	115	9.7	684	57.6	239	20.1	150	12.6
Local HMO	3.3	2.4	84	14.1	321	53.9	122	20.5	68	11.4
National HMO	5.1	4.0	40	7.5	258	48.1	153	28.5	85	15.9
Training CMH	9.5	6.8	4	3.2	57	45.6	39	31.2	25	20.0
State CMH	4.1	2.8	37	10.2	219	60.7	74	20.5	31	8.6
Total N = 6,072	4.3	3.5	496	8.2	3,448	56.8	1,272	20.9	856	14.1

Note. EAP = employee assistance program; UCC = university counseling center; local HMO = health maintenance organization in Utah; national HMO = outpatient psychotherapy clinics and practitioners from across the United States; training CMH = clinical psychology training clinic; state CMH = community mental health center funded by state and local government. From "The Psychotherapy Dose–Response Effect and Its Implications for Treatment Delivery Services," by N. B. Hansen, M. J. Lambert, and E. V. Forman, 2002, *Clinical Psychology: Science and Practice, 9,* p. 337. Copyright 2002 by the American Psychological Association.

growing number of professionals and paraprofessionals are actively involved. Judging from the coverage it gets in the media and through the Internet, psychotherapy has become widely accepted.

Despite its growing acceptance as a treatment, psychotherapy enters the current century with considerable chaos and disagreement about many of its aspects. For example, there is great disparity in what is advocated and claimed to be effective with regard to time in treatment. Arguments are made for the advantages of single-session treatment and for treatments that consist of four sessions a week extended over 4 to 6 years. Most research studies examine treatments that are delivered once weekly over 14 weeks.

Although the main purpose of this book is to describe and advocate particular intervention strategies, it is helpful to put these strategies in the context of where the field has been and appears to be going by further elaborating on some divergent viewpoints. In constructing such a context it is obvious that many conflicts are unresolved, and controversy, if not outright chaos, reigns supreme on fundamental issues that impact clinical practice. Chaos reigns with regard to the best way to help and the best way to train those who practice psychotherapy. Such chaos is an expected developmental step along the way as the field moves toward consensus on effective treatment, and this chaos also reflects an early stage of scientific development. The following section provides just a few of the many disagreements about how best to help.

Chaos in What Works

The numbers and types of psychotherapy are large and expanding. A clear trend in psychotherapeutic interventions since mid-1960 has been the proliferation of the types and numbers of psychotherapies used alone and in combination in day-to-day practice. Garfield (1982) identified 60 forms of psychotherapy in use in the 1960s. In 1975, the National Institute of Mental Research Task Force estimated that there were 125 different forms. Herink (1980) listed over 200 separate approaches, and Kazdin (1986) noted 400 variants of psychotherapy.

Research on the effectiveness of each and every emerging form of therapy is nonexistent, raising the issue of the degree to which many forms of treatment are merely experimental. The interest and ability of individuals to create new psychotherapies far exceeds that devoted to studying the effects of such treatments. Parloff (1982), for example, pointed out that "a systematic approach to dealing with a matrix of 250 psychosocial therapies and 150 classes of disorders would require approximately 47 million comparisons" (p. 723). It is not possible for clinical trials research comparing psychotherapies to guide practice. Clearly, the invention of separate psychotherapies takes place independent of research evidence, and the need for research results has not slowed the development and advocacy of various treatment methods. Obviously, in today's world there is little consensus about what works and little reason for consumers of services to feel confident that entering psychotherapy will provide a uniform process.

The proliferation of therapies has been accompanied by a trend for therapists in practice to disavow allegiance to a single system of treatment in the form of a pure theory-based approach. *Eclecticism*, representing the use of procedures from different theoretical systems, and *integrationism*, representing the theoretical joining of two or more positions into a presumably consistent approach, have replaced the dominance of major theories in therapeutic practice. Surveys of practitioners repeatedly indicate that one half to two thirds of providers prefer using a variety of techniques that have arisen from major theoretical schools (e.g., Jensen, Bergin & Greaves, 1990; Norcross, Karg, & Prochaska, 1997). Those therapists who identify with an eclectic orientation feel free to select techniques from any orientation that they deem to be in the best interest of a particular patient. Eclectic practitioners take pride in adapting interventions to client needs—in being maximally responsive to a specific patient.

Unfortunately, there appears to be little consensus among eclectic therapists about the specific techniques that are most helpful, and thus there is little likelihood that two eclectic therapists would use the same techniques were they to treat the same client. Garfield and Kurtz (1977) studied 154 eclectic psychologists and found 32 combinations of theoretical orientations were in use. Jensen et al. (1990) found comparable results but also a trend toward differences in preferred combinations across professional disciplines, with dynamic orientations more often used in psychiatry, systems theories in social work and marriage and family therapy, and cognitive and behavioral approaches in psychology. Such differences signal that professional practice is shaped by training and the world view of faculty but not by a shared and agreed upon knowledge base brought forth by academic disciplines or research results.

Because eclecticism on the whole does not represent any truly systematic approach, research on this "approach" has been minimal (Lambert, 1992), and even if studies of eclectic practice were conducted, the results would probably be nearly impossible to replicate. Nevertheless, eclecticism reflects the fact that there are many diverse theoretical orientations with varying strengths. These strengths are widely recognized and supported by research evidence from the study of single-theory approaches. The movement toward combined use and integration of these approaches is likely to continue and appears inevitable. Consider, for example, the clear trend of cognitive behavior therapy (CBT) to incorporate psychodynamic, client-centered and experiential approaches along with mindfulness practices that come from Eastern religious traditions. It is readily observed that even single-school approaches such as CBT are far more eclectic than the name implies, with substantial variations in CBT practices across the globe and over time. Even within the eclectic practice of CBT there are strong disagreements between theoreticians about the necessity and importance of specific procedures; it does not seem farfetched to suggest that two patients entering CBT treatment offered by different providers might receive nearly nonoverlapping treatments.

Another important development in the field that runs counter to eclectic practice and single-school approaches is research evidence suggesting that the most powerful aspects of treatments are common to all therapies. Theories of change can be viewed as being somewhat independent of the actual activities that therapists engage in. Therapists providing different therapies show a large degree of overlap in their behaviors across treatments so that it is possible to find more variance within name brand therapies than between them. The behaviors and attitudes that are present across treatments have been termed *common factors*. Jerome Frank (1961; Frank & Frank, 1991) considered the notion of the common factors of healing in arenas beyond psychotherapy. In a series of books, Frank explored the similarities in healing situations including psychotherapy, family therapy, group therapy, drug therapy, and religio-magical healing. He concluded that there is an underlying sameness in what appears to be curative for the client, patient, or believer who seeks alleviation from distress. Four common features were proposed. The first was a confiding relationship in which emotions were highly charged and one person was identified as a helper. The second was a healing setting or a place set aside for healing. The third was some sort of plausible framework or explanation for patients' symptoms and a ritual or procedure for their alleviation. Finally, the treatment ritual required both the helper and patient to believe that the healing ritual would work and required participation from both.

These and related common factors can be shown to account for a significant amount of patient change. They include the facilitation of hope; the opportunity for emotional release; the exploration and integration of problematic aspects of one's self; and the giving of support, advice, and encouragement to try out new behaviors and thoughts. Emphasis on common factors, a phenomenon that is distinct from eclecticism, also has the potential for reducing conflicts between particular theoretic views while minimizing the importance of theory-based interventions to a necessary but insufficient component of intervening. This supposition is supported by research findings from component studies. Such studies are designed once a treatment has been found to be effective to identify the necessary aspects of a treatment. Component studies break down the presumed active ingredients of an effective treatment to find out which elements of the treatment are essential (Lambert & Ogles, 2004).

Ahn and Wampold (2001) carried out a meta-analysis on 27 component studies. In their analysis there was no significant difference between treatments containing the purported therapeutic ingredient and those without it. Ahn and Wampold argued that this demonstrates that the specific techniques that are claimed to be the central necessary active ingredient cannot be claimed to be therapeutically beneficial, and the usefulness of therapy must derive from some other source. Certainly, the failure to find specific activities to be essential to effective practice raises questions about the wisdom of insisting that specific techniques be a mandated part of effective practice or be a means of improving effective practice. It is important to have a specific (theory-based) way of proceeding in therapy, but it matters less that it consists of particular school brand techniques.

Polarization resulting from claims of unique effectiveness for specific theoretical orientations has led to conflict within the field that has had positive consequences (e.g., stimulation of research studies, reconsideration of positions) but has also caused considerable defensiveness and slowing of progress (e.g., through the overstatement of claims of success). Eclectic or integrationist and common factor movements reduce polarization and reflect attempts by many practitioners to be flexible in their approach to working with patients but have largely failed to reduce chaos with regard to what is most helpful. Funding agencies and policymakers are moving ahead with mandates to use specific treatments for specific disorders despite the fact that little evidence exists that this is necessary or even possible.

Chaos in Training

One might think that if it were possible to agree on the most effective treatments, then there might be some agreement as to the training and qualification of providers, at least with regard to maximizing the ability to provide some of the common factors. Unfortunately, the practitioners of psychotherapy have increased in number and diversity along with training programs. In America, the practice of psychotherapy, which was at one time the purview of psychiatry, was usurped by clinical psychology by the 1950s and eventually by newer professions, such as counseling psychology, school psychology, marriage and family therapy, social work, addiction treatment, and "licensed professional counselors" (not to mention the extensive use of nursing and paraprofessionals), all of whom disagree about the type and extent of training needed to engage clients in psychological treatment. In the United States, as much as 60% of the psychotherapy that is conducted is now provided by social workers whose master's degree training in psychotherapy, at least from the point of view of psychology, is inadequate. A common practice in Europe and the United Kingdom is to license professionals within psychotherapy training programs that are single-theory based rather than profession based and typically require a master's degree (in these training models the focus of training and credentialing is entirely on the practice of psychotherapy). Given such diverging views about ideal or even adequate training and necessary qualifications (in the United States and abroad), confusion reigns supreme with regulatory bodies and a public unsure about differences and advantages that might come from selecting an available provider. Selecting a provider on the basis of knowledge of that provider's treatment effects is emerging as a possibility, but it is as rare in psychotherapy as it is in medicine to know the likely consequences of being treated by a particular provider or kind of treatment.

THE EMERGENCE OF EVIDENCE-BASED PRACTICE

In recognition of the great divergence and chaos in psychotherapeutic practices, practitioners in today's world are expected to provide treatments that have empirical support. Virtually every professional organization, regulatory body, and health-related government agency has now embraced the idea of evidence-based practice (EBP), a broad term that implies the need for scientific evidence but does not limit evidence to controlled experiments on specific treatments. Ambitious efforts to formally identify and recommend evidenced-based treatment guidelines for specific psychological disorders (agoraphobia, depression, schizophrenia, and obsessive–compulsive disorder) were first undertaken more than 25 years ago in the Quality Assurance Project (1982, 1983, 1984, 1985a, 1985b) headed by Gavin Andrews and associates in Australia. These researchers combined evidence from meta-analytic reviews of outcome research and expert clinician panels to provide treatment guidelines for these disorders. Surprisingly, many of the efforts to narrow treatment choices did not follow this pattern of integrating evidence and instead defined evidence in a much more narrow way by considering only highly controlled experiments.

The most notorious of efforts in this area were those developed by Division 12 (Clinical Psychology) of the American Psychological Association (APA), which created criteria for what constitutes empirical support for treatments. The agenda of the original APA Task Force on Promotion and Dissemination of Psychological Procedures (1995) was to consider methods for educating clinical psychologists, third-party funders, and the public about effective psychotherapies. This task force (now called the Standing Committee on Science and Practice) generated and disseminated criteria for levels of empirical support, identified relevant treatment outcome studies, and weighed evidence according to defined criteria. This resulted in highly controversial lists of treatments that met criteria for different levels of empirical support (Chambless, 1996; Chambless & Hollon, 1998; Chambless et al., 1996) and lists of resources for training and treatment manuals (Woody & Sanderson, 1998). A more practical goal, given the number of disorders, treatment research paradigms, and means of measuring treatment effects, might have been to inform both practitioners and the public of developments in the field based on current research. Lists of "empirically validated treatments" are static and seem to offer a false guarantee of effectiveness, thus possibly doing more harm than good in the long run.

The controversies generated from the initial reports of the task force came mainly from practitioners who saw the report as rigid, if not dogmatic, and as having an agenda that was biased in favor of therapies that were promoted by task force members (e.g., criteria were set up that would give an advantage to highly structured short-term behavioral and cognitive–behavioral treatments advocated by many task force members). But strong criticism came from psychotherapy researchers as well (Garfield, 1996; Nathan, 1998; Strupp & Anderson, 1997). For example, Gavin Andrews (2000) stated his view of empirically supported treatments in a commentary:

> This is not to deny that identifying empirically supported treatments carried out by a profession does not have important political advantages for the profession. Funders, providers, and consumers all like to pretend that efficacy is the same as effectiveness, and lists of empirically supported treatments feed this delusion. (p. 267)

The task force's initial response to these criticisms appeared defensive to many—they insisted on retaining terms such as *empirically validated therapies* (later changed to *empirically supported therapies*; Chambless, 1996) and refused to recognize the limitations of their own work while being especially harsh on practitioners whose practices were often seen as not being based on empirical knowledge. This "methodolatry" did not seem like a hopeful way of bridging the gap between practice and research, creating greater conflict rather than greater consensus. A more recent Committee on Science and Practice pursued a broader view with a three-part agenda (Weisz, Hawley, Pilkonis, Woody, & Follette, 2000): (a) reliability of review procedures through standardization and rules of evidence, (b) improved research quality, and (c) increased relevance and dissemination to the professions and public. The work of this committee was much more circumspect in its assertions than the original committee (Weisz et al., 2000). Nevertheless, the committee continued toward the goal of developing "a single list of empirically supported treatments" and setting "standards of practice" (Weisz et al., 2000, p. 249).

Unfortunately, the very clinical trials designed to identify specific treatments for specific disorders have consistently failed to return much evidence of specificity (Lambert & Ogles, 2004; Wampold, 2001). Meta-analysis—the critical investigative tool to synthesize data—has shown conclusively, from the initial applications of the procedure by Smith and Glass (1977; Smith, Glass, & Miller, 1980) to numerous contemporary analyses, including treatments that are designated as empirically supported, that almost no particular treatment or approach is demonstrably superior to another across or within disorders (Wampold, 2001; Wampold, Minami, Baskin, & Tierney, 2002; Wampold et al., 1997). Further, any trend toward finding differences between treatment approaches in recent studies is conspicuously absent—a result that is contrary to what would be expected with improvements in research design and diagnostic-specific treatment approaches (Wampold et al., 1997).

As mentioned earlier, meta-analysis also has shown that adding or removing purported critical components of so-called demonstrably efficacious treatments does not attenuate their benefits (Ahn & Wampold, 2001). To illustrate, CBT is currently identified and listed as a "well-established" empirically supported treatment for depression by the APA Task Force on Promotion and Dissemination of Psychological Procedures (1995; Chambless et al., 1998). Nevertheless, when researchers in the Jacobson et al. (1996) study— the very study cited by the task force as evidence of empirical support for CBT—carefully and systematically dismantled the approach, removing the cognitive component of the treatment, they found the remaining elements to be as effective as the package containing all of the supposed active ingredients (Jacobson et al., 1996).

Research on the use of treatment manuals has only added to the mounting evidence against specificity. Manuals, like the molecular structure of a pharmaceutical preparation, are supposed to identify the ingredients (e.g., techniques, strategies, principles) responsible for the efficacy of a particular psychotherapy. Judging by their numbers and influence, the guidebooks have been a staggering success. Required for funding and publication of psychotherapy outcome research, the count has been estimated at slightly over 100 different manualized therapies for adults (Duncan & Miller, 2005). And yet, the evidence indicates that adherence to the protocols specified in the manuals does not usually result in better outcomes. In reality, strict adherence may even undercut the action of important curative factors (e.g., the alliance, therapist competence) and result in poorer outcomes (Wampold, 2001).

Currently, psychology as a discipline has increased its emphasis on what is commonly referred to as EBP in psychology (APA Presidential Task Force on Evidence-Based Practice, 2006). Key terms that are used to discuss treatments and the use of evidence reflect the differences and priorities of the various parties involved. For example, empirically supported or *evidence-based treatment* (EBT) refers to the specific interventions or techniques (e.g., exposure-based therapy for panic disorders) that have produced therapeutic change in controlled trials. EBP is a broader term and refers to clinical practice that is informed by evidence about interventions; clinical expertise; and patient needs, values, and preferences and their integration to make decisions about individual care (e.g., APA, 2005; Institute of Medicine, 2001).

Despite the clash between "science" and "practice," the common goal of ensuring positive patient outcomes and the dialogue between advocates of the two positions will, I hope, prove to be in the long-term best interests of the recipients of psychotherapy. Certainly, there have been serious attempts to bridge the gap and find common ground; perhaps the most important of these was undertaken by Alan Kazdin while he was president of APA. Kazdin (2008) noted that

> in the evolution of attempts to place psychotherapy practice on a stronger empirical footing the discussion of preferred treatment and delivery of services has moved into the public domain as part of the larger health-care landscape. There is an effort to provide resources that inform and make available current evidence-based interventions. (p. 146)

For example, on web-based sites a single link can encompass over 30 federal, state, professional, and university sites that enumerate these interventions (http://ucoll.fdu.edu/apa/lnksinter.html). The Substance Abuse and Mental Health Services Administration (http://www.nrepp.samhsa.gov/) has provided an active and ever expanding web-based site that regularly evaluates and adds new treatment options.

One can applaud efforts to provide resources to agencies and practitioners for the purpose of improving services, but it is also clear that some are eager to be more forceful in insisting EBTs be used. There are efforts among third-party payers and states to prescribe what treatments are to be allowed and reimbursed. According to the Campaign for Mental Health Reform—a national group of mental health organizations, including the American Psychiatric Association and APA—the only remaining impediment to widespread use of EBPs is "resistance to change by entrenched and threatened organizational structures, outdated reimbursement rules, lack of effective provider training, and, most importantly, lack of resources" (http://www.mentalhealthcommission. gov/reports/Finalreport/FullReport.htm; see Section 5.2).

Still, it is not difficult to see dangers in prescriptive and inflexible treatments and an evidence base that is short on data showing that such treatments are adequate, sufficient, and generalizable to practice situations. Beutler (2000) provided an overview of efforts to set scientific standards both in the United States and abroad. He noted, however, that scientific standards for practice have been typically based on the subjective impressions of committee members rather than on the evidence itself (e.g., Nathan, Gorman, & Salkind's, 2002, *Treating Mental Disorders: A Guide to What Works*; Roth & Fonagy's,

2005, *What Works for Whom? A Critical Review of Psychotherapy Research*). In addition, serious questions can be raised about who (professionals, managed care agencies, government agencies, or administrators) should be empowered to make treatment decisions when the evidence applies to a specific client. Researchers, practitioners, and health care policy advocates continue to debate the merits of the evidence in behalf of various interventions, what counts as evidence, and how the evidence is to be used and integrated (e.g., Burns & Hoagwood, 2005; Goodheart, Kazdin, & Sternberg, 2006; Hunsley, 2007; Tanenbaum, 2005; Wampold, 2001; Westen, Novotny, & Thompson-Brenne, 2004).

Unfortunately, EBPs have not been studied with great frequency by researchers, and, as yet, not much evidence has been provided for EBP. In routine care, judgments and treatment decisions are made by individual clinicians "informed by evidence," expertise, and patient considerations.

THE PROBLEMS AND PROMISE OF RESEARCH IN CLINICAL PRACTICE

Research on the processes and effects of psychotherapy remains much less known and, to some degree, a minor aspect of the endeavors falling under the rubric of psychotherapy with its emphasis on philosophy, theory, and personal preferences. For example, a study of American psychotherapists found that only 4% ranked research literature as the most useful source of information on how to practice, with 48% giving top ranking to "ongoing experiences with clients," 10% ranking theoretical literature as the most useful source, and 8% ranking their own experiences as clients most highly (Morrow-Bradley & Elliott, 1986, p. 188). There are many reasons for the low impact of psychotherapy research, not the least of which is that most clinical trials research, and even many correlational studies, are aimed at a scientific audience. As highly important as personal experience is in guiding future behavior with clients, it is obvious that cherished beliefs built through personal experience need to be examined through scientific methods and that research findings can play a much larger role, albeit a limited one, in guiding practice.

Psychotherapy research can be seen as a vital and evolving enterprise that can ideally provide a supplementary role in the theory-based activities of therapists, if not a foundation for practice. In contrast to issues that were dominant in the 1950s, 1960s, and 1970s, researchers are now searching for ways of maximizing known treatment effects rather than establishing that there are such effects. We know that for at least a minority of patients the effects can be attained with small doses of treatment, and they are lasting (see Chapter 9, this volume, for elaboration).

Alternate and Complementary Paradigms for Enhancing Treatment Effects: Efficacy, Effectiveness, Practice-Based Evidence, and Patient-Focused Research

Two traditional research paradigms that have dominated conclusions about which treatments are most effective have been described as efficacy studies and effectiveness studies. Together they make up a large share of what is thought of as EBT and practice. Efficacy studies are synonymous with randomized clinical trials. These studies isolate to the highest degree possible the treatment of interest and compare outcomes with control groups of various kinds to isolate the causes of change. Effectiveness studies aim to identify whether efficacious treatments can have a measurable beneficial effect when implemented across broad populations and in other service settings where the degree of experimental control is much less. Generally, an efficacy study reveals, in an optimal situation, treatment effects, whereas effectiveness research finds out if the results still hold under suboptimal conditions, such as when patients are not meeting criteria for a specific disorder. Both these forms of evidence depend on single discrete studies.

The evidence from efficacy and to a lesser extent from effectiveness studies is peer reviewed and published, continuously building and feeding meta-analytic and systematic reviews of specific literatures. This whole process cannot possibly test all the competing approaches and is so slow to emerge in published literature that treatments have been modified before the results of such studies are published and put into practice, a process that can take years, if not decades. Citing the many differences in clients, therapists, and treatment conditions typically observed between research-based services and usual clinical care, Weisz and colleagues (1995) indicated that the most valid answers to questions about treatment outcome and change processes are more likely to come from research in "real-world" service settings than from controlled lab studies.

Efficacy studies tell one about what was accomplished in some setting other than one's own when certain procedures were followed. However, the questionable relevance of such evidence in applied settings has led to other research paradigms that assume that to best maximize treatment effects it is important to study the effects of treatment as continuously practiced in one's own setting of care.

In addition to the term *effectiveness research*, a broader term, *practice-based evidence*, has also been referred to in recent years. Barkham and Margison (2007) provided a definition for this term:

> Practice-based evidence is the conscientious, explicit, and judicious use of current evidence drawn from practice settings in making decisions about the care of individual patients. Practice-based evidence means

integrating both individual clinical expertise and service-level parameters with the best available evidence drawn from rigorous research activity carried out in routine clinical settings. (p. 446)

Practice-based research examines how and which treatments or services are provided to individuals within service systems and evaluates how to improve treatment or service delivery. The aim is not so much to isolate or generalize the effect of an intervention but to examine variations in care and ways to disseminate and implement research-based treatments. The aspiration of this broader based approach has been documented in several articles. *Bridging Science and Service: A Report by the National Advisory Mental Health Council's Clinical Treatment and Services Research Workshop* (National Institute of Mental Health, National Advisory Mental Health Council, 1999), written under the auspices of both the National Institutes of Health and the National Institute of Mental Health, suggests, along with the APA, a vision of the role and kinds of research paradigms most likely to deliver a relevant evidence base for mental health services. They advocate practice-based data as part of the evidence base.

Targeting research to investigate what makes for an *effective practitioner* (see Chapter 7, this volume) can also be considered a crucial component of practice-based evidence because it shifts the focus of attention on to the *practitioner* as much as on the *treatment*. This is also supported by the APA report (APA Presidential Task Force on Evidence-Based Practice, 2006), which considered the role of clinical expertise and patient characteristics, culture, and preferences as the subject of EBP. In relation to the former, the report made clear that the "individual therapist has a substantial impact on outcomes, both in clinical trials and in practice settings" (p.276) and cited a range of supporting research concerning the contribution of therapists themselves (e.g., Crits-Christoph et al., 1991; Huppert et al., 2001; Wampold & Brown, 2005). Indeed, the fact that evidence from successive meta-analytic reviews and from the empirically supported treatment tradition delivers small and apparently discrepant results may, in itself, be sufficient reason to question whether the current model of evidence is best serving psychology's collective needs in terms of the psychological therapies.

As detailed elsewhere (Haaga & Stiles, 2000; Stiles, 2005), the advantage of studying therapists lies within the concept of *responsiveness* (Stiles, Honos-Webb, Surko, 1998). Responsiveness refers to therapist behaviors that are affected by the emerging context of care, including others' behavior. For example, therapists are being responsive when they make an out-of-office assignment based on a client's particular situation or design homework assignments taking into account a client's abilities rather than assuming a standard homework activity will suffice. Effective therapy depends on the therapist's ability to rephrase an explanation that a client seemed not to understand the first time. Therapists and clients are responsive to each other on time scales that range from months to milliseconds. Though far from perfect, therapist responsiveness promotes desired outcomes in ways consistent with a general approach that must be tailored to each individual. In effect, then, the anticipated outcome (the dependent variable) feeds back to influence the delivery of the treatment (the independent variable) on all time scales.

Practice-based studies place few limitations on included data. That is, rather than controlling variables as in a randomized clinical trial, they aim to "capture" data drawn from routine practice such that the subsequent research endeavor is molded to reflect everyday clinical activity. Although there may be no restrictions on data inclusion, there are clear requirements relating to the basic tenets of measurement, namely, the use of well-designed, valid, and reliable measurement systems and procedures. Importantly, experimental control and establishing causal relationships are not the primary concerns. Instead, logic, feasibility, and plausibility govern the planning, data collection, and perhaps most crucially, interpretation of the results. Hence, data can be used not only to investigate the application of results from randomized controlled trials (efficacy studies) to routine practice (effectiveness studies) but also to consider questions of service quality and delivery. One of the key roles of the measurement systems used for this kind of research is to deliver large data sets using standard measures that can be used for a variety of administrative and clinical purposes (see Chapter 8, this volume).

The concept of practice-based evidence includes the idea that research questions are grounded in the practice context and, for this reason, need to be relevant to practitioners and the delivery of routine services in particular settings. Moreover, *practice* is the core driver of the process, driven by practitioners' and managers' desires to provide quality services to their clients. At this level, the issue of *ownership* of the research activity by practitioners becomes crucial as they strive to innovate and generate solutions to their issues. Although provider buy-in is often difficult at first, the fact that practitioners may have an important voice in shaping the questions of interest facilitates their participation in data collection and applications. The information and solutions that arise are of their choosing rather than imposed on them (Chapter 8, this volume, provides several good examples of this process).

At a broader level of service delivery a typical aim of practice-based research often is to *locate* the processes and outcomes of targeted services against a standard or benchmark, that is, against evidence outside of the targeted settings but within a similar delivery service or configuration at a single point in time (e.g., Evans, Connell, Barkham, Marshall, & Mellor-Clark, 2003) or by comparing across years (e.g., Barkham et al., 2001). Such benchmarks become standards that are indicators of quality improvement. Good examples of benchmarks can be found in a special issue of *Counselling and Psychotherapy Research* (Trusler, Doherty, Mullin, Grant, & McBride, 2006), including completion rates for measures, frequency of unilateral termination, recovery and improvement rates, and waiting times. Benchmarking can also take the form of comparing effectiveness in a particular clinical setting against the outcomes obtained in efficacy studies (e.g., Barkham et al., 2008; Merrill, Tolbert, & Wade, 2003; Minami, Wampold, Serlin, Kircher, & Brown, 2007).

Patient-Focused: An Emerging Foundation for Clinical Practice

In contrast to the preceding kinds of practice-based evidence, which are generally used by administrators and managers of services, *patient-focused research* is aimed at enhancing ongoing treatment in real time. This promising line of research is the central focus of this book with early efforts to apply this alternative psychotherapy research paradigm reported in a special section of the *Journal of Consulting and Clinical Psychology* (Lambert, 2001). It has several distinguishing characteristics. The first is that the subject of interest is the individual client. Rather than focusing on group means and *group-based* inferential statistics, this research relies heavily on the individual client's response to treatment and the concept of clinically meaningful change as applied to specific clients (such as those elaborated on by the late Neil Jacobson and his colleagues; Jacobson, Follette, & Ravenstorf, 1984; Jacobson & Truax, 1991 and discussed in Chapters 2 and 3, this volume).

A second important characteristic of patient-focused research is the repeated assessment of client mental health during the course of care. Rather than using pretest–posttest assessments, it is essential in this paradigm that repeated testing occur before the patient leaves treatment. In Chapter 2, issues and practices surrounding outcome measures are discussed. Outcome assessment within patient-focused research requires significant modifications to the procedures that are considered standard in efficacy and effectiveness studies. Assessments cannot be extensive or lengthy. Practicality in measurement is necessary and preferred over comprehensive coverage.

A third important characteristic of patient-focused research is reliance on longitudinal data analytic techniques for modeling expected patient treatment response (or comparable methods) and alerting therapists that the client is not responding to treatment as intended. Reports are generated for the use of clinicians, patients, and perhaps supervisors rather than for administrative reports. The focus is on patient progress and modification of poor progress in real time.

THE INFLUENCE OF REIMBURSEMENT SYSTEMS

Reimbursement systems have changed dramatically and emerged as a powerful force in theory, practice, and research. How providers are reimbursed for their services is an important contextual factor that is influencing both the nature of psychotherapy and its study. Reimbursement systems and calls for accountability of clinical services by the government favor the use of practice-based and patient-based research paradigms. Wielding the power of making referrals and paying for services, managed care organizations have had an enormous influence in the United States by taking on the role of decision makers with regard to which therapists offer services and which therapies they practice. The same trends are emerging in Europe and the United Kingdom. In situations in which managed behavioral health care organizations compete with each other for contracts from employers to manage benefits, price becomes a major issue. Thus, selecting therapists who are the least expensive and deliver the least amount of treatment has been common.

Managed care organizations make policy decisions about treatment practices in the absence of empirical evidence or with the use of selective evidence and in the service of economic concerns or competitive pricing to those who pay the bills (often private companies who provide insurance for employees). Unfortunately, employers may fail to see psychotherapy as a service that increases employee productivity and that actually returns company expenditures. Instead, employers see mental health benefits as a cost that lowers their profit margins, thus the less spent the better. Managed health care companies have emphasized uniform treatments (best practices) as long as the costs are low. Providers who are dependent on income through managed care have lost considerable autonomy in how they practice; just what effect this is having on patient well-being is largely unknown.

In a most remarkable cultural shift, some managed care companies have grasped the idea that psychological treatment is not the commodity that is sold, but instead it is positive treatment outcomes that are sold. In this regard, recounting changes in reimbursement practices, veteran industry observers J. Brown, Dreis, and Nace (1999) noted,

> In the emerging environment, the outcome of the service *rather than the service itself* is the product that providers have to market and sell. Those unable to systematically evaluate the outcome of treatment will have nothing to sell to purchasers of health care services. (p. 393; see also, Herz, 2009; Lambert, 2009)

Managing mental health services on the basis of outcomes and selling services on the basis of measured outcomes is an appealing idea: Paying for what works and paying more for what works better would seem to be in the best interest of patients, but it is not the norm.

There continues to be a disappointing emphasis placed on cost reductions by insurance companies and the government (rather than treatment outcome), but such an emphasis has rekindled the drive toward reducing chaos through an emphasis on brief EBP and, to a lesser extent, psychotherapy outcomes. Irrespective of the problems created by misplaced financial emphasis, the resulting attention to acquiring and using evidence of effective and efficient practice promises to benefit patients in the long run if evidence on outcomes is in fact collected and then translated into policy and practice. But collecting outcome data and using it for client benefit as suggested by J. Brown et al. (1999) is not typical, and managed care has placed much more emphasis on providing the "right" and most often briefest treatments.

SUMMARY

Psychological suffering is painful and widespread. There are effective interventions that at the very least substantially speed recovery. A portion of clients do not respond to treatment or even worsen as a result of the nature of their illness, social support network, failed treatment practices, and the like. Given these negative outcomes, and despite the consequences of economic forces to contain costs, it is important to address negative outcomes and quality of care. Professionals, the scientific community, and policymakers have not always addressed these problems. From the material presented in this chapter it is obvious that at this time in history the imagined solution by most of the concerned parties lies in providing EBPs and more specifically EBTs. It is suggested here that fostering the use of EBTs will not go far in reducing negative outcomes (even if it were possible for every patient to receive one). Practice-based evidence and patient-focused research offer strategies that may be most relevant to assuring the best patient care. Regardless of the treatment a patient is receiving and the type of provider offing treatment, it is important to monitor treatment effects. Before I turn to methods created for this purpose, in Chapter 2, I provide a more general discussion about outcome measurement, a topic that is extremely important if one wants to use outcomes to evaluate and manage treatment services.

2

WHAT IS PSYCHOTHERAPY OUTCOME AND HOW IS IT MEASURED IN CONTRASTING RESEARCH PARADIGMS?

In this chapter, I lay a historical foundation by discussing how psychotherapy outcome has been measured in times past. Issues related to outcome measurement are described along with some important findings that have come from past research. *Ideal* assessment of outcome is presented on the basis of practices that characterize clinical trials and effectiveness studies and contrasted with practices that characterize patient-focused research. The topic of clinically significant change is given special attention as a central feature of patient-focused research. These topics lay the groundwork for understanding the operational definition of the change measures presented in Chapter 3.

EVOLUTION OF OUTCOME ASSESSMENT IN PSYCHOTHERAPY

The problems associated with assessing the changing psychological status of patients in research studies are, as Luborsky (1971) suggested over 35 years ago, a "hardy perennial" in the field of psychotherapy. Historically (and even today) psychotherapists have devoted themselves to defining and perfecting treatments rather than systematically assessing the consequences of these treatments. Personality psychologists have been more interested in stable or static traits and stability than in change. Although occasional exceptions to this trend can be found (e.g., Worchel & Byne, 1964), personality psychology has developed and contributed to psychologists' knowledge about human functioning without expending effort on developing measures for the purpose of measuring change in functioning.

Within the context of studying the consequences of psychological interventions (change), the earliest attempts were characterized by little scientific rigor. These formal attempts consisted of *therapists'* retrospective ratings of patient's status at termination. Despite the lack of scientific rigor, the reader should not assume that psychotherapists in this era were not serious about judging patient change. Psychoanalytic therapists who engaged in research were very ambitious about the goals of treatment and conservative in judging those goals as having been reached; they simply did not use procedures that promoted reliable ratings or independent judgments, as would be expected today. The field gradually moved from sole reliance on these therapist retrospective ratings of general improvement (i.e., is the patient recovered, much improved, slightly improved, unchanged) to the use of outcome indices of specific symptoms that are quantified from a variety of viewpoints, including the patient, outside observers, significant others, physiological indices, and even environmental data such as employment records.

Although the data generated from these multiple perspectives are hardly impervious to methodological limitations, the multimeasure and multisource approach represented in today's clinical trials research is a notable improvement over previous measurement methods that relied solely on the subjective impressions of therapists. The use of operational definitions and systematic collection of data, including follow-ups, is an additional advancement. This improvement has not only fostered the possibility of replicating studies but also has allowed researchers to demonstrate the generality of previous findings across the world. Thus psychotherapy outcome assessment moved from simple posttherapy ratings to complex multifaceted assessments of patient functioning prior to and following treatment.

In the past, attempts at measuring change reflected the zeitgeist of the period. The assessments used in many early studies were developed from Freudian psychology. These early instruments (e.g., Rorschach, Thematic Apperception Test) have largely been discarded as measures of outcome because of their poor psychometric qualities, reliance on inference, and emphasis on unconscious processes that have importance to mainly those who subscribe to a psychodynamic theoretical orientation. The time-intensive nature of these measures prohibits their repeated use, especially over short periods of time (weeks or months). The use of dynamic measures was followed by the application of instruments consistent with other specific theories: client-centered theory (e.g., the ideal self/real self Q-sort technique), personal construct theory (e.g., repertory grid), behaviorism (behavioral monitoring), cognitive behavior therapy (e.g., Automatic Thoughts Questionnaire), and the like. Psychotherapy outcome studies continue to be influenced by the theoretical interests of investigators (e.g., psychodynamic interventions examining quality of object relations), but they also focus on measures that are important to the practical needs of clinics and institutions.

Though prevailing theoretical perspectives are likely to continue to influence the assessment of outcome, a legacy of the theory-based examination of change is a seemingly diverse and plentiful pool of measures that seriously challenge psychologists' ability to make outcome comparisons between theory-specific treatments. An Outcome Measures Project sponsored by the Clinical Research Branch of the National Institute of Mental Health attempted to solve this dilemma—to bring consensus from chaos. The purpose of this project was to identify a uniform or core battery of instruments for studying psychotherapy outcome. As conceived by those involved, additional measures could be added as called for by the interests and questions raised by particular investigators (Waskow & Parloff, 1975). The relative ineffectiveness of this attempt to bring some uniformity to assessment practices across studies and settings is notable by its failure to generate enthusiasm and general use. Even researchers who acknowledged the project were likely to select a few measures from the battery rather than the battery as a whole. They preferred to use measures that they were already familiar with or ones that were more closely aligned with the theoretical propositions they were interested in testing.

Despite this failure to use the battery of tests that was recommended, another attempt at building consensus was initiated some 20 years later—partly because of the earlier failure and partly reflecting changes in the diagnostic classification system—with core batteries being built around diagnostic clusters. In 1994, the American Psychological Association (APA) supported a conference at Vanderbilt University with this objective in mind. Three panels of experts convened with the purpose of developing three core batteries to measure progress and outcome in individuals with anxiety, mood, and personality disorders. Despite the expected divergence in instruments thought useful in each of the three areas, there were many common themes endorsed by each panel. All three panels supported the use of *multiple perspectives* rather than reliance on therapist or client reports. Additionally, each panel concluded that severity of patient distress, degree of patient impairment in life functioning, and frequency of specific and critical diagnostic-specific symptoms represented domains that are essential in measuring outcome (Horowitz, Strupp, Lambert, & Elkin, 1997). Moreover, the groups agreed that instruments comprising the battery should be psychometrically sound, appropriately normed, theory free, and efficient so that they could be routinely applied in clinical settings. Finally, these panels deemed administration of the battery before, midway through, and after treatment as important. They recognized that a core battery that might be appropriate for a clinical trial would not be suitable for assessing change in routine care but did not specify what modifications would need to be made. Although one must consider that this second attempt to build consensus failed on the grounds that the batteries have not been frequently adopted, at least some consensus was reached with regard to basic practices.

The history of outcome assessment (e.g., C. E. Hill & Lambert, 2004; Lambert, 1983) as well as the Vanderbilt Conference suggests several recommendations for the use of assessments in future research studies. Some of the more important of these suggestions are noted here: (a) clearly define the construct measured; (b) measure change from multiple perspectives; (c) use different types of rating scales and methods; (d) use symptom-based atheoretical measures; and (e) examine, to some extent, patterns of change over time. These practices are an improvement over the distant past and are further elaborated on in the sections that follow.

THE CURRENT STATE OF OUTCOME ASSESSMENT IN EFFICACY AND EFFECTIVENESS STUDIES: DO COMMON MEASURES OF OUTCOME EXIST?

As the historical material suggests, attempts have been made to reach consensual measures. One method for doing so is to identify frequently occurring measures in the research literature that used outcome measures. Although all measures of outcome have inherent strengths and weaknesses, an advantage of using *frequently used* instruments is that comparisons between studies examining different interventions are possible, whereas it is more difficult to understand the implications of infrequently used measures. Scores based on frequently used measures can be compared across treatment sites and help unravel whether different outcomes are due to the measure used or some other factor. Despite the merit of reaching agreement about the best measures to assess outcome and the identification of a core battery based on expert ratings, the application of a core battery, and therefore a limited set of measures, remains elusive. In a review of 21 separate American journals published between 1983 and 1988, Froyd, Lambert, and Froyd (1996) summarized instrument usage data from 334 outcome studies. The most frequently used self-report scales were the Beck Depression Inventory (BDI; Beck, Ward, Mendelson, Mock, & Erbaugh, 1961), State–Trait Anxiety Inventory (Spielberger, 1983), Symptom Checklist-90-Revised (SCL-90-R; Derogatis, 1983), Locke–Wallace Marital Adjustment Inventory (Locke & Wallace, 1959), and the Minnesota Multiphasic Personality Inventory—2 (Butcher, Dahlstrom, Graham, Tellegen, & Kaemmer, 1989).

A more recent review of studies measuring outcome in the *Journal of Consulting and Clinical Psychology* from 1995 to 2000 reported the BDI, State–Trait Anxiety Inventory, SCL-90-R, and Inventory of Interpersonal Problems (Horowitz, Rosenberg, Baer, Ureno, & Villasenor, 1988), respectively, as the most commonly used self-report instruments in psychotherapy research (Farnsworth, Hess, & Lambert, 2001). Based on the results of these two general reviews (Farnsworth, Hess, & Lambert, 2001; Froyd et al, 1996), there appear to be some frequently used measures but only within the category of self-report instruments.

Although on the surface the results of these reviews suggest some uniformity in instrument choice, further scrutiny reveals a startling conclusion. Of a total of 1,430 outcome measures identified by Froyd and colleagues (1996), 840 different instruments were used just once and never again during the 5-year period. Unfortunately, the heterogeneous nature of the studies included in this review (e.g., patient diagnoses, treatment modalities, and therapy approaches) cannot account for the diversity of the measures used. Reviews of studies with similar patient populations and treatment interventions suggest a similar conclusion. For example, Ogles et al. (1990) reviewed the agoraphobia outcome literature during the 1980s. Though a majority of the 106 studies included in their review used behavioral and cognitive–behavioral interventions, 98 unique outcome measures were used to assess outcome. E. A. Wells, Hawkins, and Catalano (1988) reported similar findings, identifying more than 25 ways to measure drug *usage* in addiction outcome research.

The seeming disarray of instruments is partly a function of the complex and multifaceted nature of psychotherapy outcome, which is represented by the divergence in clients and their problems, various treatments and their underlying assumptions and techniques, and the multidimensionality of the change process itself. However, the lack of consensus is also indicative of the inability of scientists to agree on how to operationalize valued outcomes. The result, it appears, is that problems associated with measuring the outcomes of psychotherapy promises to be a hardy perennial for years to come.

CONCEPTUALIZING MEASURES AND METHODS OF OUTCOME ASSESSMENT

It can be of some value in understanding past and current outcome practices in efficacy and effectiveness research to have an organizing scheme for viewing outcome measurement. Ogles, Lambert, and Masters (1996), following Lambert (1983), introduced a broad conceptual model that proposed that measures can be characterized by their content, social level, source, methodology (or technology) of data collection, and time frame of each instrument

(See Exhibit 2.1). In the remainder of this section, I discuss each of these factors in detail. Other writers have also made attempts to organize the outcome measurement enterprise (e.g., McGlynn, 1996; Rosenblatt & Attkisson, 1993) but with less comprehensive schemes.

Content

Outcome measures are typically designed to assess specific domains, traits, or characteristics of individuals that are of interest. In the case of psychotherapy outcome assessment, these constructs are generally of a psychological nature, such as the symptoms of depression, anxiety, or interpersonal difficulties. The domain that an instrument assesses is referred to as the *content* of a measure. Depending on the scope of the psychological areas of interest, a measure may address a broad area of content, such as symptoms of many of the most common psychological disorders, or a rather specific domain, such as symptoms relevant to a single disorder. Regardless of the primary content area, three com-

EXHIBIT 2.1
Scheme for Organizing and Conceptualizing Outcome Measures

Content	Source	Technology	Time Orientation
Intrapersonal Cognition	Self	Global	Trait
1	1	1	1
2	2	2	2
*	*	*	*
Affect	Therapist	Specific	State
1	1	1	1
2	2	2	2
*	*	*	*
Behavior	Trained Observer	Observation	
1	1	1	
2	2	2	
*	*	*	
Interpersonal		Relevant Other	
1		1	
2		2	
*		*	
Social Role		Status	
1		1	
2		2	
*		*	

Note. The numbers and asterisks below each area represent the notion that there can be subcategories such as types of intrapersonal events or types of interpersonal measures, etc. From "Choosing Outcome Assessment Devices: An Organizational and Conceptual Scheme," by M. J. Lambert, B. M. Ogles, and K. S. Masters, 1992, *Journal of Counseling and Development, 70*(4), p. 529. Copyright 1992 by the American Counseling Association. Reprinted with permission.

mon broad domains of interest are represented in most efficacy and effectiveness research-based outcome assessments: cognition, affect, and behavior. Thus, although unique measures of depression and anxiety exist, for example, it is likely that these both have in common items that address the cognition, affect (including physiological arousal), and behavior of depressed and anxious individuals.

Selecting an outcome instrument is contingent on the constructs that one wishes to measure. In addition to choosing a measure that emphasizes a psychological domain of interest, the user must determine the components of this domain that are important. Are cognition, affect, and behavior of equal interest, or is a measure emphasizing behavior a more appealing domain? In general, and to the extent possible, all three areas are considered essential to a complete study of change.

Social Level

The first dimension listed in Exhibit 2.1 refers to areas of content that are often addressed by outcome measures. This dimension is divided into intrapersonal, interpersonal, and social role performance. Thus, social level is a dimension that reflects changes that occur within the client, in the client's interpersonal relationships, and in the client's participation in the community through social roles (e.g., work, homemaking). This dimension can be considered a continuum ranging from qualities inherent to the individual such as subjective discomfort, intrapsychic attributes, and bodily experiences to characteristics of the individual's participation in the interpersonal world of intimate contacts to the degree to which and ways in which individuals participate in work, school, and leisure activities. The results of outcome studies are generally considered more impressive when multiple levels of social focus are measured in part because changes in functioning can help determine whether individual progress is deemed meaningful in the context of society.

Social level has important implications for the measurement of change in outcome assessment because it tends to be a reflection of the values and interests of clients, mental health providers, third-party payers, government agencies, and society at large (Strupp & Hadley, 1977). It is apparent that when clients enter treatment they are typically interested in reducing subjective psychological pain, such as panic, extreme sadness, or very frequently disruptions in their primary relations that may be connected to such pain. Disturbances in social role performance, on the other hand, may be more of a concern to others, such as employers who might be concerned with poor work performance or disruptive behavior while on the job. If persons are not able to work, the community at large in the form of government may have to expend considerable amounts of money that may have been better spent elsewhere. It is clear that researchers have not provided an even balance in assessing these areas because outcome assessment even in the best designed studies has overwhelmingly emphasized the intrapersonal level (74% of measures) at the expense of the interpersonal (17%) and social role performance level (9%; Froyd et al., 1996). This is largely due to the difficulty and costs associated with measuring these latter two areas.

As in the content dimension, users must determine which level or levels of social assessment matter most to them. In a community mental health center, functioning in social roles such as work may be considered central because impairment at this level has not only a terrible cost to the individual and her or his family but to society as well. In contrast, in the assessment of clients with eating disorders, eating behaviors (intrapersonal) may be considered most essential because damage to physical health is paramount. Although the literature suggests that most instruments target subjective well-being and symptomatology, it is important to understand the *social level* actually assessed and the inherent value judgments that are associated with these levels. In addition to limiting the conclusions one can make about treatment gains, the social level of assessment provides support for the societal merits of treatment.

Source

In the ideal study of change, all of the parties and sources who have information about a client's functioning are represented. This includes the client, therapist, relevant (significant) others, trained judges (or observers), and societal agencies that collect information such as employment or educational records. Multiple sources are considered superior because of the validity they lend to the estimates of change. Two or more reasonable judgments of improvement are more credible than a single perspective of improvement. Furthermore, there is less concern about the potential bias of independent sources of data such as ratings provided by individuals independent of the therapeutic intervention (Smith, Glass, & Miller, 1980). On the basis of the extant literature, there is good reason to be cautious about interpreting the results of outcome studies using single and potentially biased perspectives of outcome.

The practice of applying multiple criteria measures in research studies has made it clear that multiple measures from different sources do not yield unitary results (Lambert, 1983). Indeed, relying on single sources of assessment can result in questionable conclusions. For example, a specific treatment used to reduce fears may result in a decrease in behavioral avoidance of the feared object (provided by observers) while having seemingly little effect on the self-reported level of discomfort associated with the feared object (provided by the patient; Mylar & Clement, 1972; Ross & Proctor, 1973; Wilson & Thomas, 1973). Conversely, despite marked improvement in self-reported fear, an intervention may have no effect on a physiological indicator of fear (Ogles et al., 1990). For example, in a review of the effects of relaxation training, Glaister (1982) found a similar departure from agreement. Compared with exposure techniques, relaxation training primarily affected *physiological* indices of change, proving superior to other treatments in 11 of 12 outcome comparisons. In contrast, using patients' verbal reports of self-improvement, exposure techniques were superior in 28 of 38 comparisons. Only behavioral assessments of change that included assessor ratings revealed no differences between the relaxation and exposure conditions.

The lack of convergence between measurement sources is further supported by older factor analytic studies that have examined the agreement between numerous outcome measures (Cartwright, Kirtner, & Fiske, 1963; Forsyth & Fairweather, 1961; Gibson, Snyder, & Ray, 1955; Shore, Massimo, & Ricks, 1965). Pilkonis, Imber, Lewis, and Rubinsky (1984) collected trait and symptom data from clients, therapists, expert judges, and significant others using 15 different scales. A factor analysis of these data reduced to three factors most closely representing the source of the data rather than the content of the scales; in other words, it matters who does the ratings.

To investigate assessment source in efficacy and effectiveness studies, Lambert and McRoberts (1993) examined 116 outcome studies reported in the *Journal of Consulting and Clinical Psychology* between 1986 and 1991. The outcome measures used were classified into five source categories: self-report, trained observer, significant other, therapist, and instrumental (e.g., societal records and physiological recording devices). A self-report scale was used alone or in combination in over 90% of the studies, with 25% of the studies using client self-report data as the single source of evaluation. A combination of two data sources—self-report and observer ratings, self-report and therapist ratings, self-report and instrumental—was used simultaneously in 20%, 15%, and 8% of the studies, respectively. Significant other ratings were rarely used, occurring alone or in combination with other data sources in approximately 9% of the reviewed studies. In contrast to the general pattern, 30% of the studies used six or more instruments to reflect changes in patients. The most ambitious effort used a combination of 12 distinct measures to assess change following psychotherapy.

Although the ratings of therapists, trained raters, significant others, and institutional records as well as other methods such as brain imaging are ideal for understanding patient change, there are considerable costs in the adoption of multiple perspectives. Moreover, it is often impractical to obtain assessments from others given the additional effort required from already burdened parties (e.g., therapists). Even in the best-designed efficacy studies the ideal often cannot be reached. Arguably, it is the patients' perspective that matters most and is most easily obtained (Ogles, Lambert, & Fields, 2002); thus, it is not surprising that the most popular source for outcome data has been the client.

The lack of consensus between sources of outcome measures coupled with the financial and practical consequences associated with implementing multiple sources of data presents a challenging dilemma for those interpreting the findings of research. It is important for researchers and clinicians alike to consider the advantages of diverse perspectives while acknowledging the consequences of using limited sources. Given the importance of assessing the patients' perspective of change, researchers seldom question the necessity of including the patient's perspective, but how many and which additional sources are included in the assessment of outcome remain open questions.

Technology of Change Measures

In addition to selecting different sources to reflect change, the technology (methodology) used to develop measures impacts its assessment (Smith et al., 1980). Exhibit 2.1 lists several different technologies or procedures that have been used to measure outcome. These include global ratings (e.g., measures of client satisfaction), specific (specific symptom indexes), observation (behavioral counts), and status (physiology, neuroimaging, institutional records) procedures.

Because procedures for collecting outcome data on patient change usually vary simultaneously on several dimensions, it is difficult to isolate the aspect of the measurement approach that may be the most important. An underlying limitation relevant to the technology of measures is the extent to which raters of outcome are able to consciously manipulate their responses. This factor is also connected to the advantages and disadvantages inherent to global, specific, behavioral, and institutional assessments of outcome.

Global Ratings

Traditionally, global ratings of outcome have consisted of rating of overall improvement rather than the overall severity of patient distress at the time of its assessment. Generally, patients are requested to respond to questions that broadly assess their perceived progress in treatment, but therapists and significant others can also provide these ratings. Moreover, global ratings typically provide a summary evaluation of the complex matter of patient functioning or general well-being using one or a few items. For example, patients may be asked to rate their level of agreement with the statement, "Therapy helped me feel less distressed."

There are a number of advantages to using a global approach. First, complex constructs can be assessed with simply a few items. Because global ratings are easily designed, they serve as a flexible approach to measure nearly any construct of interest (Kazdin, 1998). In addition, global ratings are adaptable to various sources of outcome.

However, global measures have many limitations. Because global measures are usually face valid (questions ask specifically about improvement), it is not difficult for respondents to consciously manipulate their responses; this is even likely to be the case if such questions are asked in front of the therapist. Expectancy effects loom large under such circumstances. Furthermore, because the construct of interest is global, only general rough conclusions can be drawn from the findings. The lack of psychometric qualities (such as reliability) is an additional limitation of most global ratings. As a result, it is frequently unclear whether a global rating is measuring what it purports to measure. The well-known survey conducted by *Consumer Reports* (CR; 1995) represents the advantages and disadvantages to a typical global measure. The findings of this survey indicated that respondents were satisfied and benefited greatly from psychotherapy and that longer more intense therapy was more "effective." The psychometric properties of the items used in this survey and the retrospective nature of data collection (asking patients to reflect on how much they improved as a result of therapy that had been terminated years ago), prevented definitive conclusions about the meaning of these findings from the point of view of a number of commentators (e.g., Hollon, 1996; Jacobson & Christensen, 1996).

Nielsen et al. (2004; further discussed in Chapter 8, this volume) replicated the survey among a group of clients who provided both the retrospective rating of satisfaction and improvement using the CR global items as well as pretherapy, posttherapy, and follow-up ratings on a 45-item scale of more specific disturbance, collected both prospectively and retrospectively. In this study, the CR retrospectively perceived emotional change scores sharply overestimated prospectively measured change on the basis of the more specific Outcome Questionnaire-45 (OQ-45). They also found that treatment length was correlated with satisfaction but not with CR-item perceived change, CR-item perceived problem resolution, or with OQ-45 measured change. Overall, it appears that outcomes based on retrospective ratings and broad scales meant to provide overall global evaluations of change overstate the benefits of therapy, are overly optimistic, and are too general, at least in relation to the standardized scales typically used in psychotherapy research.

Specific Ratings

Because of the many deficiencies that characterize general outcome measures (e.g., global therapist ratings) used for posttreatment evaluations, they have all but disappeared as outcome measures in psychotherapy research protocols. Their reemergence can be observed in inpatient practice and other settings, often taking the form of satisfaction ratings. Typically these are "homemade" devices used in one study or after a single treatment session, making it difficult to evaluate their adequacy and meaning. A number of measures meeting the global rating objective of an overall assessment of outcome have been developed. Unlike global ratings in which instruments rely on one or several general items, specific instruments use numerous specific items, usually 30 to 70, to address the severity of patient disturbance before, during, and after treatment (Ogles et al., 2002).

Specific ratings of outcome also assess particular (e.g., depression) or multiple psychological constructs of interest (psychiatric symptoms). Additional differences between global and specific rating approaches are the number of items used to measure the construct of interest and psychometric information demonstrating the reliability and validity of the scales. Specific ratings typically include multiple items to measure the domain of interest, and the construct validity of the items often has been supported. Although longer in length (often 10–15 min) than global ratings, the relative brevity of these instruments facilitates data collection. The mode of assessment for many of these specific scales is self-report, which is conducive to the accumulation of information that only patients can provide (their subjective experience of psychic pain). Consequently, specific assessments typically provide clinically relevant and meaningful information.

Like global scales, however, specific scales of outcome are subject to distortion. Most of these instruments are face valid, with their purpose being obvious (e.g., how sad have you felt this last week?). However, because these scales focus the person's attention on the status of specific symptoms and signs, as opposed to general questions about the benefits of therapy, there is likely less risk of patients distorting their responses to please or meet the expectancies that are created by care settings, practitioners, or researchers. Specific scales also produce a more complicated assessment of functioning because patient ratings across many specific items can show areas of improvement and deterioration within a single scale. For example, with the BDI it is possible to examine changes in somatic expressions of depression separately from mood. Thus, specific scales provide a much richer source of data.

Observer Ratings

Ratings based on observers' observations, often applied in behavior therapy with children, offer an important methodology for outcome assessment. The frequency with which specific behaviors are performed is often the goal of treatment or, at least, of relevance to treatment goals. Provided that observer ratings have little influence on the behavior of those watched, observational ratings offer an objective assessment of an individual's behavior at the time of its occurrence. An advantage of observational procedures is that persons' actual behavior can be observed in the context of realistic situations, allowing generality of the effects of treatment to a person's natural environment (e.g., classroom behavior). In addition, behaviors of interest can be formally defined and customized to the individual's presenting concerns. Furthermore, observational procedures are especially useful in situations in which the client is unable to provide a valid self-report (e.g., children, adolescents, people with serious disabilities).

Although observational approaches are among the most relevant assessments of outcome, there are limitations to their use. Change in cognition and affect is frequently of interest as well as behavior, two constructs that may be essentially unobservable by others. Furthermore, some overt behaviors occur infrequently (e.g., particular phobias) or typically are not performed in public (e.g., sexual performance). In addition, it is not always accurate to assume that the performance of an individual in a single situation is representative of how that person customarily interacts or reacts when under stress.

Status

The last approach to be introduced is referred to as *status* and represents measures of outcome that are less subject to distortion. For the sake of this discussion, status is composed of physiological, neuroimaging, and institutional assessments of outcome. For example, devices that measure physiological arousal (e.g., heart rate, blood pressure) can be used to determine the effectiveness of treatments designed to reduce symptoms of anxiety. There is emerging interest in changes in brain imaging measures that are now becoming widespread (Grawe, 2007). Challenges to this approach are the cost of assessment equipment and the expertise required to reliably read images, not to mention the meaning of such changes. Though individuals are less able to consciously manipulate their responses to such procedures, care must be taken to ensure that the measurement setting, which is almost always an analogue, is not affecting estimates of outcome. Furthermore, like many measures of outcome, it is important to scrutinize the construct validity of physiological and neuroimaging assessments (Tomarken, 1995).

Institutional assessments of outcome are, perhaps, the least subject to conscious distortion related to psychotherapy because they are collected for other purposes and remote from psychotherapy settings. Typical examples of such measures are agency records that provide information relevant to the construct of interest. For example, juvenile criminal records prior and subsequent to a therapeutic intervention can be reviewed to evaluate the success of treatment, or grade point average across semesters can be examined to understand academic recovery following treatment. A particular advantage of this approach is that the consequences of overt behavior can be evaluated in actual life circumstances. In addition to being relevant to the individual receiving treatment, it is often relatively simple to generalize the importance of findings to society in general. However, in the case of institutional assessments, specific indicators of outcome are subject to the data collected and may represent a combination of many related constructs, including the accuracy or completeness of the data (e.g., arrest records). For example, in a recent study examining the effects of psychotherapy on work productivity, Trotter et al. (2009) found supervisor ratings of employee work performance to be useless because all employees were rated at the highest level possible despite other evidence that their performance was below expectations. This is not an uncommon problem because no efforts are expended to make such ratings reliable and valid, as would be done if they were subjected to the usual scientific standards. Many other examples could be given. For example, readmission to a hospital, despite the fact that it is seriously needed, may not occur because of a lack of financial resources rather than set criteria for readmission. Or standards for hospital admission may dramatically change, and readmission rates are a reflection of policy changes rather than patient change.

The preceding characteristics were presented according to how susceptible each is to manipulation by the individual being rated and also included the strengths and limitations of these four basic procedures for measuring outcome. Additionally, an underlying quality of the methodology used in assessing outcome is the general flexibility of the approach. The global rating approach provides the evaluator of outcome with the most freedom, requiring only the construction of a few items that purportedly measure the desired construct. In contrast, a status rating approach is the least flexible because an evaluator is confined to the precision of developed data bases or the availability and relevance of collected data. A careful weighing of the procedural strengths and limitations addressed in this discussion will facilitate the selection of outcome measures and address some of the limitations connected with their use.

Time Orientation

The final characteristic introduced to help conceptualize instruments, *time orientation*, refers to the extent to which an instrument measures psychological traits or states. Traits are defined as enduring characteristics that tend to distinguish one individual from another, whereas states reflect attributes that temporarily describe an individual. The relevance of this characteristic is that it governs the time frame to which assessments refer. Instruments assessing less malleable individual qualities are designed for infrequent use (i.e., pre- and postassessment), provided that the length of the time interval in between measurements allows for change in stable characteristics. In contrast, more frequent intervals of assessment are possible with instruments developed to measure states. Such assessments also allow researchers to study patterns of change over time because they can be collected at multiple times during psychotherapy.

Certainly in some situations it is important to measure frequently. For example, in treating substance abuse, daily or weekly monitoring of blood or urine samples is important, especially if the information is going to be used to modify treatment. In studying children who are delinquent (and rearrest is an indicator of outcome), however, it makes no sense to reassess frequently—a more suitable time frame might be 6 months or 1 year. It is extremely important for those measuring outcome to consider if they are measuring things that can change over the relatively brief periods most individuals are in treatment. These are design issues of obvious importance, but time frame emerges in more subtle forms as well. Test instructions often provide time periods to be considered when answering questions. The most obvious example can be found in the State–Trait Anxiety Inventory in which state anxiety is conceptualized as momentary arousal, and trait anxiety is seen as a stable disposition to react to some situations. The actual items making up the original scales are identical; the state scale asks how a person is feeling right now, whereas the trait scale seeks to quantify how people generally feel by getting at the frequency of anxiety feelings looking back. In most psychotherapy studies it is the trait scale that is used as an outcome indicator, whereas in laboratory studies that are intended to provoke anxiety, the state scale is more useful.

Despite test instructions that may call for the person to reflect back over the past week or the past 2 weeks, it is hard to argue that scores of individuals would vary markedly given either of these instructions. Only the most (overly) conscientious individual will attempt to count back just 7 days or 14 days. Most people will take both time frames as indicating the recent past. But at some point, time frame will make a difference and the time orientation individuals take on will affect the answer they give. The way the items themselves are worded can provide a time frame that can affect the degree to which measuring change becomes impossible. Consider the statement "I have never been arrested" or "I have had a time in my life when my thoughts were coming so fast that I could not stay organized." Either statement may be highly valuable diagnostically, but each has a time frame that makes measuring change impossible. It is possible to know how likely it is that an assessment question will reflect changes in functioning. Certainly in the case of the State–Trait Anxiety Inventory, dozens of studies were devoted to this topic (Spielberger, Sydeman, Owen & Marsh, 1999), and much is known. Unfortunately, much less is known about other measures with regard to time orientation.

CHANGE SENSITIVITY: A CONSTRUCT OF UNIQUE IMPORTANCE TO OUTCOME ASSESSMENT

As the preceding discussion suggests, a central issue in outcome assessment is the degree to which different measures and measurement methods are likely to reflect changes that actually occur as a result of participation in therapy. Many factors influence the sensitivity of the items composing a measure, including the relevancy, scaling approach, stability of constructs assessed, and ability of individual items to detect change at the extremes of the construct of interest. For example, items assessing abuse of substances in a general mental health sample rarely show any endorsement, and therefore it is difficult to show any improvement for groups and individuals on these items are more difficult on the scale as a whole. In general, not all items within an outcome instrument are relevant to each individual. However, the sensitivity of a specific instrument is contingent on the endorsement of a sufficient number of items relevant to the individual; consequently, a sensitive instrument is likely to have few irrelevant items.

Additionally, the scale used to document responses determines the change sensitivity of an instrument. Categorical (e.g., *yes–no*) or limited scale range minimizes the potential detection of change (Lipsey, 1990). As mentioned earlier, the static nature of some constructs also prohibits the measurement of change. For the purposes of psychotherapy outcome, change that occurs on a specific item during the course of treatment should reflect an actual change in functioning manifest in the patient. In addition, the positive change measured in treated samples of patients should exceed the positive change measured in untreated patients. In essence, items that fail to distinguish the improvement made in patients and nonpatients are not ideal because the change scores may simply reflect spontaneous remission. In Chapter 3, I address this topic further and provide a method for gaining greater understanding of test characteristics.

A common approach to determining the sensitivity of an *instrument* is to focus on the global index it produces. From a pre- and posttest assessment of outcome, one can calculate an effect size within a group of individuals. An advantage of an effect size is that it is a metric that transforms the magnitude of the difference between assessments of outcome into standard deviation units. As a result, comparisons between independent measures are presumably possible because the scores are calibrated using the same standard score unit. A growing body of meta-analytic literature suggests that there are reliable differences in the change sensitivity of instruments (Lambert, Hatch, Kingston, & Edwards, 1986; Ogles et al., 1990) and that it is not safe to assume that effect size statistics accurately standardize effect sizes across studies using different measures—a basic purpose of the statistic.

An Illustration of Differences in Measure Sensitivity to Treatment Impact

Table 2.1 presents data from the Ogles et al. (1990) review of agoraphobia outcome studies. These table data illustrate the remarkable disparity in estimates of improvement that can occur with different instruments or methods of measurement. The two extremes based on the Fear Survey Schedule (mean effect size [ES] = 0.99) and Phobic Anxiety and Avoidance Scale (mean ES = 2.66) suggest different conclusions. The "average patient" taking the Fear Survey Schedule moved from the mean (50th percentile) of the pretest group to the 16th percentile after treatment. In contrast, the average patient being assessed with the Phobic Anxiety and Avoidance Scale moved from the 50th percentile of the pretest group to the .001 percentile of the pretest group following treatment. If a study estimated treatment effects by using the Fear Survey Schedule, the treatment would not look as effective as it would look if the measure of phobic anxiety and avoidance had been chosen.

Comparisons between the measures depicted in Table 2.1 are confounded somewhat by the fact that the data were aggregated across all studies that used either measure. However, similar results can be found when only studies that gave both measures to a patient sample were aggregated. Examining data comparing three frequently used measures of depression, the BDI and Zung Self-Rating Scale for Depression (ZSRS), both self-report inventories, and the Hamilton Rating Scale for Depression (HRSD), an expert judge rating Lambert et al. (1986), found discrepant results. The meta-analytic results suggest that the most popular dependent measures used to assess depression following treatment provide reliably different pictures of change. It appears that the

TABLE 2.1
Overall Effect Size, Mean, and Standard Deviation by Scale

Scale	n[a]	M	SD
Phobic anxiety and avoidance	65	2.66	1.83
Global Assessment Scale	31	2.30	1.14
Self-rating severity	52	2.12	1.55
Fear Questionnaire	56	1.93	1.30
Anxiety during Behavioral Avoidance Test	48	1.36	.85
Behavioral Avoidance Test	54	1.15	1.07
Depression measures	60	1.11	.72
Fear Survey Schedule	26	.99	.47
Heart rate	21	.44	.56

Note. Adapted from "Agoraphobia Outcome Measurement: A Review and Meta-Analysis," by B. M. Ogles, M. J. Lambert, D. G. Weight, and I. R. Payne, 1990, *Psychological Assessment: A Journal of Consulting and Clinical Psychology, 2*, p. 321. Copyright 1990 by the American Psychological Association.
[a]n = the number of treatments whose effect were measured by each scale.

HRSD, as used by trained professional interviewers, provides a significantly larger index of change in depressive symptoms than the BDI and ZSRS. Because the amount of actual improvement that patients experience after treatment is never known, these findings are subject to several different interpretations. It may mean that the HRSD overestimates patient improvement; it could be argued just as easily, however, that the HRSD accurately reflects improvement and that the BDI and ZSRS underestimate the amount of actual improvement. It is also possible that true change falls somewhere in between the HRSD estimate and estimates provided by the BDI and ZSRS. In any case, if the HRSD is selected as an outcome measure (as is typical of studies examining psychoactive medications), treatments would appear maximally effective. These findings go against clinical lore by demonstrating that self-reported estimates of improvement do not exaggerate treatment effects (compared with expert ratings of functioning).

Summary of Change Measures and Conclusions

Although it is virtually impossible to eliminate the various challenges that are faced when measuring outcome or to choose the perfect instruments to measure change, by understanding how content, social level, source, technology, and time orientation affect estimates of patient improvement, users of outcome instruments will be less likely to misinterpret their findings and the comparative meanings of those findings. Moreover, because not all instruments are equivalent in their ability to reflect change, an awareness of the complexity inherent in measuring it sheds further light on the strategy of choosing appropriate instruments. Among the things that have been learned from assessing outcomes in efficacy and effectiveness studies, the following tentative conclusions are offered here (the interested reader is invited to read C. E. Hill & Lambert, 2004, for more complete documentation): (a) Therapist and expert-judge-based data, even when such raters are not aware of the treatment status of clients, produce larger effect sizes than self-report data, data produced by significant others, or institutional records; (b) gross ratings of change produce larger estimates of change than ratings on specific symptoms; (c) change measures based on the specific targets of therapy (such as individualized goals or anxiety-based measures taken in specific situations) produce larger effect sizes than more distal measures, including tests of personality; (d) life adjustment measures that tap social role performance in the natural setting (e.g., grade point average) produce smaller effect sizes than more laboratory-based measures; (e) measures collected soon after therapy show larger effect sizes than measures collected at a later date; and (f) physiological measures, such as heart rate, usually show relatively small treatment effects compared with all other ratings.

MEASURING CHANGE IN PATIENT-FOCUSED
AND PRACTICE-BASED EVIDENCE PARADIGMS

Outcome measurement approaches the ideal in well-funded efficacy and effectiveness studies. Practices within patient-focused research and practice-based evidence studies in routine care do not. The research questions addressed in such studies are very different, as are funding sources. In patient-focused research outcome assessment is conducted for the purpose of enhancing ongoing treatment by providing feedback to clinicians. In practice-based evidence studies the assessments that are thus collected are summed across groups of patients for the purpose of improving care at the system level. Outcome measurement in these domains has shifted from being largely a research enterprise carried out by scientists to a part of routine care mandated through public policy demands for accountability, the desire of agencies to improve and change their routines, and sometimes, albeit rarely, by practitioners themselves (see, e.g., Clement, 1996). Measures used in routine care settings are typically self-report, brief (5–10 min), symptom based, and given on repeated occasions. Although there is a case for multiple sources and methods, it has to be said that the implementation of multimethod, multisource measurement is unrealistic in routine care settings and in all but the best funded research protocols. The rule of thumb for routine care is to succeed with measuring outcome from at least a single source, the patient, before attempting to collect outcome information from multiple sources. The development of easily administered, inexpensive, and multiple-sourced measures of outcome is beyond the reach of most agencies even with all the advances in information technology.

From the principles laid out in the prior section, one can classify the usual procedure in these routine care studies as likely to measure *content* that includes symptoms in the form of affect, thoughts, and behaviors (including physiological functioning) at the intraindividual *social* level from a single *source* (self-report) with a *technology* that gets at the specific rather than gross level and with a *time orientation* that calls for recent functioning (over the last week). This is the general picture. Variations, of course, exist. For example, Australia has adopted a system that relies on clinician ratings of client functioning in the public health sector and only recently added a self-report measure of anxiety and depression. Although outcome assessment is not as widespread as desirable, several systems have gained some popularity.

Illustrative Routine Care Outcome Measurement Practices

Several outcome measurement systems have been developed and are suitable for tracking patient treatment response and providing mental health vital sign information. These measures were developed for use in routine care, where brevity is at a premium, rather than for purely research purposes.

COMPASS

The first outcome management system was developed by Howard, Moras, Brill, Martinovich, and Lutz (1996), using an instrument known by the acronym COMPASS. The COMPASS includes 68 items broken down into three scales: Current Well-being, Current Symptoms, and Current Life Functioning. These scales are summed, and the total score designated the Mental Health Index. Instructions call for clients to rate items on a 5-point scale about their functioning in the preceding month. Supporting scales include a measure of the therapeutic bond and presenting problems and their significance to the client, including clinician ratings on the *Diagnostic and Statistical Manual of Mental Disorders* (4th ed., text rev.; American Psychiatric Association, 2000) Global Assessment of Functioning scale and Life Functioning. Clients and therapists are expected to complete the measure monthly throughout the course of treatment.

Using a variety of statistical modeling techniques, this feedback system provides an expected treatment response. It is modeled for each client on the basis of degree of initial disturbance and several client variables such as chronicity of problems. Significant negative deviations from the expected treatment response are used as one aspect of alerting therapists to potential treatment failure. In addition, the expected treatment response model uses several indicators of poor outcome. For instance, it monitors the discrepancy between client reported (good) health and clinician reported (poor) health and the failure to improve reliably by the 12th session. Lueger et al. (2001) provided ample data on the ability of this system to identify treatment failures. As an advantage, the COMPASS provides for the collection of data from both clinician and client. Disadvantages of this system entail the amount of time required of therapists and clients to complete forms, the need to submit assessments to a third party for scoring and interpretation, and its time orientation. In many treatment settings the last drawback is especially important because in many clinical settings 50% of clients will have terminated after 4 weeks.

CORE

Barkham and colleagues (2001) created the Clinical Outcomes in Routine Evaluation (CORE) system widely used in the United Kingdom. The CORE consists of three independent tools. The CORE Outcome Measure (CORE-OM) is a 34-item client self-report questionnaire administered before and after therapy (10- and 5-item versions are also commonly used for tracking treatment response on a more frequent basis). Ratings are rendered on a 5-point scale regarding how the person has been feeling over the last week. It provides a score indicating current global psychological distress. Pre-and post-treatment scores indicate how much change has occurred while a client has been in treatment. The second tool, a Therapy Assessment Form, is completed by practitioners to profile the client, presenting concerns and a pathway into treatment. An End of Therapy Form is also completed by the practitioner. It highlights the process during therapy, termination, and subjective impressions of outcome.

The use to date emphasizes grouped data over individualized reports on clients. Benchmark data are grouped and analyzed along specific categories. The data can assess whether cases are falling outside of service targets by monitoring time on waitlists, clinical deterioration, poor attendance, and early termination. Anytime the CORE-OM is re-administered, another tool (CORE-PC) can show which cases have deteriorated, remain unchanged, or have entered the ranks of normal functioning. Progress is monitored and the information fed back to clinicians, if this is desired. Yet, the strength of the system principally resides in the data it provides to administrators and managers of service delivery systems.

TOPS

Kraus and Horan (1999) developed the Treatment Outcome Package System (TOPS), which includes numerous evaluation tools covering child and adult functioning. Time of administration ranges from 2 to 25 min. TOPS, like CORE, has primarily focused on administrative uses rather than feedback to therapists. Managers can examine progress throughout treatment and compare outcomes with appropriate benchmarks.

The functioning of adults and children is quantified across a variety of areas and includes diagnostic aids, historical information, and written statements of treatment goals. The report for clinicians includes ratings on 23 high-risk-related questions. Considerable emphasis is placed on the use of the report for treatment planning, individualization of treatment goals, and tracking these goals. Client satisfaction, too, is measured and used as a quality assurance index. TOPS requires users to send off forms for scoring and reporting. This procedure limits rapid turnaround of feedback for clinicians and the frequency with which the response to treatment can be tracked. The adult symptom scale is long, around 85 items, and has considerable redundancy within each area of disturbance (e.g., sleep, anxiety, mood). For these reasons, the TOPS provides reliable information for estimating degree of disturbance. The length of TOPS, however, does not make it ideal for tracking treatment response on a weekly or even biweekly basis unless tracking is limited to specific subscales. For clients whose subscales are elevated, Kraus and Horan (1999) recommend using their tracking system each week. Overall, this practice has the advantage of targeting specific problems for specific clients, but it also carries the disadvantage of leaving untracked many items measuring symptoms. It is also hard to compare across patients when different targets are being tracked for each. This practice may also overestimate improvement while underestimating negative change.

PCOMS

Duncan and associates created an ultrabrief assessment package—the Partners for Change Outcome Management System (PCOMS; Miller, Duncan, Sorrell, & Brown, 2005). The PCOMS uses two 4-item (visual analogue) scales, one focusing on outcome (Outcome Rating scale) and the other aimed at assessing the therapeutic alliance (Session Rating scale). Measures are also available for use with children and adolescents (Duncan, Sparks, Miller, Bohanske, & Claud, 2006). Although brief, the Outcome Rating scale correlates modestly with other outcome measures such as the SCL-90-R (.57), the CORE-34 (.67), and the OQ-45 (.58; Duncan & Miller, 2008). Owing to its brevity, the Outcome Rating scale provides a more general description of change (global rating) rather than the more usual specific symptoms the longer scales previously mentioned provide. It has the advantage of directly involving both clinician and client in the process of measuring and discussing both progress and the working relationship. Each session, the therapist provides the measures to the client. Furthermore, as scoring takes place in the session, feedback is immediate.

Frequency of Use and Impact on Practice

An accurate estimate of the frequency of use of these instruments (COMPASS, CORE, PCOMS) is not currently available, but it is likely that they far surpass the frequency of use of the traditional scales used in efficacy and effectiveness research. This is because efficacy and effectiveness studies typically include rather small samples (e.g., 100 individuals), whereas measures used in routine care are given by the thousands. Given the large numbers of clients who complete measures on a weekly basis in routine care and the likelihood that such large data sets and research procedures will eventually have a strong impact on clinical practice, studying their psychometric properties and related characteristics (the degree to which they can be relied on to accurately reflect change and current functioning) is a matter of great importance. Before I turn to the measures used in the patient-focused procedures as outlined in this book, I discuss two final issues that are central to patient-focused research.

EVALUATING THE MEANINGFULNESS OF CHANGE—A CORE CHARACTERISTIC OF PATIENT-FOCUSED PRACTICE: STATISTICAL VERSUS CLINICAL SIGNIFICANCE

Much of psychotherapy research is aimed at answering questions of theoretical interest, such as, "Is dynamic therapy more effective than cognitive therapy?" or "Is exposure in vivo necessary for fear reduction?" These and a host of similar questions have given rise to research designs that emphasize the use of statistical tests of significance. Typically, the within-group and between-groups variability are estimated; group means are compared; and the resulting numerical result is compared with a preset critical value. The occurrence of a sufficiently large difference, defined as one that is unlikely to occur as frequently as the predetermined critical value (e.g., $p < .05$), demonstrates statistical significance.

Limitations of Inferential Statistics and Effect Size

Although this common approach is an essential part of the scientific process, there are limitations to this strategy (Jacobson, Roberts, Berns, & McGlinchey, 1999). First, a statistically significant result may have little practical meaning. For example, a behavioral method of treatment for obesity may create a statistically significant difference between treated and untreated groups if all treated subjects lost 10 pounds and all untreated subjects lost 5 pounds. However, the clinical utility for health-related benefits of an extra 5-pound weight loss is debatable, especially in clinically obese patients. Second, the focus on group averages that often accompanies statistical techniques makes it difficult to generalize the results to the outcome of a specific individual. Third, statistical significance does not clarify the strength of a demonstrated effect (Kazdin, 1998), only that it is not likely due to chance. A second less commonly used technique, an effect size, aims to address this last limitation. However, an effect size is unable to convey the meaningfulness of an effect. For instance, the preceding example comparing a weight loss intervention for a treated group of individuals to an untreated group is likely to have a moderate effect size despite its lack of practical meaning for health.

Such limitations are not lost on the practicing clinician because the question "How likely is it that a client with a particular problem will leave therapy without that problem?" (Jacobson, et al., 1999, p. 306) remains of central importance to most therapists. Clinical significance is a concept that was introduced to provide a solution to this dilemma (Jacobson, Follette, & Revenstorf, 1984; Jacobson & Truax, 1991). In the past 2 decades, a number of methods have been proposed to determine the clinical significance of interventions (e.g., Blanchard & Schwarz, 1988; Gladis, Gosch, Dishuk, &

Crits-Christoph, 1999; Kendall, 1999; Kendall & Grove, 1988; Kendall & Norton-Ford, 1982), and a broader approach referred to as *social validity* has its proponents as well (Kazdin, 1977; Wolf, 1978). Although the former approach considers meaningfulness of change according to criteria identified by clinicians–researchers with the use of standardized assessments, the latter method defines the practicality of change using the perspectives of clients and societal members (Ogles, Lunnen, & Bonesteel, 2001).

The definition of clinical significance is synonymous with a return to normal functioning (Jacobson et al., 1999). To be labeled such an outcome, two criteria must be met: (a) The magnitude of change is considered reliable, and (b) the improvement results in the client being "indistinguishable," on the measure of interest from individuals defined as functioning normally. The purpose of the first criterion is to ensure that measured change exceeds what is possible from chance fluctuations in scores, or measurement error. Alone it is referred to as the *reliable change index* (Jacobson et al., 1984; Jacobson & Truax, 1991) and identifies clients who have reliably improved but not necessarily recovered following treatment (Jacobson et al., 1999). When each of the individual criteria is met, change is referred to as *clinically significant* and is reserved for those clients who reliably improve and who cross into the functional range after beginning treatment in the nonfunctional range.

Like any methodological approach, the concept of clinical significance has numerous assumptions and issues. For example, the very use of the preceding criteria is contingent on the availability of an instrument that has been psychometrically tested and normed. Reliability coefficients are necessary for the calculation of the reliable change index, and normative data corresponding to functional and dysfunctional populations are required for the calculation of a cutoff value that discriminates between these two groups (although Jacobson and colleagues have suggested cutoff calculations when normative data are missing; Jacobson et al., 1984; Jacobson et al., 1999; Jacobson & Truax, 1991). Given the magnitude of change necessary for a client to receive the label *recovered*, it is conceivable that some groups of individuals (e.g., those with schizophrenia) may only rarely meet the necessary criteria, suggesting the need for samples representing a continuum of improvement (Tingey, Lambert, Burlingame, & Hansen, 1996). The complexity of these issues is beyond the scope of this chapter; however, there are many sources that readers may find interesting (e.g., Bauer, Lambert, & Hansen, 2007; Kendall & Grove, 1988; Kendall, Marrs-Garcia, Nath, & Sheldrick, 1999; Ogles et al., 1996; Ogles et al., 2001; Tingey et al., 1996). Presumably, with the availability of test manuals, users can either obtain or if need be, calculate cutoff and reliable change scores corresponding to clinically significant criteria.

The following example illustrates how the concept of clinical significance can be used in practice and forms a cornerstone of patient-focused research. The BDI (Beck et al., 1961) has a reliable change index of 9 points and a cutoff score of 14 that separates the dysfunctional and functional population (Seggar, Lambert, & Hansen, 2002). On the basis of these criteria and pre- and posttreatment assessments of outcome from the BDI, a client's final outcome status can be categorized. For example, assume that Client A began treatment with a score of 34 and ended treatment with a score of 32. A change score of 2 represents the client's improvement, suggesting that reliable improvement was not attained and also that the client cannot be classified as within the range of normal functioning. Suppose that Client B began treatment with a score of 26 but ended treatment with a score of 20. In this case, Client B also has not made reliable change and is also categorized as unchanged because of the failure to change by 9 or more points. Client C began treatment with a score of 50 and ended treatment with a score of 18, experiencing reliable improvement but failing to cross the cutoff for normal functioning despite improving by 32 points. Client D represents an instance of deterioration by beginning treatment with a score of 20 but leaving treatment with a score of 38. Client E represents a client who achieves clinically significant change by virtue of beginning in the dysfunctional range, improving more than 9 points, and leaving treatment in the functional range. The results of this example are presented graphically in Figure 2.1. Because patient-focused research procedures are aimed at characterizing changes made by individual clients, using each individual patient's scores to classify his or her outcome is clinically invaluable.

Similar and Related Procedures

Additional examples of estimating clinically significant change have been published over the years. These methods have emphasized the use of normative comparison. Examples include the use of social drinking behaviors as criteria for outcome in the treatment of problem drinking or the use of definitions of adequate sexual performance (e.g., ratio of orgasms to attempts at sex or as time to orgasm following penetration; Sabalis, 1983). These criteria are based on data about the normal functioning of individuals and can be applied easily and meaningfully with a number of disorders in which normal or ideal functioning is readily apparent and easily measured (e.g., obesity, suicidal behavior).

Normative comparisons also can be used to evaluate the clinical significance of treatment by comparing posttreatment status of treated clients with samples of nondistressed individuals. This approach is highly advantageous to examining practice-based evidence through the use of benchmarks. For example, Trull, Nietzel, and Main (1988) reviewed 19 studies of agoraphobia that used the Fear Questionnaire (Marks & Mathews, 1978). The normative

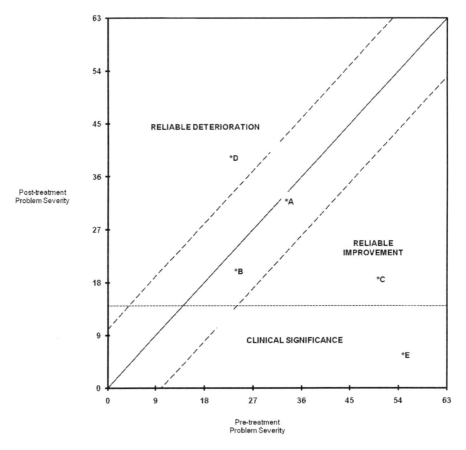

Figure 2.1. Graphical example of using the reliable change index and clinical significance change criteria.

samples were based on university students and individuals randomly selected from the community. Because the community sample appeared more distressed than the university sample, estimates of clinically significant change were a function of which normative sample patients were compared with. In a comparison with the university sample, the average agoraphobic patient began treatment at the 99th percentile and ended at the 98.7th percentile following treatment. In contrast, the average agoraphobic patient began treatment at the 97th percentile of the community sample but progressed to the 68th percentile at the end of treatment, a large discrepancy.

Using similar methodology, Nietzel, Russell, Hemmings, and Gretter (1987) studied the clinical significance of psychotherapy for unipolar depression. In all, 28 published studies were used to calculate composite BDI norms for three groups: a nondistressed group, a general population group (consisting mostly of collegiate subjects), and a situationally distressed group (e.g., pregnant women), which turned out to be very similar to the general population samples. These norms were then used in comparison with outcomes from 31 studies that yielded 60 effect sizes. Comparisons contrasting the depressed patients with the normative samples suggested that the various treatments (all of which appeared similar in their effectiveness) produced clinically significant changes in relation to the general population norms. In fact, the average depressed patient moved from the 99th percentile of the general population norms to the 76th percentile of these reference samples. These gains were maintained at follow-up. In reference to the nondistressed group, the same improvements were much less remarkable. The average depressed patient only moved from the 99th percentile to the 95th percentile of the nondistressed sample.

Normative comparison approaches provide a number of advantages. Numerous measures have normative data that facilitate comparisons between distressed and nondistressed groups of individuals, saving researchers and clinicians alike from collecting data on normal individuals. Additionally, provided that specific normative samples exist, finer comparisons between treatment progress are possible, particularly for psychological disorders that are somewhat resistant to change (i.e., schizophrenia). However, the meaningfulness of these narrower comparisons becomes less clear as well. From the preceding examples, the extent of improvement depends on the comparison group used. An additional methodological weakness with using such an approach is a reliance on the distribution of the normative sample. Samples that are not normally distributed (e.g., floor and ceiling effects) present serious problems. A potentially common problem is the fact that many tests are developed with those who have psychological disorders and thus are not as applicable for measuring less severely distressed individuals.

Nevertheless, clinicians preferring to evaluate the meaningfulness of patient gains using a normative comparison approach have available a number of instruments with published normative data. Brief lists of some of the more common measures with available norms have been made available: BDI, SCL-90-R, Fear Questionnaire, Child Behavior Checklist, HRSD, OQ-45, and Inventory for Interpersonal Problems. Cutoffs and reliable change indices for these instruments and others have been reported in Ogles et al. (1996) and Ogles et al. (2002).

COST-EFFECTIVE CARE AS AN OUTCOME

Among those outcomes that are measured, the cost-effectiveness of treatments is an interesting but rarely studied phenomenon. In societies that are becoming more preoccupied with cost containment, the cost-effectiveness of treatments is an important outcome to consider. The *value* of care is often defined as the trade-off between quality of care (or traditional clinical outcomes) in relation to dollars spent on care. To health plans, governments and employers (if not patients), the value of care, or its cost-effectiveness, may be as important as absolute costs for deciding which treatments to offer. Cost-effectiveness data are particularly important when the effects of different treatments are equal—a state of affairs that is common in psychotherapy and pharmacotherapy (Lambert & Ogles, 2004).

Perhaps the best example of research on this topic is that provided from the RAND Medical Outcomes Study, which examined outcomes in depression (K. B. Wells, Sturm, Sherbourne, & Meredith, 1996). This study examined systems of care, patient case mix, process of care, use, and clinical outcomes in an indirect structural analysis to develop models that inform policy and treatment decisions. These authors found that treatment increases mental health services use and costs regardless of provider specialty (general practitioner, psychiatrist, or other mental health specialist). The lowest cost but also the worst outcomes for depression were found in the general medical sector; the highest costs but also the best outcomes occurred in psychiatry. When cost-effectiveness ratios were calculated, the greatest value was to be found in the other mental health specialist provider group (psychologists, etc.). These authors also estimated that quality improvement programs or decisions could make substantial improvements in cost-effectiveness or value. Without quality improvement that takes into account the cost–benefit ratio of different treatments, the current tendency to shift treatment toward general medical practitioners who mainly offer psychoactive drugs may continue because it reduces costs—not because it is cost-effective.

Although the results of the RAND study are highly complicated and complex (depending on type of depression, follow-up time period, etc.), it is obvious that the results provide a rich source of data. With the data analytic procedures used by K. B. Wells and colleagues (1996), it is possible to calculate the amount of money it costs to reduce a single symptom by a particular amount (e.g., what it costs to reduce the number of headaches a person has by one per week through the use of medication versus biofeedback). It also would be possible to estimate the cost of bringing a depressed patient into a normal state of functioning (and keep him or her there). Moreover, one could compare the costs associated with specific treatment strategies—say, the cost-effectiveness of group versus individual cognitive behavior therapy.

The RAND study of depression was a large-scale, extensive effort costing approximately $4 million to complete (K. B. Wells et al., 1996). Numerous other studies have been conducted on a variety of other disorders such as chronic pain (Texidor & Taylor, 1991) and psychosomatic disorders (Pautler, 1991), but none have reached the scope of the RAND study. The limited number of studies and their diversity make it difficult to identify the best methods of estimating costs. Like the area of clinical outcome measurement, there are few agreed-upon methods of estimating treatment costs.

The RAND study defined *health* as the number of serious functioning limitations. Costs were based on the "direct" costs of providing services to treat depression, and the value of care was estimated for the cost of reducing one or more functioning limitations. Other researchers estimate cost as an average cost of providing treatment for an episode of illness per patient by adding up staff expenses (including benefits) and then dividing by the number of patients treated in a year (Melson, 1995). Researchers have also attempted to estimate social costs such as those that arise from lost productivity, use of social services and the criminal justice system, use of other health services, and the like. Cost–benefit analysis combined with estimates of outcome based on clinical significance could be usefully applied in the managed mental health setting or other payer policies to understand the consequences of rationing treatment. What is the value of fewer sessions versus more sessions on the long-term adjustment of patients or tax revenue collections?

Addressing the complexity of these issues is, again, beyond the scope of this chapter. Suffice it to say that estimates of the cost, cost-effectiveness, and medical cost offsets of psychotherapy are important topics in the assessment of psychotherapy outcome. McKenzie (1995), for example, argued that the relative equivalence of outcome in group and individual psychotherapy can be a powerful argument for the use of group therapy when either the cost of delivering treatment or the cost–benefit of group therapy is considered. At the very least, this finding emphasizes the importance of research aimed at selecting patients who are most suitable for group treatment.

SUMMARY AND CONCLUSIONS

Through the examination of some of the most important considerations in the complex area of operationalizing the outcomes of current treatments, I hope that the reader has grasped the complexities of making choices about measuring outcomes. The topic of measuring outcomes has demanded the attention of researchers since the inception of research on the effects of psychotherapy itself and certainly for the last 70 years. Much has been learned, and yet no standards or means of measuring outcomes have been agreed upon. Researchers can say that measures vary with regard to their content (e.g., affect, cognition, behavior), intra- and interpersonal focus, source, the type of rating scale used, and the time perspective that they tap. Each of these domains has an important impact on what researchers come to know and conclude. With such complexity, it is easy to see why no single study of treatment effects can provide definitive answers about how to be most helpful to those in need of psychologists' professional services and why this field is consumed with the kind of chaos and conflict noted in Chapter 1.

From among the thousands of measures available to psychologists to make client outcome more explicit, they have seemingly unlimited choices and frequently some foreknowledge of the consequences of choosing a measure. In Chapter 3, I move from the general considerations summarized in this chapter to the development of outcomes measures for the purpose of improving mental health services based on client outcomes in routine care. In this context it will become quickly apparent to the reader that the practical necessities of feasible application, even more than scientific principles, will determine how psychologists measure outcomes and how they use this information to better ensure that clients receiving routine care are well served.

II

MEASURING AND PREDICTING TREATMENT OUTCOME

3

MEASURES FOR TRACKING PATIENT TREATMENT RESPONSE AND THEIR CHARACTERISTICS

Given the serious problems of patient deterioration and nonresponse to treatment highlighted in Chapter 1, and given the general principles for outcome measurement overviewed in Chapter 2, several outcome measures were developed for use in routine care. These measures were created by my colleagues and me over a period of several years. Some important characteristics of these assessment tools are presented in this chapter. Methods of using these measures to predict patient treatment response are presented in Chapter 4. Here the aim is to describe measures and methods that are used to enhance treatment outcomes for psychological disorders, especially for patients whose progress and eventual positive outcome is in doubt. The detailed presentation of this material provides the reader with an understanding of how patient problems are defined and problems are quantified and how the resulting information is used in routine care.

Table 3.1 provides a summary overview of the measures and their functions. The interested reader can consult the administration and scoring manuals for extensive reviews of the measures psychometric properties and normative data. Some of this information is provided here—enough, I hope, so that the reader can evaluate some of the strengths and limitations of the scales.

TABLE 3.1
Outcome Questionnaire (OQ) Instrument Overview

Instrument	No. items	Completed by	Subscales	Change metrics	Treatment failure alert	Community normative scale range	Clinical score range
OQ 45.2 —adult outcome measure (ages 18+)	45	Self	3	X	X	0 to 63	64 to 180
Y-OQ 2.01—youth outcome measure (ages 4–17)	64	Parent	6	X	X	–16 to 46	47 to 240
Y-OQ 2.0 SR—youth outcome measure (ages 12–18)	64	Self	6	X	X	–16 to 46	47 to 240
OQ 30.1—adult outcome measure (ages 18+)	30	Self	3	X	X	0 to 43	44 to 120
Y-OQ 30.1—omniform youth outcome measure (ages 12–18)	30	Parent	6	X	X	0 to 23	30 to 120
Y-OQ 30.1 self-report —youth outcome measure (ages 12–18)	30	Self	6	X		0 to 30	31 to 120
S-OQ 2.0—outcome measure for the severely and persistently mentally ill	45	Self or clinician	2	X		0 to 59	60 to 180
Brief Psychiatric Rating Scale—outcome measure for the severely and persistently mentally ill	24	Clinician	3	X		0 to 30	30 to 50 (outpatient) 51 to120 (inpatient)
Assessment for Signal Clients—adult clinical support tool to help assess problems with therapeutic alliance, motivation, social supports, and life events.*	40	Self	4	NA	X	NA	NA

Note. Copyright 2004 by OQ Measures, LLC. Reprinted with permission.
*More fully described in Chapter 6.

OUTCOME QUESTIONNAIRE-45.2

The central measure within those listed in Table 3.1 is the Outcome Questionnaire-45 (OQ-45), first developed and distributed in the United States in 1993. According to a survey conducted by Hatfield and Ogles (2004), by 2001 it had become the third most frequently used self-report instrument of mental health functioning used by clinicians for measuring adult patient outcome in the United States. Unlike most psychological tests, it was developed specifically for use in monitoring patient well-being on a weekly basis during routine care. In this regard it was expected to provide a mental health "vital sign" at each administration.

Following the usual practices in patient-focused methods presented in Chapter 2, it is a brief self-report scale measuring problems with specific items rather than providing a global evaluation of treatment effects. The OQ-45 attempts to measure three broad areas of functioning suggested by the social level described generally in Chapter 2. It can be argued that it would be best to track treatment response with diagnostic specific scales. Whereas scales that attempt to measure a single construct such as depression or anxiety have the advantage of concentrating items around a single diagnosis and therefore allow more broad coverage of symptoms within a disorder, it is important to note that the initial administration of an instrument in relation to interventions (including intake) is best if it precedes any treatment activity such as a diagnostic interview. Delay in first administration reduces the amount of change that is documented because of these diagnostic procedures. In addition, scales that purport to measure a single construct such as depression are highly correlated with scales that purport to measure a different diagnostic classification such as anxiety. These facts suggest the value of an omnibus scale that includes items that cover the most important and common aspects of adult functioning but less comprehensively than these monoconstruct scales.

The OQ-45 was designed to be taken no more than once weekly and for reasons that will become clear, just prior to each treatment session. It requires about 5 to 7 min of patient time and is tolerated well at this length provided that patients believe that it is being done in their behalf and will be used for furthering the aims of treatment. In this regard it is important for staff and providers to communicate the reason for administering the scale. Often the rationale that is provided includes reference to the need to monitor the patient's well-being just as taking blood pressure or acquiring lab test data is common at office visits to a physician.

The OQ-45 went through several iterations before it was distributed in its current version, the OQ-45.2. OQ-45 respondents estimate frequencies of occurrence of 45 symptoms, emotional states, interpersonal relationships and social role functioning with reference to the preceding week including the day of administration. Thirty-six negatively worded items (e.g., Item 5, "I blame myself for things") are scored: *never* = 0; *rarely* = 1; *sometimes* = 2; *frequently* = 3; and *almost always* = 4; scoring is reversed for 9 positively worded items (e.g., Item 13, "I am a happy person"): *never* = 4; *rarely* = 3; *sometimes* = 2; *frequently* = 1; and *almost always* = 0. This yields a total score ranging from 0 to 180. Higher scores reveal more frequent symptoms, distress, interpersonal problems, and role dysfunction and less frequent positive emotional states, pleasant experiences, successful social relationships, and adaptive role functioning. The positive items were included in an attempt to overcome the ceiling effects found in scales (e.g., Beck Depression Inventory) that only quantify degree of pathology.

Norms and Psychometrics

The OQ-45 manual (Lambert, Morton, et al., 2004) documents excellent internal consistency: Cronbach's α = .93, test–retest reliability (e.g., 3-week r = .84), and good-to-excellent correlations between the OQ-45 and a wide variety of other instruments that are frequently used in traditional psychotherapy outcome research (e.g., Beck Depression Inventory, .80; Symptom Checklist-90, .78; State–Trait Anxiety Inventory, .80; Social Adjustment Rating Scale, .71; Inventory of Interpersonal Problems, .74). These relatively high validity coefficients are typical across a variety of patient and normal samples and hold up across cultures. The OQ-45 distinguishes between patient and psychologically healthy samples and has been normed on patient and nonpatient samples across the United States and throughout much of the world through translations into 17+ non-English languages. Normative information is presented graphically in Figure 3.1. Correlations between the subscale scores and total score indicate a high degree of overlap between subscales, suggesting that individuals who have problems in one area of functioning probably have problems in the other areas as well.

Men and women in clinical and nonclinical samples suggest slight gender differences. There do not appear to be systematic differences across age groups. The OQ-45 has been shown to be useful across a variety of ethnically diverse populations across cultures and ethnic minorities within the United States.

Given the means and standard deviations for nonpatient samples, it appears that about two thirds of people will obtain an OQ-45 total score between 27 and 63, whereas about two thirds of patients at the inception of treatment will score between 99 and 61.

Clinically Significant Change

Normative comparisons have been used to provide markers for individual patient progress based on Jacobson and Truax's (1991) formulas for reli-

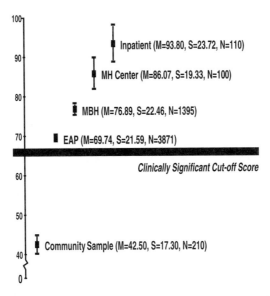

Figure 3.1. Graphic representation of patient and non-patient samples (with cutoff line demarking normal functioning). MH Center = mental health center; MBH = managed behavior health; and EAP = employee assistance program. Copyright 2004 by OQ Measures, LLC. Reprinted with permission.

able and clinically significant change (as introduced in Chapter 2, this volume). Jacobson and colleagues' work has been used with standardized scales to estimate where the patient stands in reference to normal functioning and how much change needs to occur to regard the person as reliably improved. Jacobson, Roberts, Berns, and McGlinchey (1999) cautioned that "any method of defining clinical significance can be no better than the measuring instruments and their psychometric properties" (p. 306). The use of clinically significant change formulas and concepts is a necessary development in patient-focused and practice-based work because at the foundation of outcome management at the individual patient level is an operational definition of return to healthy functioning.

Applying the Jacobson and Truax (1991) formulas to calculate the Reliable Change Index (RCI) and cutoff point for normal functioning, Lambert, Morton, et al. (2004) estimated that a client taking the OQ-45 must improve by at least 14 points to be regarded as improved and score below 64 to be regarded as recovered (see the horizontal line in Figure 3.1). These markers are used with individual clients to judge the clinical significance of their participation in treatment (i.e., clinically meaningful treatment outcome). Support for the validity of the OQ-45's reliable change and clinical significance cutoff scores have been reported by Lunnen and Ogles (1998), Beckstead et al.

(2003), and Bauer, Lambert, and Nielsen (2004). This research suggests that the Jacobson and Truax (1991) formulas provide a sound basis for estimating cutoff scores and that classification of change based on other measures such as the Symptom Checklist-90 results in considerable consensus with OQ-45 classifications of the same patients. For example, Beckstead et al. (2003) examined outcome classification using four measures: the Symptom Checklist-90, Social Adjustment Rating Scale, Inventory for Interpersonal Problems, and Quality of Life Inventory. Classification of clients as being part of a clinical or nonclinical population suggested considerable concordance between measures, with any three of the measures agreeing about 85% of the time. The OQ-45 was the most likely to classify client change as clinically meaningful, with 32% of patients recovered compared with 23% for the Symptom Checklist-90. The implications of validation data for classification of patients as recovered, improved, unchanged, or deteriorated are that the OQ-45 classifications would be nearly duplicated had another self-report scale been used in its place.

Although factor analysis was not used as a way of developing the subscales of the OQ-45, confirmatory and exploratory factor analytic studies suggest that the best factorial description of the scale supports the presence of three subscales: symptomatic distress (with anxiety, depression, and somatic anxiety components), interpersonal problems, and social role functioning (de Jong et al., 2007; Mueller, Lambert, & Burlingame, 1998). For the purposes of tracking patient treatment progress information on each subscale is typically provided, but the major emphasis has been on the total score, which is based on all 45 items. Figure 3.2 provides a screenshot from the OQ-Analyst software for administration, scoring, and provision of feedback of a fictional patient's intake OQ-45. As can be seen, this client's score on the measure is graphed in relation to normative samples that have different levels of functioning ranging from inpatient to nonpatient samples and also in relation to the Jacobson and Truax (1991) cutoff score for normal functioning.

The normative means and standard deviations are also provided numerically for normative samples and for the subscale scores. The use of subscales for tracking may be stretching the limits of the psychometrics needed for tracking because of problems associated with scales composed of few items, such as poor reliability and validity, and the fact that the intended use of the OQ-45 involves comparisons of an individual's scores over time. Difference scores are less reliable than scores examined at only one point in time. At the same time, valid subscales have the advantage of differentiating and refining the results of treatment evaluation, much the same as the use of multiple specific scales does. In the case of the OQ-45, subscales make it possible to track the degree to which symptoms may change at a different rate than interpersonal problems and work-related functioning (as described in Chapter 4, this volume). Providing this information to those who use the

Clinician Report
Red Alert – Part 1

Name:	Adult, Melanie, R	ID:	ASDF0195
Session Date: 2/16/2006		Session: 5	
Clinician:	Clinician, Bob	Clinic:	North Clinic
Diagnosis:	Panic Disorder		
Algorithm:	Empirical		

Alert Status:	**Red**
Most Recent Score:	104
Initial Score:	89
Change From Initial:	Reliably Worse
Current Distress Level:	Moderately High

Most Recent Critical Item Status:

8. **Suicide** - I have thoughts of ending my life. — Sometimes
11. **Substance Abuse** - After heavy drinking, I need a drink the next morning to get going. — Frequently
26. **Substance Abuse** - I feel annoyed by people who criticize my drinking. — Almost Always
32. **Substance Abuse** - I have trouble at work/school because of drinking or drug use. — Almost Always
44. **Work Violence** - I feel angry enough at work/school to do something I might regret. — Sometimes

Subscales	Current	Outpat. Norm	Comm. Norm
Symptom Distress:	63	49	25
Interpersonal Relations:	25	20	10
Social Role:	16	14	10
Total:	**104**	**83**	**45**

Clinician Report Red Alert – Part 2

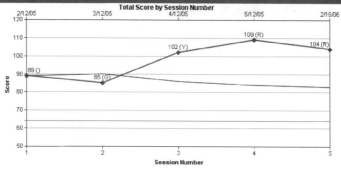

Total Score by Session Number

Graph Label Legend:
(R) = Red: High chance of negative outcome   (Y) = Yellow: Some chance of negative outcome
(G) = Green: Making expected progress   (W) = White: Functioning in normal range

Feedback Message:
The patient is deviating from the expected response to treatment. They are not on track to realize substantial benefit from treatment. Chances are they may drop out of treatment prematurely or have a negative treatment outcome. Steps should be taken to carefully review this case and identify reasons for poor progress. It is recommended that you be alert to the possible need to improve the therapeutic alliance, reconsider the client's readiness for change and the need to renegotiate the therapeutic contract, intervene to strengthen social supports, or possibly alter your treatment plan by intensifying treatment, shifting intervention strategies, or decide upon a new course of action, such as referral for medication. Continuous monitoring of future progress is highly recommended.

Figure 3.2. OQ-Analyst clinician report showing a patient who deviated from expected response (ascending line) and who is off-track for a positive treatment response (horizontal line = normal functioning). Copyright 2004 by OQ Measures, LLC. Reprinted with permission.

scales allows them to track changes in each domain albeit with a tentative attitude.

The use of a 5-min measure like the OQ-45, as short as it is relative to what is needed for covering the three domains, was still seen by some individuals and organizations as too lengthy; they often administered other forms to patients at the time of intake and did not want to overburden patients. This led to shortening the scale to a 30-item version for use by organizations that found the 5 min needed for administration of the OQ-45 excessive.

OUTCOME QUESTIONNAIRE-30

The Outcome Questionnaire-30 (OQ-30; Lambert, Vermeersch, Brown, & Burlingame, 2004) is a derivative of the OQ-45 originally created for use by a behavioral health company (PacifiCare) managing the care of patients from a pool of about 5 million customers. For their use the measure was titled the Life Status Questionnaire, and it has been administered to thousands of patients undergoing psychological and medication treatments. Its development reflects the consistent interest shown in very brief assessments. Despite interest in and the advantages of short measures, the time saved is miniscule (1–2 min by taking a 30-item instead of a 45-item measure). Generally speaking, it takes no more time for administrators or clerical staff to use short or long measures provided that they are scored through automated systems such as with scan forms or handheld computers.

The OQ-30 was derived from the OQ-45 in an attempt to shorten test administration time while maintaining the OQ-45's psychometric properties of reliability, validity, and sensitivity to change. Choices of which items to retain were largely based on analysis of item "sensitivity to change" by Vermeersch and colleagues (Vermeersch, Lambert, & Burlingame, 2000; Vermeersch, et al., 2004). Within this research, *item sensitivity* was defined as the degree to which an item score remained constant in the absence of treatment but declined in the presence of treatment. As noted in Chapter 2, this is an essential component of outcome measures because their purpose is to serve as a mental health vital sign, rather than to help clinicians understand personality dynamics, make diagnostic judgments, or formulate treatment plans (other than estimating the likely length of treatment that will be needed to return a patient to a state of normal functioning as described in Chapter 8, this volume).

Each item within the OQ-45 was rated with regard to the steepness of the slope of an item (speed of change), and those with the steepest slope (relative to untreated individuals) made up the OQ-30. The OQ-30 assesses the same domains as the OQ-45: subjective discomfort and symptoms, problems in interpersonal relationships, and problems in social role performance but without calculating subscale scores. Some items assessing positive aspects of functioning were retained. Each item is scored on the same 5-point scale with the total score yielding a range of possible scores of 0 to 120 with higher values indicating higher levels of client distress and pathology.

Completion of the OQ-30 takes approximately 4 min. An RCI and normal functioning cutoff score have been calculated for the OQ-30. On the basis of normative data from community nonclients ($n = 904$) and clients entering outpatient treatment ($n = 8,410$), the RCI was estimated to be 10 points. Thus, clients who change by at least 10 points are regarded as having made reliable change. The cutoff on the OQ-30 for demarking the point at which a person's score is more likely to come from the nonclinical population than a clinical population was estimated to be 44. This score turns out to be about a standard deviation higher than the mean of the nonclient sample ($M = 31.50, SD = 14.22$). When clients' scores fall at 43 or below, it is concluded that their functioning is at that time more like nonclients' than clients' (Lambert, Vermeersch, et al., 2004). When the client improves by 10 or more points and passes below 44, the client has met criteria for making clinically significant change.

A comparison of the OQ-45 and OQ-30 with regard to classifying a patient into functional and nonfunctional populations was made by Ellsworth, Lambert, and Johnson, (2006). This comparison suggested that there was excellent agreement between OQ-45 and OQ-30 classifications of clients as being in the functional or dysfunctional range at both pre- and posttreatment. Agreement in classification of individuals as in the clinical range at pretreatment was 93%. At posttreatment, agreement was 88%. At pretreatment the interclass correlation was $\kappa = .851$, and at posttreatment it was $\kappa = .866$. The OQ-45 classified a slightly higher percentage of individuals as functional at intake (135/447, 30%) than the OQ-30 (118/447, 26%). At intake the OQ-45 is more likely to classify individuals as being in the functional range, whereas the OQ-30 is more likely to classify individuals as being in the dysfunctional range. The same discrepancy was also present at posttreatment (OQ-45, 55.3%; OQ-30, 49.9%).

Although there is a high degree of agreement between the OQ-45 and the OQ-30 in their classification of clients as being in the functional or dysfunctional range at pre- and posttreatment, there were also some differences in the way these instruments classified some clients. A closer look at the data indicated that the discrepancies were due in large part to slight variations around the cutoff scores. In cases in which the OQ-45 and OQ-30 differed in classification, the scores were typically tightly clustered around the cutoff scores of 64 and 44, respectively.

The analysis of OQ-45 and OQ-30 agreement on posttreatment classifications of change indicated substantial agreement ($\kappa = .753$). Classifications of clients at posttreatment as recovered, improved, not changed, or deteriorated between OQ-45 and OQ-30 suggest considerable overlap, with discrepancies occurring when one measure classified the client as recovered and the other measure classified the client as improved; the individual improved by the RCI or more on both measures. Disagreement occurred because the scores for one of the measures were typically quite close to the cutoff score for one of the four classifications in the wrong direction. For example, if a client started treatment in the dysfunctional range using the OQ-30 and the functional range using the OQ-45, it was not possible for the person to meet the criteria for recovery using the OQ-45. The difference between final treatment classifications was a matter of very few points in most cases. In every other category of disagreement, the discrepancy was not due to differences in classification of the client as being in the functional or dysfunctional range. Rather, the discrepancy was due to variation in the amount of change demonstrated by the client on each measure. Typically, a client barely met the RCI on one measure and barely missed the RCI cutoff on the other measure. In general, the kind of classification "errors" that were observed are those that can be expected when dichotomous classification is used instead of continuous scores. Because cutoff scores and dichotomous classification are essential in patient-focused research, these types of errors cannot be avoided, only minimized.

The OQ-30 is a widely used instrument, and its total score can be used in place of the OQ-45 as a mental health vital sign. There is, of course, some loss of information using the shorter scale. However, most past research related to the effects of providing progress feedback to therapists and patients has been based on the OQ-45 total score rather than the subscales. Table 3.2 presents data on the concordance between classifications of progress during the course of treatment. Data suggest considerable overlap.

As the OQ-45 and OQ-30 began to be applied in public mental health settings, including long- and short-term inpatient settings where the patients were seriously and persistently mentally ill, some clinicians were concerned that

TABLE 3.2
Session-by-Session Feedback on the OQ-45 and OQ-30

OQ-45 feedback	OQ-30 feedback				
	White	Green	Yellow	Red	Total
White	**1,252**	170	11	4	1,437
Green	32	**884**	80	95	1,091
Yellow	2	18	**21**	76	117
Red	0	11	12	**215**	238
Total	1,286	1,083	124	390	2,883

Note. OQ = Outcome Questionnaire. From "A Comparison of the Outcome Questionnaire-45 and Outcome Questionnaire-30 in Classification and Prediction of Treatment Outcome," by J. R. Ellsworth, M. J. Lambert, and J. Johnson, 2006, *Clinical Psychology and Psychotherapy, 13*, p. 386. Copyright 2006 by Wiley. Reprinted with permission.

none of the scale items measured the symptoms and functioning peculiar to these severe disorders. They hypothesized that the scales might be missing some of the effects of treatments (including medication) on these more serious problems. To address this concern an attempt was made to identify items that could be used for this purpose. This eventually led to the development of the Severe Outcome Questionnaire.

SEVERE OUTCOME QUESTIONNAIRE

The Severe Outcome Questionnaire (S-OQ) is composed of the 30 items from the OQ-30 and an additional 15 items that were created to capture symptoms and functioning of patients who have severe psychopathology such as bipolar disorder, schizophrenia, and other psychotic illness (e.g., "I have been told by others my behavior is out of control"; "I can't stop thinking, moving, or doing things"; "My temper leads me to act without thinking or say things I do not mean"). The S-OQ was heavily influenced by use of the OQ-45 and the OQ-30 for tracking patient improvement at the Utah State Mental Hospital and the Salt Lake Valley Mental Health Center. In the state hospital setting most patients experienced such severe psychopathology that their hospitalization was based on involuntary commitment proceedings. The S-OQ was created with the intention of being especially appropriate for use in this and related settings, such as community mental health centers, where highly impaired patients seek treatment.

As a derivative of the OQ-45 and OQ-30, the S-OQ attempted to focus on symptoms, and interpersonal and social role functioning. The 15 "severely mentally ill" items of the S-OQ were based on the test developers' understanding of features that characterize individuals classified under the seriously mentally ill (SMI) rubric. This understanding was influenced by guidelines found in literature about inpatient and SMI populations (Carey, 2000) and by the need to track the changing aspects of an SMI patient's functioning throughout the treatment process from inpatient, day care, outpatient care, and the like.

It was intended that the combination of these 15 SMI items and the items from the OQ-30 would make the S-OQ a practical and relevant measure that patients could complete multiple times (at least monthly) over the course of treatment. Carey (2000) evaluated the validity of the S-OQ by calculating correlations between the S-OQ and the Behavior and Symptom Identification Scale, the Brief Psychiatric Rating Scale (BPRS-E), and the Nurses' Observation Scale for Inpatient Evaluation. Table 3.3 depicts the results. The S-OQ was significantly correlated with the total scores from each of the criteria measures, two of which were based on outside observer ratings. Additionally, the S-OQ was correlated with the Affect subscale of the BPRS-E at a

TABLE 3.3
Correlation of the Severe Outcome Questionnaire With Criterion Measures

	BASIS-32 (n = 147)	BPRS-E (n = 83)					NOSIE-30 (n = 79)
Prediction measures	Total	Thought	Anergia	Affect	Disorganizaton	Total	Total
S-OQ	.90*	0.04	0.07	.55*	0.00	.43*	−.44*
OQ-30	.86*	−0.03	0.03	.58**	−0.04	.37*	−.44*
SMI-15	.87*	0.152	0.15	.41*	0.08	.47*	−.38*

Note. BASIS = Behavior and Symptom Identification Scale; BPRS = Brief Psychiatric Rating Scale; NOSIE = Nurses' Observation Scale for Inpatient Evaluation; OQ-30 = Outcome Questionnaire 30; SMI = seriously mentally ill. From *Administration and Scoring Manual for the Severe Outcome Questionnaire* (p. 15), by G. M. Burlingame, J. Lee, P. Nielsen, and M. J. Lambert, 2005, Salt Lake City, UT: OQ Measures, LLC. Copyright 2005 by OQ Measures, LLC. Reprinted with permission.
*p < .05., **p < .01.

significant level but, surprisingly, not with factors of disorganization and thought disturbance as rated by clinicians. As expected, the S-OQ correlated negatively with the Nurses' Observation Scale for Inpatient Evaluation because a higher score on the Nurses' Observation Scale for Inpatient Evaluation indicates higher levels of functioning.

At this time the S-OQ is available as an experimental scale. Its development lags behind the other measures. An alarm-signal warning system for alerting clinicians to deviations from a course of expected treatment response has not yet been developed. Despite the inclusion of items for assessing severe disturbance, little evidence suggests that it provides a different (more sensitive) measure of change than the OQ-30 or OQ-45 with these populations. Further details regarding its characteristics can be found in the test manual (Burlingame et al., 2007).

Patient outcome is being tracked with the S-OQ, which provides reasonable estimates of change for about 60% to 70% of the patients in the most restrictive settings of care. In this context, many of the patients (about 30%–40%) must be primarily tracked with staff ratings rather than a self-report measure. This is because a sizable minority of patients are too ill to rate their functioning or believe that not admitting to psychopathology will result in early release from the hospital. For purposes of tracking this subset of patients the BPRS was incorporated into the OQ-Analyst for examining progress. The recommendation is that providers track patients with the clinician-rated BPRS if clients cannot complete a self-report or produce a score that is obviously inconsistent with their current level of functioning. Given the costs associated with training clinical staff to make reliable ratings, the cost in staff time associated with making the ratings, and the loss of morale associated with placing the burden of more paper work on the staff, it is an advantage to reduce (from 100%)

tracking with a clinician-rated scale. In addition, from the perspective of providing feedback to clinicians that is a usual part of patient-focused methods, there is little advantage to providing feedback to clinicians based on their own ratings of patient functioning.

YOUTH OUTCOME QUESTIONNAIRE

In addition to extending measurement and tracking to severely disturbed patient populations, measures and methods have been extended downward from adults to children and adolescents. For the purpose of tracking their treatment response, the Youth Outcome Questionnaire (Y-OQ) was created. As those who do research with children are well aware, measurement is more difficult in this area. The conceptual scheme that was used for adults, which is based on the fact that regardless of which disorder a patient has most adults experience anxiety and depressive symptoms, could not be applied with children. In addition, research with children is difficult because of their relatively rapid development and because they present for treatment at different presenting ages that can range from infant to near adult. They will have problem behaviors clearly linked to age (e.g., behaviors quite normal in a child would be abnormal in an adolescent).

The Y-OQ consists of 64 items that describe the symptoms and functioning of children from the ages of 4 to 17. It is available in formats suitable for parent and guardian report as well as self-report for children age 12 and older. When working with children under the age of 11 or 12, parent-report data are the most frequently used method of assessment (Burlingame, Wells, Cox, Lambert, & Latowski, 2005). This preference is based on the difficulty of obtaining reliable self-report data from children and the assumption that parents are the most suitable source for obtaining data about a young child's functioning and behavior. In contrast, it is usually preferable to collect data from both parents and adolescents. When both self-report and parent-report data are collected on adolescents, Achenbach (1991) showed that the major difference between parent-report and self-report data is that adolescents tend to underreport their behavior problems (e.g., oppositional attitude, externalizing behaviors, school failures) but that they are more accurate informants regarding their subjective states (e.g., anxiety, depression, feelings of loneliness). Measuring outcomes with youths requires the development of separate formats for youths' self-report and their parents' perceptions.

Parents or other adult caretakers (e.g., grandparents, foster parents) with reasonably extensive interaction with the client complete the parent report at an initial evaluation (e.g., intake or admission interview) to establish a baseline level of severity for symptom distress. They then complete the parent report at later sessions or time periods to track the child's progress; the self-report is completed by the adolescent in a similar manner.

The Y-OQ was created by mutual effort from individuals representing a university-based research team, administrators from a large managed health organization, parents and child patients, and clinicians treating children. Initially, a comprehensive review of the literature was performed of both narrative and meta-analytic reviews of the general psychotherapy treatment literature for children and adolescents having heterogeneous diagnoses. This review's aim was to search for content domains that had empirical support as being sensitive to change in clinical work with children and adolescents. From recent meta-analytic reviews, content domains were considered in which a .5 effect size was obtained (e.g., Baer & Nietzel, 1991; Russell, Greenwald, & Shirk, 1991; Shirk & Russell, 1992; Weisz, Weiss, Alicke, & Klotz, 1987). In other words, content domains in which the average treated child or adolescent was .5 standard deviation better off than untreated children or adolescents were initially considered.

The second element of the Y-OQ development protocol entailed gathering information from focus groups made up of consumers (former clients and their parents) as well as inpatient and outpatient provider focus groups (psychologists, psychiatrists, and other support staff). Both consumers and providers were drawn from a large western health care corporation. Professional focus group leaders led 10 separate focus groups to identify characteristics of change thought to be the direct results of treatment. Audio tapes of the focus groups were transcribed and became part of the material reviewed. Focus groups from providers of inpatient care were particularly valuable in the construction of the Critical Items subscale, which assesses characteristics necessitating inpatient treatment and which must be ameliorated or stabilized prior to referral to outpatient services.

Hospital records were examined to assess the characteristic behavior change goals that were being addressed in treatment planning for both inpatient and outpatient clients. A manifest content analytic process was used to delineate the most frequently occurring change themes noted by providers in these two settings. The intersection of content from the literature reviews, focus groups, and hospital charts constituted the sources from which the final content domains for each of the six subscales were developed. Frequently, final item wording directly reflected change terminology used by parents in their description of a child or adolescent. Although most of the items were formatted to describe various levels of behavior difficulty, 7 of the 64 items were written positively to describe and track healthy child and adolescent behaviors.

Youth Outcome Questionnaire Subscales

The following sections describe each subscale.

Intrapersonal Distress

The purpose of this subscale is to assess the amount of emotional distress in the child or adolescent. Anxiety, depression, fearfulness, hopelessness, and self-harm are aspects measured by the Intrapersonal Distress subscale. Because depression and anxiety are frequently correlated in assessment instruments (Burlingame, Lambert, Reisinger, Neff, & Mosier, 1995), no attempt was made at differentiating these symptoms. High scores indicate a considerable degree of emotional distress in the patient.

Somatic

This subscale assesses change in somatic distress that the child or adolescent may be experiencing. Items address symptoms that are typical presentations, including headaches, dizziness, stomachaches, nausea, bowel difficulties, and pain or weakness in joints. High scores indicate a large number of somatic symptoms, whereas low scores indicate either absence or unawareness of such symptoms.

Interpersonal Relations

The purpose of this subscale is to assess issues relevant to the child's or adolescent's relationship with parents, other adults, and peers. Assessment is made regarding attitude toward others, communication and interaction with friends, cooperativeness, aggressiveness, arguing, and defiance. High scores indicate significant interpersonal difficulty, whereas low scores reflect a cooperative, pleasant interpersonal demeanor.

Critical Items

This subscale describes features of children and adolescents often found in inpatient services where short-term stabilization is the primary change sought. It assesses change in paranoia, obsessive–compulsive behaviors, hallucinations, delusions, suicide, mania, and eating disorder issues. High scores are indicative of those who may need immediate intervention beyond standard outpatient treatment (inpatient, day treatment, or residential care). A high score on any single item should receive serious attention by the provider.

Social Problems

This subscale assesses problematic behaviors that are socially related. Many of the items describe delinquent or aggressive behaviors that are frequently the cause for bringing a child or adolescent into treatment. Although aggressiveness is also assessed in the Interpersonal Relations scale, aggressive content found in this scale is of a more severe nature, typically involving the breaking of social mores. Items include truancy, sexual problems, running away from home, destruction of property, and substance abuse.

Behavioral Dysfunction

This subscale assesses the child's or adolescent's ability to organize tasks, complete assignments, concentrate, and handle frustration, including times of inattention, hyperactivity, and impulsivity. Although many of the items on this scale tap features of specific disorders (e.g., attention-deficit/hyperactivity disorder), the scale is not intended to be diagnostic.

Youth Outcome Questionnaire Total

The total score is simply a summation of items from all six subscales. It reflects total distress in a child's or adolescent's life. Like the OQ-45 this value tends to be the best index to track change and has the highest reliability and validity.

Psychometrics and Norms

Multiple normative groups have been studied to provide a sound basis for judging the health and well-being of youths. Besides children who were from normal community samples, those seeking services in outpatient, school, day treatment, residential, and inpatient samples were included.

Collectively across samples (community normal, outpatient, and inpatient), males outnumber females (approximately 60% to 40%, respectively), with approximately 29% of the total sample coming from the community normal sample, 60% coming from outpatients, and 11% coming from inpatients. As expected, there are very large differences on the total scores among the three samples. Community sample total means were substantially below those taken from clinical settings (inpatient and outpatient). Reliable differences also exist between the two patient populations with inpatients demonstrating more overall symptoms than outpatients. Furthermore, residential patients exhibit the highest levels of symptom severity.

The reliability data suggest excellent internal consistency ($\alpha = .94$) and test–retest reliability correlation coefficients (2-week $r = .84$, 4-week $r = .81$) in both patient and nonpatient samples (Burlingame, Wells, Lambert, & Cox, 2004). Concurrent validity studies suggest moderate to high correlations with scales aimed at measuring similar constructs. Table 3.4 provides an example of findings from such studies. The typical finding is that the Y-OQ has convergent validity with the Child Behavior Checklist (CBCL); the Y-OQ total score and the CBCL Total Problems score have a .78 correlation (Burlingame, Wells, et al., 2005).

TABLE 3.4

Criterion-Related Validity Estimates for the Youth Outcome Questionnaire
Using a Normal Elementary School Sample (N = 423)

Criterion	Youth Outcome Questionnaire subscales					
	ID	S	IR	SP	BD	Total
	Child Behavior Checklist					
Delinquent behavior	.48*	.37*	.49*	*.58**	.53*	.60*
Attention problems	.48*	.36*	.41*	.32*	*.64**	.58*
Total problems	.73*	.57*	.61*	.42*	.69*	*.78**
	Conners Parent Rating Scale					
Anxious, shy	*.67**	.48*	.44*	.25*	.46*	.62*
Psychosomatic	.38*	*.62**	.22*	.15*	.32*	.41*
Conduct disorder	.60*	.39*	*.60**	.44*	.61*	.68*
Antisocial	.35*	.25*	.42*	*.48**	.41*	.41*
Hyperactive, immature	.52*	.40*	.48*	.38*	*.67**	.64*
Restless-disorganized	.60*	.46*	.48*	.31*	*.59**	.64*

Note. Italic values denote correlations that were expected to be statistically significant as they reflect the same construct. ID = Intrapersonal Distress; S = Somatic; IR = Interpersonal Relations; SP = Social Problems; and BD = Behavioral Dysfunction. From *Administration and Scoring Manual for the Youth Outcome Questionnaire* (p. 26), by G. M. Burlingame, J. G. M. Wells, J. Cox, M. J. Lambert, and M. Latowski, 2005, Salt Lake City, UT: OQ Measures, LLC. Copyright 2005 by OQ Measures, LLC. Reprinted with permission.
*$p < .01$.

The sensitivity to change of the Y-OQ adolescent self-report version of the Y-OQ and the parent version were tested relative to two youth scales commonly used to assess treatment outcome (although these latter scales were initially designed for other purposes, such as providing categorical descriptions of symptoms or assigning a diagnosis): the CBCL and the Behavior Assessment System for Children. Both measures have excellent general psychometric properties. Warren, Nelson, Mondragon, Baldwin, and Burlingame (in press) tracked the treatment response of 936 parents recruited from a community mental health system in the intermountain west. Parents of children ages 6 to 17 completed parent-report forms, and adolescents ages 12 to 17 completed self-report forms. Hierarchical linear modeling was conducted for three major comparisons: an adult informant comparison, an adult and adolescent dyad comparison, and an adolescent informant comparison. Results indicated that the Y-OQ was most change sensitive, whereas the Behavior Assessment System for Children and the CBCL were not statistically different from each other. In addition, ratings from adult informants were more change sensitive than those from adolescent informants.

The Jacobson and Truax (2001) methods for calculating clinically significant change in the Y-OQ were done in the same manner as for the OQ-45. Using this method the RCI was calculated to be 13 and the cut-off for normal functioning was 46. Using these scores the clinician knows that the parent sees the child as having reliably changed and behaving "within normal limits" and can adjust treatment accordingly (e.g., work to consolidate gains, prepare for termination).

Burlingame et al. (2001) examined consequences of using these cutoff scores in a large sample of outpatient and inpatient youths compared with a community normal sample. The samples consisted of 81 normal youths, 675 outpatients, and 174 inpatients. The sample ranged from age 4 to 17 ($M = 11.17$; $SD = 3.43$). Y-OQs were administered at the 3rd, 5th, and 10th sessions of treatment. Using the cutoff of 46 and the RCI of 13, Burlingame et al. (2001) designated 17% of their clinical sample as recovered (falling below the cutoff while changing more than 13), 37% as improved (symptom scores improving by more than 13), 31% as unchanged, and 15% as deteriorated (symptom scores increasing by more than 13). They reported an average change between pre- and posttest scores for the clinical sample of 17.7 points ($SD = 34.8$), whereas the student normal sample difference score mean was 4.34 ($SD = 2.48$). This difference was significant indicating that the Y-OQ is likely to reliably detect changes in symptom levels across short periods of treatment and supporting the conclusion that the Y-OQ demonstrates good construct validity.

As with the OQ-45, some users desired a briefer measure. Sixty-four items is quite long for a measure that would be given weekly or even every other week. This is especially true if it is being taken by an adolescent who is a poor reader. As a consequence, a shorter form was developed.

YOUTH OUTCOME QUESTIONNAIRE-30

The Youth Outcome Questionnaire-30 (Y-OQ-30) is a brief version of the Y-OQ that maintains the content areas of the Y-OQ without providing subscale information. Like the OQ-30, it was originally developed for use by the same managed care company (and named the Youth-Life Status Inventory) that used the OQ-30. The progress of thousands of children throughout the United States has been tracked using this instrument. The 30 items for the Y-OQ-30 were chosen from the full length Y-OQ (Burlingame, Wells, et al., 2005) on the basis of their individual sensitivity to change as estimated from a large-scale study of patients undergoing treatment in a variety of settings (Berrett, 1999). Questions are written in language appropriate to a fourth-grade reading level.

Relevant Issues

As described in the section that follows, psychometric calculations from the normative database permit determination of the client's symptom distress

similarity at each measurement interval with several normative populations including inpatient, outpatient, and community samples. Using cutoff
scores and an RCI, clinicians, parents, guardians, clients and administrators
can determine if and when the client's mental health functioning has entered
the normal range. Although there is no question that a self-report measure is
appropriate for tracking change in most adult clinical populations (Lambert,
Gregersen, & Burlingame, 2004), it is not as clear whether a parent-report or
a self-report measure is best for child and adolescent populations. In addition
to developmental considerations (verbal skills and reading ability), factors
such as motivation for treatment, social desirability, and perception of
problem behavior or feelings (i.e., whether the child sees a particular symptom as problematic or his parents or teacher see it as problematic), all influence the decision to use parent-report or self-report data with children.

Normative Data and Psychometrics

Normative data based on patient and nonpatient samples provide the
basis for evaluating the clinical significance of change as well as interpreting
the meaning of scores. Two separate parent-report inpatient and outpatient
samples were collected through the intake offices of a large multistate western
health care corporation. Specifically, all children and adolescents who presented for treatment at outpatient and inpatient facilities located in Utah and
Idaho that were owned and operated by this corporation completed the instrument as part of their initial screening. By collecting data at intake from all new
patients, initial level of disturbance for these populations was captured. Over
500 protocols were collected from four inpatient and outpatient sites. One additional sample contributed to the inpatient grouping, a private residential treatment facility also in the western United States ($n = 242$).

Two community mental health centers also contributed to the outpatient
data. These centers are operated by state-funded public mental health systems
in the western United States (one services a city of approximately 1 million,
and the other covers a diverse western county). These two samples contributed
approximately 600 protocols in the analyses. Another segment of the outpatient clinical sample came from a western state's youth protection and reform
system. This state system typically requires psychosocial interventions as well
as detention or probation. A total of 719 adolescents (64% male, 36% female)
from this state system were part of the analyses.

Additional outpatient samples were obtained from two other managed care companies, one servicing clients throughout the United States
and another along the eastern seaboard. These clinical samples consisted
of 577 clients. Protocols were simply given to parents of adolescents presenting for treatment within the care system at intake and predetermined points

TABLE 3.5
TABLE 3.5
Parent-Report Normative Groups for the Youth Outcome
Questionnaire-30 Total Score

Sample	n	Total score M	SE
Inpatient	435	68.1	.96
Outpatient	2,297	43.3	.46
Community	1,091	17.3	.43
Juvenile justice	719	32.6	.76

Note. From *Administration and Scoring Manual for the Youth Outcome Questionnaire-30* (p. 7), by G. M. Burlingame, T. Dunn, M. Hill, J. Cox, M. G. Wells, M. J. Lambert, and G. S. Brown, 2004, Salt Lake City, UT: OQ Measures, LLC. Copyright 2004 by OQ Measures, LLC. Reprinted with permission.

throughout treatment. Finally, a population sample of all juveniles entering the intake system for the state of Utah completed the Y-OQ-30 (Gray et al., 2000). The majority were male (70%) with (84%) ranging from 11 to 17 years of age. A small number (13.6%) fell above this range—18 to 19 years of age, and 2.4% were 6 to 10 years of age. The means and standard errors for the normative groupings are depicted in Table 3.5.

Collectively across the four samples (community normal, juvenile justice, outpatient, and inpatient), males outnumber females (approximately 64% to 36%, respectively) with approximately 24% of the total sample coming from the community normal sample, 51% coming from outpatients, 16% coming from juvenile justice, and 10% coming from inpatients. The cutoff score for the parent report that distinguished membership between a normal community sample (Dunn, 2004) and a clinical sample (inpatient and outpatient combined) using the Jacobson and Truax (1991) formula for the total score and nearly 10,000 outpatient cases (cf. Hill et al., 2004) produced a value of 30. This value was also supported for the self-report cutoff score. The RCI derived with community and clinical samples is 10, meaning that an individual's score must change by at least 10 points on the Y-OQ-30 to be considered reliably changed. As with the cutoff score, the use of the RCI presented here is recommended for most general purposes as it is based on large and diverse normative samples.

Reliability

The internal consistency reliability of the Y-OQ-30 parent report was tested using Cronbach's alpha with a parent-report community normative sample of 1,091 and a parent-report patient normative sample (inpatient and outpatient combined) of 2,732. A high internal consistency estimate of .96 was attained with the combined sample. The internal consistency reliability of the self-report was tested using Cronbach's alpha with a community normative sample of 494 patients (day treatment and outpatient combined) and 773 normal youths. The self-report also had high internal consistency.

Concurrent Validity

The validity of the Y-OQ-30 parent report was examined by comparing it with the total score of the CBCL (Achenbach, 1991) in a community sample of the parents of 423 elementary children (age 6–12); a moderately high correlation of .76 was found between the total score and the CBCL total score, indicating adequate convergent validity.

Given that the Y-OQ-30 parent report maintains the psychometric qualities of the longer Y-OQ, it is reasonable to prefer it as a tracking measure to the Y-OQ, particularly from the point of view of systems of care adoption of this measure. However, users of the measure who have tried both the full version and the short version, particularly if they are psychologists, show a preference for the longer scale. The reason for this appears mainly to be their familiarity with psychological tests delivering information that can be used for clinical purposes other than tracking—such as diagnostic formulations, personality assessment, and treatment planning. As the shorter Y-OQ-30 provides less of this kind of information than the longer version, it is not as highly valued.

SUMMARY

In this chapter several instruments appropriate for use with children and adults were presented along with some of their characteristics. Because the instruments were created to operationalize patient mental health functioning, their ability to serve this purpose was emphasized. To do this job, tests need to be reliable, measure what they purport to measure, discriminate between groups that are functioning poorly and well, reflect improvements when they occur, and assist in classifying individual patients as improved or deteriorated. In addition, such tests need to be suitable for frequent readministration. The evidence reported supports the presence of these characteristics. In relation to self-report scales that enjoy a preferred status in clinical trials for measuring psychological disturbance, the OQ measures perform similarly and are used in controlled outcome studies as well as patient-focused research. Treatment effects can be monitored well using the OQ scales.

Because patient-focused methods also rely on the ability of instruments to predict treatment failure, and because this is their major function in improving patient outcome, this complex but critical topic is addressed in a separate chapter. Chapter 4 focuses on predictive methods and their accuracy.

4

PREDICTING NEGATIVE TREATMENT OUTCOME: METHODS AND ESTIMATES OF ACCURACY

One of the likeliest ways of improving the effects of psychotherapy is to identify cases at risk of a negative outcome and intervene with the patient before he or she leaves the therapist's care. This procedure stands in contrast (but is complementary) to the contemporary practice of ensuring that patients are provided with an empirically supported treatment. The assumption here is that therapists are providing the highest level of care if they select the right psychotherapy for the right disorder. As noted earlier in this book (see Chapter 1, this volume), even when an empirically supported treatment is offered to individuals who have the same disorder and who see therapists who have been carefully selected, monitored, and supervised, 30% to 50% of patients fail to respond to treatment (Hansen, Lambert, & Forman, 2003). This means that even if there were a right treatment or best practice for an individual, therapists would need to identify patients who were failing to respond to this treatment. In addition to providing best practices, it is essential that therapists monitor clients while they are in treatment and take actions if a client is not benefiting from the services. The major assumption of this practice is that therapists can identify poorly responding clients in a timely fashion and then take corrective actions: Can we predict treatment failure before it occurs?

Once efficient measures (as presented in Chapter 3) were developed to operationalize treatment response on a session-by-session basis, it became possible to examine patterns of change over time (also discussed in Chapter 8) and to use this information to predict negative change. Prediction is the cornerstone of patient-focused research, but such prediction needs to be practical in that the predictive information needs to be quickly gathered, inexpensive, and available very early in the treatment process, before patients terminate services. The value of unique predictive systems is demonstrated if predictions can be made more quickly than other methods and if these predictions are more accurate. The reader is reminded that the prediction that is of interest here is not the general ability to predict patient outcome but the specific ability to predict negative outcome.

PREDICTION OF NEGATIVE CHANGE

As is shown in Chapters 5 and 6, maximizing patient outcomes through monitoring patient mental health and feeding back this information to therapists is specifically helpful for patients who are having a negative treatment response. It should be emphasized that prediction of negative outcomes using psychological tests and systematic actuarial methods would not be a necessary or important activity if therapists could accomplish the task based on their clinical intuition.

The Surprising Failure of Clinicians to Accurately Predict Negative Outcomes

Prior to a discussion of the accuracy of rational and empirical methods of predicting deterioration, it may be helpful to understand how well clinicians can do this task on the basis of their clinical wisdom and experience with the client. After all, why develop elaborate means of predicting negative outcomes if clinicians can do the task? To examine therapist predictive accuracy, Hannan et al. (2005) examined therapist accuracy by asking 40 therapists (20 trainees and 20 experienced professionals) at the end of each session with each of their clients if they believed the client would leave treatment in a deteriorated state and, in addition, if the client was worse off at this particular session than when he or she entered treatment. Hannan et al. expected that experienced clinicians, given their extensive contact with clients over the years, would be more accurate in their judgments than trainees (who ranged from 1st-year graduate students to intern level providers).

Therapists were aware of the purpose of the study, understanding it to be a contest between experienced and less experienced providers compared with statistical methods that they had used in the recent past. They also under-stood that there was no consequence to the client for making any prediction, as the research was aimed at understanding how well clinicians could forecast negative final treatment outcome. They were aware that the dependent meas-ure used to categorize patient change was the Outcome Questionnaire-45 (OQ-45) and understood the cutoff scores for judging deterioration, but they did not have access to the patients OQ-45 scores. They were reminded that the base rate for deterioration was likely to be 8%. So the phenomenon they were to predict was relatively rare, perhaps 1 in 10 of their clients. Most therapists had experience receiving predictive information based on both rational and empirical predictive methods described later in this chapter. So the experiment was a straightforward contest between licensed providers with an average of 10 years postdoctoral experience, novice providers (mostly psy-chology trainees), and empirical algorithms.

During a 3-week period predictions were made for 550 clients who par-ticipated in therapy sessions. In some cases therapists made three predictions, two predictions, or a single prediction based on the number of sessions a client attended over the 3 weeks. In every other way treatment continued as usual and clients' progress was followed until they terminated treatment, at which time their intake OQ-45 score could be compared with their end of treatment OQ-45 score. Although 40 clients had deteriorated at the termination of treatment, only 3 of 550 clients (.01%) were predicted by their therapist to leave treatment worse off than when they began, one of whom actually dete-riorated. In general, clients' eventual deterioration was not forecast by clini-cians who were attempting to do so. Rather than experienced clinicians being more able to predict the phenomenon, they did not identify a single client who deteriorated; the only accurate prediction out of the three that were made was made by a trainee. In contrast, 36 of the 40 (90%) clients who dete-riorated were predicted to do so on the basis of applying actuarial predictive methods to data from the same time period.

The actual deterioration rate for this sample was 7.3%, very close to the 8% Hannan et al. (2005) expected and informed therapists of at the incep-tion of the study. Despite being armed with base-rate information and having familiarity with the outcome measure used in the study, therapists showed an inability (unwillingness?) to accurately forecast negative outcome. Their pre-dictions would have improved markedly if they had simply used their judg-ment that a patient was worse off relative to his or her intake status at any particular session (16 such clients), but they did not interpret their percep-tion of patient worsening in this way. One might hope that the results of this study are limited to a single clinic consisting of poor or below average thera-pists, but it seems unlikely that this could explain these results. The therapists were well trained, and, as a group, demonstrated patient outcomes that were on a par with other treatment centers (information on this latter point is provided in Chapter 7, this volume).

Collaborating information has been found in a related study that applied different methodology. Hatfield, McCullough, Plucinski, and Krieger (2009), using an archival database from a large Midwestern university, identified cases that had deteriorated during routine care offered by 13 licensed professionals, nearly half of whom had a doctorate with the remaining having a master's degree or completing a predoctoral internship. Outcome was measured with the OQ-45, and the selected clients were in the clinical range and seen by the same therapists from intake through treatment termination. No feedback was given to therapists in a systematic way, although session-by-session scores were present in many client files. The deterioration rate at the center among clients in the clinical range was 9% (386/4,253). Of these cases, 214 were randomly selected and further reduced by eliminating clients who had seen more than one therapist, leaving 70 clients whose case files were examined to see if therapists made any note indicating clients had worsened from the time they entered treatment. The files that were rated corresponded to those sessions in which the OQ-45 score had increased by 14 points or more (the reliable change index). Case notes were classified as either mentioning change or not and if worsening was noted. For those case notes in which worsening was noted, the actions of therapists were recorded.

Therapists noted deterioration in 15 of the 70 clients (21%) with no mention of progress occurring in 41 (59%) of the cases. The OQ-45 score was referred to in 9% of cases. Two (3%) of the clients were rated as improved. With regard to new treatment decisions for the clients whose negative change was noted by the therapist and those who mentioned the OQ-45 score ($n = 21$), many were noted in the record. The most common actions were referral for medication (24%), continue treatment as usual (24%), and change treatment implementation (19%).

The most severe cases of negative change were further examined by looking only at cases whose negative change was 30 or more points, an extreme deviation from entry levels of distress. Among 41 (4.4% of those entering treatment) clients who met this criterion, deterioration was recorded in a case note in 32% of the cases. In contrast to the Hannan et al. (2005) study in which therapists were asked to predict the eventual outcome of treatment and virtually never imagined it happening, the Hatfield et al. (2009) study estimated awareness of negative change as indicated in written notes. In this latter instance, even in situations involving very serious symptom worsening, therapists made no mention of it in about 70% of the cases, and even when it was noted did not bring up supervision or consultation as an appropriate action in a single instance, although changing strategies and referral for medications were noted. These results are similar to results in Hannan et al.

with regard to asking therapists to judge client status after specific sessions. Of 55 clients who were identified by the OQ-45 as signal-alarm cases at a specific session, 21 were judged by their therapist as "recovered" or "improved." So the fact is that Hatfield et al. drew conclusions that may have underrepresented therapist awareness of client worsening because they relied on case notes (which may have been incomplete), whereas the Hannan et al. study provides evidence that therapists not only cannot predict final outcome but see nearly 40% of clients as in an improved state when they are reporting more symptoms than they had when they started treatment.

It seems clear on the basis of therapists' perceptions of client worsening that therapists are overly optimistic about their positive effects on clients.

The Lake Woebegone Effect

On his radio program, *A Prairie Home Companion*, Garrison Keillor describes all of the children from Lake Woebegone as being above average, a rosy picture indeed. Previous research has consistently found not just a parental bias toward one's own children but a positive self-assessment bias. Positive self-assessment bias (an overly positive assessment of personal performance) is present in a wide variety of occupations from engineers to policemen. Walfish, McAlister, O'Donnell, and Lambert (2009) studied the self-perceptions of 129 therapists in private practice. This investigation extended self-assessment-bias research with a multidisciplinary sample of mental health professionals. Respondents were asked to (a) compare their own overall clinical skills and performance levels with others in their profession and (b) estimate what percentage of their clients improved, remained the same, or deteriorated as a result of treatment with them.

Results (see Table 4.1) indicate that psychotherapists are not immune from self-assessment bias in terms of (a) comparing their own skills with those of their colleagues and (b) estimating the improvement and deterioration rates that likely occur with their clients. Among mental health professionals, 25% viewed their skill level to be at the 90th percentile when compared with their peers, and none viewed themselves as below average. Psychotherapists may have little problem identifying colleagues they believe are below average and to whom they might never consider referring a client for psychotherapy. At the same time, they overestimate their own abilities.

The information found in the Walfish et al. (2009) investigation regarding therapist self-perception and therapist perception of client improvement and deterioration is somewhat troubling and potentially problematic. As noted in Chapter 1, outcomes in routine care across a variety of treatment settings suggest a mean of 8% of clients leave deteriorated (Hansen, Lambert, & Forman, 2002). In the Walfish et al. survey of psychotherapists, on average,

TABLE 4.1
Distribution of Percentiles of Self-Rated Psychotherapy Skill Levels

Percentile	%
50	3.9
60	.7
65	.7
70	3.1
75	33.1
80	15.1
85	15.1
87	.7
89	1.6
90	17.3
95	7.9
100	.7

From "Are all therapists from Lake Wobegon?: An investigation of self-assessment bias in mental health providers," by S. Walfish, B. McAlister, P. O'Donnell, and M. J. Lambert, 2009. Manuscript submitted for publication. Printed with permission of the authors.

clinicians probably underestimated client deterioration rates (3.66%), with nearly half (47.7%) of the psychotherapists reporting that none of their clients regressed in their symptoms as a result of treatment with them.

Erhlinger and Dunning (2003) found a significant portion of performance estimates from a variety of situations unrelated to psychotherapy to be based on a chronic view of a person's ability within a particular domain. They were able to demonstrate how overreliance on inaccurate self-assessments may result in negative behavioral consequences. There is no reason to believe that psychotherapists, and by proxy their clients' well-being, would not be subject to the same consequences of overly positive self-assessments. Dunning, Heath, and Suls (2004) stated that underlying self-assessment bias is that "people are often motivated to reach flattering conclusions about themselves and their place in the world. Thus they mold, manage, and massage the feedback the world provides them so that they can construe themselves as lovable and capable people" (p. 78). It may also be just an unconscious attempt to stay motivated in the face of very difficult client problems and circumstances. Whatever motivations may be involved, the problem is heightened by research suggesting that individuals who are less competent may be the least likely to accurately assess the quality of their performance (Erhlinger & Dunning, 2003; John & Robbins, 1994). Most important for the client, the failure to recognize client worsening lessens the chance that such a phenomenon will be acted on by the therapist in a timely manner. Because psychotherapists who are truly below average may not recognize that their skills are deficient and even above average psychotherapists may not recognize that their patients are regressing, an argument may be made that all psychotherapists need to formally monitor client progress and outcomes. The implication for practice based on the results of the Walfish et al. (2009) survey and related literature is that psychotherapists, as a result of self-assessment bias, will likely overestimate their skill level and positive client outcomes and underestimate client deterioration rates.

A dilemma of providing feedback to clinicians about their effects on client outcome is that most will be unhappy with the findings, a topic that is returned to in Chapter 8. In general, because clinicians view themselves as near the top in effectiveness and as having a greater positive impact on client functioning than the data will show, disappointment seems inevitable. Another implication of self-assessment bias for improvement of psychotherapy outcomes that is extremely important is that therapists will look for reasons that the data are flawed and discount the data, rather than seek to improve. Under such conditions it is likely that clinicians will see little need to change routine practice patterns to include methods for monitoring client treatment response and will resist routine study of client outcomes. Therapist optimism about the eventual end of treatment functioning of those they treat is a very good thing for clients because it allows therapists to continue working productively with very difficult clients whose lives are out of control. Clients are less likely to benefit from treatment offered by discouraged providers, so failures to predict an impending negative outcome may have its advantages. But the cost of such optimism appears to be high (i.e., failure to recognize and deal with factors causing negative change).

In fact, the results are consistent with, if not more extreme than, findings from hundreds of studies comparing clinical prediction with actuarial methods. Examples regarding the limitation of clinicians' ability to make accurate judgments without feedback are plentiful. For example, a review comparing human judgment and diagnosis abilities versus statistical methods consistently shows that statistical methods are much more accurate (Grove, Zald, Lebow, Snitz, & Nelson, 2000). Despite the evidence suggesting that clinical decision making may not always be accurate, professionals are typically very confident about their eventual clinical decisions (Garb, 1998). Owing to the extant research documenting the superiority of actuarial over clinical methods in making such predictions (Garb, 2005), there is little doubt that the greatest predictive success will come through real time, clinic-based application of computer-assisted actuarial methods. Indeed, in the future, such psychological "lab test" or "vital sign" data will be as important in behavioral health as in medicine.

The Rational Method: A First Attempt
at Actuarial Prediction of Deterioration

In researchers' initial attempts at prediction, information about early response to treatment, the dose–response relationship, and clinically significant change was used by two clinical judges to create rational algorithms for identifying patients who were predicted to leave treatment with a negative treatment outcome. In essence this predictive strategy relied on three important variables to make predictions: (a) initial level of disturbance, (b) how much change had occurred (and in which direction), and (c) how many sessions of care a patient had received. The judges created a matrix for identification of these signal-alarm or not-on-track cases. The vertical axis was used to plot severity at intake (intake OQ-45 scores across the possible range of scores from 0 to 180). The horizontal axis consisted of OQ-45 score at the session of interest, with each cell color coded to indicate the raters consensual judgment of satisfactory progress at this time (green), return to normal functioning (white), worrisome progress (yellow), or highly problematic (red) progress at the session of interest.

It proved difficult to make decisions about satisfactory patient progress for every session that a patient received, and such a procedure would have necessitated 20 or more separate matrices of the kind just described, each dealing with the effects of that session and one varying only slightly from the next. Therefore, it was decided to lump sessions into groupings, creating three matrices. These matrices grouped the number of treatment sessions as 2–4, 5–9, and 10 and above. The reasoning used to create three matrices was that insufficient change after 2–4 sessions of treatment would not be as alarming as the same insufficient progress after 5–9 or more sessions of treatment. These decision rules could be applied as soon as the patient had a single session of psychotherapy (had an intake score and a second score following the second treatment session).

The judges used their clinical experience and knowledge of the OQ-45 to imagine specific scenarios with the intent of classifying specific patients into the four classifications on the basis of the colored signals. After scenarios for Sessions 2–4 were created, the same procedures were repeated for the imagined patient who had received 5–9 sessions of treatment, and again for patients who had 10 or more sessions of treatment. The two raters would imagine a patient who started at a specific OQ-45 score and then imagine the patient worsening by 1 point, 2 points, 3 points, and so on. At a given point, depending on the patient's intake score, a degree of worsening would become large enough that the raters would reach a consensus that a yellow signal was warranted and then a red signal. As noted previously, movement in a positive direction (or small movement in a negative direction) was given a green signal indicating patients were making satisfactory progress or a white categorization when the patients' change score put them in the functional range (i.e., below a score of 64 on the OQ-45).

Some examples of the procedures will help clarify the way cutoff points were devised. A patient could be imagined who began treatment with an OQ-45 score of 75. This score is an average score for patients entering treatment in outpatient clinics and about 1.5 standard deviations above the mean of non-patients. The raters considered the patient's worsening after having 2–4 sessions of treatment (1 point, 2 points, 3 points, etc.) and agreed that if the patient had made a negative change of 1 point (after this dosage of therapy) a yellow warning was appropriate, and that getting worse by 9 points (about 2/3 of the reliable change index of 14 points) would qualify him or her for a red warning.

In contrast to this patient, consider a patient who enters treatment with a score of 96 (a score that is close to the mean of inpatients, about a standard deviation above outpatients, and 2.5 standard deviations above nonpatients). This score suggests severe distress and a need for immediate relief. The raters agreed that an improvement of less than 7 points after 2–4 sessions of treatment should signal a yellow caution, no change or any worsening should result in a red signal. A white signal categorization was given if patients changed by 32 points or more (indicating their score at the session of interest had moved to 63 or below).

Similar decisions were made to form the matrices for Sessions 5–9 and 10 and above. The rules for classification for these matrices were based on the meaning of changing or not changing after this higher dosage of treatment. For example, a patient who starts treatment with a score of 70 on the OQ-45 and does not change after two treatment sessions was not considered to be as "alarming" as this patient's same failure to change after nine treatment sessions.

An Empirical Method for Prediction

Traditionally, empirical outcome prediction has used baseline characteristics of patients, therapists, and the treatment context to predict treatment outcome. These variables are useful in creating models for case-mix adjustment and can guide the placement of patients into services (Hendryx, Dyck, & Srebnik, 1999; Kramer et al., 2001) at the system level but only if there are unlimited options available. For example, if a patient is best suited to be seen by a Latino therapist, then one must be available for the information to profit a client. In general, the traditional empirical predictive elements tell researchers what would be ideal to maximize outcome but little about how to make the information work in practice (possibly one reason clinicians do not find traditional psychotherapy research an important influence in their work).

A more empirical or purely statistical method of prediction became possible after repeatedly assessing clients with the OQ-45 following sessions of treatment. Survival statistics used for the dose–response research are ideal for providing analysis that can affect policy decisions that consider the occurrence of an event of interest, such as recovery and the sessions needed for that event to materialize. In contrast, a large database provides enough information to use hierarchical linear modeling (HLM) to model the shape and speed of average change over time using session-by-session data produced by patients. HLM is especially useful in analyzing longitudinal data from routine care (in contrast to clinical trials in which treatment length is fixed), a situation in which patients begin treatment at diverse levels of initial disturbance and have treatment lengths that are highly varied. The results of such modeling can be examined for subsets of patients who meet criteria for an event such as clinically significant or reliable change (or deterioration) but are most valuable as a means for establishing session-by-session expectations for a course of psychotherapy in relation to unique levels of initial disturbance.

Finch, Lambert, and Schaalje (2001) used the PROC MIXED functions of the Statistical Analysis System to apply HLM to a large database consisting of 11,492 patients treated in a variety of settings including employee assistance programs, university counseling centers, outpatient clinics, private practice, and a clinical psychology training clinic. An initial graphical analysis of the data revealed decelerating growth curves similar to those identified in dose–response studies—a lawful linear relationship between the log of the number of sessions and the normalized probability of patient improvement, again illuminating the tendency for larger and larger doses (number of sessions) to find a higher percentage of recovered patients.

To compare an individual patient's change with that of similar patients, it would be ideal to generate a recovery curve for every possible initial level of disturbance, degree of motivation, expectancy of a positive outcome, diagnosis, type of treatment, and the like. Although the data set used for this purpose was large, it was not of sufficient size to be able to establish an individual recovery curve for each intake OQ-45 score (score range 0–180) because the statistical techniques require a large number of cases at each score for reliable modeling. In addition, other variables that could be used for prediction, such as diagnosis, were either unreliable, missing, or did not improve predictive accuracy (e.g., professed treatment orientation did not relate to outcome). Scores falling at the extremes of the continuum of disturbance are quite rare. Therefore, the full range of scores was divided into distinct groups by percentiles. This yielded 50 groups identified by intake score with no fewer than 220 patients in each band and represented approximately 2% of the total sample. The resulting distribution across intake scores was approximately normal with intake score increments as small as 1 point at the group average and a larger spread between intake scores at the two extreme tails (e.g., patients seldom score below 30 or above 130 at intake).

The resulting groups of data were analyzed to generate a linear model for recovery curves. Administrations of the OQ-45 were nested within an individual patient, who was nested within a specific therapist, who was nested within a specific treatment site, and so forth. Each of these hierarchical levels can potentially contribute randomly to the variance of the final estimates. Mixed modeling identified statistically significant differences in error variance between random variables, such as between psychotherapy outcomes at different sites. When a statistically significant difference was found, the amount of variance attributable to this difference was identified and combined with the fixed effects in the linear equation used to establish the estimates and confidence intervals. When patients in this data set did not have OQ-45 administrations at every session, a linear model of their course in therapy was still produced, accounting for the within-subject variance of the missing data points. This linear model allowed comparisons of individuals even when OQ-45 scores were missing at different sessions and even when the ultimate number of sessions, length of time between sessions, and overall length of therapy was different between clients. Essentially, a separate regression line and error estimate was generated for each patient in the analysis.

Error estimates from the fixed effects, random effects, and correlations were combined into an aggregate error term for the estimates of the OQ-45 total score at each session. This combined error term was then used to establish the upper and lower bounds of tolerance intervals for each of the coefficients. The tolerance interval is a quality control protocol often used in engineering applications. Tolerance intervals determine the probability that a given OQ-45 score at a given session will fall within a specified interval. The tolerance intervals allowed for the identification of OQ-45 total score values that have an established probability of falling outside of the upper and lower limits of the tolerance interval. Specifically, this means that the tolerance intervals calculated in this model allowed for the identification of the 10% (red signal) and 15% (yellow signal) of patients in a given sample whose rate and trajectory of progress deviated significantly from what was the predicted course of recovery for others entering therapy with a similar intake score.

The tolerance intervals created were aimed primarily at identifying this 10% of the patient population who deviate from the recovery track. These coefficients and tolerance intervals formed the core of the "empirical warning system" by providing table values and charts of predicted therapeutic gains against which any given patient could be compared at any session of psychotherapy. After an individual has completed a given OQ-45 administration, the total score can then be compared with the corresponding session value for others beginning therapy with a comparable pretreatment score. If at any session following intake the OQ-45 total score for a patient does not exceed the tolerance interval, then therapy is judged as proceeding as anticipated for this particular patient and a green message can be given as feedback for the therapist to proceed as he or she has been. If the same OQ-45 score falls outside of the upper 15% and does not surpass the upper bound of the 10% tolerance interval, the patient is considered to be deviating by greater than 1 standard deviation from what is expected of a typical person at this point in therapy, and the therapist would receive a yellow message as a warning to attend to this patient's progress. If this same OQ-45 score falls above the upper limits of the 10% interval, then the patient is deviating significantly in a negative direction from what is predicted for patients at this point in therapy. The 10% boundary is consistent with the estimate that about 10% of patients deteriorate following psychotherapy (Lambert & Ogles, 2004). At this point the therapist would receive a red warning message that therapy may be heading toward an unsuccessful conclusion and that the therapist may need to consider an alternative course of action. In this program of research Finch et al. (2001) considered patients whose treatment response crosses either the yellow or red boundary to be alarm-signal or *off-track* cases. Such patients are predicted to leave treatment deteriorated unless preventive actions are taken.

Abbreviated messages associated with predictions are as follows:

- White feedback: "The client is functioning in the normal range. Consider termination."
- Green feedback: "The rate of change the client is making is in the adequate range. No change in the treatment plan is recommended."
- Yellow feedback: "The rate of change the client is making is less than adequate. Consider altering the treatment plan by intensifying treatment, shifting intervention strategies, and monitoring progress especially carefully. This client may end up with no significant benefit from therapy."
- Red feedback: "The client is not making the expected level of progress. Chances are he or she may drop out of treatment prematurely or have a negative treatment outcome. Steps should be taken to carefully review this case and consider a new course of action such as referral for medication or intensification of treatment. The treatment plan should be reconsidered. Consideration should also be given to seeking supervision on this case."

ACCURACY OF PREDICTING TREATMENT FAILURE

After methods for predicting negative treatment outcome were developed for adults and children, a series of studies tested their accuracy in routine care settings in which the OQ measures were administered, but the results were withheld from clinicians and clients.

Accuracy of Predicting Treatment Failure in Adults

In contrast to clinician accuracy, the accuracy of researchers' actuarial methods has been tested in five separate studies (Ellsworth, Lambert, & Johnson, 2006; Hannan et al., 2005; Lambert, Whipple, Bishop, et al., 2002 ; Lutz et al 2006; Spielmans, Masters, & Lambert, 2006), and these methods appear to be successful at predicting which patients will have negative treatment outcomes. These studies vary with regard to patient populations, methods, and findings and are now briefly reviewed.

Lambert, Whipple, Bishop, et al. (2002) examined predictive accuracy of both the rational and empirical methods with 492 clients who were in treatment at a university counseling center. Of these cases, 36 (7.3%) were reliably worse or had deteriorated at termination. The empirical method correctly identified all 36 (100%), most of whom (86%) were identified by the third treatment session. Thus, the empirical method was highly effective at identifying clients who went on to deteriorate, and such a prediction could be made very early (although in this setting about 90% of clients have left treatment by the 15th session). At the same time, the empirical method misidentified 83 (18%) clients as likely to deteriorate (not on track) when they did not. The outcome of these misidentified cases (false alarms or false positives) was further studied and contrasted with the outcome of clients who were not identified as signal-alarm cases (predicted positive outcome). Of the 83 misclassified signal-alarm cases, 18% improved or recovered at termination, whereas 74% showed no reliable change. In contrast, of the 373 cases that the empirical method did not identify as signal-alarm cases, 50% recovered or improved and 50% showed no reliable change. These findings offer further support for the signal-alarm method in that they suggest that even the false alarms have a poorer outcome than cases that are not identified as likely treatment failures. That is, if an alarm (red or yellow warning) is given, the client has less than a 1 in 5 chance of having a positive outcome compared with a 50 in 50 chance if no signal alarm is generated.

Unlike some medical decisions in which the cost of overidentification of signal cases may result in intrusive and even health-threatening interventions such as surgery, the signal alarm in psychotherapy merely alerts the therapist to the need for reconsidering the value of ongoing treatment rather than mandating specific changes. Thus, researchers see the signal alarm as supporting clinical decision making rather than supplanting it. Because the signal alarm alerts therapists to the possible need for action rather than triggering a negative chain of events such as termination or referral, the current level of misidentification would seem to be tolerable.

Further analyses explored the difference between red and yellow warnings: What was the relative outcome for clients receiving a red versus a yellow signal? Outcome for these clients was classified into three categories: reliably improved or recovered, no reliable change, or deteriorated. Of the 36 deteriorated cases, the empirical method's red alarm picked up 34 of the 36 deteriorated cases, whereas the yellow signal picked up the remaining two deteriorated cases. The red alarm is indeed a more serious indicator for deterioration, one that should generate greater cause for concern to clinicians than the yellow signal.

In a replication of this study, Spielmans et al. (2006) examined the predictive accuracy of the rational and empirical methods in two treatment centers, a state university counseling center ($n = 216$) and a university-based graduate student training clinic ($n = 83$) where psychotherapy was provided to community members. When reliable worsening (OQ-45 worsening of 14 or more points) was used as the negative outcome criterion, the empirical method was accurate in 81% of cases. Of the 16 (5%) clients who reliably worsened, the empirical method identified 13. When deterioration (leaving treatment in the clinical range and worsening by 14 or more points) was used as the negative outcome criterion, 10 of 13 cases were correctly identified.

When transformed into a standardized mean difference effect size (ES; intake OQ-45 score − endpoint OQ-45 score / pooled standard deviation of intake and endpoint OQ-45 scores), those clients predicted to fail by the empirical method improved by an ES of .17, which is slightly less than the ES of .20 widely considered to represent a small ES (Cohen, 1988). This indicates that little improvement, on average, occurred for those clients who were identified as not on track (signal alarms) by the empirical method. Clients predicted to have a nonnegative outcome (i.e., *not* to have a negative response to treatment) showed positive outcomes on average (ES = .90). In contrast to the original study, which had an identification rate of 100%, this study showed less accuracy (81%). A likely reason for this is the amount of missing data. Although HLM can model recovery with missing data, it is more difficult to identify cases that may be in trouble if data are not collected often. Such was the case in the Speilmans et al. (2006) study.

Lutz et al. (2006) modeled recovery in 4,365 clients using a variation of calculating the expected treatment response called the nearest neighbor methodology. This rather creative approach had been applied in avalanche research (Brabec & Meister, 2001) to predict future avalanches—a fitting metaphor for deterioration in psychotherapy—and was applied to cases in which clients had undergone serious decompensation. In avalanche prediction research the best predictors are characteristics of the snow that surrounds an avalanche. Lutz et al. (2005) found that this methodology worked well to predict rate of change, although they did not examine deterioration itself. In this study deterioration as measured by the OQ-30 was predicted with client responses to the 15 items ("nearest neighbors") that make up the rest of the OQ-45. In essence the method uses the intake scores of previously treated clients to make predictions about subsets of similar clients. Predictions based on this model were compared with predictions made using the rational method.

Three questions were addressed: (a) How well do the rationally derived and empirically derived decision rules predict outcome? (b) How early in treatment can the decision rules identify negative developments, and which method is better? and (c) Is the number of warning signals provided from these decision rules predictive of therapy outcome? Unlike past research on prediction from our research group (e.g., Lambert, Whipple, Bishop, et al., 2002), Lutz et al. (2005) lumped reliable improvement and clinically significant change as positive outcomes and no change and reliable negative change as negative outcomes. Past predictive studies have only examined the ability to predict negative reliable change, with all other categorizations of patient change considered positive (i.e., nonnegative).

Results showed that the nearest neighbor technique had a specificity of 86% but sensitivity of only 41% at the 90% level of confidence, whereas the rational method had 66% specificity and sensitivity of 57%. As shown in Figure 4.1 (illustrating the progress of a case in relation to confidence intervals set at the 67%, 75%, 84%, 90%, 95%, and 99.5% levels that could be provided as feedback to therapists), the advantage of providing feedback with varied confidence intervals rather that at a fixed level (e.g., 90% only) is that

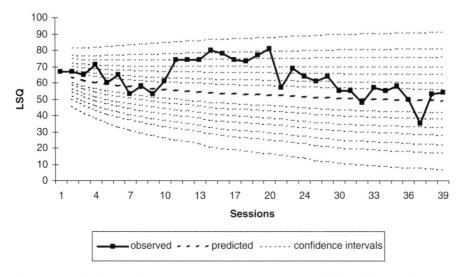

Figure 4.1. Predicted individual treatment response and confidence intervals (example) for the Outcome Questionnaire-30 (LSQ) and nearest neighbor predictive methods. From "The Probability of Treatment Success, Failure, and Duration—What Can Be Learned From Empirical Data to Support Decision Making in Clinical Practice?" By W. Lutz, M. J. Lambert, S. C. Harmon, A. Tschitsaz, E. Schurch, and N. Stulz, 2006, *Clinical Psychology and Psychotherapy, 13,* p. 227. Copyright 2006 by Wiley. Reprinted with permission.

the clinician can choose how sure to make the prediction. The nearest neighbor method also identified a significantly greater proportion of clients sooner than the rational method. Multiple alarm signals given to individual patients indicated a greater likelihood that the patient would deteriorate. It should be noted that these results suggest the nearest neighbor method far exceeds clinical judgment, but the hit rates are not comparable to researchers' usual studies in which deterioration is the predicted state of interest. Counting those who do not reliably change as having a negative outcome makes logical sense because psychotherapy is intended to provide measurable positive change (except in some clinical circumstances in which preventing deterioration is all that can be expected), but it is a difficult task.

Essentially the same methods were used to formulate the predictive system for the OQ-30 as with the OQ-45, with the exception that a completely independent database consisting of 8,815 patients with two or more OQ-30 administrations was used (Thompson, 2004). The total sample was split in half using a random number table to provide an initial data set for modeling as well as a cross-validation sample for testing predictive accuracy. The full range of scores (0–120) was divided into distinct groups on the basis of severity of disturbance. This yielded 20 groups identified by intake score with no fewer than 100 clients in each band, representing approximately 2% of the total sample. The resulting data were analyzed to generate a linear model for expected treatment response.

The cross-validation sample consisted of 4,136 clients who received treatment in a variety of settings across the United States; one half had a mood disorder, and 29% were diagnosed with an adjustment disorder or anxiety disorder (13%). The clients were seen in a variety of private or public treatment settings, including private practice. Of the 4,136 clients who received services 367 (9%) left treatment deteriorated. Of these, 350 (95%) were identified through expected recovery curves using a score a 10% confidence interval. In addition to failing to identify 17 clients who went on to deteriorate, the algorithms used falsely identified 672 patients who were predicted to have a negative outcome who did not. As noted earlier, the tendency to overidentify individuals as at risk for treatment failure appears similar across studies; for every two to three clients predicted to deteriorate, one does so. The empirical and rational predictive systems are able to identify most of the patients who deteriorate, whereas clinicians fail to recognize nearly all.

Accuracy of Predicting Treatment Failure in Children

Predicting treatment failure in children undergoing psychotherapy is more difficult than it is for adults. One reason for this is that in children's services there are more missing data. Often the schedule for administration of the measures is less frequent than weekly. In addition, in outpatient settings the child may be accompanied to their session by a person who did not bring the child to intake, such as a father or sister instead of the mother. Prediction is dependent on tracking change with a single informant, such as an adolescent, or in many cases the mother. These difficulties are unfortunate because the problem of deterioration in youth is double or triple that found in adults (as noted in Chapter 1, this volume). Four studies have been published extending the work with adults to children. As with the prediction methods used with adults, those with children have used a variety of techniques, including rational and statistical.

The first published study in this line of research was by Bishop et al. (2005), who tested the accuracy of expert judge rational algorithms in a sample of 300 residential and outpatient clients ages 3 to 18. The average age of patients was 12.2 years with the majority (56%) being males. Of the 300 patients, 145 were in residential treatment receiving a variety of interventions on a daily basis, including educational programs. Outpatients were seen through a managed care network through private practice providers. Patient progress was tracked using the Y-OQ parent or guardian report form. Patients from a larger archival database were excluded if more than 14 days between administrations of the Y-OQ had occurred or more than one unaccounted for therapy session had occurred between consecutive administrations of the Y-OQ. This ensured that patient distress could be followed in a systematic way. The average intake score indicated that the typical patient was judged by the rater as experiencing a level of distress between inpatient and outpatient means.

Of the 300 patients who were followed throughout Treatment 22, 7.3% deteriorated. In this group, 17 of these 22 (77%) were accurately predicted to be treatment failures. The algorithms accurately identified 82% of the individuals who did not deteriorate and had an overall hit rate of 82% (the outcome of 244 patients was correctly predicted). Examination of unsuccessful prediction indicated that 51 (18%) patients were false alarms and that many of these patients began treatment in the normal range; otherwise the algorithms were equally successful at other levels of initial disturbance.

Bybee, Lambert, and Eggett (2007) developed and tested empirical algorithms for identification of treatment failure using the Y-OQ-30. In this investigation the treatment progress of 3,712 child and adolescent patients who sought services through a managed care corporation was drawn from an archival database. These children, ages 4 to 18, were randomly split into two groups of 1,856 each. HLM was performed on the first group in order to establish the alarm system using techniques to model expected recovery as was done by Finch et al. (2001). Models drawn from the first sample were replicated on the second sample for purposes of cross-validation. Both samples produced equivalent warning cutoffs, and their accuracy was explored using the entire sample of 3,712 patients.

Results indicated that 429 in 3,712 children deteriorated by the time they left treatment, a rate of 12%. At the 90% confidence interval (red signal), 72% (307 in 429) of the deteriorators were identified. For the 84% cutoff (yellow and red cases), the figure increased to 85% identification but nearly doubled the number of false alarms. Of those cases predicted to have a positive outcome (3,283), 2,966 (90%) attained this outcome, making the overall hit rate 88%. The signal-alarm method identified 624 of the 3,712 (17%) cases as at risk of treatment failure, whereas the actual number of deteriorated cases was 429 (12%). This indicates that if the red signal is used, for every two patients identified as off track, only one will actually deteriorate. As already suggested, this level of over predicting failure is probably tolerable because false-alarm cases appear to benefit from this inaccurate feedback. Nevertheless, increased accuracy should remain a goal for future predictive methods. In this particular study the data used to model expected treatment response included both self-report and parent report combined, a shortcoming that was corrected in the following study.

Cannon, Warren, Nelson, and Burlingame (in press) examined the predictive accuracy of change trajectories using the Y-OQ parent or guardian form on 363 child or adolescent patients 4 to 17 years of age who received treatment in a western outpatient community mental health center. Multilevel modeling procedures, rather than HLM, were used with a randomly selected subgroup of the whole sample (n = 181) and then applied for predictive purposes to the other subgroup (n = 182). Treatment for the entire sample was offered by 115 therapists employed by the agency, who provided a variety of treatments with systems theories being the most common. The mean age of the sample was 11 years, with 62% being males. Of the sample, 31% were minorities (largely Latino), 53% received medication, and 52% were receiving Medicaid.

Of the predictive sample of 182 cases, 40 (22%) deteriorated by the time they left treatment, with the cutoff scores identifying 28 (70%). An additional 34 cases were predicted to deteriorate but did not, suggesting that for every correct prediction an incorrect prediction of deterioration was made. In the overall predictive process, the hit rate was 75%. These results were similar in regard to the Bybee et al. (2007) study just described. Recall that three major differences in these studies were that the Bybee et al. study used the rational method for prediction, with the Y-OQ-30, and the patients studied were treated in a managed care setting. It is important to note that the base rates for deterioration were quite discrepant, 12% versus 22% in the current study, and Bybee et al.'s sample also had an 88% overall hit rate, much higher than the current study. Both studies managed to identify about 70% of deteriorated cases with both studies having similar rates of false positive identifications.

Warren, Nelson, Mondragon, Baldwin, and Burlingame (2009) compared symptom change trajectories and treatment outcome categories in children and adolescents (ages 4–17) receiving outpatient mental health services in a public community mental health system ($n = 936$) and a private managed care organization ($n = 3075$). Archival longitudinal outcome data from parents completing the Y-OQ were analyzed using multilevel modeling and partial proportional odds modeling to test for differences in change trajectories and final outcomes across the two service settings (the attempt here was to find out if different settings needed separate predictive models). Results indicated that although initial symptom level was comparable across settings, the rate of change was significantly steeper for cases in the private managed care setting. In addition, 24% of cases in the community mental health setting demonstrated a significant increase in symptoms over the course of treatment compared with 14% of cases in the managed care setting, a startling contrast. Results from this study are presented graphically in Figure 4.2.

These two major types of service systems share many common features, but a number of distinctions can be observed: Community mental health centers in the United States are often supported by government assistance programs such as Medicaid and serve more youth from lower income families

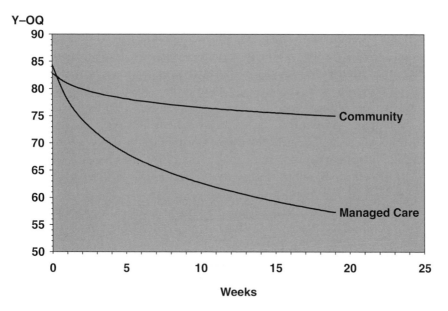

Figure 4.2. Trajectories for community and managed care settings, controlling for initial severity using data matched by baseline score. From *Administration and Scoring Manual for the Outcome Questionnaire-45* (p. 15), by M. J. Lambert, J. J. Morton, D. Hatfield, C. Harmon, S. Hamilton, R. C. Reid, K. Shimokowa, C. Christopherson, and G. M. Burlingame, 2004, Salt Lake City, UT: OQ Measures, LLC. Copyright 2004 by OQ Measures, LLC. Reprinted with permission.

with more severe constellations of stressors and negative circumstances that often go along with financial disadvantage. Therapists in this setting were expected to accrue 20 to 25 billable client hours per week and reportedly maintained a typical open caseload of 90 to 110 clients.

Private managed health care organizations are more likely to serve youths from families that can afford employer-provided or private health insurance and treatment from a more highly trained single (as opposed to team) mental health professional in individual psychotherapy. Mental health treatment provided by the managed care organization was described by clinical supervisors as being multidisciplinary and eclectic with short-term cognitive–behavioral interventions being most emphasized and encouraged by supervisors. Individual psychotherapy, family therapy, group therapy, and medication management were the most common modes of treatment provided. Parent involvement in youth treatment was reported to be strongly emphasized. Of the 55 clinicians from this setting who provided services to cases used in this study, their professional backgrounds were as follows: 27% social workers, 18% psychiatrists, 13% psychologists, 4% licensed professional counselors, and 38% other or unknown. Therapists in the managed care setting were expected to accrue at least 25 billable client hours per week and reportedly maintained an open caseload of approximately 100 clients. Services in the private sector were more often based on weekly sessions rather than spaced over longer time periods. Furthermore, given the increased emphasis in managed care on providing quality services while minimizing costs, the average duration of treatment was shorter in managed care than in the community mental health setting. This finding is reinforced by a common criticism of the traditional managed care model as being ill-suited for treating persons with chronic mental health conditions (Anderson, 2007).

Whatever the reasons for such different trajectories of change, it is apparent that being off track for a positive mental health outcome can be modeled within patient populations and provide more specific (albeit relative) identification of signal-alarm cases. This study did not provide estimates of predictive accuracy within these specific samples.

Cannon, Warren, Nelson, and Burlingame (in press) examined outcome in community mental health and managed care samples using data from the preceding study for the purpose of modeling change and predicting treatment failure on the basis of parent ratings and self-report ratings as well as those provided by other individuals. Within the combined sample of 2,715 children, and with the use of multilevel modeling, expected recovery curves were developed for each of the data sources. A sample graph displaying the initial degree of disturbance and change over time has been reproduced in Figure 4.3. As can be seen, adolescents report themselves as least disturbed at the beginning of treatment and at the end, whereas others rate patients at the highest level at both time points, with parents taking a middle position.

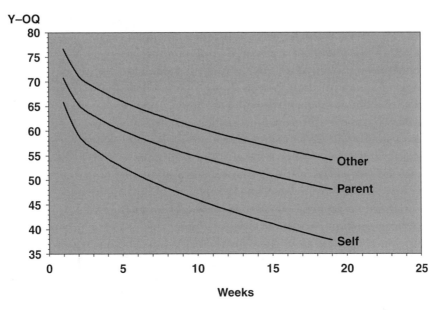

Figure 4.3. Trajectory differences by respondent. Self-report Y-OQs demonstrate a lower elevation on average and a faster rate of change. Parent-report Y-OQs demonstrate a higher elevation and slower rate of change than self-report. Y-OQs completed by respondents other than self or parent demonstrate the highest elevation yet a rate of change equal to that of Y-OQs from parent respondents. From "Change trajectories for the Youth Outcome Questionnaire Self Report: Identifying youth at risk for treatment failure" by J. Cannon, J. Warren, P. Nelson, and G. Burlingame, in press, *Journal of Clinical Child and Adolescent Psychology.* Copyright American Psychological Association.

Although not obvious at a glance, self-reported change shows improvement over time that is more rapid than the other two sources.

In this large sample of patients treated in multiple settings the deterioration rate was 15% (*n* = 177). Accuracy of prediction of deterioration varied somewhat on the basis of data source, from 54% for self-report, 57% for parent report, and 62% for other report. When all three sources' cutoff scores were combined, 70% of those who deteriorated were identified. For every correct prediction of deterioration that was made, there were about one to one and one half false alarms, depending on source.

SUMMARY

Consistent findings suggest a deterioration rate of 5% to 10% across samples of adult patients undergoing psychotherapy. The negative change problem is even more serious among child and adolescent patients who seem to deteriorate at rates closer to 12% to 24% depending on the population. There are serious problems with clinicians' ability to recognize which of their clients are likely to leave treatment worse off and also which might be having notable worsening at a particular time in treatment. Both awareness problems could be overcome, increasing the probability that therapists could provide better care through the use of actuarial and statistical methods. Final deterioration can be predicted before it occurs through the use of information about patients' *initial level of disturbance* and their *treatment response* following sessions of psychotherapy (both rational and empirical algorithms). Once these variables are taken into account, little improvement in predictive accuracy has been achieved by adding such variables as diagnosis, sex, age, ethnicity, type of treatment, experience of therapist, and the like. It appears that what matters most is how disturbed a patient is—not which disorder they have or if they have more than a single diagnosis—because these variables correlate with degree of disturbance.

Several studies were presented that illustrated methods for predicting treatment failure and their success. The sensitivity of these predictive methods for adult clients, defined as the proportion of people who ultimately deteriorate in treatment and who were predicted to fail by the predictive system, typically results in a figure around .88 with a range of about 80% to 100% (and with statistically based algorithms outperforming the rational). This means that for every 100 deteriorated individuals, the OQ-45 (or OQ-30) predictive system would identify 88. The hit rate (overall correct classification rate) for the OQ-45 and OQ-30 appears to be around .80. Because deterioration rates for adults undergoing psychotherapy usually hover around 5% to 10%, hit rates for predicting failure must exceed the baseline judgment that deterioration will not occur (e.g., always predicting no deterioration will lead to accuracy 90%–95% of the time). The reader may recognize the practical futility of making predictions by always alerting the population to impending disaster by noting this procedure with Homeland Security alerts. The United States has been on heightened alert since September 11, 2001, effectively making the alert signal valueless. With regard to prediction with adults, it appears that the systems have a good share of false positives with the ratio of false alarms to correct identification hovering around 2 to 1.

With children and adolescents predictive accuracy is not as high. The predictive systems are able to identify closer to 70% of those who deteriorate (with a range of 54%–85%) and produce rates of false alarm similar to adults. It may be that is just more difficult to make these predictions with children, but it is also true that the data used to model child expected treatment response is based on fewer sessions and has more missing data. Importantly, child self-reported psychological and social functioning proved to be as accurate at identifying negative outcomes as parent-based data.

The algorithms researchers have developed show that if a patient never signals red or yellow, it is almost certain that he or she will not deteriorate. At the same time the negative predictive power (the proportion of people who are predicted not to deteriorate in treatment who, in fact, do not deteriorate in treatment) typically is around .90+. The quality of the positive predictive power values is much lower, somewhere around .20. There is about a 20% increase (over baseline rates of 8% in adults) in ability to predict treatment failure by using the predictive system (in children it is closer to .30–.40). These results are consistent with validity coefficients that can be expected when base rates (such as in suicide) are very low (Steiner, 2003).

As illustrated in Chapter 3, practical change sensitive measures can be developed and are suitable for monitoring mental health vital signs as patient progress in treatment. In this chapter it has been shown that these tests can be administered on a weekly basis and expectations for an adequate and inadequate treatment response can be created for the purpose of providing therapists with "lab test" feedback to supplant their questionable ability to identify cases at risk of treatment failure. Just what happens to clients when this is routinely done is the subject of Chapters 5 and 6. It is theoretically interesting to better understand patterns of patient change, but can any of this knowledge be used in behalf of client welfare?

III

THE EVIDENCE BASE

5

USING PROGRESS FEEDBACK TO INFORM TREATMENT: CONCEPTUAL ISSUES AND INITIAL FINDINGS

Chapters 5 and 6 provide the reader with experimental (clinical trial) evidence on the effects of providing various types of feedback (mainly) to clinicians for the purpose of improving patient functioning. In these two chapters, six clinical trials are reviewed. In Chapter 5 the focus is on delivering progress feedback, whereas in Chapter 6, progress feedback as well as problem-solving feedback is studied. Inasmuch as the interventions (changes in practice patterns) recommended in this book rely on feedback, this chapter begins with a general discussion of the broader topic of how well feedback works in various situations and what researchers know about how to make it most effective. Given that there are many forms that feedback can take, just what was fed back for the purpose of maximizing patient outcome is then spelled out, followed by the consequences of the feedback.

TOWARD A GENERAL MODEL OF FEEDBACK TO PSYCHOTHERAPISTS

The basic rationale behind the concept of providing feedback is based on common sense. If therapists get information about what works, and perhaps more importantly what does not, their performance will improve. This is true for most people in many venues of their lives, from learning to speak to shooting basketballs into a hoop. In many situations, performance and feedback are intertwined and obvious; in others a certain degree of blinding occurs such that the association is not so temporally connected and the effects of performance are harder to discern, making it much more difficult to learn and improve.

In obvious as well as more subtle situations, providing feedback to improve performance has been studied quite extensively in a variety of areas and confirms common sense expectations. In evaluating the magnitude of impact for feedback interventions, Kluger and DeNisi (1996) conducted a meta-analysis of feedback interventions published since the 1930s. They found interventions that used feedback to have a small to medium effect (.41). To put it another way, two thirds of individuals given feedback had similar or better performance than people in the control group who were not given feedback. But it should also be noted that there were instances in which feedback was especially helpful and others in which the effects were actually negative.

Unfortunately most of the studies examined in this meta-analysis were analogue situations involving motor performance, puzzle solutions, memory tasks, and the like, rather than based in actual clinical practice, and of the few that tested feedback to professionals, not one study provided feedback on patient's status to health professionals. Nevertheless, this review does suggest that a broad array of feedback interventions consistently improves performance and encourages the idea that feedback will enhance performance.

In a meta-analysis more closely related to treatment effects, Sapyta, Riemer, and Bickman (2005) examined 30 randomized clinical trials that evaluated the effectiveness of client health status feedback to health professionals in community settings. The studies under consideration varied considerably. Feedback varied from giving general practice doctors depression and anxiety screening information regarding clients with undiagnosed mental health problems to providing doctors and clinicians physical or mental health status feedback of clients each time they arrived for treatment. The average effect size of feedback interventions of this nature was .21, a small effect, with the average client in the feedback group being better off than 58% of the control group. In general, this research supports the conclusion that feedback improves patient outcome. This review suggests that the effectiveness of feedback is likely to vary as a function of the *degree of discrepancy* between expected progress and actual progress and that the greater the discrepancy the more likely feedback will be helpful. This finding is consistent with feedback theories and the role of negative feedback in regulatory systems (Bandura, 1997; Lord & Hanges, 1987); feedback about poor progress is expected to have a greater impact than feedback indicating positive progress, and also, a key element of effective feedback is bringing into the recipient's awareness the discrepancy between what is thought and what is reality, thereby prompting corrective action.

When comparing the effect of feedback on *flagged* clients (e.g., not progressing well in therapy) versus clients who were not flagged (e.g., samples of clients progressing through treatment typically), flagged clients responded much better to the feedback intervention. Feedback to flagged samples in the Saptyta and Bickman (2004) meta-analysis achieved an effect size of .31, which indicates that 62% of treatment group participants had equal or better outcomes than the flagged control group. At the same time, it appears that the feedback of client's health status is mainly beneficial to clients who may require changes to their current treatment. This finding is consistent with feedback theories that suggest feedback will only change behavior when the information provided indicates the individual is not meeting an established standard of practice (e.g., Riemer & Bickman, 2004). Riemer and Bickman (2004; Riemer, Rosof-Williams, & Bickman, 2005) have developed a clinical model (contextual feedback intervention theory) to explain how feedback is interpreted and made useful. Basic tenets of this model are that clinicians (and professionals, generally) will benefit from feedback if they are committed to the goal of improving their performance and aware of a discrepancy between the goal and reality (particularly if the goal is attractive and the clinician believes it can be accomplished); if the feedback source is credible; if feedback is immediate, frequent, systematic, and unambiguous; if feedback provides them with concrete suggestions of how to improve; and if feedback is cognitively simple (e.g., graphic in nature).

If the clinicians do not consider feedback credible, valid, informative, or useful, they are more likely to dismiss it whenever it does not fit their own preferences. As researchers know from research on cognitive dissonance, people can change attitudes rather than keep attempting to reach goals, thus regarding the goal as less important, or see a client as too resistant or injured to benefit from an intervention (e.g., disown personal responsibility for meeting the goal of positive functioning). As the preceding model suggests, the value of monitoring and systematic feedback through psychological assessments hinges on the degree to which the information provided goes beyond what a clinician can observe and understand about patient progress without such information. It is important for the information to add something to the psychotherapist's view of patient well-being.

As pointed out in Chapter 4, a reasonable conclusion from research in the area of patient treatment response is that clinicians overlook negative change and have a limited capacity to make accurate predictions, particularly with clients who are failing to improve (Hannan et al., 2005; Mumma, 2004; Ziskin, 1995). This is not surprising given therapist optimism, the complexity of persons, and a treatment context that calls for considerable commitment and determination on the part of the therapist who actually has very little control over the patient's life circumstances and personal characteristics. Patients' response to treatment is, especially in the case of a worsening state, a likely place for outside feedback to have the greatest chance of having an impact. Helping with the task of identifying potential treatment failures and feeding back this information to therapists could be a welcome advance in the practice of psychotherapy.

As discussed in Chapter 1, the American Psychological Association (APA) Presidential Task Force on Evidence-Based Practice (2006) made explicit psychology's stance to consider a "full range of evidence that policymakers must consider" and its "fundamental commitment to sophisticated evidence-based psychological practice" (APA Presidential Task Force on Evidence-Based Practice, 2006, p. 273). In this task force's report, the following definition for evidenced-based practice was set forth: "*Evidence-based practice in psychology* (EBPP) is the integration of the best available research with clinical expertise in the context of patient characteristics, culture, and preferences" (p. 273). Regarding the phrase *clinical expertise* in this definition, the task force expounded the following:

> Clinical expertise also entails the monitoring of patient progress (and of changes in the patient's circumstances—e.g., job loss, major illness) that may suggest the need to adjust the treatment (Lambert, Bergin, & Garfield, 2004a). If progress is not proceeding adequately, the psychologist alters or addresses problematic aspects of the treatment (e.g., problems in the therapeutic relationship or in the implementation of the goals of the treatment) as appropriate. (APA Presidential Task Force on Evidence-Based Practice, 2006, pp. 276–277)

TOWARD APPLYING FEEDBACK IN PRACTICE

The preceding definition acknowledges the importance of monitoring and feedback, and such an emphasis can be traced back to research results presented in this chapter and Chapter 6. As noted in Chapter 3, reliable and valid measures suitable for collecting client ratings of their functioning have been created. Collecting this information from the client on a session-by-session basis provides the clinician with a systematic way of monitoring life functioning from an independent point of view. This 5 to 10 min assessment provides a summary of symptoms, interpersonal, and social role functioning that is not otherwise available to the therapist unless the therapist spends time within the treatment hour to systematically inquire about all the areas of functioning covered by the self-report scale. An important additional piece of information that is not otherwise (accurately) available to the therapist is a prediction of final functioning in relation to the direction and amount of change experienced since the patient entered treatment. The predictive information has the specific intent of identifying clients whose positive outcome is in doubt and alerting clinicians to this problematic progress. As noted in Chapter 4, this predictive information is based on a large number of similarly disturbed patients treated in a variety of settings by a variety of providers and is far more accurate than the therapist's judgment. It is these two novel pieces of information fed back to therapists that are hypothesized to improve treatment outcome.

To provide feedback that was most effective it was decided that it should be graphic in nature. As already displayed in Figure 3.2, the clinician feedback report included a graph of patient progress over sessions of psychotherapy, plotted in relation to normal functioning (the possible target of treatment) and in relation to the progress of similar patients (expected treatment response), another possible target of treatment. In addition to the graphic information in the top right-hand corner is the predicted outcome based on current functioning in relation to expected functioning—an alert. The alert is colored and bolded (red, yellow, green, or white). The color coding is seen as an important aspect of effective feedback; whereas providing numbers requires interpretation and thought, the colors may have an effect on therapists that is more emotionally provocative—thus it was hoped that the color red would be emotionally arousing and more likely to lead to action. Like a traffic light system, the yellow carries with it a cautionary reaction whereas red suggests a more urgent reaction. Green suggests the idea of carrying on in the journey, with the implicit sense of things going well.

A written message for the therapist, which is placed at the bottom of the report, interprets the patient's current score (e.g., that the patient is functioning in the clinical range and continues to need help) and the prediction of final outcome based on how close the patient is functioning to the expected recovery curve (e.g., the patient is expected to leave treatment a deteriorated case unless steps are taken to change his or her treatment response). Also provided and highlighted in red are current responses to critical items, such as thoughts of suicide. Clinicians can view the patient's response to any specific item at any administration of the questionnaires if they choose (see Chapter 3, Figure 3.2, this volume).

In general the feedback system my colleagues and I developed appears to meet the fundaments of effective feedback in the model suggested by Bickman and his colleagues. The feedback is immediate (available within seconds of the patients' completing the questionnaire) frequent (weekly), systematic, unambiguous (to the extent possible for complex information), and cognitively simple (graphic and color-coded). Importantly, it makes therapists aware of a potential discrepancy between hoped for treatment response and actual response. Certainly therapists are highly invested in reducing suffering, and to the extent that they believe the questionnaire's index of suffering and ability to predict ultimate treatment response, they can be expected to welcome and use the feedback. Some problems and limitations with this assumption that limit the effects of feedback within the current paradigm are addressed in this chapter and again in Chapter 9. After methods for feedback were developed, it was time to test the consequences of using these methods in a series of outcome studies to see if client outcome was actually enhanced.

EVIDENCE ON THE EFFECTS OF FEEDBACK

In the clinical trials designed to test the effects of feedback we wanted to mimic, as far as possible, the way feedback methods would be applied in routine practice rather than create a laboratory application of feedback research in which we exercised the highest degree of control. Our thinking here was that we would save a step in implementation if we could find an effect in routine care, rather than the usual method of finding an effect in a highly controlled study and doing additional effectiveness studies to see if the research protocol could be transferred to the clinical setting.

What this meant in practical terms was that we would not recruit and pay therapists to implement the feedback intervention and we would honor their personal preferences for use of the feedback, allowing them to discuss the clients test scores in treatment sessions or not as they preferred. No attempts were made to manage clinicians' actions in relation to the feedback. No record was kept with regard to the number of patients who were on medication or other concomitant treatments. In this regard the intervention tested in this study was minimal but consistent with the intent to examine findings in routine clinical practice. It consisted of giving therapists patient Outcome Questionnaire-45 (OQ-45) scores on a graph as well as information about expectations for client outcome based on the OQ-45 but no mechanism to ensure that the data be used in any systematic way, including whether the client's progress graph or expected level of progress was shared with the client. This was done in an attempt to impose as little as possible on the manner in which therapists practiced therapy and in a way that would be consistent with using feedback in routine practice where experimental control would be nonexistent. The atmosphere of the research was one of minimal control and intrusion. Another important difference between this research and the usual clinical trial is that treatment length was not determined by some preset time limit such as 12 weeks. Treatment length was free to vary on the basis of client and therapist needs and preferences.

Study 1

Lambert et al. (2001) conducted the first study in 1998 and 1999. Participants were 609 consecutive clients treated in a university counseling center. The sample ranged in age from 17 to 57 (M = 22.23) and were 70% female, 88% Caucasian, 4% Hispanic, 3% Pacific Islander or Asian, and 5% of mixed ethnicity. Approximately one half (n = 307) were randomly assigned to an experimental (feedback) group and one half (n = 302) were randomly assigned to the control (no feedback) group. All random assignment was within therapists' case loads so that the same therapists practiced both treatment-as-usual as well as feedback-assisted treatment. The risk with such a design is that the feedback information applied in the experimental condition may help therapists with their treatment-as-usual clients and thereby wash out any treatment effects that might be present. An advantage of such a design is that it allows control of any effects that might be due to the therapists themselves.

Statistical tests revealed no significant differences between the experimental and control groups on any of the demographic variables. The clients were all referred or self-referred for personal concerns rather than career or academic counseling. Patients in the counseling center are routinely diagnosed by the treating clinician, and no attempt was made to have clients undergo research-based diagnostic evaluations. In this study, 80% of clients were diagnosed, and 20% had their diagnosis deferred at intake and never had a formal diagnosis recorded in the database. Those receiving a formal clinical diagnosis had a mood disorder (27%), adjustment disorder (14%), anxiety disorder (9%), or somatoform disorder (5%). Of clients, 19% had a *Diagnostic and Statistical Manual of Mental Disorders* (4th ed., text rev.; DSM–IV–TR; American Psychiatric Association, 2000) V-code diagnosis, whereas the rest of the clients (26%) received a variety of other disorder classifications.

Therapists were 31 counseling center staff consisting of 16 doctoral-level psychologists and 15 doctoral students in training, including interns. An additional 7 therapists refused participation in this study; the rest gave informed consent, although they were skeptical about the value of the feedback intervention and in that sense did not meet many of the necessary feedback conditions recommended by Bickman (e.g., did not see the need for feedback; Riemer, Rosof-Williams, & Bickman, 2005; Sapyta et al., 2005). Therapists had a variety of treatment orientations, with most subscribing to an integration of two or more theoretical systems. The most common orientations were cognitive–behavioral (42%), psychodynamic and interpersonal (19%), humanistic and existential (16%), behavioral (6%), or other (16%). Therapists were either salaried employees of the university or students in training and did not receive a direct fee for the services provided.

It was explained to participating therapists that the purpose of the study was to test the effects of feedback and that they would only receive feedback on approximately one half their client load. During the course of the study the status of all clients was routinely measured on a weekly basis with the OQ-45, but only information for the experimental cases was made available to therapists. To assess therapists' experiences as recipients of feedback, a post-experimental questionnaire and interview were conducted with therapists following termination of data collection. Interviews were conducted after completion of the questionnaire. The questionnaire and interview were used as an informal procedure aimed at improving the feedback procedures to be used in subsequent studies.

At the inception of the study the number of clients who would be predicted treatment failures was not known. Once OQ-45 data collection commenced, it continued until at least 30 patients in both the experimental and control groups had received a yellow or red warning (about 20% of the total sample). Patients who received only green or white messages (i.e., who progressed as expected) and whose therapists received feedback were referred to as the on-track feedback (OT-Fb) group. Patients who were on track but whose therapists were not informed were referred to as the on-track no feedback (OT-NFb) group. Patients who were not progressing as expected (i.e., received red or yellow warnings) and whose therapists were informed were referred to as the not-on-track feedback (NOT-Fb) group. Those clients who were not progressing as expected and whose therapists did not receive feedback are referred to as the not-on-track no feedback (NOT-NFb) group. Because treatment length was indeterminate and termination was frequently initiated by the client, the final outcome status of the client was determined by the last available OQ in the client's file (with OQs completed before each treatment session). This procedure probably underestimated the total amount of change because OQ data following the final session of treatment were not collected, but it ensured much greater data collection than pretest–posttest methods typically used in routine care.

Clients completed their first OQ prior to their intake appointment and subsequent OQs prior to each treatment session. Completed OQs were then scanned, graphed, and a white, green, yellow, or red dot was placed on the client's chart and on a graph that included all the patient's scores to that time. The counseling center had an informal policy of limiting treatment to 14 sessions but no mechanism to ensure that therapists and clients stayed within this guideline. Therapists were free to use their judgment to terminate treatment when it seemed appropriate. There was some pressure to be efficient but no urgency about efficiency or contingencies rewarding efficiency (as are sometimes seen in managed care). Treatment in university-based clinics is often suspended at the end of the school year because of the necessity for many of the students to return home during the summer months. Most decisions to terminate treatment were client initiated or jointly agreed upon. Unlike clinical trials in which patients commit to therapy for a specific duration and dropouts are often replaced, patients in the present study had varying lengths of treatment, and treatment length itself was a dependant variable of interest.

The results of this study are presented in Table 5.1. The mean pretreatment OQ total score for the experimental (feedback) group and the control (no-feedback) groups was nearly identical. The NOT groups had significantly higher OQs at intake than their OT counterparts ($M = 77.56$; $SD = 19.68$ and $M = 68.10$; $SD = 23.16$, respectively). These differences reached statistical significance and suggest, as expected, that the NOT cases were more disturbed as a group at the beginning of treatment than OT cases. Patients most likely to go off track during therapy and complete treatment in a deteriorated state are more impaired and experience more pain. Although 59.5% of the OT patients began treatment in the dysfunctional range, 89.3% of the NOT participants began in this same range. Within feedback and control conditions, NOT-Fb and NOT-NFb participants had equivalent OQ pretreatment scores.

The patients seen at the counseling center ($N = 609$), ignoring their assignment to experimental or control conditions, improved over the course of therapy with an average change of 4.99 OQ points ($d = 0.64$). For

TABLE 5.1

Study 1 Means, Standard Deviations, and Comparisons of Experimental and Control Group Outcome Questionnaire-45 (OQ-45) Scores

Group	n	Pretreatment OQ-45		Posttreatment OQ-45		ANCOVA[a]	
		M	SD	M	SD	F	p
Total Fb	307	69.18	23.49	63.32	24.12	2.221	.137
Total NFb	302	69.08	22.48	65.13	23.09		
NOT-Fb	35	77.57	20.04	74.57	19.81	4.937	.030
NOT-NFb	31	77.55	19.60	83.13	18.92		
OT-Fb	272	68.10	23.72	61.88	24.29	.707	.401
OT-NFb	271	68.10	22.62	63.06	22.66		
Total	609						

Note. NOT-Fb = patients who were not on track and whose therapists received feedback; NOT-NFb = patients who were not on track and whose therapists did not receive feedback; OT-Fb = patients who were on track and whose therapists received feedback; OT-NFb = patients who were on track and whose therapists did not receive feedback. From "The Effects of Providing Therapists With Feedback on Patient Progress During Psychotherapy: Are Outcomes Enhanced?" by M. J. Lambert, J. L. Whipple, D. W. Smart, D. A. Vermeersch, S. L. Nielsen, and E. J. Hawkins, 2001, *Psychotherapy Research, 11,* p. 58. Copyright 2001 by Taylor & Francis. Reprinted with permission.
[a]An analysis of covariance using the pretreatment OQ score as the covariate was used to compare treatment effects between groups.

patients ($n = 371$, 61%) who began treatment in the dysfunctional range, the improvement was even larger ($M = 7.99$; $d = 1.04$). Of these patients in the dysfunctional range, 17% reliably improved by the end of therapy, with an additional 11.2 % of clients in the dysfunctional range showing clinically significant gains. After receiving an average of 3.3 sessions of treatment, 49% of clients scored within the functional range (i.e., at or below an OQ total score of 63). Treatment effects of this magnitude are typical of those reported in other college counseling centers. For example, Drum and Baron (1998) reported the preliminary results of a national study of counseling centers (Research Consortium of Counseling Services in Higher Education) that examined outcomes across 35 centers that used the OQ-45. They found nearly identical pretreatment scores and slightly lower posttreatment scores, with the same dosage ($M = 3.3$ sessions) of therapy as reported in the current study.

The Effect of Feedback on Outcome

If the feedback was to be considered effective, my colleagues and I expected the posttherapy OQ total scores of the NOT-Fb group to be lower than the posttherapy scores for the NOT-NFb group. As expected, the NOT-Fb group had lower OQ scores at termination than the NOT-NFb group (who actually showed an overall worsening). This difference reached statistical significance on the basis of ANCOVA with pretreatment scores as the covariate. The effect size for the NOT-Fb versus NOT-NFb group was .44, a medium effect according to Lipsey's (1990) criteria. These changes are presented graphically in Figure 5.1. This figure illustrates that the NOT-NFb patients, on average, worsened to the point at which their therapists could have been warned about their poor progress and then showed some improvement. Likewise, the NOT-Fb patients showed a similar, although not as severe, worsening to the point of feedback, followed by more dramatic improvement.

To further explore outcome in the NOT groups, patients were categorized with regard to the clinical significance of their change at termination (see Table 5.2). The impact of feedback on outcome was rather striking for the frequency that cases met criteria and were regarded as deteriorated (6% versus 23%). Of the NOT-NFb group, 16% reached Jacobson and Truax's (1991) criterion for reliable or clinically significant change, whereas 26% of the NOT-Fb cases reached this same degree of success.

The results of this study are quite interesting and potentially important as a method of maximizing treatment effects; but it is also worth noting that 75% of patients in the NOT-Fb condition remained within the dysfunctional range on the OQ (above 63), suggesting that they were in need of further treatment despite being better off as a group when compared with the NOT-NFb controls. The relatively small sample size of NOT groups also limited certain

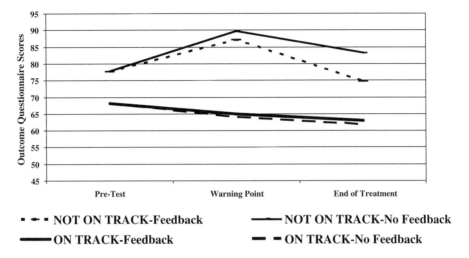

Figure 5.1. Study 1: change from pretreatment to posttreatment testing of not-on-track (signal-alarm) and on-track clients. From "The Effects of Providing Therapists With Feedback on Patient Progress During Psychotherapy: Are Outcomes Enhanced?" by M. J. Lambert, J. L. Whipple, D. W. Smart, D. A. Vermeersch, S. L. Nielsen, and E. J. Hawkins, 2001, *Psychotherapy Research, 11,* p. 59. Copyright 2001 by Taylor & Francis. Reprinted with permission.

TABLE 5.2
Percentage of NOT-Fb and NOT-NFb Cases Meeting Criteria
for Clinically Significant Change at Termination

| | Group | | | | |
| | NOT-Fb | | NOT-NFb | | |
Outcome classification	*n*	%	*n*	%	chi-square
Deteriorated[a]	2	6	7	23	$\chi^2 = (2, N = 66)$
					4.257, $p = .118$
No change	24	69	19	61	
Reliable or clinically significant change[b]	9	26	5	16	

Note. NOT-Fb = patients who were not on track and whose therapist was given feedback; NOT-NFb = patients who were not on track and whose therapist did not receive feedback. From "The Effects of Providing Therapists With Feedback on Patient Progress During Psychotherapy: Are Outcomes Enhanced?" by M. J. Lambert, J. L. Whipple, D. W. Smart, D. A. Vermeersch, S. L. Nielsen, and E. J. Hawkins, 2001, *Psychotherapy Research, 11,* p. 62. Copyright 2007 by Taylor & Francis. Reprinted with permission.
[a]Worsened by at least 14 points on the Outcome Questionnaire from pretreatment to posttreatment.
[b]Improved by at least 14 points on the Outcome Questionnaire or improved and passed the cutoff between dysfunctional and functional populations.

comparisons (e.g., differences between trainees and licensed professionals) that might be possible in a larger study. Such a comparison might help reveal if seasoned professionals could better use progress and alarm feedback to turn around the negative changes in alarm-signal cases.

Therapist Attitudes Toward Feedback

As part of this investigation my colleagues and I tracked therapists' attitudes toward the study and their use of the OQ feedback by having them rate statements about their attitudes and activities with regard to use of the OQ and OQ feedback. Six 5-point Likert scale statements (0 = never; 1 = rarely; 2 = sometimes; 3 = frequently; 4 = almost always) were used: (a) "The information and suggestions for clinical practice associated with the feedback messages were helpful in providing possible courses of action in therapy"; (b) "I found it helpful to share OQ feedback (e.g., graphs, warning messages) with clients"; (c) "The individual OQ items are helpful in providing me with information I would not typically gather through my interactions with clients"; (d) "I look to see how clients respond to Item 8, which states, 'I have thoughts of ending my life'"; (e) "I look to see how clients respond to Item 23, which states, 'I feel hopeless about the future'"; and (f) "I look to see how clients respond to Item 44, which states, 'I feel angry enough at work/school to do something I might regret.'" Outcomes of NOT-Fb clients whose therapists obtained an additive score of 21 or above in their responses to these questions (i.e., high users of OQ data and OQ feedback whose average response was "frequently") were compared with outcomes of NOT-Fb clients whose therapists scored below 21 (i.e., low users of OQ data and OQ feedback). Results indicated that for therapists who were high users of OQ data and OQ feedback, clients had better outcomes, and that was especially true when therapists reported sharing test results directly with clients.

One unexpected finding was that therapists were unaware of the fact that when they viewed yellow and red feedback, they saw clients for nearly twice as many sessions compared with their NOT-NFb clients and that the feedback cases had better outcomes. This finding is important in that it addresses the therapists' perceived need for receiving progress and alarm information. Despite fairly dramatic improvements in their clients' outcome and a dramatic drop in deterioration, therapists perceived no real benefit for clients and thus would not be motivated to use the feedback in future studies. To this point, therapists in general saw participation in the feedback research as a mild annoyance (with nearly 50% of the licensed staff refusing participation, mainly on philosophical grounds). Objections were based largely on the idea that outcome is too complex to be measured and that weekly measurement would be a burden to clients.

To deal with the refusal to participate by some therapists and the lack of awareness that the feedback changed some therapist behaviors and resulted in keeping negatively changing clients in treatment longer and improving their outcome, the results of the study were reported to the entire staff and administration. Most people were surprised and intrigued by the results, and permission was given to replicate the study.

Study 2

Lambert et al. (2002) reported a replication of Study 1 by examining outcome of 1,020 participants from the same university counseling center setting. Most details of the replication remained the same as those used in Study 1 with the exception that more therapists (22 doctoral level and 27 trainees) agreed to participate (only 2 of the professional staff refused). Many of the student therapists who participated in Study 1 rotated out of training or took professional positions and were replaced by new trainees. Most important, participating clients were assigned to the experimental (Fb) group and the control (No-Fb) group, depending on the semester in which they sought services. Thus, random assignment was not used.

Approximately one half the clients ($n = 528$) were assigned to the Fb group, and one half ($n = 492$) were assigned to the No-Fb group. Clients were assigned to the Fb condition if they attended school during winter or spring semester 2000 or to the No-Fb condition if they attended school summer or fall semester 1999. Finally, to assess therapists' decisions and actions as recipients of feedback, a tracking form was created and given to therapists when a client was identified as an alarm-signal case. This survey form was seen as both a method for identifying the actions therapists took as a result of having received feedback and as part of the experimental manipulation because it suggested actions that could be taken (e.g., meeting more frequently) and, therefore, might affect the way therapists' treated clients who were not showing adequate progress. In this regard it was seen as a method of increasing therapist use of feedback information.

The results of Study 2 (see Table 5.3) were very similar to those reported in Study 1. The mean pretreatment OQ total scores for the experimental (Fb) groups and the control (No-Fb) groups were 69.87 ($SD = 22.74$) and 72.77 ($SD = 22.19$), respectively. This difference between groups was statistically significant. This was unexpected and suggested some slight differences in clients seeking treatment in the summer and fall semesters versus the winter and spring semesters.

As expected, the NOT cases were more disturbed as a group at the beginning of treatment than the OT cases. Whereas 57.2% of the OT clients began treatment in the dysfunctional range, 82.5% of the NOT participants

TABLE 5.3
Study 2 Means and Standard Deviations of Outcome Questionnaire (OQ)
Scores and Treatment Duration for Experimental and Control Groups

Group	n	Pretreatment OQ M (SD)	Posttreatment OQ M (SD)	OQ change M (SD)	Total duration M (SD)
Total feedback	528	69.87 (22.74)	56.84 (22.48)	−13.03 (19.36)	4.60 (3.58)
Total no feedback	492	72.77 (22.19)	61.74 (24.53)	−11.03 (20.13)	4.44 (3.06)
Total NOT	240	80.85 (19.08)	78.96 (23.69)	−1.89 (22.55)	3.79 (2.71)
Total OT	780	68.32 (22.68)	53.13 (21.52)	−15.19 (17.68)	6.93 (4.00)
NOT-Fb	116	79.25 (19.64)	73.87 (25.34)	−5.38 (23.53)	7.47 (4.29)
NOT-NFb	124	82.35 (18.50)	83.72 (21.05)	1.36 (21.61)	6.43 (3.67)
OT-Fb	412	67.23 (22.88)	52.04 (22.00)	−15.18 (17.45)	3.80 (2.88)
OT-NFb	368	69.54 (22.42)	54.34 (20.93)	−15.20 (17.96)	3.77 (2.51)
Total	1,020				

Note. NOT = clients who were not on track; OT = clients who were on track; NOT-Fb = clients who were not on track and whose therapists received feedback; NOT-NFb = clients who were not on track and whose therapists did not receive feedback; OT-Fb = clients who were on track and whose therapists received feedback; OT-NFb = clients who were on track and whose therapists did not receive feedback. From "Enhancing Psychotherapy Outcomes via Providing Feedback on Client Progress: A Replication" by M. J. Lambert, J. L. Whipple, D. A. Vermeersch, D. W. Smart, E. J. Hawkins, S. L. Nielsen, and M. K. Goates, 2002, *Clinical Psychology and Psychotherapy, 9,* p. 96. Copyright 2002 by Wiley. Reprinted with permission.

began in this same range, nearly identical proportions to Study 1. Fortunately, no OQ pretreatment differences were noted between the NOT participants in the control (NOT-NFb $M = 82.35$; $SD = 18.50$) and treatment conditions (NOT-Fb $M = 79.25$; $SD = 19.64$). Therefore, despite the decision to forgo randomization and the overall pretreatment differences between the experimental and control groups noted previously, the comparison groups of central interest in the test of hypotheses (NOT-Fb vs. NOT-NFb, OT-Fb vs. OT-NFb) were equivalent on the dependent variable prior to the experimental manipulation.

Over the course of therapy, 1,020 out of a possible 1,422 clients seen at the counseling center were followed until they left treatment. These clients improved with an average change of −12.06 OQ points ($d = 1.22$). Those who began therapy in the functional range ($N = 376$, 36.9%) had an average change of −5.72 points ($SD = 15.48$). For clients who began treatment in the dysfunctional range (those who started counseling with an OQ score of 64 or greater; $N = 644$, 63.1%), the improvement was even larger ($M = -15.77$; $d = 1.54$). Of the clients in the dysfunctional range, 36.6% were classified as having achieved clinically significant change by the end of therapy, whereas an additional 15.1% achieved reliable change.

After receiving an average of 5.25 sessions of treatment, 41.8% of clients scored within the functional range (i.e., at or below an OQ total score of 63). Descriptive statistics for OQ scores and attendance data are presented in Table 5.3. Treatment effects of this magnitude are typical if not higher than those reported in other college counseling centers.

The Effects of Feedback on Outcome

If the feedback was to be considered effective, my colleagues and I expected the Fb group to have lower posttherapy OQ scores than the NFb group and more precisely the pre–post change in OQ scores for the NOT-Fb group to be greater (in the direction of improvement) than the pre–post OQ change scores for the NOT-NFb group. The results are presented in Table 5.4. The difference in pre–post outcome between the 528 clients of therapists receiving feedback and the 492 clients of therapists not receiving feedback reached statistical significance. The effect size for the NOT-Fb versus NOT-NFb group was .40 (compared with .44 for Study 1), a medium effect according to Lipsey's (1990) criteria. These changes are presented graphically in Figure 5.2. This figure illustrates that the NOT-NFb clients, on average, worsened to the point at

TABLE 5.4
Means Adjusted by Covariate and Standard Deviations of Outcome
Questionnaire Change Scores for Comparisons of Significant ANCOVA Results

Therapist	Feedback			No feedback		
	OT M (SD)	NOT M (SD)	Total M (SD)	OT M (SD)	NOT M (SD)	Total M (SD)
Staff	−16.99 (17.18) $n = 195$	−4.99 (17.06) $n = 57$	−11.00 (20.32) $n = 252$	−16.18 (17.00) $n = 204$	7.76 (17.22) $n = 63$	−4.21 (20.26) $n = 267$
Trainee	−16.42 (17.09) $n = 217$	.10 (17.21) $n = 59$	−8.16 (20.77) $n = 276$	−15.43 (17.03) $n = 164$	3.16 (17.18) $n = 61$	−6.13 (19.20) $n = 225$
Total	−16.71 (17.25) $n = 412$	−2.45 (17.23) $n = 116$	−9.58 (20.68) $n = 528$	−15.81 (17.17) $n = 368$	5.46 (17.37) $n = 124$	−5.12 (19.83) $n = 492$

Note. ANCOVA using pretreatment Outcome Questionnaire as the covariate. OT = clients who were on track; NOT = clients who were not on track. From "Enhancing Psychotherapy Outcomes via Providing Feedback on Client Progress: A Replication" by M. J. Lambert, J. L. Whipple, D. A. Vermeersch, D. W. Smart, E. J. Hawkins, S. L. Nielsen, and M. K. Goates, 2002, *Clinical Psychology and Psychotherapy, 9,* p. 97. Copyright 2002 by Wiley. Reprinted with permission.

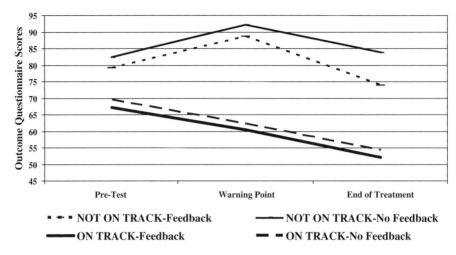

Figure 5.2. Study 2: change from pretreatment to posttreatment testing of not-on-track (signal-alarm) and on-track clients. From "Enhancing Psychotherapy Outcomes via Providing Feedback on Client Progress: A Replication" by M. J. Lambert, J. L. Whipple, D. A. Vermeersch, D. W. Smart, E. J. Hawkins, S. L. Nielsen, and M. K. Goates, 2002, *Clinical Psychology and Psychotherapy, 9,* p. 98. Copyright 2002 by Wiley. Reprinted with permission.

which their therapists could have been warned about their poor progress and then showed some improvement despite an overall worsening from pre- to posttreatment. Likewise, the NOT-Fb clients showed a similar (although not as great) worsening to the point of feedback, followed by more noticeable improvement.

Although Study 1 lacked the power to find a statistically significant difference in client improvement between NOT groups following the point at which feedback was given, the larger sample size of the Lambert et al. (2002) study enabled such an analysis. At termination the NOT-Fb group OQ score averaged 73.87 (SD = 25.34), whereas the NOT-NFb group score averaged 83.72 (SD = 21.05). This difference reached statistical significance, $d = .34$). In addition, Study 2 confirmed that the time at which clients qualify for a yellow or red warning (early vs. later) apparently has little systematic impact on the amount of change clients report at termination.

Analysis of Clinical Significance

To further explore the clinical importance of the outcome in the NOT groups, clients were categorized with regard to the clinical significance of their change. These data are presented in Table 5.5. The differences in the frequency with which clients were assigned to outcome classification categories reached statistical significance when tested with the chi-square statistic. This

TABLE 5.5
Percentage of NOT-Fb and NOT-NFb Cases Meeting Criteria for Clinically Significant Change at Termination

| | Group | | | | |
| | NOT-Fb | | NOT-NFb | | |
Outcome classification	n	%	n	%	χ^2
Deteriorated[a]	21	18.1	29	23.4	6.552*
No change	58	50.0	73	58.9	
Reliable or clinically significant change[b]	37	31.9	22	17.7	

Note. NOT-Fb = clients who were not on track and whose therapist was given feedback; NOT-NFb = clients who were not on track and whose therapist did not receive feedback. From "Enhancing Psychotherapy Outcomes via Providing Feedback on Client Progress: A Replication" by M. J. Lambert, J. L. Whipple, D. A. Vermeersch, D. W. Smart, E. J. Hawkins, S. L. Nielsen, and M. K. Goates, 2002, *Clinical Psychology and Psychotherapy, 9,* p. 100. Copyright 2002 by Wiley. Reprinted with permission.
[a]Worsened by at least 14 points on the Outcome Questionnaire from pretreatment to posttreatment.
[b]Improved by at least 14 points on the Outcome Questionnaire or improved and passed the cutoff between dysfunctional and functional populations.
*$p < .01$.

finding is consistent with Study 1, which found only a trend in the same direction, possibly as a result of the small sample size. When data on NOT cases from the original study were combined with those in the present study, it appeared that 15.2% of those in the NOT-Fb group deteriorated and 30.5% improved or recovered compared with 23.2% deteriorated and 17.5% improved in the NOT-NFb groups.

The Effects of Feedback on Amount of Psychotherapy

Rates of attendance were significantly different for both the Fb or NFb and OT or NOT groups (regardless of receiving the feedback or no feedback manipulation). Clients in the Fb condition received significantly more sessions than clients in the NFb condition ($d = .05$), a difference that was not significant in the prior study. However, the mean difference between the Fb or NFb groups was only .52 sessions in the current study, which has practical meaning over the long run when considering large numbers of clients. Also, as in Study 1, results from Study 2 found NOT cases had significantly more sessions than OT cases, a finding that is consistent with overall high initial level of disturbance for those in the NOT group.

In contrast to Study 1, which showed an interaction between treatment conditions and number of sessions attended (with OT-NFb clients receiving more sessions than OT-Fb clients and NOT-NFb clients receiving fewer sessions than NOT-Fb clients), no such interaction effect was found in the current study. Results show that the NOT-Fb participants received more treatment than participants in the NOT-NFb condition, whereas no difference in treatment sessions was noted between the OT-Fb and OT-NFb cases. The inconsistency between the two studies with regard to the effects of the feedback intervention made the claim that feedback resulted in more cost-effective treatment ambiguous. It seemed clear that providing red and yellow alerts to clinicians for cases at risk for treatment failure resulted in delivery of more sessions to these cases but unclear if sending only green and white messages reduced the number sessions delivered to OT cases.

Study 3

The next study in this line of research was created to deal with two limitations in the foregoing projects. The first was that the original and replication studies had been conducted in the same clinical setting. This naturally raised the question of generalizability of the results to other settings and patient populations. Would progress feedback results hold up in a different setting with a different set of therapists and clients? Because university counseling centers typically see clients at the less disturbed end of the clinical population, a sample with an abundance of more disturbed clients would be ideal. Positive results in such a setting would suggest that the feedback intervention was more universally applicable and could be transportable to a place where fewer resources were available for implementation.

The second limitation dealt with in this study was the degree to which therapists were free to share or withhold feedback results with their clients and exactly what was shared with the clients. The reader will recall that my colleagues and I only provided direct progress feedback to clinicians and left it up to their discretion whether to show the graphs to clients or even talk about the results. From an experimental perspective, very little control was exercised over the independent variable. Why not give clients graphs and messages about their progress in treatment? This would mean that we could be certain clients uniformly got progress feedback and increase the likelihood that such feedback would be discussed in the therapy session. Of course therapists would still be free to modify the impact of feedback through the way they discussed it with clients.

An important issue for the study was the research task of modifying the feedback that had been given to therapists so that it was suitable for delivery to patients. This was challenging both clinically and from the perspective of creating messages that would be acceptable to review boards for research with human participants. Feedback on performance has long been used as an intervention designed to change behavior. In constructing feedback material for clients we relied on research studies that described characteristics of feedback that had been found to be effective. We relied heavily on the results of the Kluger and DeNisi (1996) meta-analysis of the effects of feedback interventions on performance. Results of this review suggested that performance results that convey change in progress since the last assessment of outcome or include a method of improving performance yielded better outcomes. Additionally, there was evidence that written and graphic performance results increased the effects of feedback, whereas verbally delivered feedback interventions reduced the effects of feedback (Kluger & DeNisi, 1996). Consistent with the findings of prior research (Flowers, 1979; Kivlighan, 1985; Kluger & DeNisi, 1996), the messages designed for patients were a blend of positive and negative language. Effort was made to avoid message content potentially perceived as threatening or discouraging to patients' self-esteem. Patients were informed of their self-reported level of distress according to the OQ-45, progress since beginning therapy, and likelihood of benefiting from treatment given the present course of progress. Additionally, patients identified as potential treatment failures were encouraged to discuss personal concerns about their progress, alternative courses of action, and goals of therapy with their therapist to further facilitate the collaborative alliance.

Nine unique patient messages, each corresponding to a particular color code (white, green, yellow, or red), were constructed. Because it was difficult to distinguish qualitative differences in feedback messages designed for patients identified as potential treatment deteriorators, patient messages corresponding to red and yellow warnings were identical for the purpose of this study.

Hawkins, Lambert, Vermeersch, Slade, and Tuttle (2004) reported the results of Study 3. The study was conducted in a hospital-based outpatient clinic operated by a regional behavioral health care company. The clinic served an urban and rural catchment area in the intermountain west. About one half the patients in the clinic were referred after brief inpatient care in the hospital.

Participants

A total of 715 adult patients seeking outpatient psychotherapy services were invited to participate in Study 3 as part of the clinic's intake procedures. Of the 313 patients initially consenting to participate, 112 were excluded from the data analyses. Of the excluded participants, 108 failed to meet inclusion criteria. To be included in the analysis, a patient was required to have received at least two sessions of treatment and completed the outcome measure for a minimum of two sessions representing the first and any subsequent session. The average treatment length for the excluded patients was 1.81 sessions (*Mdn* = 1; *SD* = 1.20), whereas the included participants attended an average of 8.21 sessions (*Mdn* = 6; *SD* = 6.91). One of the four remaining patients was removed from the study because the therapist believed the feedback to be potentially detrimental to the patient's progress and therefore did not disclose the information to the patient. The final three patients refused to complete the outcome measure prior to each session and removed themselves from the study.

The mean age of the 201 participants included in the final sample was 30.8 ($SD = 10.5$). This included 137 female participants (68%) and 64 male participants (32%). Additionally, 190 (94%) were Caucasian; 3 (1.5%) were African American; 3 (1.5%) were Hispanic or Latino; 2 (1%) were Asian American; and 3 (1.5%) were Pacific Islander or other. There were 125 (62%) married and 76 (38%) single participants. Of the participants, 140 (70%) were employed, whereas 61 (30%) were unemployed, and 195 (97%) of the participants had insurance. Without the benefit of structured diagnostic interviews, the most common diagnoses were *DSM–IV–TR* Axis I (American Psychiatric Association, 2000), with mood (74%) or anxiety (21%) disorders occurring most frequently. Sixty-five (32%) of the participants received two diagnoses. Approximately 63% of the patients had previously received psychotherapy services, and 52% of the participants were taking psychotropic medications when they entered treatment. My colleagues and I were unable to monitor patients who were prescribed new medications or a change in medications during treatment.

Three licensed psychologists and two licensed social workers provided treatments in the study. Two of the participating therapists described their treatment orientation as primarily cognitive–behavioral, whereas the remaining three therapists used a variety of treatment orientations including cognitive–behavioral, interpersonal, and humanistic. The treatment approaches practiced in the current study appear similar to those of psychologists surveyed by Division 29 (Psychotherapy) of the American Psychological Association (Norcross, Hedges, & Castle, 2002).

The average age of the therapists was 44 years ($SD = 14.3$ years), and the mean years of experience was 19.6 years ($SD = 10.9$). Patients were assigned to therapists nonrandomly, using therapist availability, clinical factors (e.g., the female therapist in this study was assigned female patients who experienced sexual trauma), and managed care factors (e.g., insurance panels) as assignment criteria. To control for potential effects of therapist assignment, patients were assigned to treatment conditions using a randomized block design, with therapists serving as the blocking variable. This approach appeared to be effective as each therapist was represented equally across all three treatment conditions. The total number of patients treated by each therapist ranged from 21 to 62.

Feedback was provided to therapists and patients according to treatment condition assignment prior to each subsequent session. Therapists in the patient/therapist condition were instructed to present the progress information to their patients at the beginning of each treatment session using the following introduction: "Patient A, to begin the session, I'd like you to look at some information about your progress. After you are finished, if you would like, we can talk about any questions you may have." The introduction of the verbal exchange between therapists and patients represented the second significant change in methodology from Studies 1 and 2. Although the procedures of the present study required that therapists verbally introduce the feedback information and provide a format for patients to discuss their treatment progress, the frequency or content of these interactions was not monitored.

Differences Between Treatment Groups at Pretreatment

A comparison between the groups on the OQ-45 was conducted, and this comparison revealed no difference between groups. In addition, the three groups had no statistically significant differences in age, gender, marital status, employment, insurance coverage, prior mental health treatment, and history of taking psychotropic medications. The mean initial OQ-45 scores of patients in the three treatment groups identified as NOT was 88.55 ($SD = 20.44$), whereas the comparable OT mean was 83.09 ($SD = 23.43$). A test for the difference between these groups was not significant. These results reveal fairly dramatic differences between this sample of patients and the clients studied in the counseling center setting. The patients in the current study scored about a standard deviation higher on the OQ-45 than the counseling center clients. This indicates their functioning is more disturbed than about 95% of the population. The diagnostic classifications indicated that they were much more likely to meet criteria for depression and anxiety and to meet criteria for multiple disorders and longer history of disturbance and treatment. Whereas about 20% of the counseling center samples were taking psychoactive medications, more than 3 times that number were doing so in the current sample. In addition, the large discrepancy between the initial functioning of OT and NOT clients found in the counseling center samples did not appear in the current setting.

Pretreatment–Posttreatment Changes

Table 5.6 shows OQ-45 pretreatment and posttreatment means, standard deviations and effect sizes for the three treatment groups. To assess the improvement from pretreatment to postreatment, paired t tests were performed to assess within-treatment effects for the treatment-as-usual, therapist feedback, and patient/therapist feedback treatment groups. The results of these analyses revealed significant improvement for each treatment group. The effect size for the treatment as usual was $d = .63$; therapist feedback was $d = .82$; and patient/therapist feedback was $d = .92$.

TABLE 5.6
Means, Standard Deviations, and Effect Sizes for Pretreatment and
Posttreatment Outcome Questionnaire Scores by Treatment Group

	Treatment as usual ($n = 64$)			Therapist feedback ($n = 70$)			Patient/therapist feedback ($n = 67$)		
Measure	Pre	Post	Change	Pre	Post	Change	Pre	Post	Change
M	83.72	69.33	14.39	88.84	69.41	19.43	84.71	62.49	22.22
SD	21.74	23.42	16.61	22.70	24.56	21.01	21.77	25.82	19.98
d			.63			.82			.92

Note. Effect size: $d = t_c[2(1-r)/n]^{1/2}$ (Dunlap, Cortina, Vaslow, & Burke, 1996); t_c = correlated t statistic; r = correlation between pre- and posttreatment score; n = sample size per group. From "The Therapeutic Effects of Providing Patient Progress Information to Therapists and Patients," by E. J. Hawkins, M. J., Lambert, D. A. Vermeersch, K. Slade, and K. Tuttle, 2004, *Psychotherapy Research, 14*, p. 315. Copyright 2004 by Taylor & Francis. Reprinted with permission.

The Effect of Feedback on Outcome

Planned comparisons were used to test the major hypotheses of the study. To obtain adjusted means and the error term used in the contrasts, a 2 (Status) × 3 (Treatment) ANCOVA with pretreatment OQ-45 score as the covariate was performed. The outcome measure used in this omnibus analysis was the change score calculated from the difference between the pre- and post-OQ-45 total score. The feedback and patient/therapist versus no feedback contrast was statistically significant and resulted in a moderate effect size ($\eta^2 = .02$). The therapist feedback versus patient/therapist feedback comparison was also statistically significant and reflected a moderate effect size as well ($\eta^2 = .02$). The largest difference between treatment groups was represented by a contrast between the treatment as usual and patient/therapist feedback group ($\eta^2 = .04$). The effects of feedback on the three treatment groups are shown graphically in Figure 5.3.

A particular aim of this research was to identify and alter the final outcome of patients identified as potential treatment deteriorators. Thus, comparisons among the three treatment groups in the NOT condition were conducted. Following the format of the comparisons mentioned previously, the feedback interventions did not reach statistical significance.

Analysis of Clinical Significance

To further determine the clinical meaningfulness of outcome, final outcomes were categorized according to the number of patients who responded to treatment (i.e., met either reliable or clinically significant change criteria) and those who did not respond to treatment (deteriorated or no change). The percentages of patients responding to treatment in the treatment-as-usual,

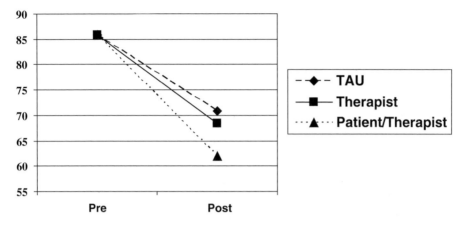

Figure 5.3. Study 3: adjusted pre- and posttreatment means of treatment-as-usual (TAU), therapist feedback, and patient/therapist feedback conditions. From "The Therapeutic Effects of Providing Patient Progress Information to Therapists and Patient," by E. J. Hawkins, M. J. Lambert, D. A. Vermeersch, K. Slade, and K. Tuttle, 2004, *Psychotherapy Research, 14,* p. 316. Copyright 2004 by Taylor & Francis. Reprinted with permission.

therapist, and patient/therapist groups was 53, 57, and 64, respectively. A comparison between the proportion of patients responding to treatment in the patient/therapist and treatment-as-usual conditions found a nonsignificant difference ($z = 1.28$; $p = .10$).

An examination of only those patients identified as potential treatment nonresponders revealed a similar pattern. The percentages of patients categorized as improved at the end of treatment was 34, 40, and 56 for the treatment-as-usual, therapist, and patient/therapist groups, respectively. However, a comparison between the proportion of patients in the patient/therapist and treatment-as-usual NOT groups revealed a significant difference ($z = 1.85$; $p < .05$). The frequencies and proportions of patients identified as potential treatment failures and meeting the outcome categories are presented in Table 5.7.

The Effects of Feedback on Amount of Psychotherapy

The mean number of sessions received by patients in the treatment-as-usual, therapist feedback, and patient/therapist feedback groups was 8.66 (*Mdn* = 7), 8.20 (*Mdn* = 6), and 7.79 (*Mdn* = 6), respectively. Contrary to expectations, the groups did not differ on the number of treatment sessions received. However, the number of sessions received by the NOT and OT groups was significantly different. On average, patients in the NOT groups attended 4.24 (*SD* = 6.08) more sessions than patients in the OT conditions.

TABLE 5.7
Percentage of Not-on-Track Patients Meeting Reliable or Clinically
Significant, No Change, or Deteriorated Criteria on the Outcome
Questionnaire-45 (OQ-45) at Final Outcome

Outcome classification	Treatment as usual		Therapist		Patient/ therapist	
	n	%	n (%)	%	n (%)	%
Deteriorated[a]	3	9	1	3	2	5
No change[b]	19	59	17	57	15	39
Reliable change[c]	7	22	9	30	13	33
Clinically significant change[d]	3	10	3	10	9	23

Note. From "The Therapeutic Effects of Providing Patient Progress Information to Therapists and Patients," by E. J. Hawkins, M. J. Lambert, D. A. Vermeersch, K. Slade, and K. Tuttle, 2004, *Psychotherapy Research, 14*, p. 317. Copyright 2004 by Taylor & Francis. Reprinted with permission.
[a]Worsened by at least 14 points on the OQ-45 from pre- to posttreatment. [b]Improved fewer than 14 points and worsened by fewer than 14 points on the OQ-45. [c]Improved by at least 14 points on the OQ-45 but did not pass the cutoff between dysfunctional and functional populations. [d]Improved by at least 14 points on the OQ-45 and passed the cutoff between dysfunctional and functional populations.

An indicator of the strength of the patient/therapist feedback intervention was that 56% of the patients identified during treatment as potential treatment nonresponders met criteria for reliable or clinically significant change, the only condition in which more than one half of such patients improved during treatment. This, coupled with the finding that compared with the treatment-as-usual condition a significantly greater proportion of patients in the patient/therapist condition responded to treatment, further suggests the benefits of patients receiving feedback regarding their treatment progress.

Consistent with the two previous studies investigating the use of feedback interventions patients identified as NOT attended significantly more sessions than OT patients. In the present study, NOT patients attended twice the number of sessions attended by OT patients. This finding seems to support the status of these patients and connotes that barriers to improved outcomes likely exist. However, it also suggests that despite little progress, these patients remained hopeful of reducing their distress.

Although my colleagues and I predicted that the feedback interventions would enhance the outcomes of the NOT patients, we expected that this would be achieved by increasing the number of sessions attended. In contrast to previous studies, the outcomes of patients in the feedback conditions surpassed the treatment-as-usual controls with no average increase in sessions attended. As a partial replication of the prior feedback studies, the present study found a relatively weak effect when only therapists were provided feedback about a patient's treatment progress. This was an unexpected and disappointing result, and it is unclear why therapist feedback did not have a more significant impact on outcomes.

In contrast to our previous investigations, the feedback interventions in the present study enhanced the outcomes of both OT and NOT patients, suggesting that provision of progress information directly to patients and therapists has more global effects than when feedback is provided only to therapists. Patients expressed a very strong interest in receiving information about their progress in treatment, and despite the fact that the patients were severely distressed, the results suggest that these patients were capable of receiving "objective" feedback about their treatment progress without being negatively affected.

SUMMARY AND CONCLUSIONS FROM STUDIES 1, 2, AND 3

The initial two studies helped us draw some basic conclusions about the clinical impact of providing therapists with client progress feedback. Although our original methods were somewhat crude compared with our current methods as described in Chapter 6 (e.g., paper-and-pencil administration, scanner scoring and hand graphing, 1-week time delay vs. computer-based electronic methods with instantaneous feedback), we were able to conduct these labor intense studies, which required daily data collection over a 1-year period. Without the advantages of the conceptual work of Riemer and Bickman (Riemer & Bickman, 2004; Riemer, Rosof-Williams, & Bickman, 2005), which were published after our design of feedback interventions, our feedback procedures were relatively immediate, credible, systematic, frequent, unambiguous, and simple (color-coded, graphic).

With regard to the degree to which therapists saw the feedback intervention as valuable, we were not quite prepared for the hesitancy with which the clinicians greeted our efforts. We underestimated the importance of having clinicians who saw a need for improving their performance (as therapists were pleased with their performance in the absence of feedback) and were unaware of a discrepancy between their perceived client outcomes and actual outcomes (they saw no need for alarm-signal feedback). It was several years before we actually undertook a study (Hannan et al., 2005) described in Chapter 4 to see if clinicians could detect a negative treatment response and compare their accuracy with that of our statistically based procedures. We did find that clinicians who were motivated to use feedback and found it valid, credible, and useful had better outcomes than those who did not.

With regard to the study findings, we were surprised that feedback was not universally helpful across clients but limited mainly to those who fell off track during their course of treatment. Because OT clients represented about

20% of the total number being treated, this was somewhat disappointing. There were hints, however, that the other 80% of clients could be helped in fewer sessions without losing any measured benefit. It appeared from the data that when off-track feedback was provided, therapists paid more attention to patients, keeping them in treatment longer. We did not know what else they did to benefit these clients. Apparently the therapists were quite capable of figuring out how to solve problems of progress with these at-risk cases by merely being informed that there was a concern. Therapists were surprised to learn that this was true and thought they were doing their very best in the absence of alarm signals. They were not aware that feedback cases had better outcomes than their treatment-as-usual cases. They generally warmed up to the idea of feedback and particularly appreciated the progress graphs they received. In this regard, the research developed a good reputation for providing therapists with something useful rather than just being used for collecting data for studies that would be published and might have eventual implications for professional practice.

The accumulated evidence made us optimistic about the use of feedback as a means of enhancing patient outcome even when the context for feedback fell short of the ideal therapist attitudes necessary for feedback to be most valuable. The methodology used endeavored to improve psychotherapy outcome by monitoring client progress in relation to expected progress as described in Chapter 4. Of greatest importance was providing this information to clinicians to guide ongoing treatment, particularly for the client who was not having a favorable response to treatment (signal-alarm cases). This methodology is an extension of quality assurance and represents one effort to bridge the gap between research and clinical practice while enhancing patient outcome before treatment termination. The methods used seemed especially well suited to models of care in which clinicians attempt to step-up or step-down treatments after assessing patient treatment response (Newman, 2000; Otto, Pollack, & Maki, 2000). Within practice of this kind, the opportunity to adjust treatment as it unfolds is especially appealing because it can make psychotherapy especially efficient by allocating more resources when they are necessary and allocating fewer when it is reasonable to do so.

The research agenda for improving outcomes for poorly responding cases had further to go; such advances are described in Chapter 6.

6

BEYOND PROGRESS FEEDBACK: THE EFFECTS OF CLINICAL PROBLEM-SOLVING TOOLS

At the end of Study 3 (described in Chapter 5, this volume) my colleagues and I were pretty confident that progress feedback improved psychotherapy outcome for clients who showed negative progress during the course of undergoing psychological treatment in a routine care setting and perhaps more generally if clients began treatment with more severe levels of disturbance. But we were also aware that a significant portion of not-on-track (NOT) clients remained distressed at treatment termination despite the fact that their therapist received progress feedback and alarm signals. We reduced deterioration substantially, but still about 13% of poorly responding cases left treatment deteriorated, and there were a large number of cases that did not budge one way or the other in terms of measured benefit. As we reflected on this situation, we decided that it would make sense to provide therapists with a problem-solving (decision support) strategy while working with such cases.

A few problems needed to be overcome. It was obvious that therapists were eclectic in their treatment orientation, and we also knew from published literature (Jensen, Bergin, & Greaves, 1990; Norcross, Hedges, & Castle, 2002) that this was also the case for the majority of clinicians who provided treatment in routine care. Despite the fact that almost all clinical trials examine the effects of applying a single theoretical orientation with a single disorder (although cognitive–behavior therapy, the most studied therapy in clinical trials, could be considered an eclectic treatment), clinical practitioners are rarely constrained to limit treatment to one theory-based treatment. We needed a problem-solving strategy that would be acceptable and language neutral enough that it could be used by a wide range of individual clinicians.

Second, we realized that therapists had been initially resistant to getting progress feedback and felt very confident in their own personal practices. It was difficult to believe that they would find any further "help" in improving their routine care a welcome development. Therapist estimates of their own patient's outcome and their confidence in their ability (as already noted in Chapter 4, this volume), although very necessary for positive client outcomes, makes therapists resistant to applying procedures they do not initiate themselves.

A third consideration in our deliberations, one related to the issue just mentioned, was to place emphasis on a simple intervention that might take just minutes to use. Whatever we developed needed to quickly lead to therapist action. There seemed no point at all in developing an elaborate intervention that required training and high levels of commitment on the part of therapists. In this endeavor, we relied on the related psychotherapy research literature, identifying variables that could be measured and had associated interventions that had been shown to be effective. We decided to create a clinical support tool (CST) intervention based on a decision tree to hierarchically organize problem solving according to a reading of the research literature (see Figure 6.1). Accordingly, we intended to ask clinicians to consider the therapeutic alliance, client motivation, social supports, and diagnostic considerations (that might lead to a referral for psychoactive medications or alteration in ongoing pharmacotherapy) in deciding how to proceed with the alarm-signal cases.

A search of the literature for suitable brief measures with good psychometric properties that could be used to measure each construct was instigated. It may help the reader to get a brief overview of why such constructs were chosen.

THERAPEUTIC ALLIANCE

The quality of the relationship between the client and therapist has been found to significantly and regularly correlate with psychotherapy outcomes and especially with client deterioration if the therapist is perceived as rejecting. This latter point should be emphasized. In an early review of therapist-induced deterioration there was clear evidence that misapplications of specific interventions seldom led to client worsening, instead such worsening was nearly always connected to aspects of the human encounter such as disrespect, neglect, and sub-

Clinical Support Decision Tree

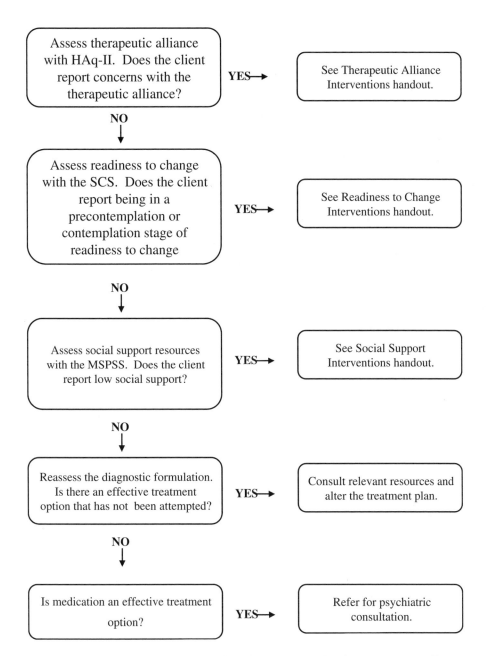

Figure 6.1. Decision tree for guiding clinical decision making for at-risk cases. From "Improving the Effects of Psychotherapy: The Use of Early Identification of Treatment Failure and Problem-Solving Strategies in Routine Practice," by J. L. Whipple, M. J. Lambert, D. A. Vermeersch, D. W. Smart, S. L. Nielsen, and E. J. Hawkins, 2003, *Journal of Counseling Psychology, 58,* p. 68. Copyright 2003 by the American Psychological Association.

tle rejection (Lambert, Bergin, & Collins, 1977). To the extent that specific therapeutic procedures could be linked to negative outcomes, the strongest evidence pointed to therapies with little structure delivered to patients who showed considerable emotional volatility.

Early relationship research focused on the traditional client-centered facilitative conditions of empathy, unconditional positive regard, genuineness, and nonpossessive warmth. More recently, the terms *therapeutic alliance* and *working alliance* have been used, and research has focused on the alliance and its relationship with outcome. The therapeutic alliance is not synonymous with the client-centered variables and has arisen from psychodynamic theory. It has various definitions, but most agree that it is composed of a positive bond (made up of the traditional client-centered conditions), agreement on the tasks (how the therapist and client work together during the hour), and agreement on the goals of psychotherapy. Alliance research, like that of the client-centered tradition, has found its way into research on all kinds of psychotherapy and is not generally viewed as theory specific.

Difficulties in the therapeutic alliance can be referred to as *alliance ruptures* (Safran & Muran, 2000), with successful psychotherapy being highly dependent on the ability of the client and therapist to resolve ruptures and strains in the alliance. Ruptures can be both negative shifts in the quality of the alliance and ongoing problems in establishing an alliance. Within psychodynamic theory, ruptures can also be understood as moments when the client's schemas or working models of relationships are acted out in the therapeutic context (negative transference)—a potentially vital part of the change process if resolved. Even in therapies that rely heavily on homework assignments, research has suggested the importance of the alliance for ensuring compliance with these out-of-office tasks.

In an effort to solve the problem of the deteriorating client, it is important to measure the quality of the relationship between client and therapist from the client's point of view because research consistently suggests that the client's perception of the relationship (rather than the therapist's) has a higher correlation with outcome. Thus the first goal of the CSTs is to assess the strength of the alliance as rated by the patient. The Helping Alliance Questionnaire was selected for the task of providing feedback to therapists. The Revised Helping Alliance Questionnaire (Luborsky, Barber, Siqueland, & Johnson, 1996) is a brief self-report instrument consisting of 19 items. We hoped to focus attention on possible problems in the relationship, not just positive qualities. This is also necessary because alliance measures that are used for the purposes of feedback to therapists are notorious for being highly skewed toward the positive end of the continuum. Although it may be reassuring to know that clients have very positive feelings about their relationship with therapists, it is more helpful in a problem-solving mode to identify ruptures in the relationship and move to repair them if possible. It is also important to note that there is research on therapist actions that repair alliance ruptures (Safran & Muran, 2000). And we sought not only to measure the construct of interest but to make suggestions to therapists about constructive actions that were empirically justified.

MOTIVATION

Therapy clients often come with similar problems but may have different levels of motivation. It should be noted that expectancy for a positive outcome is a highly related construct. Poorly motivated clients do not necessarily take responsibility for being in therapy or in taking the role of patient, which in psychotherapy means accepting responsibility for active participation in treatment sessions. Expectations for therapy usually consist of either a positive anticipation that treatment will be helpful or an understanding of the kind of self-involvement necessary to reach goals or both. Motivation, like expectation, plays an important role in changing behavior; but research on the relationship between motivation and expectation and treatment outcome has been very inconsistent, with low correlations between initial motivation and expectation and final outcome being the most likely finding. Presumably this is because motivation and expectations can be quite fluid, with poorly motivated clients changing their motivation after a single session or dropping out of treatment without changing their expectations or motivation (Garfield, 1994).

Nevertheless, identifying problematic motivation is important for designing therapeutic procedures to assist clients whose positive therapy outcome is in doubt. For the client who is manifesting negative change, we believe it is especially important to investigate motivational issues as they interact with ongoing interventions and lead to premature withdrawal from treatment. Deviations from an expected treatment response reflect the possibility that a client has entered psychotherapy in a less than favorable stage of readiness to change (Prochaska, DiClemente, & Norcross, 1992). By matching therapeutic techniques with a client's readiness to change, Prochaska and Prochaska (1999), suggested that final outcomes could be improved. Similarly, and in specific relationship to participants in Study 4 (to be presented shortly), Drum and Baron (1998) found that final outcome could be predicted and enhanced by assessing a client's readiness to change and matching it with appropriate therapeutic interventions.

Therapists have successfully improved client outcome by incorporating their understanding of motivational stages and how they interact with different types of interventions. The dominant conceptual scheme across this research is based on the stages of change model within which clients can be seen to move through motivational stages (precontemplation, contemplation, preparation, action, and maintenance; Prochaska et al., 1992). Prochaska and colleagues noted that progression through the stages rarely occurs in a linear fashion. The majority of clients may relapse into earlier stages, with many returning to the precontemplation stage when confronted with a failure to change or maintain gains.

An alternative conceptual model for motivation, self-determination theory, asserts that lower levels of motivation are based on the client's locus of motivation (Pelletier, Tucson, & Haddad, 1997). Extrinsically motivated clients, for example, are motivated by the insistence of others that they participate in therapy. Intrinsically motivated clients, however, are highly motivated to make changes in therapy because of the difficulty they feel in their personal life. The "amotivation" spoken of in self-determination theory may be analogous to the precontemplative stage within the stages of change model. As Markland, Ryan, Tobin, and Rollnick (2005) suggested, self-determination theory lends itself well to the interventions in motivational interviewing.

The Stages of Change Scale was selected to measure motivation. The Stages of Change Scale is a measure of a client's readiness to change based on the four-stage model developed by McConnaughy, Prochaska, and Velicer (1983). Eight items scored on a 5-point Likert scale measure each stage. The stage with the highest overall score determines the client's readiness to change.

SOCIAL SUPPORT

Conservative estimates indicate clients spend less than 1% of their waking hours in psychotherapy sessions. This estimate is consistent with findings that report 40% of therapy outcome variance is due to extra therapeutic factors including clients' social support network (Lambert, 1992). Consequently, clients predicted to have a poor outcome may not have adequate social support networks to initiate or maintain gains acquired in therapy. Furthermore, the adequacy of social support is directly related to a client's reported severity of symptoms and can mediate stressful life events and the development of psychological symptoms (Monroe, Imhoff, Wise, & Harris, 1983). High levels of social support can moderate the negative effects of other life events (e.g., losing a job). For clients who have poor support, therapists may need to identify the social support resources that clients already have in their current life and attempt to activate or modify them to achieve a better treatment outcome (Bankoff & Howard, 1992).

As already mentioned, research has demonstrated that adequacy of social support is directly related to the reported severity of psychological symptoms. The presence of strong interpersonal relationships has also been shown to reduce the risk of psychological disturbance and augment the effectiveness of therapy (Thoits, 1986; Zimet, Dahlem, Zimet, & Farley,1988). Another important issue to consider is the fact that the association between symptomatology and social support is reciprocal: Social support influences well-being, but on the other hand, the presence of severe psychopathology may hamper the capacity to seek social support and to benefit from it. The problem is that cause and effect are hard to disentangle. It seems probable that interpersonal conflicts and the lack of social support reinforce interpersonal sensitivity, loneliness, and depression, but it is equally possible that the psychological status of an individual will negatively affect the quality of social relationships.

Persons with certain types of psychopathology, notably, personality disorders, are characterized by disturbances in interpersonal relationships and therefore social supports. The interpersonal difficulties are reflected in the incapacity or unwillingness to seek social support and the tendency to freely vent anger. It is also true that those diagnosed as having borderline personality disorder have unusual difficulties maintaining social supports and are among the most likely patients to experience a negative psychotherapy outcome. Because a lack of social supports may be circumstantial or due to underlying processes in the patient, considerable care may need to be exercised while intervening. In contrast to instability in emotional regulation, many clients have skill deficits instead of or in addition to personality-based problems. Such deficits can be ameliorated if detected. But by-and-large it is the client's perception of social support, rather than the objective count of support that is present in a client's life, that predicts outcome.

We therefore chose the Multidimensional Scale of Perceived Social Support (Zimet et al., 1988) for the purpose of operationalization of the social support construct. The Multidimensional Scale of Perceived Social Support is a 12-item inventory designed to measure three sources of perceived social support: family, friends, and a significant other.

Once my colleagues and I organized the preceding variables of interest, constructed the decision tree, and selected the assessment measures, cutoff scores were developed for the measures. Cutoff scores were deemed as essential to moving clinicians toward areas in which there were potential problems and away from areas in which there were no problems. The general thinking here was that it would not be helpful to provide clinicians with scores on measures and to depend on clinicians to interpret these scores and then take actions. Rather, we wanted them to know if the therapeutic alliance was a problem and, if not, to quickly move toward considering motivation or other problems.

Reevaluating diagnostic formulations (e.g., Eells, Kenkjelic, & Lucas, 1998) and referring for medication (e.g., Hatfield, McCullough, Plucinski, & Krieger, 2009; Trivedi & Kleiber, 2001) was the final consideration in the decision tree. Here the emphasis was on prompting therapists to consider arranging a medication consultation if, on reflection, this might be necessary. Although this is often a consideration for therapists, it may be especially appropriate in the case of the deteriorating client. A treatment manual that explained the rationale for the intervention, included the decision tree, explained the tests, and provided a list of suggested interventions for problematic areas was created.

We were ready to initiate a study on the effects of this CST intervention for not-on-track (NOT) cases. The aim of this study was to see if this improved client outcomes for NOT cases and also to complete a replication of Study 1 and Study 2.

STUDY 4

The design of Study 4 (Whipple et al., 2003) called for three groups of clients randomly assigned to treatment as usual (no feedback; NFb), progress feedback (Fb), or progress feedback plus CSTs (Fb+CST) for NOT cases. Unfortunately, the center would not allow clients to be randomly assigned to the CST intervention and a substantial number of therapists would not agree to be part of the intervention. To gain the cooperation of those who agreed to use the CST intervention, we also had to agree that the measures would only be administered to NOT clients at the therapists' discretion. This produced a design flaw that resulted in an experimental group that was selected, rather than randomly assigned. As previously described, therapists saw the CST intervention as more intrusive than progress feedback. Therapists were not sure it was worth clients' time and effort to take the measures, even though the design of the study called for administration of the measures only to NOT cases at the time they first signaled red or yellow.

Nevertheless, the design of the study allowed us to conduct a second replication of the effects of progress feedback and to compare both of these interventions with CST feedback if the therapist thought it would be helpful. Because this procedure might prove to be the way CSTs were used in practice, and allowed the research program to move forward, we undertook Study 4.

Participants

Participants were 981 clients out of a possible 1,339 treated at the same university counseling center as in Studies 1 and 2. There were 358 clients who were not included in the sample because they did not complete an outcome measure or did not return for a second session. These figures are consistent with routine practice across settings that show the median number of sessions attended is one (Garfield, 1994) and with clinical trials, which exclude even larger numbers of participants (Westen & Morrison, 2001). Approximately one half of the clients ($n = 499$) were randomly assigned to the experimental (Fb) group, and one half ($n = 482$) were randomly assigned to the control (NFb) group. Statistical tests revealed no significant differences between the experimental and control groups on any of the variables of interest. Clients had similar characteristics as those studied in the first two studies.

Therapists were 48 counseling center staff consisting of 27 doctoral-level psychologists and 21 doctoral students in training, including interns. Three additional therapists refused participation in this study; the rest gave informed consent, as did clients. The original NOT-Fb condition consisted of 147 clients. After 59 clients were removed to form the NOT-Fb+CST group, only 88 cases remained in the NOT-Fb condition, whereas the NOT-NFb group totaled 131.

Measures

Patients were tracked with the Outcome Questionnaire-45 (OQ-45) and the CST measures described earlier. The therapeutic relationship and social support network were determined to be below average if the client scored 1 standard deviation below the reported client mean for these two measures on the basis of the published literature. Below average motivation to change was evidenced by a client's scoring in the precontemplation or contemplation stage of readiness to change. To further influence therapists' decisions and actions as recipients of feedback, a tracking form was given to therapists when a client was identified as NOT. This survey form was seen as part of the experimental manipulation because it listed actions that could be taken by therapists and, therefore, might affect the way therapists treated clients who were not showing adequate progress (e.g., Did you discuss the OQ-45 feedback with the client? Did you consult about the case with other professionals? Did you alter the treatment plan?). No tracking form was given to therapists whose clients were on track (OT) or in the control group (NOT-NFb).

As in Study 1 and 2, the mean pretreatment OQ total score for the Fb (experimental) group and the NFb (control) group were equal and the NOT clients started treatment about 10 points higher than the OT clients. Although 57.8% of the OT clients began treatment in the dysfunctional range, 74.5% of the NOT participants began in this same range. No OQ-45 pretreatment differences were noted between the NOT participants in the treatment and control conditions. As in the earlier studies, randomization procedures appeared to be effective at creating comparison groups that were reasonably equivalent at pretreatment prior to the experimental manipulations.

Over the course of therapy, clients seen at the counseling center ($n = 981$) during this study improved with an average change of -12.52 OQ-45 points ($d = .55$). Those who began therapy in the functional range ($n = 368$)

had an average change of −4.12 points. For clients who began treatment in the dysfunctional range ($n = 613$, 62.5%), that is, those who started psychotherapy with an OQ score of 64 or greater, the improvement was even larger ($M = -17.56$; $d = .98$). Of these clients in the dysfunctional range, 36.9% were classified as having achieved clinically significant change by the end of therapy, whereas an additional 17.3% achieved only reliable change. After receiving an average of 6.20 ($SD = 5.29$) sessions of treatment, 44.4% of clients scored within the functional range (i.e., at or below an OQ total score of 63).

The Effects of Feedback on Outcome

If the CSTs were to be considered effective, the NOT-Fb+CST group would have greater pretreatment–posttreatment change in OQ-45 scores (in the direction of improvement) than the NOT-Fb and NOT-NFb groups. Pretreatment and posttreatment OQ-45 scores can be seen in Table 6.1. Results from an ANCOVA with the pretreatment OQ-45 score as a covariate showed that a significant difference existed between the NOT groups. Least significant difference post hoc comparisons indicated that the NOT-Fb+CST group improved significantly more than the NOT-Fb group ($d = .28$) and the

TABLE 6.1
Means and Standard Deviations of Outcome Questionnaire-45 (OQ-45)
Scores and Duration Data

Group	n	Pretreatment OQ-45 M (SD)	Posttreatment OQ-45 M (SD)	Total sessions M (SD)	Sessions after Fb M (SD)
Total Fb	499	71.23 (23.03)	58.15 (22.25)	5.47 (4.86)	5.82 (5.76)
Total no Fb	482	70.50 (22.33)	58.56 (23.38)	5.46 (4.88)	4.50 (4.83)
Total NOT	278	78.64 (20.94)	72.81 (22.14)	8.66 (5.67)	5.20 (5.38)
Total OT	703	67.80 (22.62)	52.63 (20.41)	4.20 (3.84)	NA
NOT-Fb+CST	59	83.15 (20.51)	67.75 (23.61)	12.02 (6.73)	8.86 (6.78)
NOT-Fb	88	77.81 (21.65)	71.30 (23.23)	7.44 (4.66)	3.84 (3.92)
NOT-NFb	131	77.16 (20.51)	76.11 (20.26)	7.96 (5.21)	4.50 (4.83)
OT-Fb	352	67.59 (22.77)	53.25 (19.84)	3.88 (3.14)	NA
OT-NFb	351	68.01 (22.50)	52.01 (20.98)	4.53 (4.41)	NA
Total	981				

Notes. Fb = feedback; NOT = clients who were not on track; OT = clients who were on track; NOT-Fb+CST = clients who were not on track and whose therapists received feedback and used the clinical support tools (CSTs); NOT-Fb = clients who were not on track and whose therapists received feedback; NOT-NFb = clients who were not on track and whose therapists did not receive feedback; OT-Fb = clients who were on track and whose therapists received feedback; OT-NFb = clients who were on track and whose therapists did not receive feedback. From "Improving the Effects of Psychotherapy: The Use of Early Identification of Treatment Failure and Problem-Solving Strategies in Routine Practice," by J. L. Whipple, M. J. Lambert, D. A. Vermeersch, D. W. Smart, S. L. Nielsen, and E. J. Hawkins, 2003, *Journal of Counseling Psychology, 58,* p. 64. Copyright 2003 by the American Psychological Association.

NOT-Fb group improved significantly more than the NOT-NFb group. The mean difference in pretreatment–posttreatment change between the NOT-Fb+CST and NOT-NFb was 11.79 ($d = .70$).

Client improvement between NOT groups following the time after which feedback was given was also analyzed. Point of feedback to posttreatment differences between the three groups reached statistical significance. Least significant difference post hoc comparisons revealed that the NOT-Fb+CST group improved significantly more than the NOT-Fb group. Despite a statistical trend, the NOT-Fb group did not improve significantly more than the NOT-NFb group. These changes are presented graphically in Figure 6.2.

This figure illustrates that the NOT-NFb clients, on average, worsened to the point at which their therapists could have been warned about their poor progress and then showed some improvement. The NOT-Fb clients showed a

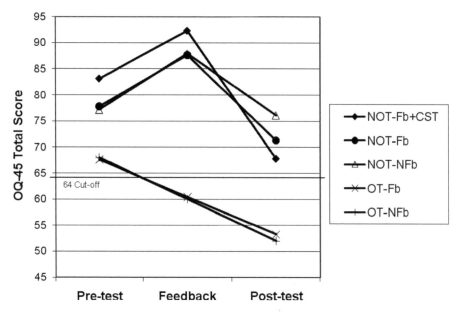

Figure 6.2. Change from pre- to post-testing of not-on-track and on-track clients. NOT-Fb+CST = clients who were not on track and whose therapists received feedback and used the clinical support tools (CSTs); NOT-Fb = clients who were not on track and whose therapists received feedback; NOT-NFb = clients who were not on track and whose therapists did not receive feedback; OT-Fb = clients who were on track and whose therapists received feedback; OT-NFb = clients who were on track and whose therapists did not receive feedback. From "Improving the Effects of Psychotherapy: The Use of Early Identification of Treatment Failure and Problem-Solving Strategies in Routine Practice ," by J. L. Whipple, M. J. Lambert, D. A. Vermeersch, D. W. Smart, S. L. Nielsen, and E. J. Hawkins, 2003, *Journal of Counseling Psychology, 58,* p. 64. Copyright 2003 by the American Psychological Association.

similar worsening to the point of feedback, followed by more noticeable improvement. Likewise, the NOT-Fb+CST clients worsened to the point of feedback but improved even more at posttreatment.

Analysis of Clinical Significance

To further explore the clinical importance of outcome in the NOT groups, clients were categorized with regard to the clinical significance of their change. These data are presented in Table 6.2. The differences in the frequency with which clients met criteria for outcome classification categories reached statistical significance when tested with the chi square statistic. Notably, only 8.5% of those in the NOT-Fb+CST group deteriorated, with 49.1% improved or recovered. In contrast, the deterioration rate for alarm-signal cases was 13.6%, with 33.0% improved or recovered. These rates can be compared with a deterioration rate of 19.1% in the treatment-as-usual group, with 25.2% recovered or improved. The impact of the CSTs and feedback on outcomes suggests that the effects are powerful enough to change the levels at which clients are classified as having met the rigorous definition of clinically meaningful change.

The Effects of Feedback on Amount of Psychotherapy

Although the rates of attendance were not significantly different between the Fb (experimental) and NFb (control) conditions, there was a significant dif-

TABLE 6.2
Percentage of NOT-Fb+CST, NOT-Fb, and NOT-NFb Cases Meeting Criteria for Clinically Significant Change at Termination

Outcome classification	NOT-Fb+CST n (%)	NOT-Fb n (%)	NOT-NFb n (%)	χ^2
Deteriorated[a]	5 (8.5)	12 (13.6)	25 (19.1)	11.782*
No change	25 (42.4)	47 (53.4)	73 (55.7)	
Reliable or clinically significant change[b]	29 (49.1)	29 (33.0)	33 (25.2)	

Note. NOT-Fb+CST = clients who were not on track and whose therapists received feedback and used the clinical support tools (CSTs); NOT-Fb = clients who were not on track and whose therapist was given feedback; NOT-NFb = clients who were not on track and whose therapist did not receive feedback. From "Improving the Effects of Psychotherapy: The Use of Early Identification of Treatment Failure and Problem-Solving Strategies in Routine Practice," by J. L. Whipple, M. J. Lambert, D. A. Vermeersch, D. W. Smart, S. L. Nielsen, and E. J. Hawkins, 2003, *Journal of Counseling Psychology, 58*, p. 65. Copyright 2003 by the American Psychological Association.
[a]Worsened by at least 14 points on the Outcome Questionnaire from pretreatment to posttreatment;
[b] Improved by at least 14 points on the Outcome Questionnaire or improved and passed the cutoff between dysfunctional and functional populations.
*χ^2 (4, N = 278) = 11.782, p < .05.

ference in the number of sessions between clients for both the OT versus all three of the NOT groups (regardless of receiving the Fb or NFb manipulation). Clients in the NOT groups received on average 4.12 ($SD = 9.80$) more sessions than OT cases. A significant interaction (Fb/NFb × OT/NOT) suggested that participants in the NOT-Fb+CST and NOT-Fb groups combined received more treatment than participants in the NOT-NFb condition, whereas OT-Fb clients received significantly fewer sessions than OT-NFb cases.

Another session-related analysis showed that all three of the NOT groups qualified for a warning at the third session, on average. The small differences between the means was not statistically significant. However, there was a significant difference in the number of sessions received after the warning feedback between the NOT groups. Least significant difference post hoc comparisons revealed that the NOT-Fb+CST group received significantly more sessions than the NOT-Fb group (mean difference = 4.92) and the NOT-NFb group (mean difference = 4.26), but the NOT-Fb group did not receive more sessions than the NOT-NFb group (mean difference = 0.66).

Therapist Effects on Outcome and Amount of Psychotherapy

Because no experimental control was exercised over which therapists used the CSTs at any time during the study, an analysis of differences in outcome and attendance rates between therapists who used CSTs and those who did not was performed. It was thought that these analyses would help to rule out therapist effects as a causal factor for the positive outcome and attendance results in the CST group. To test for therapist effects, differences between therapists who used the CSTs ($n = 26$) with at least one client and therapists who never used the CSTs ($n = 23$) were compared on outcome and session data for clients in the control conditions (OT-NFb and NOT-NFb).

ANCOVA results indicated there were no differences in outcome between the therapists who did and did not use the CSTs (mean difference in client outcome = 0.853). Similarly, ANCOVA results for the attendance data indicated there was no difference between therapists who did and did not use the CSTs (mean difference in total number of sessions attended = .349). These analyses suggest that the observed results in outcome and attendance data for the NOT-Fb+CST condition was probably not due to therapists who self-selected themselves to use the CSTs. These self-selected therapists did not have superior outcomes or increased attendance rates across other cases.

Additional therapist analyses were performed to determine if the therapist's level of training (professional staff or supervised trainees) and use of the CSTs produced significant differences in outcome or attendance rates. However, no significant main effects or interactions were found in the outcome or session related analyses.

Study 4: Summary and Conclusions

The results of Study 4 were quite encouraging. They replicated the findings of Studies 1 and 2 that progress feedback for off-track clients significantly improved outcomes, with the effect size for such an intervention around .40. Deterioration rates dropped from a baseline of 19%–21% to around 13%. More importantly, the problem-solving strategy in the form of the CST had an added benefit for NOT clients, with an effect size of .70 compared with treatment as usual and .26 compared with alarm feedback alone. Deterioration reduced to 8.5% when CSTs were added. The number of clients who reliably improved or recovered doubled from 25% to 50% compared with treatment as usual. As can be seen in Figure 6.2, those whose therapists used the CSTs, as a group, nearly returned to a state of normal functioning. Given our difficulties in getting all therapists to use the CSTs and following our report to the clinical staff about the results of the Whipple et al. (2003) study, two important developments occurred.

The first development came as a surprise in that a staff discussion ensued about the ethics of *not* providing progress feedback as part of routine care. One of the staff (not a person on the research team) raised this issue and asked: "Why after more than 3 years of research and consistent positive, if not dramatic improvements in client outcome, should we not make progress feedback routine practice in the counseling center?" After considerable discussion, a vote was taken and treatment as usual disappeared from the clinic. This was quite a change in attitudes from the beginning of the research program. Therapists were quite pleased with graphical presentations of client progress and were happy to have them. They were less than unanimous in their perceived need for the warning alerts, but because they were part of the feedback system and perceived by the research team as essential, the alerts were agreed to. Given the content of the discussion, it was apparent that many therapists thought there was clinical value in seeing graphic representations of client progress but did not think warning messages were essential or even necessary.

The second development was that the research team was allowed to conduct a replication CST study with random assignment to all conditions. This acceptance of another study and the vote to make progress feedback routine care at the Counseling and Career Center (CCC) demonstrated that the research results were persuasive and were becoming an integral part of clinical practice. All but one therapist agreed to participate in the next study. Those who had participated in Study 4 made numerous comments along the way about how to improve the CST interventions. In designing the next replication study, we made use of these suggestions.

STUDY 5

Given that Study 3 (Hawkins, Lambert, Vermeersch, Slade, & Tuttle, 2004) and Study 4 (Whipple et al., 2003) were carried out concurrently (with the Whipple study beginning and ending before Hawkins et al. completed data collection), the results of both affected the design of Study 5. Harmon et al. (2007) designed Study 5 to replicate the findings of Studies 3 and 4. Harmon et al. wanted to see if the CST intervention tested in Study 4 would be replicated when random assignment was used and all therapists participated. In addition, we wanted to know if direct client feedback would enhance outcome as it had been shown to do by Hawkins et al. (2004). There was also an interest in seeing if combining all the interventions maximized client outcome. The reader might recall that the CCC had decided to provide progress feedback to clinicians as a matter of routine care, and this resulted in the unavailability of random assignment to an NFb control group. We therefore combined the NFb clients from Studies 1, 2, and 4 for comparison purposes—a treatment-as-usual archival control. These clients formed a benchmark control, randomly assigned to this condition and composed of clients treated by many of the same therapists that would be providing treatment in Study 5.

The Study 5 research design was rather elaborate with all clients entering the CCC who agreed to participate in the study assigned to either therapist-only progress feedback or client/therapist progress feedback. A second randomization took place for each group's NOT cases, with both the preceding groups' NOT cases being randomly assigned to either a No-CST feedback or CST-feedback group. This meant that we could test the effects of a total treatment package for NOT cases that included progress feedback to clinicians and clients plus the CSTs. We expected this experimental group's outcome to surpass the other treatment groups.

Participants and Methods

A total of 1,705 adult clients seeking treatment at the university counseling center were invited to participate as part of the center's intake procedure. Of those invited, 19% ($n = 331$) declined participation, leaving 1,374. Combining the archival and new samples yielded a total sample of 2,819 clients whose outcome was examined in the present study. Of these 2,819 clients, 297 clients did not return for a second session, and 53 clients did not complete the outcome measure more than once, yielding a subset of 350 clients who did not have a second outcome measure. To examine the most conservative estimate of treatment effects and because treatment length was indeterminate (see Kendall, Holmbeck, & Verduin, 2004), all 2,819 clients who consented to be studied were included in the analysis with the pretest score carried forward and used as the posttest score for the 350 clients with a single observation on the outcome measure.

The sample collected specifically for this study was very similar to samples in Studies 1, 2, and 4 with regard to age, gender, and diagnosis. Clients were assigned to therapists through routine intake procedures regardless of their experimental group. Therapists were 72 staff consisting of 28 doctoral-level psychologists and 44 doctoral students in training. Therapists used a variety of treatment orientations as described in the earlier studies. Clients who had been assigned to NFb archival treatment control groups were seen by almost all the same cohort of doctoral-level therapists as those in this study. Trainee-level therapists in the experimental conditions had similar training and backgrounds as trainee therapists in the NFb archival control conditions, but there was little overlap in trainee therapists who participated in this study.

As in the Whipple et al. (2003; Study 4) study, when the decision rules identified a client as a predicted deteriorator (red or yellow warning), the client was administered the three CST measures at the beginning of the next session. The questionnaires were administered only after the first alarm rather than each time an alarm occurred in the case of multiple alarms. The measures were scored by a research assistant and then feedback was delivered to the therapist's mailbox on the morning of the client's next session. CST feedback consisted of a copy of the decision tree and a report of the client's scores referenced to the norms for the measure. Additionally, the feedback directed the therapist to review a copy of the CST manual (Lambert, Whipple, et al., 2004), a 22-page compilation of suggestions culled from the psychotherapy research literature for improving therapeutic alliance, motivation for therapy, and social support.

Following informed consent, clients were randomly assigned to a therapist Fb ($n = 687$) or client/therapist Fb ($n = 687$) experimental group using a randomized block design, with therapists serving as the blocking variable to control for effects associated with therapists. Clients were classified as NOT if they received a yellow or red message at any time during the course of treatment. Clients designated as NOT ($n = 369$) were further randomly assigned (again, assignment was blocked on therapist) into two groups: (a) CST Fb and (b) No CST Fb. Clients in both of these groups were administered the three CST measures following algorithm generation of the first red or yellow signal. Although clients in both groups took the CSTs, only therapists of clients in the CST Fb experimental condition received information on client scores. Information on CST response was "buried" for individuals in the No CST Fb group. This procedure was followed to exclude the possibility that simply taking the measures could account for the treatment effects.

Although therapists agreed to and were encouraged to use the CST manual, discuss the results of the CST measures with their clients, and take actions they deemed appropriate, their actions were not monitored. At the inception of the study and multiple times over the course of the investigation, therapists were reminded through memo and staff meeting announcements to use the CSTs.

Prior to testing the effectiveness of the feedback interventions, preliminary analyses were completed to test for preintervention group differences. No statistically significant between-groups differences were found. These results suggest that randomization was effective in creating groups that did not have dissimilar levels of initial disturbance.

Clients whose response to treatment resulted in classification as OT versus NOT differed in mean intake OQ-45 score. As expected, the mean NOT initial OQ-45 score ($M = 79.78$) was significantly higher than the mean score for their OT counterparts ($M = 67.98$), as was true in Studies 1, 2, and 4, suggesting that as a group, NOT clients begin therapy more disturbed than OT clients. Further, 78.9% of clients in the NOT group began treatment in the dysfunctional range (OQ-45 > 63) compared with 57.4% of OT clients. As can be seen in Table 6.3, both NOT and OT clients had similar pretreatment OQ-45 scores within their assigned feedback group conditions. The small differences between these groups did not reach statistical significance.

The Effects of Feedback on Outcome

The effects of the feedback interventions are described here by first looking at the changes that took place from pretreatment to posttreatment and then by examining outcome for OT and NOT clients separately.

Pretreatment–Posttreatment Changes

Paired t-tests were conducted to assess within-group treatment effects for the NFb archival, therapist Fb, and client/therapist Fb treatment groups. Results indicated significant improvement for each treatment group over the course of psychotherapy ($d = .37, .60,$ and $.55,$ respectively). Without regard for assignment to treatment condition, over the course of therapy clients improved with an average change of −11.01 OQ-45 points ($d = .47$). The improvement was even larger for the subgroup of clients ($n = 1,759, 62.4\%$) who began treatment in the dysfunctional range (OQ-45 > 63), as they improved by an average of −15.07 points ($d = .79$). Of the clients beginning treatment in the dysfunctional range, 33% were classified as having achieved clinically significant change by the end of treatment, with an additional 15% meeting criteria for reliable improvement.

Planned comparisons were used to test the main hypotheses under consideration regarding OQ-45 feedback: (a) Clients in both experimental feedback conditions will have better outcomes than NFb archival controls,

TABLE 6.3
Means, Standard Deviations, and Pretreatment–Posttreatment Effect Sizes for Outcomes by Treatment Group

Measure	No feedback archival (n = 1,445)			Therapist feedback (n = 687)			Client/therapist feedback (n = 687)		
	Pretreatment	Posttreatment	ES (d)	Pretreatment	Posttreatment	ES (d)	Pretreatment	Posttreatment	ES (d)
Total sample (N = 2,819)									
M	70.28	61.68	.37	71.10	57.09	.60	71.28	58.21	.55
SD	22.60	23.88		22.58	23.76		22.74	25.10	
Δ		−8.61			−14.01			−13.08	
SD		18.35			19.79			19.73	
Not-on-track sample (n = 655)									
	(n = 286)			(n = 166)			(n = 203)		
M	79.45	80.17	−.04	79.83	73.47	.31	80.21	72.60	.36
SD	19.66	20.74		19.41	22.18		19.02	22.56	
Δ		+.7168			−6.36			−7.62	
SD		20.19			22.10			23.02	
On-track sample (n = 2,164)									
	(n = 1,159)			(n = 521)			(n = 484)		
M	68.01	57.11	.48	68.32	51.87	.74	67.54	52.17	.66
SD	22.71	22.35		22.82	21.82		23.14	23.64	
Δ		−10.92			−16.45			−15.37	
SD		17.12			18.36			17.72	

Note. From "Enhancing Outcome for Potential Treatment Failures: Therapist-Client Feedback and Clinical Support Tools," by S. C. Harmon, M. J. Lambert, D. M. Smart, E. Hawkins, S. L. Nielsen, K. Slade, and W. Lutz, *Psychotherapy Research, 17*, p. 385. Copyright 2007 by Taylor & Francis. Reprinted with permission.

and (b) clients who receive formal progress feedback (i.e., feedback to both client and therapist) will have better outcomes than clients who do not receive direct feedback (i.e. feedback to therapist only). For the total sample, contrasts yielded a significant difference between the Fb (therapist Fb and client/therapist Fb, $n = 1,374$) and NFb archival ($n = 1,445$) groups. The therapist Fb versus client/therapist Fb comparison was not statistically significant.

Outcome of On-Track Clients

Owing to the significant effect for the two progress conditions, separate analyses were conducted for OT and NOT clients. Considering only those clients whose therapy response designated them as OT for a positive outcome yielded a significant effect for the feedback condition. Similar to results for the total sample, there were significant differences between the Fb and NFb archival groups ($d = .23$) and no significant differences between outcomes in the therapist Fb and client/therapist Fb groups ($d = .01$).

Outcome of Not-On-Track Clients

Planned comparisons between the three treatment groups in the NOT condition were conducted. A significant difference ($d = .33$) between the Fb (therapist Fb and client/therapist Fb, $n = 369$) and NFb archival ($n = 286$) groups was found. On the other hand, the therapist Fb versus client/therapist Fb comparison was not statistically significant ($d = .04$). These results mirror the results for the total sample and suggest that the addition of formal client feedback to therapist progress feedback did not enhance outcome for NOT clients.

Effects of Feedback on Number of Sessions

An additional interest of the study was to assess the effect of feedback on session use. ANCOVA results indicated rates of attendance were significantly different for the two progress conditions (OT vs. NOT; $d = 1.19$) and the three feedback conditions (NFb archival, therapist Fb, client/therapist Fb), with a significant interaction between progress status and feedback condition. The OT clients averaged 4.60 ($SD = 3.85$) sessions, with no significant session differences between the three feedback conditions, NOT clients averaged 10.30 ($SD = 6.71$) sessions. For NOT clients, however, there was a significant session difference between the feedback (therapist Fb and client/therapist Fb, $n = 369$) and NFb archival ($n = 286$) group ($d = .59$). This indicates that NOT clients in the feedback conditions received significantly more sessions than their NFb archival counterparts. The therapist Fb ($n = 166$; $M = 11.73$; $SD = $

8.39) versus client/therapist Fb ($n = 203$; $M = 12.38$; $SD = 8.47$) comparison did not reach statistical significance ($d = .08$).

The Effect of Clinical Support Tools on Outcome

The naturalistic nature of this study (i.e., clients can terminate treatment at any time), combined with the likelihood of NOT clients ending treatment before experiencing significant benefit, resulted in some attrition before the CST intervention was completed. Of those who signaled and were in the CST Fb condition, 10.6% ($n = 20$) did not return for any additional sessions following their first signal. An additional 11.2% did not fill out all ($n = 2$) or any ($n = 19$) of the CST questionnaires; 14.4 % ($n = 27$) failed to show up for their session on the day feedback was given to their therapist (decreasing the likelihood feedback was used in session); 11.8% ($n = 22$) had no additional OQ-45s following CST completion; and 1.5% ($n = 3$) were not given the questionnaires because of administrative error. This yielded a final CST Feedback sample of 95 clients. Similarly, of those who signaled and were in the No CST Fb condition, 11% ($n = 20$) did not return for additional sessions following their first signal. An additional 14.3% did not fill out all ($n = 6$) or any ($n = 20$) of the CST questionnaires; an additional client produced an invalid protocol ($n = 1$). This yielded a final No CST sample of 134 clients. No statistically significant mean differences in intake OQ-45 or OQ-45 at time of first signal were found between the final CST comparison sample and clients lost to attrition.

Table 6.4 shows the means and standard deviations for the CST groups and the No Fb archival condition. A one-way ANCOVA comparing the CST conditions (CST Fb, No CST Fb) was performed to test the main hypothesis that CST feedback would provide an additive outcome-enhancing effect for clients predicted to end treatment with negative change. Pretreatment OQ-45 score was included as the covariate, with OQ-45 posttreatment score as the dependent variable. Results indicated a significant effect for CST Fb versus No CST Fb ($d = .31$). The comparison between the CST Fb group and the NFb archival group yielded an even stronger effect ($d = .73$). On average, clients in the CST condition experienced 5.3 points more improvement than their No CST Fb counterparts and 14.78 points more than NFb archival controls. Statistically significant differences between CST Fb and No CST Fb were also found when OQ-45 score at time of signal-alarm was substituted for intake score as a covariate. The strengthened feedback condition (both OQ-45 and CST feedback) resulted in average posttreatment scores that were only 1 point above the cutoff for the functional range (63), in contrast with NOT NFb archival clients who ended treatment 16 points above the cutoff. Figure 6.3 is a graphical representation of the average change scores for the feedback conditions.

TABLE 6.4

Means, Standard Deviations, and Change Scores for Pretreatment,
Signal, and Posttreatment Outcomes by Treatment Group:
Not-on-Track Clinical Support Tools Comparison

Measure	Pretreatment	Signal	Posttreatment
	No feedback archival		
	(n = 286)		
M	79.45	89.90	80.17
SD	19.66	15.14	20.74
Δ	+.72		
SD	20.19		
	No clinical support tools feedback		
	(n = 134)		
M	80.84	88.60	72.07
SD	19.44	15.06	23.48
Δ	−8.78		
SD	24.12		
	Clinical support tools feedback		
	(n = 95)		
M	79.45	86.65	65.39
SD	18.56	14.08	19.33
Δ	−14.06		
SD	20.96		

Note. Total N = 515. From "Enhancing Outcome for Potential Treatment Failures: Therapist Client Feedback and Clinical Support Tools," by S. C. Harmon, M. J. Lambert, D. M. Smart, E. Hawkins, S. L. Nielsen, K. Slade, and W. Lutz, 2007, *Psychotherapy Research, 17,* p. 387.Copyright 2007 by Taylor & Francis. Reprinted with permission.

On average, clients in the CST Fb condition had 3.46 more sessions than their No CST Fb counterparts. This difference was partly due to the exclusion of clients not filling out at least one OQ-45 posttreatment delivery of CST feedback.

Analysis of Clinical Significance

To further assess the meaningfulness of the feedback and CST interventions, clients were categorized into final outcome classifications on the basis of Jacobson and Truax's (1991) criteria for reliable or clinically significant change. These data are presented in Table 6.5. Because there were no significant outcome differences between the therapist Fb and client/therapist Fb conditions, these groups were combined into a single OQ-45 Fb group. A chi-square comparison between the NFb archival, OQ-45 Fb, and OQ-45 Fb+CST groups was significant. The strengthened feedback condition resulted in a 67% (7% vs. 21%) reduction in deterioration as compared with the NFb

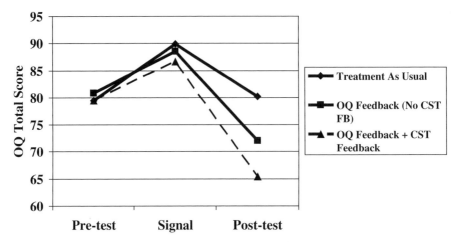

Figure 6.3. Improvement of not-on-track clients assigned to one of three treatment conditions. CST = clinical support tools. From "Enhancing Outcome for Potential Treatment Failures: Therapist–Client Feedback and Clinical Support Tools," by S. C. Harmon, M. J. Lambert, D. M. Smart, E. Hawkins, S. L. Nielsen, K. Slade, and W. Lutz, 2007, *Psychotherapy Research, 17,* p. 388.Copyright 2007 by the Taylor & Francis. Reprinted with permission.

group. Further, although 21% of clients in the NFb archival condition showed reliable improvement or clinically significant change, 29.2% in the OQ-45 Fb condition and 42.1% in the OQ-45 Fb +CSTcondition reached this same level of success. Essentially the use of CSTs doubled (21% versus 42.1%) the number of clients who were rated as recovered or reliably improved according the Jacobson and Truax criteria.

TABLE 6.5
Percentage of Not-on-Track Clients Meeting Criteria
for Clinically Significant Outcome at Termination

Outcome classification	No feedback archival ($n = 286$) n (%)	OQ feedback ($n = 274$) n (%)	OQ feedback + CST feedback ($n = 95$) n (%)
Deteriorated or reliable worsening	61 (21.3)	49 (17.9)	7 (7.4)
No change	165 (57.7)	145 (52.9)	48 (50.5)
Reliable or clinically significant change	60 (21)	80 (29.2)	40 (42.1)

Note. OQ = Outcome Questionnaire; CST = clinical support tool. From "Enhancing Outcome for Potential Treatment Failures: Therapist-Client Feedback and Clinical Support Tools," by S. C. Harmon, M. J. Lambert, D. M. Smart, E. Hawkins, S. L. Nielsen, K. Slade, and W. Lutz, 2007, *Psychotherapy Research, 17,* p. 388. Copyright 2007 by Taylor & Francis. Reprinted with permission.
$\chi^2 = 20.797, p < .001$.

Study 5: Summary and Conclusions

The Harmon et al. (2007) study replicated the Whipple et al. (2003) study with regard to the effectiveness of CST feedback. It demonstrated that clients benefited when their therapists were given problem-solving tools to help clients who were predicted to have a negative outcome and that the effect size for this effect (compared with treatment as usual) was about .70, a large effect. It failed to show an added benefit for direct feedback to clients, with the effect close to zero. This latter finding was somewhat confusing as Hawkins et al. (2004) had found an effect using the same methods.

On the basis of feedback from therapists about the nature of the CST intervention and developments in our ability to deliver more timely feedback to therapists, we were eager to conduct a replication study. Therapists in the CCC were becoming more interested in the CST intervention and in receiving information to help them problem solve with the failing case. This presented an opportunity to conduct yet another study.

STUDY 6

Study 6 was conducted by Slade, Lambert, Harmon, Smart, and Bailey (2008). As the different research studies progressed, a software product (OQ-Analyst) was developed. This software came into being after Studies 1–5 were conducted, and we felt confident progress feedback for at least NOT cases was an intervention that was evidence based, practical, and made clinical sense. The major reason for developing software was to ease the manual work involved in passing out hard copies of the OQ-45, collecting them, scanning or hand scoring them, using the scores to estimate alarm-signal status, graphing the results, and placing the appropriate colored message on the client's chart. This manpower-heavy procedure made feedback reports available to clinicians 1 week after the client completed the OQ-45 rather than at the session the test was completed. More immediate feedback was hypothesized to improve outcomes in that it would allow more timely discussions of progress.

Qualitatively, therapists who have participated in this feedback program indicated that they would be more motivated to view feedback and take action if the progress feedback they were receiving was more pertinent to that week's session, rather than information that was based on the client's responses to the OQ-45 collected the week before. Feedback theory also indicates that more immediate feedback is likely to have a greater influence on performance than feedback that is delayed. Furthermore, providing progress feedback to the therapist in a more immediate manner increases the likelihood that alarm-signal cases will be identified faster and appropriate action will be taken sooner rather than later. A major purpose of conducting this study was to examine the effects of immediate electronic OQ-45 feedback (IEF) through the use of OQ-Analyst software, with the goal of ameliorating the constraint of delayed progress feedback.

Because of the discrepant findings in Studies 4 and 5 with regard to the advantages of direct feedback to clients, this study also sought to replicate the previous therapist versus therapist/client feedback findings. Another major goal of this study was to replicate the differential effects of CST feedback on NOT clients' outcome (making it a second replication of the Whipple et al., 2003, study) while strengthening the intervention by replacing less sensitive problem-solving measures and adding a measure of perfectionism to the CST. This later suggestion came from several of the therapists who felt that some negatively changing clients had problems in this area.

The following hypotheses were tested: (a) NOT clients whose therapists received IEF will have better outcomes compared with NOT clients whose therapist received 1-week-delayed progress feedback, (data for the latter group were archival, based on Study 5); (b) NOT clients whose therapists received IEF or 1-week-delayed feedback will have better outcomes compared with NOT clients in the treatment-as-usual (No Fb) condition (data for the latter group were archival and came from Studies 1, 2, and 4); (c) the IEF experimental group in which both NOT clients and their therapists received feedback will have better outcomes than the experimental IEF group in which only therapists received feedback on client progress; (d) the IEF experimental group in which both NOT clients and their therapists received feedback will have better outcomes than the NOT treatment-as-usual condition (data for the treatment-as-usual condition were archival); and (e) NOT clients whose therapists received the CST feedback will fare better than clients whose therapists did not receive the CST feedback. Put more simply, we expected faster progress and problem-solving delivery to produce improved client outcomes.

Participants and Methods

A total of 1,294 adult clients seeking treatment for personal problems at the same counseling center as in Studies 1, 2, 4, and 5 were invited to participate as part of the intake procedure. From this group, 17% ($n = 192$) declined to participate (did not provide informed consent) at intake, and 1 client requested to be removed midstudy, reporting he did not want to complete the CST measures (leaving 1,101 clients). These patients received IEF, and their outcome was compared with archival clients ($n = 1,445$ used as archival treatment-as-usual controls from Studies 1, 2, and 4) and 1,373 clients from four prior feedback studies in which progress feedback had been delayed by a week (Study 1, Lambert, Whipple, et al., 2001; Study 2, Lambert, Whipple,

Vermeersch et al., 2002; Study 4, Whipple et al., 2003; Study 5, Harmon et al., 2007). This yielded a total sample of 3,919 clients.

For the IEF group ($n = 1,101$), 118 clients did not return for a second session. All clients who consented to be studied were included in the data analysis with last-observation-carried-forward procedures used for the 118 clients with a single observation on the outcome measure. The remaining clients completed the outcome measure more than once. The IEF sample was similar in their demographics, gender, age and diagnosis to the comparison samples.

Of the total sample (archival and current dataset combined; $n = 3,919$), 416 clients did not return for a second session, and 53 clients who did return for a second session did not complete the outcome measure. All clients who consented to the study were included in the data analysis with last-observation-carried-forward procedures used for the 469 clients with a single observation on the outcome measure, providing a conservative estimate of the impact of the experimental treatment within a naturalistic setting. The last-observation-carried-forward procedure was not followed with the CST Fb comparison cases in the NOT clients. It is necessary for NOT clients to attend at least three sessions to receive an OQ-45 progress feedback message indicating they are not on track, and on receiving their first alarm-signal, they must attend two more sessions to assess the impact of the CST feedback intervention.

Therapists were 74 counseling center staff consisting of 28 doctoral-level psychologists and 46 doctoral students in training (including interns). There was substantial overlap in therapists across all studies, except for student therapists.

Measures

The CSTs consisted of four measures: the Client Motivation for Therapy Scale (Pelletier et al., 1997) with revisions for the current study (in place of Stages of Change Scale used in earlier studies); the Revised Helping Alliance Questionnaire (Luborsky et al., 1996); and the Multidimensional Scale of Perceived Social Support (Zimet et al., 1988), all of which were also used in earlier studies; and the Perfectionism Inventory (Hill et al., 2004), which was added for this investigation. The Revised Helping Alliance Questionnaire feedback was modified for use in this study by providing therapists information on specific items that were endorsed in a negative manner regarding the alliance as well as subscale and the overall scale with cutoff scores for areas of problematic functioning.

The Client Motivation for Therapy Scale—Revised is a 12-item scale adopted for the current study as a hypothesized solution to the limitations of the previous motivation scale used by Whipple et al. (2003) and was used to assess clients' motivation to engage in therapy rather than their readiness to change a specific behavior. The original scale is a 24-item scale that measures six different types of motivation. Those subscales deemed most able to assess differences in clients' motivation for therapy were included in the shortened version. Intrinsic motivation has been reported to be associated with more positive outcomes, whereas external regulation and amotivation have been reported to be associated with less positive therapeutic outcomes (Pelletier et al., 1997). The domain with the highest score was identified as the client's current type of motivation. Those falling in the amotivation or external regulation domain were identified as having motivation for seeking treatment that was hypothesized to be related to unfavorable outcomes that needed to be addressed by therapists.

The Perfectionism Inventory (Hill et al., 2004) was added to the current study after a thorough review of the literature, which suggested that perfectionism is an additional factor that contributes to poor outcomes as well as mediating the quality of the therapeutic relationship (Blatt, 1995; Blatt & Zuroff, 2002; Johnson & Slaney, 1996; Zuroff et al., 2000). For purposes of this study, clients who scored 1.25 standard deviations or more above the client sample mean were designated as having problematic perfectionism.

An informal fidelity check was conducted periodically by sending an e-mail, asking therapists, "Over the last week, for what percentage of clients did you view OQ feedback?" It was hoped that this general reminder would encourage therapists to view the progress feedback reports.

When the decision rules identified a client as NOT (red or yellow warning), feedback was speeded up by e-mailing clients the following: "Dear [Client], please click on the link below and complete the questionnaire prior to your next scheduled appointment so that your therapist may better help you."

In contrast to the progress feedback that is administered at each session, the CST measures were administered only once (upon advent of their first alarm signal) to each NOT client. The measures were scored and CST feedback was delivered to the therapist's work mailbox the evening before the client's next session and thus delayed by 1-week from the time the client completed the OQ-45 with an alarm signal. The CST feedback consisted of a copy of the decision tree and a report of the client's scores referenced to the norms for the measure with intervention suggestions at the bottom of the feedback targeting the CST domains that were problematic or needed attention. Additionally, the feedback directed the therapist to review a copy of the CST manual (Slade, Lambert, Harmon, Smart, & Bailey, 2006). For example, if a NOT client was given the clinical support measure and scored below average on the alliance assessment, the therapist was notified and given feedback regarding the subscales that were endorsed in a negative manner. The therapist was also encouraged to examine the list of suggestions for strengthening the relationship (e.g., discuss the client's ratings of the relationship, explore relationship ruptures). If the client's alliance rating was not below average, the therapist would proceed to evaluation of the client's motivation, social support, perfectionism, and last diagnosis and the possible need for a medication consultation.

Therapist use of the suggested clinical support interventions was not prescriptive; therapists used their clinical judgment to decide how to use the CSTs to maximize therapy response. This procedure was used to maximize the external validity of the CST feedback intervention but at the cost of some internal validity. Upkeep was performed daily to ensure that all NOT cases were given the CSTs immediately following their first alarm in an effort to reduce the time (in terms of sessions) it took to deliver feedback to the therapist. The CST intervention was not yet available as part of the OQ-Analyst software and was delayed 1 week but was provided 1 week sooner than in previous feedback studies in which CST feedback was delivered 2 weeks after the client's initial signal.

Follow-up was conducted to see that the clients did indeed attend the session in which CST feedback was given to their therapist. If a client "no showed" to a session, attempts were made to redeliver the CST feedback to the therapist prior to the next scheduled appointment. Therefore, feedback was still able to be delivered at the visit following the initial signal alarm (designating them as NOT). If feedback was unable to be delivered to the session immediately following the signal session, thereby diluting or negating the possible effects of the immediacy of the CST feedback intervention, the client was removed from the final CST condition before analysis.

Over a 16-month period of data collection, clients were randomly assigned to one of two treatment conditions after consenting at intake: A therapist only Fb condition, and a client/therapist Fb condition. To test for the effects of CST Fb on client outcome, this first randomization was followed by a second randomization for all clients whose progress indicated they were NOT. Clients who were NOT (had received a red or yellow warning) were divided into two groups; therapist CST Fb and no therapist CST Fb. Thus, the second randomization occurred continuously as signal cases were identified.

In all, there were 14 experimental groups. Because of the complicated nature of this study only the most important findings are highlighted here. In general, experimental groups looked at two variables: feedback timing (immediate or delayed) and feedback type (therapist vs. therapist/client).

Initial Differences

Prior to testing the effectiveness of the feedback interventions, a one-way ANOVA was conducted to assess for comparability of the mean OQ-45 score at pretreatment for each type of feedback group and for each feedback timing group. Table 6.6 shows the means and standard deviations of the three feedback groups (therapist Fb, client/therapist Fb, and treatment as usual), and three feedback timing groups (treatment as usual, 1-week-delayed Fb, and IEF). No statistically significant between-groups differences were found for both feedback type, and feedback timing. These results suggest that randomization was effective in creating groups that had similar levels of initial disturbance and that the clients in the different feedback timing groups had essentially equivalent scores at intake. As can be seen in Table 6.7, NOT clients had equivalent pretreatment OQ-45 scores within their assigned feedback type conditions (TAU, client OQ-45 Fb, client/therapist OQ-45 Fb) and within their assigned feedback timing conditions (treatment as usual, 1-week-delayed OQ-45 Fb, and IEF), providing support for equivalence of these groups at pretreatment.

The Effects of Feedback on Outcome

The effects of the feedback interventions are described here by first looking at the changes that took place from pretreatment to posttreatment and then by examining outcome as a function of feedback type and session use.

Pretreatment–Posttreatment Changes

Table 6.7 shows means and standard deviations of OQ-45 pre- and posttreatment scores. Paired t-tests were conducted to assess within-group treatment effects for the feedback type and feedback timing groups. Results indicated significant pre- to posttreatment improvement for each feedback group and the treatment-as-usual control group (treatment as usual, $d = .37$; therapist IEF, $d = .50$; client/therapist IEF, $d = .53$); and each feedback timing group (treatment as usual, $d = .37$; 1-week-delayed Fb, $d = .57$; IEF, $d = .50$). Without regard for assignment to treatment condition, over the course of therapy, clients improved with an average change of -11.17 OQ-45 points ($d = .48$), the equivalent of complete remission of almost three full symptoms (e.g., moving from having headaches, feeling no interest in things, and irritation *almost always* to *never*). The improvement was even larger for clients ($n = 2,461$, 62.8%) who began treatment in the dysfunctional range (OQ-45 ≥ 64), with an average change of -15.3 OQ-45 points ($d = .82$).

The Effect of Feedback Type

For feedback type, a 2×3 MANCOVA was conducted, comparing the two progress conditions (OT vs. NOT) and the three feedback type conditions (treatment as usual, therapist Fb, client/therapist Fb). When compared with clients in the feedback type conditions, clients in the treatment-as-usual

TABLE 6.6
Means, Standard Deviations, and Effect Sizes for Pretreatment and Posttreatment Outcomes by Treatment Group

Not-on-track sample—feedback type (n = 614)

Measure	Treatment as usual (n = 286)			Immediate electronic OQ-45 therapist feedback (n = 164)			Immediate electronic OQ-45 client/therapist feedback (n = 164)		
	Pretreatment	Posttreatment	ES (d)	Pretreatment	Posttreatment	ES (d)	Pretreatment	Posttreatment	ES (d)
M	79.44	80.17	−.04	77.08	70.83	.31	80.83	71.57	.44
SD	19.64	20.74		18.65	21.37		20.17	22.06	
Δ		−.72			6.25			9.21	
SD		20.19			19.36			20.61	

Not-on-track sample—feedback timing (n = 983)

Measure	Treatment as usual (n = 286)			1-week-delayed OQ-45 feedback (n = 369)			Immediate electronic OQ-45 feedback (n = 328)		
	Pretreatment	Posttreatment	ES (d)	Pretreatment	Posttreatment	ES (d)	Pretreatment	Posttreatment	ES (d)
M	79.44	80.17	−.04	80.04	72.99	.34	78.96	71.20	.38
SD	19.64	20.74		19.17	22.36		19.49	21.68	
Δ		−.72			7.05			7.73	
SD		20.19			22.59			20.02	

Note. OQ-45 = Outcome Questionnaire-45. From "Improving Psychotherapy Outcome: The Use of Immediate Electronic Feedback and Revised Clinical Support Tools," by K. Slade, M. J. Lambert, S. C. Harmon, D. W. Smart, and R. Bailey, 2008, *Clinical Psychology and Psychotherapy, 15*, p. 294. Copyright 2008 by Wiley. Reprinted with permission.

TABLE 6.7
Session Means for Not-on-Track Clients by Treatment Group

Measure	Treatment as usual ($n = 286$)	Immediate electronic OQ-45 therapist feedback ($n = 164$)	Immediate electronic OQ-45 client/ therapist feedback ($n = 164$)
	Sessions: Not-on-track clients—feedback type ($n = 614$)		
$M (SD)$	7.98 (4.49)	9.36 (6.17)	9.68 (6.07)

$(F_{(2, 610)} = -6.28, p < .01)$

Treatment as usual versus feedback: Contrast estimate $= -1.54$ ($p < .001$)

Measure	Treatment as usual ($n = 286$)	1-week-delayed OQ-45 Feedback ($n = 369$)	Immediate electronic OQ-45 feedback ($n = 328$)
	Sessions: Not-on-track clients—feedback timing ($n = 983$)		
$M (SD)$	7.98 (4.9)	12.09 (8.43)	9.52 (6.12)

$(F_{(2, 979)} = 31.70, p < .01)$

1-week-delayed feedback versus immediate electronic feedback:
Contrast estimate $= 2.57$ (p $< .001$)

Treatment as usual versus combined feedback: Contrast estimate $= -2.83$ ($p < .001$)

Note. OQ-45 = Outcome Questionnaire-45. From "Improving Psychotherapy Outcome: The Use of Immediate Electronic Feedback and Revised Clinical Support Tools," by K. Slade, M. J. Lambert, S. C. Harmon, D. W. Smart, and R. Bailey, 2008, *Clinical Psychology and Psychotherapy, 15*, p. 296. Copyright 2008 by Wiley. Reprinted with permission.

condition left treatment with a change score that was 5.4 points lower (less improvement), whereas the difference for therapist Fb versus client/therapist Fb did not reach statistical significance. For feedback timing, results indicated significant effects for the two progress conditions (OT vs. NOT) and the three feedback type conditions (treatment as usual, therapist Fb, Client/therapist Fb). When compared with clients in the feedback type conditions, clients in the treatment-as-usual condition left treatment with a change score that was 5.8 points lower (less improvement). The difference between 1-week-delayed OQ-45 Fb and IEF did not reach statistical significance.

The following hypotheses were tested using planned comparisons for feedback type within the NOT group: (a) NOT clients in both IEF conditions will have better outcomes compared with NOT clients in the treatment-as-usual condition; (b) NOT clients in the IEF condition who receive direct feedback in addition to therapist feedback will have better outcomes than NOT clients who do not receive direct feedback (therapist IEF only). Significant differences between combined feedback groups (therapist IEF and client/therapist IEF, $n = 328$) and treatment as usual were found but with no significant differences between therapist IEF and client/therapist IEF for NOT clients. These results suggest that the addition of direct client feedback to therapist feedback did not improve outcomes for clients who were NOT. This finding was consistent with Study 5 but inconsistent with Study 3.

The following hypotheses were tested using planned comparisons for feedback timing, within the NOT group: (a) NOT clients whose therapists received IEF will have better outcomes compared with NOT clients whose therapists received 1-week-delayed Fb, (data for the latter group was archival), and (b) NOT clients whose therapists received IEF or 1-week-delayed Fb will have better outcomes compared with NOT clients in the treatment-as-usual condition (data for the latter group were archival). There were significant differences between treatment-as-usual ($n = 286$) and combined feedback timing conditions (1 week delayed and IEF combined, $n = 697$), but there were no differences between 1 week delayed and IEF. These results indicate that speedy delivery of progress information is not necessary for enhancing client outcomes.

Session Effects

Table 6.7 shows average number of sessions for feedback type and feedback timing conditions. There were significant session differences between feedback type, with clients in the combined feedback conditions (client/therapist and therapist only Fb) receiving 1.5 sessions more, on average, compared with their treatment-as-usual counterparts. The therapist IEF ($n = 164$) versus client/therapist IEF ($n = 164$) comparison did not reach statistical significance. For feedback timing, NOT clients in the feedback groups received significantly more sessions than their treatment-as-usual counterparts. Results also indicated significant session differences between feedback timing conditions, including between the treatment-as-usual group ($n = 286$) and the feedback timing conditions combined ($n = 697$). Significant differences were also found between 1-week-delayed OQ-45 Fb and IEF. These results suggest that equivalent outcomes can be reached in fewer sessions if progress feedback is delivered immediately preceding a treatment session.

The Effects of Clinical Support Tools on Outcome

An additional aim of this research was to test the following hypotheses for feedback type within the NOT group: NOT clients whose therapists received the CST feedback 1 week earlier will fare better than clients whose therapists received the CST feedback 1 week later.

Prior to testing the effectiveness of the CST intervention, a one-way ANCOVA with pretreatment OQ-45 as covariate was conducted to assess for equivalence of groups following random assignment into a CST condition (i.e., at session of first alarm signal). No significant differences on OQ-45 scores at time of random assignment were found.

Given that the setting of the study is naturalistic (e.g., therapists decide what to do with the feedback and clients may terminate at any time), combined with the fact that NOT clients are traditionally likely to end treatment before experiencing significant benefit, there was some attrition within the NOT sample before the CST feedback intervention was offered. For example, if a client signals at Week 3 of therapy and then completes the measure during the week before his or her next appointment, he or she may not return, thereby making it impossible to deliver an intervention based on the client's CST responses. Furthermore, if the client signals at Week 3 of therapy, completes the measure during the week, and returns for the next session, he or she will still need to attend yet another session to complete the OQ-45 so as to measure the effects of the CST feedback and the interventions that the therapist may have used. A client is considered to have completed the course of the CST intervention if he or she completed at least three of the four CST domains of interest (alliance, motivation for therapy, social support, and perfectionism) and attended two or more sessions of therapy after the CST feedback was delivered to his or her therapist.

For feedback type, of those who signaled and were in the CST feedback condition ($n = 168$), 14.3% ($n = 24$) did not return for any additional sessions following their first signal. An additional 14.9% ($n = 25$) did not complete the CST questionnaires; 16.1 % ($n = 27$) failed to attend their session on the day feedback was given to their therapist (decreasing the likelihood feedback was used in session); 4.8% ($n = 8$) completed the CSTs but never returned to therapy; and .6% ($n = 1$) were not given the questionnaires as a result of administrative error. This yielded a final CST type feedback sample of 83 clients. Similarly, of those who signaled and were in the No CST Fb condition ($n = 160$), 14.4% ($n = 23$) did not return for additional sessions following their first signal. An additional 8.8% ($n = 14$) did not complete the CST questionnaires. This yielded a final No CST Fb sample of 126 clients in addition to the NOT treatment-as-usual sample ($n = 286$).

For feedback timing ($n = 356$), of those who signaled and were in the CST Fb timing conditions (1-week-delayed CST Fb and 2-week-delayed CST Fb), 12.4% ($n = 44$) did not return for any additional sessions following their first signal. An additional 12.6% ($n = 45$) did not complete the CST questionnaires; 15.5 % ($n = 55$) failed to attend their session on the day feedback was given to their therapist (decreasing the likelihood feedback was used in session); 8.4% ($n = 30$) completed the CSTs but never returned to therapy; and 1.1% ($n = 4$) were not given the questionnaires as a result of administrative error. This yielded a final CST Fb timing sample of 178 clients in addition to the NOT treatment-as-usual sample ($n = 286$).

Table 6.8 shows the means and standard deviations for the CST groups. Analysis of covariance for feedback type was performed with intake OQ-45 score as the covariate to test the hypothesis that delivery of CST Fb would provide an additive outcome-enhancing effect for clients predicted to end treatment with negative change compared with those clients whose therapists did not receive CST Fb. Results indicated significant effects. Clients in the OQ-45 Fb+CST condition left treatment with 7.57 points more improvement than their OQ-45 Fb No CST Fb counterparts and 17.87 points more improvement than those who received treatment as usual. These results are presented graphically in Figure 6.4.

Another analysis of covariance comparing CST feedback timing conditions with pretreatment OQ-45 score as the covariate was performed to test the main hypothesis that earlier delivery of CST feedback would provide an added outcome-enhancing effect for clients predicted to end treatment with negative change. The client's OQ-45 change score was the dependent variable. A comparison between the feedback timing indicated significant effects compared with treatment as usual; combined feedback groups (2 weeks delayed and 1 week delayed) yielded a significant effect as well, but the differences between 1-week-delayed CST Fb and 2-week-delayed CST Fb groups did not reach statistical significance. The week-delayed CST Fb timing condition resulted in average post scores that were .3 points below the cutoff for the functional range (63) in contrast with the 2-week-delayed CST Fb condition in which clients ended treatment on average 2.8 points above the cutoff, and treatment-as-usual clients ended treatment 17 points above the cutoff. These results suggest that the use of the CST intervention had a substantial effect on the outcome of psychotherapy but that delaying their use by a session had no effect on outcome.

Session Effects

Those in the treatment-as-usual group attended an average of 4.7 fewer sessions than those in the CST group. Those in the OQ-45 Fb without CST Fb group attended 2.5 fewer sessions on average than those in the OQ-45 Fb+CST Fb group. Differences were also significant for the feedback timing conditions between combined feedback timing conditions for 1-week-delayed and 2-week-delayed CST Fb ($n = 178$) and treatment as usual ($n = 286$) and for 1-week-delayed ($n = 85$) and 2-week-delayed CST Fb ($n = 95$; contrast estimate = 3.5, $p < .001$) with clients in the 1-week-delayed CST Fb condition attending 3.5 fewer sessions than their 2-week-delayed CST Fb counterparts and 4.7 sessions more than their treatment-as-usual counterparts. It should be noted that these session differences are partly due to the fact that clients in

TABLE 6.8

Means, Standard Deviations, and Effect Sizes for Pretreatment and Posttreatment Outcomes by Treatment Group: Not-on-Track Clinical Support Tools (CSTs) Comparison by CST Feedback Type and CST Feedback Timing

Not-on-track CSTs Completers—feedback type (n = 209)

Measure	Immediate electronic OQ-45 feedback + no CST feedback (n = 126)			Immediate electronic OQ-45 feedback + 1-week-delayed CST feedback (n = 83)		
	Pretreatment	Posttreatment	ES (d)	Pretreatment	Posttreatment	ES (d)
M	78.45	69.23	.47	83.59	64.42	.93
SD	20.34	21.37		18.54	21.59	
Δ		9.13			19.04	
SD		20.37			19.77	

Not-on-track CSTs Completers—feedback timing (n = 178)

Measure	1-week-delayed OQ-45 feedback + 2-week-delayed CST feedback (n = 95)			Immediate electronic OQ-45 feedback + 1-week-delayed CST feedback (n = 83)		
	Pretreatment	Posttreatment	ES (d)	Pretreatment	Posttreatment	ES (d)
M	79.45	65.39	.69	83.59	64.42	.93
SD	18.56	19.33		18.15	21.24	
Δ		14.06			19.05	
SD		20.96			19.83	

Note. OQ-45 = Outcome Questionnaire-45. From "Improving Psychotherapy Outcome: The Use of Immediate Electronic Feedback and Revised Clinical Support Tools," by K. Slade, M. J. Lambert, S. C. Harmon, D. W. Smart, and R. Bailey, 2008, *Clinical Psychology and Psychotherapy, 15*, p. 297. Copyright 2008 by Wiley. Reprinted with permission.

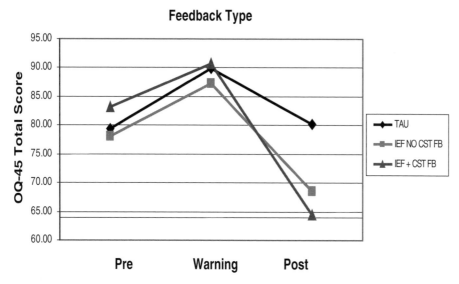

Figure 6.4. Improvement of not-on-track clients assigned to one of three treatment conditions. TAU = treatment as usual; EF NO CST FB = electronic feedback with no clinical support tools feedback; EF+CST FB = electronic feedback and clinical support tools feedback. From "Improving Psychotherapy Outcome: The Use of Immediate Electronic Feedback and Revised Clinical Support Tools," by K. Slade, M. J. Lambert, S. C. Harmon, D. W. Smart, and R. Bailey, 2008, *Clinical Psychology and Psychotherapy, 15,* p. 294. Copyright 2008 by Wiley. Reprinted with permission.

each condition were required to attend an unequal number of sessions to be considered completers in their respective conditions and because clients in the CST Fb condition who did not fill out at least one OQ-45 (attend an additional session) post delivery of CST feedback were excluded from analyses. These results suggest that equivalent outcomes can be reached in fewer sessions if CST feedback is delivered 1 week rather than 2 weeks after the initial NOT signal.

Analysis of Clinical Significance

To further assess the meaningfulness of the progress feedback and CST intervention, clients were categorized into final outcome classifications based on Jacobson and Truax's (1991) criteria for reliable or clinically significant change. These data are presented in Table 6.9. Because there were no significant outcome differences between the therapist Fb and client/therapist Fb type conditions within the IEF condition, these groups were combined into a single OQ-45 IEF group. Because there were no significant outcome differences between the therapist Fb and client/therapist Fb conditions within the 1-week-delayed OQ-45 Fb groups, they were also combined into a single 1-week-delayed

TABLE 6.9
Percentage of Not-on-Track Clients Meeting Criteria for Clinically Significant Outcome at Termination

Outcome classification	Feedback timing		
	Treatment as usual ($n = 286$) n (%)	2-week-delayed CST feedback ($n = 95$) n (%)	1-week-delayed CST feedback ($n = 83$) n (%)
Deteriorated or reliable worsening	61 (21.3)	7 (7.4)	4 (4.8)
No change	165 (57.7)	48 (50.5)	26 (31.3)
Reliable or clinically significant change	60 (21)	40 (42.1)	53 (63.9)

	Feedback type		
	Treatment as usual ($n = 286$) n (%)	No CST feedback ($n = 126$) n (%)	CST feedback ($n = 83$) n (%)
Deteriorated or reliable worsening	61 (21.3)	12 (9.5)	4 (4.8)
No change	165 (57.7)	67 (53.2)	26 (31.3)
Reliable or clinically significant change	60 (21)	47 (37.3)	53 (63.9)

Note. CST = clinical support tool. From "Improving Psychotherapy Outcome: The Use of Immediate Electronic Feedback and Revised Clinical Support Tools," by K. Slade, M. J. Lambert, S. C. Harmon, D. W. Smart, and R. Bailey, 2008, *Clinical Psychology and Psychotherapy, 15*, p. 299. Copyright 2008 by Wiley. Reprinted with permission.

OQ-45 Fb group. A chi-square comparison between the feedback type groups (treatment as usual, IEF No CST Fb, and IEF+CST Fb) was significant. The CST Fb type condition resulted in 16.5% fewer clients deteriorating (4.8% of clients in this group deteriorated) as compared with the No CST Fb group. This latter group had 11.8% fewer clients deteriorating (9.5% of clients in this group deteriorated) compared with the 21.3% deterioration rate for clients in the treatment group.

Further, although 21% of clients in the treatment-as-usual condition showed reliable improvement or clinically significant change, 37.3% in the No CST Fb condition reached this same level of improvement, and 63.9% in the CST Fb condition improved or recovered. Essentially, the use of IEF plus CST tripled (63.9% vs. 21%) the number of clients who were rated as recovered or reliably improved according to the Jacobson and Truax's (1991) criteria.

Differences between feedback timing conditions were also significant. Compared with treatment as usual, 1-week-delayed CST Fb resulted in 16.5%

fewer clients deteriorating (4.8% of clients in this group deteriorated). Compared with 2-week-delayed CST Fb (7.4% of clients in this group deteriorated), 1-week-delayed CST Fb resulted in 2.6% fewer clients deteriorating. Further, although 21% of clients in the treatment-as-usual condition showed reliable improvement or clinically significant change, 63.9% in the IEF with 1-week-delayed CST Fb timing condition and 42.1% in the 1-week-delayed OQ-45 Fb with 2-week-delayed CST Fb group reached this same level of improvement in therapy. In short, providing therapists with information about the client's responses on the CST measures 1 week following the initial signal (rather than 2) nearly doubled the percentage of clients who showed reliably improved or clinically significant change (21.8% difference between groups) compared with clients whose therapists received CST Fb 2 weeks after the time of first signal.

Study 6: Summary and Conclusions

The results of this complex study suggested that adding direct client progress feedback did not enhance treatment effects. This finding suggests that it may not be necessary for clients to get progress feedback beyond that already provided by therapists. It also suggests that what is important is for therapists to get progress feedback along with the problem-solving material. In this circumstance patients stay in treatment longer and substantially improve. The study results show that speed of delivery of feedback was an important variable with regard to making treatment more efficient.

SUMMARY AND CONCLUSIONS

A variety of procedures aimed at reducing deterioration rates and enhancing positive outcomes in patients predicted to have negative psychotherapy outcome have been tested. Based on the three studies summarized in Chapter 5 and the Whipple et al. (2003; Study 4), it was obvious that progress feedback with alert signals reliably reduced patient deterioration and enhanced positive outcomes when compared with treatment as usual delivered by the same therapists. It was also clear that many patients predicted to have a negative outcome were not substantially helped by this intervention. In our attempt to further enhance outcome for these struggling clients we studied two diverse interventions: directly providing progress feedback to clients (and encouraging them to discuss it with their therapists) and creating and using problem-solving tools for these cases.

In the case of providing graphical and written progress feedback directly to clients, the jury is still out, with two of the three studies failing to find an effect. It can be concluded that direct client feedback *can* be beneficial, but this effect is unreliable. It is undoubtedly related to the extent to which therapists engage their clients in discussions about progress when they alone (the therapists) are recipients of the progress feedback.

In contrast, the use of CSTs to assist clinicians problem solve with NOT cases is a practice innovation with reliable and substantial clinical success above that obtained through using warning feedback alone. Using these methods appears to keep patients in treatment longer, and in our last study (Slade et al., 2008) reduced deterioration from the baseline of 21% to only 4.6%. Our research findings suggest that we can provide clinicians with client assessment data that, when used, will improve outcomes in routine care.

The various interventions we have examined had different impacts on the number of sessions clients attended. For clients who are responding positively throughout the course of therapy (about 75%), progress feedback usually shortens treatment while maintaining the degree of progress made. For the negatively responding client (about 25%), progress feedback tends to but does not inevitably lengthen therapy while reducing deterioration and enhancing positive outcomes. Immediate progress feedback was not more helpful than 1-week-delayed progress feedback, but it did shorten therapy, giving it an economic "time suffering" advantage.

Our program of research on the CSTs has evolved over time in response to feedback from clinicians and our own observations about how to most effectively deliver actionable information to clinicians.

IV

ILLUSTRATIONS OF PRACTICE-BASED EVIDENCE FOR OUTCOMES MANAGEMENT AT THE SYSTEM LEVEL

7

THERAPIST EFFECTS

Part IV of this book is devoted to the ways in which administrators of services can use the information that was collected for the purpose of helping therapists manage ongoing cases for outcomes management at a system of care level. A variety of diverse strategies and studies are provided in Chapter 8, whereas this chapter concentrates on the contribution of specific therapists to outcome and its implication for service delivery. An entire chapter is devoted to therapists because their contribution is viewed as central in what happens to patients, second only to the patient's contribution.

As noted in Chapter 1, outcome research in the last two decades has extensively focused on the effects of specific treatments for specific disorders, so-called clinical trials. Researchers using this methodology typically attend to the individual therapist as an important factor to control before under-taking their primary analysis of treatment effects. Such research uses consid-erable resources to diminish variability in outcomes that could be attributed to the therapist. This is typically accomplished through careful selection of therapists, extensive training, and supervision of therapists who are using treatment manuals to guide their interventions (Lambert & Ogles, 2004; Wampold, 2001). The intent of such procedures is to maximize the likeli-hood of finding effects due to treatments, independent of the therapists who offer them. This has resulted in an "oddly personless" view of psychotherapy (Norcross, 2002, p. 4).

Such designs do not necessarily ignore the importance of therapists' capacity to both build a relationship with the client and flexibly tailor therapeutic treatment (techniques) to meet the needs of the individual client as well as to reduce variability in these important capacities that are so central in service delivery in everyday practice. Considering the therapist and the client as central elements in the process of therapy does not detract from psychotherapy itself as having important healing ingredients but expands the possibilities for understanding the human encounter as connected with rather than incidental to therapeutic techniques (Bergin, 1997; Stiles & Shapiro, 1994; Wampold, Ahn, & Coleman, 2001). In a field dedicated to the understanding of human behavior it is paradox that half the human element of therapy, the therapist, has been largely relegated to the category of an extraneous variable in clinical trials. Such design tactics make perfect sense when the goal of a study is to maximize the contribution of theory-based interventions on patient outcome but make little sense in routine care in which the importance of the person offering treatment is a central consideration for a client who enters treatment or administrators who hire providers who in routine care are not expendable (i.e., they are not merely hired for the duration of a study). Reliance on the medical or drug trial methods of psychological research does not address the complexity of the human interaction involved in therapeutic change as it unfolds outside of the laboratory (Slife, 2004).

Despite attempts to eliminate the therapist as an important outcome variable, some evidence suggests that the individual therapist can have a substantial impact on patient outcome even when extensive efforts are made to suppress this impact. For example, Luborsky, McClellan, Woody, O'Brien, and Auerbach, (1985) studied outcome for opiate addiction in a clinical trial comparing cognitive behavior therapy, supportive-expressive psychotherapy, and drug counseling. The outcome effect size for groups of patients varied across the nine therapists (three in each condition), ranging from .13 to .79 despite the usual attempts to minimize variance across therapists. Luborsky et al. (1985) concluded that "profound differences were discovered in the therapists' success with the patients in their caseload" (p. 602).

Along similar lines, data from other clinical trials have been reanalyzed with the intent of quantifying the contribution of the individual therapist to outcome. Among these the National Institute of Mental Health Treatment of Depression Collaborative Research Program has been examined extensively. Analysis based on advances in the application of statistical analyses (i.e., multilevel or hierarchical modeling) have yielded mixed results about the effect of individual therapists on client outcomes in this large multisite study. For example, two recent reanalyses of the National Institute of Mental Health

Treatment of Depression Collaborative Research Program resulted in mixed findings with regard to therapist effects. Wampold and Bolt (2006) found significant therapist effects using hierarchical linear analysis, whereas Elkin, Falconnier, Martinovich, and Mahoney (2006) did not find therapist effects using the same data and a similar data analytic tool. Estimation of the most appropriate statistical model and the different statistical treatment of outliers appear to be partly responsible for the emergence of these discrepant conclusions (Elkin, Falconnier, & Martinovich, 2007; Wampold & Bolt, 2007). Regardless, the majority of therapist effects research with clinical trials data supports the hypothesis that individual therapists differentially impact client outcomes, and depending on type of analysis, no differences have been found between types of psychotherapy in the face of statistically significant, albeit small, effects attributable to specific therapists (Elkin, 1999).

Meta-analytic reviews have documented important, even if less dramatic, therapist contributions to outcome across a variety of treatments and methodologies that have been summed across individual studies. For example, Crits-Christoph and Mintz (1991) meta-analyzed data from 10 clinical trials and noted the surprisingly high contribution of therapists to outcome, suggesting that the size of their contribution posed a challenge to attributing differential treatment effects to the specific therapies that were under study and the need to take these effects into account when analyzing outcomes. At the same time, Crits-Christoph and Gallop (2006) have cautioned about overstating the effects of individual therapists in clinical trials because no effects attributable to therapists have also been reported. They suggest that the therapist effects in such studies, despite being statistically significant, are usually small. A significant problem in clinical trial research is that such studies were not designed with the goal of finding the therapists' contribution in mind (e.g., patients are not randomly assigned to therapists), and a limited number of therapists are included in such studies (often only 5 or 10).

Therapist effects have also been reported in the context of effectiveness research conducted within routine care. Such effects might be expected to be larger because such research typically uses available therapists without the extensive controls that are used in clinical trials. Crits-Christoph and Gallop (2005) estimated that such studies appear to produce small to moderate effects attributed to specific therapists.

Within the context of providing care in routine practice, the fact that outcomes vary as a function of who is providing treatment provides an opportunity to improve services by examining, understanding, and acting on these differential outcomes. Within this context, Okiishi, Lambert, Nielsen, and Ogles (2003) analyzed the psychotherapy outcome of 1,841 patients seen by 91 therapists delivering routine care. Outcome by therapist showed considerable variability, with the most effective therapists' patients showing both rapid and substantial treatment response, whereas the least effective therapists' patients showed an average worsening in functioning. In contrast there was no evidence that the same degree of variability and superiority could be found for outcomes analyzed on the basis of therapist self-identified treatment orientation. Client outcomes were unrelated to the type of therapy a therapist claimed to practice even when the therapist held strong allegiance to a particular theory-based approach.

Whether making a referral, hiring a new therapist at a group practice, selecting a therapist for inclusion in a panel of providers, or deciding who to go to for one's own therapy, judgments about the best providers are being made on a daily basis. Despite the need for making these important decisions (about who is and who is not an effective therapist or who will be an effective therapist with a particular client), little effort has been expended on using empirical data to help make decisions. Using actual treatment outcomes based on the effects of the individual therapist to directly improve patient outcome is almost never attempted. Hesitancy to use such information is hardly limited to behavioral health care. Millenson (1997) has documented a plethora of examples in the field of medicine in which resistance to analyzing outcomes within hospitals and physicians has had disastrous consequences for patients. The historical evidence for medical institutions to use evidence from quality of care studies includes ignoring important findings on the variability of outcomes across hospitals and clinicians and the regular failure of institutions (and the researchers involved) and providers to make use of such information to directly improve patient outcomes. No one has yet documented such failures in the area of psychological treatments, but it is obvious the field is content to use informal judgments instead of patient outcome data to evaluate therapists.

HOW VARIABLE ARE CLIENT OUTCOMES BASED ON WHICH THERAPIST A CLIENT SEES?

The variability in client outcomes attributable to individual therapists in routine care provides an opportunity to manage and improve outcomes. Examples of using outcome data for this purpose are beginning to emerge and are proffered as a quality management tool independent of theoretical considerations. For example, Brown, Jones, Lambert, and Minami (2005) ranked 2,459 individual clinicians on the basis of their patients' outcomes (using the Outcome Questionnaire-30 [OQ-30]) during a 2-year period. Clinicians were included in their analysis if they had at least 10 cases with change scores in the database. The clinicians were sorted after adjusting for case mix on the basis of the degree of patient initial disturbance and analyzed by examining residualized gain scores (i.e., raw scores adjusted for initial level of disturbance). Therapists were sorted into quartiles. Clinicians in the top quartile and bottom quartile were compared. At-risk patients seen by the top quartile clinicians averaged greater change and tended to use fewer sessions. In contrast, the at-risk cases treated by bottom quartile clinicians had poorer outcomes despite averaging more sessions at the final assessment. PacifiCare Behavioral Health used such information to reward superior outcomes by publicly recognizing the most effective clinicians (or group practices) and offering each a cash award of $1,000. This practice was apparently preferred over the alternative of focusing on the bottom quartile because positive reinforcement and recognition might motivate providers to wonder why their practices fell short off the best. Of course, a managed health care company could use such information to increase referrals to top therapists while decreasing referrals to the bottom ranking therapists. Clinics that employ therapists would have to look at other procedures such as identifying practice patterns that cause the difference or creating personal development programs.

Some have proposed using similar information in other kinds of incentive schemes such as pay for performance in which more efficacious providers are paid at a greater hourly rate or less effective therapists are simply excluded from provider panels. Such actions would seem premature in most settings because they need to be based on the outcomes of a large number of clients per therapist and possibly random assignment of clients to therapists—problems that threaten the wisdom of using such information even when ample information is available. Even so, the obvious variability of outcomes across individual therapists and clinics raises important questions about what to do about the situation. Should psychologists just ignore such findings? What can be learned from examining outcomes on the basis of the specific therapists who see clients? What can be done for therapists whose clients routinely have unusually poor outcomes?

Routine monitoring of client treatment response eventually results in a large archival database that can allow a view into client-by-therapist outcomes. Outside of my colleagues' and my efforts in a managed care environment (PacifiCare), our research group has published two studies analyzing such data from the Counseling and Career Center (CCC).

THE SUPERSHRINK STUDIES

Okiishi et al. (2003) examined outcome by therapist and replicated the study as more clients became available for each clinician (Okiishi et al., 2006). Because the second study was essentially a replication and extension of the first, the emphasis here is on the findings of that study. Presentation of the results is followed by further exploration of a subset of the data that was used to explore differences in therapists' characteristics that could explain why some therapists' clients are more successful than those seen by other therapists.

Use of the word *supershrink* has precedence in the literature thanks to the work of David Ricks (1974) who reported dramatic differences in the psychological adjustment of adults who were treated in their adolescence by one of two therapists. The boys nicknamed the more effective therapist supershrink; the other therapist was undergoing personal problems that left him somewhat depressed during the time the children were treated. The case notes indicated that the supershrink devoted more time and energy to the most disturbed children and included parents more often in his treatment. In contrast the therapist of boys who had very poor adult outcomes had case notes suggesting he felt overwhelmed and discouraged by the more severe cases, investing himself more extensively with the easier cases.

Within the context of the Ricks (1974) study as well as the Okiishi et al. (2003, 2006) studies reported here, it is important to remind the reader that the study of therapist effects has taken place in the absence of random assignment of clients to therapists. This common state of affairs (including clinical trial investigations that randomize clients to treatments, not therapists) results in difficulty interpreting the findings—are any differences found the result of therapist effects or selection of cases that favors one therapist over another. The usual method for handling the selection problem is to adjust results by statistically equalizing caseloads for difficult cases. Prior investigation within this clinic and in psychotherapy outcome research in general (Garfield, 1994) has clearly demonstrated the most important predictor of final outcome status (e.g., normal functioning in initial level of patient severity). Severity is often estimated by psychological test scores or diagnosis as well as diagnostic comorbidity, with severity associated with more serious diagnostic classifications (e.g., Axis II diagnosis; American Psychiatric Association, 2000) or multiple diagnoses (Lueck, 2004). In our experience, once severity is accounted for by measures of psychological disturbance (e.g., as measured by the OQ-45), other patient variables, including diagnosis, added little to predicting outcome.

Thus, in the present study initial level of disturbance was examined across each therapist's caseload. Second, characteristics of the treatment (theoretical orientation) and therapists (gender, experience, professional background) that might be related to treatment success were examined. Once these variables were analyzed, this study examined differences in the rate of patient treatment response (efficiency), the size of the treatment response (effectiveness), differences between therapists in terms of the number of sessions they provided patients, and differences in the degree to which patients within therapist caseloads met criteria for clinically significant change. The results of the Okiishi et al. (2003, 2006) studies were then used to create feedback to therapists about their effects on clients in relation to other therapists in the clinic. The Okiishi studies thereby provide a good example of how systems of care can use outcome data to improve services within the context of a single clinic and in the spirit of helping clinicians to become more knowledgeable about the clients seen in the clinic and variability in patient outcome that could be attributed to therapist efforts.

Participants

The patient sample for this study consisted of college students seen at the CCC for individual psychotherapy over a 6-year period. Treatment was available to full-time students of the university. Patients at the center presented with a wide range of problems from simple homesickness to personality disorders and more serious problems. The most common diagnoses in the final data set (see explanation that follows) were mood disorders ($n = 1,961$, 36 %), anxiety disorders ($n = 1,200$, 22 %) and adjustment disorders ($n = 913$, 17%).

Students were initially seen in a 30-min intake interview and then assigned to a particular therapist on the basis of therapist availability and possibly the patient's perceived needs. No experimental control was exercised over this routine procedure. There were no session limits imposed, but therapists were expected to be as efficient as possible. The range of sessions in this sample was 1 to 203, with a mean of 8.74 ($SD = 14.3$).

Although 11,736 students were seen at the center over the 6-year period of data collection, the analysis being used for this study required at least three data points (a pretest and two additional measurements), so individuals with fewer than three treatment sessions including the intake were not included in the sample. This selection criterion yielded a data set of 7,628 patients who had been seen for a total of 64,103 sessions.

In this study, 149 therapists contributed data to the entire data pool of 7,628 patients. In the original study (Okiishi et al., 2003), the minimum number of patients per therapist was set at 15. To gain a more reliable assessment of patient improvement, the second study set the minimum number of patients at 30. With this criterion as well as the three data-point minimum described previously, 71 therapists who had seen a total of 5,427 patients were left in the sample. The therapists in this final data set had seen an average of 76 patients each for an average of 9.71 sessions. Data were also collected on a variety of therapist variables: level of training (preinternship, internship, and postinternship), type of training (clinical psychology, counseling psychology, social work, marriage and family therapy), sex (male, female), and primary theoretical orientation (cognitive–behavioral, behavioral, humanistic, psycho-dynamic). The modal therapist was a male, licensed, counseling psychology doctorate-level psychologist who identified his primary theoretical orientation as cognitive–behavioral.

Patient progress in this study was tracked using the OQ-45 (Lambert, Morton, et al., 2004) using the standard cutoff scores for normal functioning of 64/63 and reliable change of 14 points. At the end of treatment clients who had improved by 14 points and passed the cutoff for normal functioning were considered *recovered,* whereas those who only showed reliable change were considered *improved.* Patients who did not change more than 14 points in a positive or negative direction were considered to have not changed, and patients who worsened by 14 points were considered to have *deteriorated.*

Procedures

The database, in addition to providing information about the progress of the patients, made it possible to identify the patient, the therapist, and the date of the session. As often as possible, the OQ-45 was administered to patients before each session, but the statistical methods being used in this study did allow for missing values and collection of data at variable times. Therapist identities were protected by a nontherapist consultant randomly assigning each therapist a number so that identifying individual therapists would be impossible by viewing the data set. Patient identities were removed prior to data analysis.

Data were analyzed using random coefficients modeling or hierarchical linear modeling (HLM). The computer software used for this analysis was SAS for Windows, Version 9.1. HLM has been demonstrated to have a number of advantages over other multivariate repeated measures methods (Bryk & Raudenbush, 1992; Singer, 1998). HLM is ideal for a naturalistic study such as this in that missing and erratic data can be accounted for. As long as three or more data points are available, HLM allows for computation of estimates for missing data. HLM is a *nested regression* and provides a line of best fit with a slope and intercept for each patient, which can then be averaged within each therapist.

An initial HLM was performed taking into account therapist variables (level of training, primary theoretical orientation, type of training, and gender). This was done to answer the question: Do available therapist variables account for differences in patients' outcome? Given past effectiveness research it was not anticipated these variables would contribute significantly to the outcome of a patient, however, in case that they did, this fact needed to be considered before drawing conclusions about therapist outcomes. Furthermore, an ANOVA was performed on patient's initial OQ-45 scores by therapist to answer the question: Do some therapists see patients whose average initial disturbance is greater than other therapists?

Following this initial check of therapist variables my colleagues and I used two ways of ranking therapists. Our first method was to use HLM slopes to examine the modeled rate at which patients' OQ-45 scores decreased over sessions of psychotherapy. This gave an indication of which therapists' patients improved significantly more rapidly than expected and which therapists' patients improved at a rate much slower than expected. Once these slopes had been computed, therapists were rank ordered by HLM slope with the steepest slope being # 1 and the shallowest slope being # 71. Because HLM slopes look at rapidity of symptom alleviation (not length of treatment), this method was considered best for determining the "efficiency" of a therapist (the therapists' whose patients improve most rapidly). As HLM slope gives important information about the speed at which therapists' patients improve, it provides a modeled picture of outcome in which data from any specific case are affected by data from all other cases. In such models, the growth curve of a therapist's cases shrinks toward an average slope. Slopes are also plotted on a common, uniform number of sessions that is somewhat arbitrarily chosen but that does not directly take into account the fact that some therapists have longer or shorter average number of sessions they provide to patients. This is an important index both from a cost–benefit perspective in which improvement is accomplished with fewer sessions and also with regard to length of suffering, with ranking closer to 1 indicating a facilitated reduction in the burden of illness faster.

Another method of examining therapist effectiveness that could be calculated was the traditional pretreatment–posttreatment change score. These were computed for each patient by subtracting the patient's last OQ-45 score from his or her initial OQ-45 score. These change scores were averaged for all patients within therapists. This provided the actual amount of change experienced by patients seen by a therapist rather than a change index based on a statistical model of change (line of best fit as computed by the HLM analysis). This index ignores speed of change (number of sessions delivered to patients). Once these average change scores had been computed, therapists were again ranked from most to least effective. The disadvantage of this index of change is not only the fact that it does not take speed of change into account but also that it is based on only two scores (first and last), perhaps a less reliable estimate. It has the advantage that it expresses the self-reported change of patients at the beginning and the end of therapy, rather than an estimate of change as produced by HLM.

After average rank ordering by effectiveness was accomplished, this rank ordering was combined with HLM rank. The outcome of the top 10%

$(n = 7)$ of therapists and the bottom 10% $(n = 7)$ was examined to illustrate the size of the differences in patient outcome in terms of clinical significance criteria of recovered, improved, no change, or deteriorated using Jacobson and Truax's (1991) criteria. A chi-square analysis was performed to determine if there were statistically significant differences between top therapists' and bottom therapists' patients.

Results

Before describing the degree to which there is variability in outcome attributable to individual therapists, an analysis of variables usually considered important in determining outcome is reported.

Therapist Variables

The initial HLM analysis of therapist data was aimed at seeing if therapists differed from one another on outcomes based on four therapist variables: type of training, amount of training, theoretical orientation, and gender. The results of this analysis indicated that the type of training (counseling psychology, clinical psychology, marriage and family therapy, social work), the years of training (preinternship, internship, postinternship), theoretical orientation (behavioral, cognitive–behavioral, humanistic, psychodynamic), and gender did not change the slope of improvement across therapists. These findings are consistent with psychotherapy research in general and inconsistent with some widely held beliefs, such as more experienced therapists have better outcomes (e.g., Stein & Lambert, 1995). These findings also suggest that any differences found in client outcomes between individual therapists are the result of variables other than these. These results had practical implications from the point of view of the clinic administrator. They justified hiring and funding practicum students and interns as well as suggested that preferring to hire staff with specific degrees, specific theoretical orientations, or gender cannot be justified on the basis of patient outcome.

Initial Outcome Questionnaire-45 Scores

An ANOVA was performed on patient's initial OQ-45 scores by therapist. Results of this procedure indicated that there were no significant differences between therapists' patients' initial OQ-45 scores. In other words, therapists did not have unequal caseloads on the basis of initial OQ scores, suggesting that significant differences in outcome between therapists would not be due to variation in *difficulty of caseload*. The average initial OQ score for all patients was 66.61.

Differences Between Therapists

The HLM analysis indicated that patients' HLM lines had an average intercept OQ-45 = 63.26, with a mean slope of −.75. The negative slope indicates a decrease in OQ-45 points (i.e. a lessening of endorsed patient distress) over the course of psychotherapy of about .75 points per session.

HLM slopes were also generated on the basis of all of the patients in each therapist's caseload to compare therapists' outcomes with each other and to the general growth curve for the center. Slopes, intercepts, and average number of sessions for all the therapists in the sample are shown in Table 7.1. The HLM analysis indicated that therapists' patients differed significantly on their rate of change. The therapists' growth curve slopes (i.e., rate at which patients' growth curves moved in a negative direction, indicating less endorsed psychopathology) showed a statistically significant range of variability. This finding suggests differential rates of change for patients depending on which therapist they saw. Slopes by therapist ranged from −2.07 OQ-45 points dropped per session (Therapist Composite # 1, HLM rank = 1) to −.15 OQ-45 (Therapist Composite # 66, HLM rank = 71) points dropped per session. A typical client seeing the first therapist would need between six and seven sessions of treatment to recover, whereas the average client seeing the second therapist would need 94 sessions, nearly 2 years of weekly treatment. The preceding illustration is hypothetical, but it dramatizes the meaning of this data. Even though the previously described therapists had differences in the rate at which their patients changed and such differences could be highly important, these figures do not represent the therapists' practice pattern.

Therapists do differ in how many sessions they have with patients and the state of functioning those patients have when they leave treatment. The average number of sessions that therapists actually saw patients is shown in Table 7.1. The extremes of the average number of sessions ranged from 22.03 for Therapist # 72 to 4.94 for Therapist # 89. Such a wide range of sessions delivered suggests the individual practice patterns were widely varied and that little control was exercised by the clinic to make treatment uniform in length. To fairly judge the impact of therapy on patients the final outcome also needs to be considered.

Pretreatment–Posttreatment Change Scores

The overall results of judging patient outcome through the use of pretreatment–posttreatment change scores are also presented in Table 7.1. As can be seen, using pretreatment–posttreatment change to examine therapist effectiveness, the therapist whose patients had the largest pretreatment–posttreatment change (Therapist # 46) had an average OQ point drop of 14.93. The therapist whose patients had the least amount of pretreatment–posttreatment OQ change was Therapist # 21, whose patients reported an

TABLE 7.1
Composite Therapist Ranking, Slopes, Sessions, and Mean Pretreatment
Minus Posttreatment Outcome Questionnaire-45 (OQ-45) Score Across
71 Therapists in a University Outpatient Clinic

Composite therapist rank and identification no.[a]	Average intake OQ-45 total	Average no.of sessions	Pretreatment–posttreatment change/**rank**	HLM slope/**rank**
1/**43**	67.74	5.26	13.55/**6**	2.07/**1**
2/**39**	65.36	5.72	13.46/**7**	2.00/**2**
3/**86**	71.47	7.30	13.89/**5**	1.49/**6**
4/**84**	70.56	11.9	14.19/**4**	1.20/**8**
5/**34**	65.59	4.94	12.79/**10**	1.89/**3**
6/**36**	65.97	12.58	14.19/**3**	1.08/**13**
7/**85**	66.84	7.64	12.13/**14**	1.38/**7**
8/**36**	67.08	10.47	12.17/**13**	1.17/**9**
9/**39**	67.41	11.85	14.61/**2**	0.95/**24**
10/**84**	70.50	6.45	10.76/**23**	1.51/**4**
11/**34**	67.62	8.91	12.52/**12**	1.06/**15**
12/**36**	66.00	8.77	11.14/**19**	1.09/**12**
13/**75**	68.89	10.10	13.03/**9**	0.98/**23**
14/**171**	69.70	12.35	11.60/**16**	1.02/**21**
15/**49**	68.90	8.06	11.06/**21**	1.06/**17**
16/**174**	71.11	7.89	10.03/**29**	1.15/**10**
17/**35**	68.46	9.00	12.70/**11**	0.92/**28**
18/**62**	59.97	8.53	11.11/**20**	1.03/**20**
19/**53**	69.87	12.58	13.36/**8**	0.82/**34**
20/**55**	64.98	7.20	9.58/**32**	1.13/**11**
21/**227**	67.66	7.71	9.46/**34**	1.06/**16**
22/**97**	70.39	8.32	10.77/**22**	0.88/**30**
23/**46**	66.41	11.26	14.93/**1**	0.66/**53**
24/**378**	69.45	9.03	10.42/**25**	0.82/**35**
25/**167**	65.07	7.55	8.78/**42**	1.04/**19**
26/**119**	68.40	7.55	9.13/**40**	1.01/**22**
27/**31**	56.52	7.34	10.36/**26**	0.80/**36**
28/**67**	66.84	7.91	11.51/**17**	0.75/**46**
29/**41**	63.68	15.88	9.40/**37**	0.94/**26**
30/**51**	69.43	10.27	10.69/**24**	0.78/**40**
31/**42**	67.48	7.36	9.29/**39**	0.95/**25**
32/**41**	69.22	7.10	5.93/**63**	1.50/**5**
33/**38**	65.42	6.50	7.53/**54**	1.04/**18**
34/**138**	70.10	7.46	9.42/**36**	0.80/**38**
35/**48**	62.17	14.79	10.20/**27**	0.74/**47**
36/**53**	61.81	8.15	8.41/**48**	0.92/**27**
37/**32**	67.38	6.85	9.72/**31**	0.76/**44**
38/**196**	68.94	9.35	10.11/**28**	0.71/**50**
39/**50**	62.44	14.66	11.32/**18**	0.57/**61**
40/**30**	61.87	7.67	8.74/**43**	0.80/**37**
41/**115**	62.32	14.00	5.23/**66**	1.08/**14**
42/**51**	66.37	6.80	7.67/**52**	0.89/**29**
43/**56**	65.73	6.07	7.98/**51**	0.88/**31**
44/**130**	66.20	5.05	12.02/**15**	0.38/**68**

TABLE 7.1
Composite Therapist Ranking, Slopes, Sessions, and Mean Pretreatment Minus Posttreatment Outcome Questionnaire-45 (OQ-45) Score Across 71 Therapists in a University Outpatient Clinic (*Continued*)

Composite therapist rank and identification no.[a]	Average intake OQ-45 total	Average no. of sessions	Pretreatment– posttreatment change/**rank**	HLM slope/**rank**
45/**274**	70.27	10.00	8.45/**46**	0.79/**39**
46/**171**	64.02	9.57	8.70/**44**	0.77/**42**
47/**327**	66.10	11.5	8.26/**50**	0.77/**41**
48/**159**	66.87	11.43	9.57/**33**	0.59/**58**
49/**154**	69.32	12.03	6.36/**61**	0.85/**32**
50/**46**	65.70	9.39	9.39/**38**	0.65/**55**
51/**115**	64.79	12.51	8.33/**49**	0.75/**45**
52/**53**	70.26	8.50	9.87/**30**	0.54/**65**
53/**32**	65.16	13.22	5.72/**64**	0.83/**33**
54/**54**	63.35	8.44	6.82/**59**	0.77/**43**
55/**94**	67.62	11.97	9.44/**35**	0.42/**67**
56/**178**	69.29	11.26	8.93/**41**	0.55/**63**
57/**38**	66.68	22.03	7.58/**53**	0.67/**52**
58/**57**	67.56	8.09	6.54/**60**	0.73/**48**
59/**130**	68.84	8.80	6.97/**57**	0.69/**51**
60/**43**	68.53	9.63	8.63/**45**	0.49/**66**
61/**48**	64.83	9.81	6.85/**58**	0.65/**54**
62/**32**	62.15	9.25	8.44/**47**	0.34/**69**
63/**167**	68.13	17.63	4.72/**69**	0.72/**49**
64/**318**	63.64	8.45	5.98/**62**	0.57/**60**
65/**44**	63.82	8.82	7.28/**56**	0.27/**70**
66/**50**	62.56	8.22	7.36/**55**	0.15/**71**
67/**165**	67.08	12.15	2.66/**71**	0.62/**56**
68/**43**	66.46	12.19	4.23/**70**	0.61/**57**
69/**39**	66.97	9.18	4.87/**68**	0.59/**59**
70/**45**	68.89	13.13	5.67/**65**	0.55/**64**
71/**69**	65.39	10.41	5.23/**67**	0.56/**62**

Note. HLM = hierarchical linear modeling. From "An Analysis of Therapist Treatment Effects: Toward Providing Feedback to Individual Therapists on Their Patients' Psychotherapy Outcome," by J. C. Okiishi, M. J. Lambert, D. Eggett, S. L. Nielsen, D. D. Dayton, and D. A. Vermeersch, 2006, *Journal of Clinical Psychology, 62*, pp. 1165–1166. Copyright 2006 by Wiley. Reprinted with permission.
[a]The identification number (in bold) indicates the number of patients evaluated during the study period.

average drop of 2.66 points over the course of treatment. It can be noticed that when pretreatment–posttreatment change is used as an index of outcome, therapist rank ordering changed, and in some cases, dramatically. For example, Therapist # 70, whose patients had the steepest HLM curve of all the therapists in the sample, dropped in ranking from 1st to 6th when pretreatment–posttreatment test ordering was used. Conversely, Therapist # 46 went from being ranked 53rd using just HLM slope to # 1 when using pretreatment–posttreatment difference scores. Therapist # 46 had patients who showed less impact per session but kept patients in treatment longer. In terms of amount of change, patients, even if the cost of treatment would be higher, would be best off if they saw this therapist. An obvious lesson from this data is that the index of change used to value therapists matters, and both indices are necessary for an accurate picture of therapist effectiveness.

Average Ranking

The therapists in Table 7.1 are ordered on the basis of their average rank on both efficiency and effectiveness among the 71 therapists. The average ranking provided a third method of gauging outcome by therapist that was sometimes different from the variables alone. For example, the average patient seeing the top average ranked therapist, could expect to begin treatment in the dysfunctional range on the OQ, be seen for 5 sessions, drop 14 points on the OQ, and cross the clinical significance cutoff line of 64. In short, patients seeing this therapist could, on average, expect to meet clinical significance criteria for recovery. At the other end of the therapeutic spectrum, patients seeing the worst average ranked therapist (# 69) would be expected to enter treatment with an equivalent OQ score to the top ranked therapist, be seen for 10 sessions, and improve by 5 points on the OQ. On average, patients seen by this therapist would leave therapy not having experienced reliable clinically significant change.

Extreme Group Comparison

Using the average ranking as the estimate of therapists' outcomes, the top and bottom 10% of therapists were identified—the seven most and seven least effective therapists. The most effective therapists had an average HLM slope of −1.5 points per session and a pretreatment–posttreatment average change score of −13.18. The least effective had an average HLM slope 3.5 times less (−0.42 points per session), and a pretreatment–posttreatment average change score of 6.83, one half that of the more effective therapists. Table 7.2 shows average rankings, slopes, and pretreatment–posttreatment OQ-45 scores for these extreme groups.

For patients seen by these most and least effective therapists, outcome was classified according to the clinical significance of patients' change (recovered, improved, no change, or deteriorated) based on their pretreatment–posttreatment scores. Once this had been done, a chi-square value was computed. Results of this procedure indicated that there was a statistically significant difference between the proportion of the top and bottom therapists' patients who fell into each category, with top therapists having significantly more in the recovered and improved classification and significantly fewer in the deteriorated classification than the bottom therapists. Top therapists had an average recovery rate of 22%, whereas bottom ranked therapists had a recovery rate of 15%. Conversely, bottom ranked therapists had an 11% rate of deterio-

TABLE 7.2
Upper and Lower 10% of Therapists Based on Patient Outcome
(Average Rank Order)

Therapist identification no.	Average therapist ranking	HLM slope	Average session	Pretreatment–Posttreatment OQ-45 change
Top 10%				
176	4.67	−1.20	11.90	−14.19
161	6.33	−1.08	12.58	−14.19
163	6.33	−2.00	5.72	−13.46
70	7.00	−2.07	5.26	−13.56
159	8.67	−1.49	7.30	−13.90
116	9.67	−1.17	10.47	−12.17
92	10.33	−1.51	8.91	−10.77
Average	7.57	−1.50	8.87	−13.18
Bottom 10%				
164	58.67	−0.49	9.63	−8.63
94	61.33	−0.34	9.25	−8.44
146	62.00	−0.57	8.45	−5.98
135	62.67	−0.56	10.41	−5.23
124	63.00	−0.59	9.18	−4.87
100	65.00	−0.27	8.22	−7.28
45	65.67	−0.15	8.82	−7.36
Average	62.62	−0.42	9.14	−6.83

Note. HLM = Hierarchical linear modeling. Data from "An Analysis of Therapist Treatment Effects: Toward Providing Feedback to Individual Therapists on Their Patients' Psychotherapy Outcome," by J. C. Okiishi, M. J. Lambert, D. Eggett, S. L. Nielsen, D. D. Dayton, and D. A. Vermeersch, 2006, *Journal of Clinical Psychology, 62,* pp. 1166–1167. Copyright 2006 by Wiley. Reprinted with permission.

ration, whereas the top ranked therapists only had 5% of their patients deteriorate. A graph of rates of recovery, improvement, no change, and deterioration for top and bottom ranked therapists is shown in Figure 7.1.

An advantage of examining the outcomes on clients by extreme groups of therapists is that one can get a better idea of the consequences of variability. If a patient were to see a top ranked therapist, he or she would improve his or her chance of recovering by 30% and cut his or her chance of deteriorating in half. Within the context of studying differences between therapists who compose extreme groups, the reader is reminded that outcome by therapist is normally distributed and that most psychotherapists are average regarding the effects they have on clients. Therapists cannot be distinguished on the basis of clients' outcomes. It is hoped that therapy, as provided by the average clinician, is "good enough" therapy for most patients despite being average. Nevertheless one can learn from considering the two ends of the continuum—most and least effective therapists.

Given the goal of using the results of the current study to provide a basis for giving therapists feedback about the progress of their patients in relation to

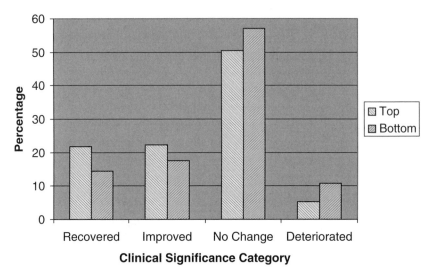

Figure 7.1. Percentage of patients in four outcome categories by the top and bottom 10% of therapists. Adapted from "An Analysis of Therapist Treatment Effects: Toward Providing Feedback to Individual Therapists on Their Patients' Psychotherapy Outcome," by J. C. Okiishi, M. J. Lambert, D. Eggett, S. L. Nielsen, D. D. Dayton, and D. A. Vermeersch, 2006, *Journal of Clinical Psychology, 62,* p. 1167. Copyright 2006 by Wiley. Reprinted with permission.

the progress at the center as a whole and the fact that the feedback would not provide the same rank ordering, it was decided that therapists should be given information about their rank on both efficiency and effectiveness as well as a composite ranking with the two pieces of information combined. A methodological issue in providing this kind of feedback to therapists is the Okiishi et al. (2003, 2006) studies guaranteed anonymity to therapists. This prevented the use of the data by administrators who might otherwise have used it as a consideration for annual raises, for recommending remedial actions to be taken by specific therapists, or even to reassign therapists to different job roles, such as shifting the top therapists toward seeing more patients while asking the less effective therapists to carry a higher burden of administrative assignments.

Given these limitations the decision was made to make personal feedback available to clinicians and leave it up to them to decide what, if anything, they wished to do. As noted in Chapter 5, feedback is most effective when information is provided that includes corrective actions because information that is discrepant from overly positive self-assessment biases may simply be discouraging or lead to anxiety and defensiveness. Therapists who wanted a feedback report on their clients' performance were able to obtain it by presenting a secretary in the statistics department with an identity number that matched that on a sealed envelope. This meant therapists could view the feedback in privacy and at their leisure, giving them time to absorb the information. In some cases therapists sought the support of their colleagues to help them digest the information; in others the report was shared in weekly case conferences. No attempts were made to study the consequences of this feedback at either a personal level or a program level.

Given the usual case that therapist relationship skills and client alliance ratings correlate with patient outcomes, a further study was conducted to measure these therapist qualities and provide feedback to therapists who were willing to participate. It was thought that such an action may have value in helping some therapists identify problems in this area of their functioning. In addition, the most successful and unsuccessful therapists were asked about their willingness to self-identify their rank ordering and to allow future sessions with clients to be tape-recorded, a study that has not been completed as of this writing.

Therapist Interpersonal Skills: A Distinguishing Characteristic of the Most Effective Therapists?

In general the Okiishi et al. (2003, 2006) studies of therapist outcomes were highly informative with regard to the amount of variability attributable to therapists but uninformative in illuminating the source of therapist effects. Just what is it that the most effective therapists have in common? Past research demonstrates that variables such as therapist emotional adjustment and certain aspects of therapist personality (e.g., dominance) fail to predict client outcome but that characteristics specific to in-session therapist activities more often do (Beutler et al., 2004). Empirical findings in this area highlight the need for studies that move beyond measuring therapists' demographic characteristics and general traits to include measures of therapist characteristics that have a more solid theoretical and empirical link to client outcomes. For example, numerous studies support the presence of relationships between psychotherapy process variables, such as empathy and the alliance, with clinical outcomes (Norcross, 2002; Wampold, 2001). Therefore, a potentially promising approach for identifying the sources of therapist effects would be to operationalize and examine therapists' skills in facilitating therapy processes (e.g., empathy and the alliance) that are theoretically and empirically related to therapy outcome.

THE ANDERSON STUDY

In theory, indicators of the therapist's contribution to therapy processes can be identified through somewhat subtle interpersonal messages (Strupp & Anderson, 1997). For example, cases in which therapists communicated subtle interpersonally disaffiliative messages were shown to result in worse clinical outcomes than when there was an absence of such communication (Henry, Schacht, & Strupp, 1990). Another illustration involves the therapeutic alliance, which has commonly been viewed as partly a therapist's skill in facilitating a collaborative relationship with his or her client (e.g., Norcross, 2002; Safran & Muran, 2000). Another process variable, empathy, refers to the therapist's skill in accurately understanding and reflecting a client's thoughts and emotional experience (Bohart, Elliott, Greenberg, & Watson, 2002). Because the therapist is by definition a major contributor to the facilitation of the processes of therapy, Anderson and colleagues operationalized and examined the relationship between therapists' facilitative interpersonal skills (FIS; Anderson, Ogles, & Weis, 1999; Anderson, Patterson, & Weis, 2007) and clinical outcomes in the CCC where the Okiishi et al. (2003, 2006) study data were collected.

In this study, aimed at further understanding the sources of therapist effects, Anderson, Ogles, Patterson, Lambert, and Vermeersch (2009) examined the relationships between a broad spectrum of therapist characteristics, which included therapists' demographic characteristics, general traits (e.g., theoretical orientation), social skills, and FIS (Anderson et al., 1999; Anderson et al., 2007), and client outcomes, in a subset of the sample studied by Okiishi and colleagues (2003, 2006). Available therapists in these two studies were invited to complete a self-report social skills measure and a performance task that consisted of responding to video-recorded analogue therapy segments. Ratings of therapists' responses to the performance task constituted the measure of FIS. The expectation was that that therapists' interpersonal skills (i.e., FIS) would account for a significant amount of variance in client outcomes. An important aspect of this methodology was that this material was collected independent of the services provided and was remote in time from the collection of client outcome data. Using this methodology assumes that the skills measured are traitlike and would also be present in the psychotherapy offered.

Participants

An archival database of clients seen in the CCC was available for this study. Clients were included in the analyses if they completed at least three therapy sessions and their therapist agreed to complete the therapist measures. Clients in the analyses had been seen prior to the therapist assessment on the measures of interest. A total of 1,141 clients were included in the final sample. Clients had a mean age of 23.0 years ($SD = 4.1$ years; range 18 to 56 years). The majority of the clients were female (62.8%), and most of the clients were Caucasian (85.5%). All of the clients attended or were associated or employed by the university where the counseling center was located.

Clients in the sample attended therapy for a range of 3 to 72 sessions, with a mean attendance of 9.09 sessions ($SD = 8.79$).

Initially, 32 therapists currently working in the CCC were invited to participate in the study. Of these, 28 therapists agreed to participate in the study and completed self-report measures and the FIS performance task. Of these therapists, 1 was excluded because of incomplete FIS performance assessment data. Additionally, 2 therapists were excluded because data for fewer than 10 clients were available in the archival data set. Thus, 25 therapists (16 men, 9 women) were initially included in the analyses. Therapists treated a mean of 45.6 clients (ranging from 13 to 141 clients) for whom data were available in the archival data set. Therapists had a mean age of 43.9 years ($SD = 10.9$ years) and were predominantly Caucasian (96%). Therapists self-identified their theoretical orientation as primarily cognitive–behavioral ($n = 8$), humanistic ($n = 8$), eclectic ($n = 5$), and psychodynamic ($n = 4$). In regard to level of training, the 25 therapists who completed the performance assessment included 17 licensed doctoral-level therapists, 2 postdoctoral but not fully licensed therapists, 3 predoctoral interns, and 3 graduate trainees. Therapists had 11.5 mean years ($SD = 10.1$) of clinical experience. Therapists estimated that they spent 42.9% of their professional hours in direct clinical practice (ranging from 8% to 70%).

Therapist Measures

The Social Skills Inventory (SSI; Riggio, 1986) is a 90-item self-report questionnaire that assesses self-reported social skills. Items are scored using a 5-point Likert scale, with response options ranging from $1 = not\ at\ all\ like\ me$ to $5 = exactly\ like\ me$. The SSI measures skills in expressivity, sensitivity, and control in verbal (social) and nonverbal (emotional) domains. The SSI yields a global score and six subscales with 15 items each, though only the global score was used in this study. Coefficient alphas range from .62 to .87 for each of the subscales and test–retest correlations range from .81 to .96 for a 2-week interval (Riggio, 1986).

In the Facilitative Interpersonal Skills Performance Task (Anderson et al, 2007), FIS is defined as a set of qualities that correspond to a person's ability to perceive, understand, and communicate a wide range of interpersonal messages as well as a person's ability to persuade others with personal problems to apply suggested solutions to their problems and abandon maladaptive patterns. A performance task was designed as a means of measuring therapists' abilities to respond to challenging interpersonal situations in a therapy setting. The development and use of a performance task, as opposed to self-report measures of facilitative interpersonal skills, is advantageous in that this task has a high level of ecological face validity.

Four problematic therapy process segments were selected from the videotaped archives of a study that focused on problematic interpersonal interactions between patients and therapists (Strupp, 1993). In addition, unique interpersonal patient styles were selected to represent a range of challenging interpersonal patterns, including (a) a confrontational and angry patient ("You can't help me"), (b) a passive, silent, and withdrawn patient ("I don't know what to talk about"), (c) a confused and yielding patient (only the therapist's opinion matters), and (d) a controlling and blaming patient (implies that others, including the therapist, are not worthy of him or her). Thus, two cases were designed to include patients who were highly self-focused, negative, and self-effacing, and the remaining two cases were designed to be highly other-focused, friendly, but highly dependent clients. Two brief segments (approximately 2 min each) were selected for each problematic patient–therapist interaction, and hence the final performance task consisted of eight of these brief segments. Actors were hired to enact the eight scenarios. These actors memorized the transcripts from actual sessions and were coached on how to capture the interpersonal style of the patients they were enacting. Using therapy transcripts, actors enacted the scenarios and practiced for multiple sessions before the enactments were video-recorded.

Therapists in this study were presented with these eight brief situations and were prompted to respond to the patient-actors (who were filmed directly facing the camera) at predefined moments "as if" they were the therapist in the situation. The video clips were presented via a computer program that allowed therapists to make their responses in the privacy of their offices at the counseling center. Therapists were asked to leave the audio recorder running to capture the therapists' initial, nonpracticed responses to the video scenarios.

FIS item content was selected from the clinical and research literature (e.g., Norcross, 2002) on common therapist interpersonal skills and facilitative conditions. Specifically, the 10 FIS items included ratings of verbal fluency, emotional expression, persuasiveness, hopefulness, warmth, empathy, alliance bond capacity, and problem focus. Each item was scored using a 5-point Likert-type scale in which ratings of 1 or 2 represent deficiencies in the skill; 3 indicates a neutral level; and ratings of 4 and 5 denote proficiencies of the skill being rated.

Two licensed doctoral-level research clinicians rated each of the eight recorded responses for each therapist. Raters were provided with a manual for rating the FIS items. After studying the manual, the two raters (one of whom developed the manual) met for 2 days to discuss and practice ratings with sample responses, none of which included therapist responses from the present study. Then from two separate locations, the doctoral-level research clinicians rated all participating therapists' responses to each of the 10 items. The mean score for the two raters on each item was then summed to obtain one

FIS performance rating for each therapist. Hence, possible scores ranged from 5 to 50, and the mean total FIS rating was 29.8 ($SD = 4.52$) and ranged from 19.8 to 36.8. In a replication of previous research involving the FIS rating system (e.g., Anderson, Crowley, & Carson, 2001), each of the FIS items had acceptable interrater reliabilities (all were $r > .70$). In a prior research study, Anderson et al., (2001) documented that therapists' who achieved high FIS ratings had better outcomes measured posttherapy and at follow-up than therapists who achieved low rankings.

After therapists completed their assessment, they placed their questionnaires and tape-recorded responses to the performance analysis in an envelope, which they were instructed to seal and sign before returning the envelope to the on-site researcher. Once therapist assessments were completed, all therapist assessments were sent to a second university site. The two raters of the therapist performance task were located at different university sites, neither of which was where the client data were collected. To protect therapist identities, a nontherapist research assistant used randomly assigned therapist identification numbers so that identifying individual therapists would not be possible when viewing the data set.

Results

Data were analyzed using HLM. An initial HLM was examined using an unconditional model with sessions nested within clients and clients nested within therapists. Although the first session intake was sometimes conducted by a different therapist, this intake was attributed to the treating therapist. After an examination of the unconditional model, a second analysis was conducted taking into account therapist variables (level of training, primary theoretical orientation, type of training, and gender). This analysis focused on traditional demographic variables. A final analysis examined the relationship of therapist FIS on client outcome. These analyses were followed with further exploration of differences in outcome among therapists and their relationship to therapist characteristics.

An examination of the unconditional model with sessions nested within clients and clients nested within therapists indicated that on average clients started treatment with an OQ-45 score of 68.24 ($SE = 0.68$) and that the average slope across therapists was approximately 1 OQ-45 point of improvement per session. There were no significant differences among therapists in terms of initial OQ-45 scores (intercepts) prior to treatment onset. However, there were differences among therapists in terms of average outcomes (slope) across clients. The next HLM analysis of therapist data was conducted to see if any of the four traditional therapist variables (age, sex, theoretical orientation, and percentage of work time conducting therapy) might account for differences in outcomes among therapists. The results of this analysis indicated that the sex, theoretical orientation (cognitive–behavioral, humanistic, eclectic, dynamic), and percentage of time conducting treatment did not significantly account for variation in outcomes among therapists. In contrast, the age of the therapist did account for differences in outcome, with older therapists having better outcomes than younger therapists.

To examine the variable of interest, FIS, a third HLM analysis was conducted with age, self-report of social skills (using the SSI), and the FIS performance assessment ratings as predictors of outcome. Age was included because it was a significant predictor in the first stage of the analysis. FIS was the lone predictor of variation in outcome slope among therapists. In the context of SSI and FIS, age was no longer a significant predictor of therapist slope. To further explore the relationship between therapist characteristics and client outcome in this naturalistic setting, a scatter plot was examined and a simple correlation between the FIS total score for each therapist and the HLM estimated outcome slope for each therapist's caseload of clients was calculated. Although this analysis is somewhat counterintuitive to the HLM design in that the hierarchical nature of the data is lost when aggregating at the therapist level, it does allow for another perspective on the relationship between slopes and FIS. As can be seen in Figure 7.2, therapists with higher facilitative interpersonal skills had clients with greater change rates (slopes). The simple correlation between therapist FIS sum and outcome slope was significant, $r = .47$ ($n = 24$).

This surprisingly high relationship, if replicated, suggests that it may be a great advantage to measure therapist interpersonal skills in relation to especially problematic client presentations. A usual problem with ratings of the therapeutic alliance is that the alliance ratings within and across therapists is uniformly high, reducing the chance of finding significant correlations because of the restriction in the range of scores. FIS vignettes and associated training may provide a method of intervening with cases predicted to deteriorate because they focus on the resolution of ruptures that may be the cause of deterioration.

Future research will help clinicians understand the situations in which the therapists' interpersonal skills influence the progress of therapy as well as identify the relative importance of competencies for therapist training. Certainly the procedures used could be applied by administrators as a method of hiring therapists. But as Chapter 6 suggests the most impactful way of maximizing patient outcome is probably through ratings of relationship variables with individual clients who are having a negative treatment response during the course of their ongoing treatment. The FIS requires considerable time to collect and analyze and is not suitable as a clinical support tool. It was found suitable for providing individual therapists with information about their

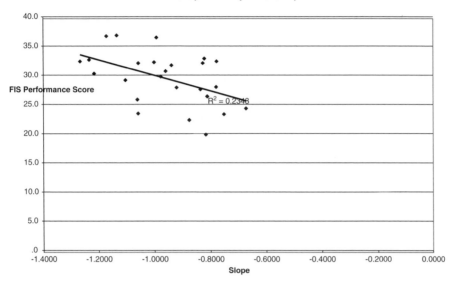

Figure 7.2. The relationship between speed of recovery and therapist interpersonal skills. FIS = facilitative interpersonal skills. From "Therapist Effects: Facilitative Interpersonal Skills as a Predictor of Therapist Success," by T. Anderson, B. M. Ogles, C. L. Patterson, M. J. Lambert, and D. A. Vermeersch, 2009, *Journal of Clinical Psychology, 65,* p. 763. Copyright 2009 by Wiley. Reprinted with permission.

behavior in these vignettes of problematic cases. This was in fact done with therapists who requested feedback from the research team. Individual appointments were made, and the therapist ratings were provided in relation to average ratings of therapists in the CCC. No attempt was made to evaluate the effects of this feedback or to connect this feedback with poor performers from the Okiishi et al. (2003, 2006) studies. So the degree to which such feedback improves the performance of therapists remains unknown.

SUMMARY AND CONCLUSIONS

The purpose of the supershrink studies was to systematically examine a large sample of therapists who had seen a large number of patients to answer the question: Are there some therapists who produce better or worse outcomes than others? This is a question that has rarely been investigated and never with patient samples within therapists of the size of those used in the Okiishi et al. (2003, 2006) studies (Crits-Christoph & Gallop 2006). Patients in the Okiishi et al. (2006) study experienced statistically significant gains during treatments that lasted an average of 9.7 sessions. The patients seen at the center showed a broad range of initial symptomotology and varying rates of improvement. Patients had a similar level of symptomotology at intake across therapists. In fact, the similarity in degree of disturbance across therapist caseloads called into question the necessity of case-mix adjustments for the purpose of fairly contrasting therapists in this sample. There were no significant differences in patient outcome between therapists on the basis of the four therapist variables of sex, level of training, type of training, or theoretical orientation. This reinforces the findings of existing empirical literature that emphasizes the unimportance of training in specific techniques to enhance treatment unique outcomes.

Something else, perhaps the qualities of individual therapists themselves and especially their interpersonal skills with difficult clients are more responsible for variation in patient outcomes (Anderson et al., 2009; Lambert & Okiishi, 1997). This is consistent with the idea that selection into training programs deserves consistent attention from researchers but also the idea that trainees' effects on clients should be used in advancement and retention decisions. It also provides administrators and, perhaps more importantly, practicing clinicians themselves reason to improve their own functioning in this important area of clinical practice.

There was a significant, sometimes dramatic difference when improvement curves and pretreatment–posttreatment test change scores were compared. On the basis of the average of these indices of efficiency and effectiveness, the top and bottom 10% of therapists saw patients whose outcome was statistically and clinically different. For example, the rate of deterioration in the bottom-ranked therapists was double that found in the top-ranked therapists. Unfortunately, patients were not randomly allocated to therapists, and there remains the possibility that differences between therapists were caused by factors that were not investigated. At the center where data were collected, case assignments were made by individuals (full-time professionals and interns) doing intakes and were routinely assigned on the basis of schedules that matched and, to a lesser extent, patients' perceived level of pathology, difficulty, or personally perceived but discordant views about the goodness of personality fit with a particular therapist. These assignments were made at the discretion of the intake interviewer and without regard to OQ-45 scores at intake. This method of deliberate, albeit unsystematic, case assignment could pose a threat to the validity (meaning) of the findings. Without random assignment, it could be possible for a particular therapist to be given a disproportionate number of "easy" or "hard" cases, thus inflating or deflating his or her measured level of effectiveness.

Another limitation apparent in the Okiishi et al. (2003, 2006) investigations was the researchers' inability to more closely examine information about and treatment practices of therapists. Identifying information describing therapists was masked to protect the confidentiality of therapists and access to client data that were linked to therapists.

In the interest of using the accumulated data to enhance patient outcome, provisions were made to give confidential individualized feedback to each therapist who met criteria for inclusion in this study. A sample therapist feedback report is presented in Figure 7.3. As can be seen, the therapist is given information that allows comparisons on categories of effectiveness and rankings. This procedure made it so none of the center research staff or administrators knew the outcomes of individual therapists, and the therapists received feedback from a person (the statistical consultant) who did not know the identities of specific therapists.

Feedback to the bottom quartile of therapists included the recommendation the therapist consider seeking supervision to sort out ways of improving patient outcome. Feedback to therapists may be repeated on a yearly basis, allowing for the opportunity to examine what, if any, impact such feedback might have on patient outcome. However, the idea that "Big Brother" is studying therapist's performance created considerable anxiety and, in the short term, may be detrimental to therapists and therefore patients. The field is yet to understand how to use the information obtained in a way that maximizes patient outcome (with the exception of not referring patients to them). Certainly books from the popular press such as *Better* or *Demanding Medical Excellence* provide evidence that linking outcomes to providers, clinics, and hospitals has a great potential for improving the quality of care by allowing an examination of what the best practices are. And certainly my colleagues' and my research is moving toward an examination of what supershrinks actually do that makes their clients improve faster or more completely.

Actually measuring patient change as a method of identifying gifted practitioners and practices stands in contrast to identifying "master therapists" through processes such as peer nomination. For example, in one study of master therapists (Jennings & Skovholt, 1999), "expert" therapists (i.e., those who had written books on psychotherapy or who had been involved in training therapists) nominated colleagues (a) to whom they would apply the term *master therapist*, (b) to whom they would refer a family member or close friend, and (c) in whom they would have full confidence in seeing for their own personal therapy. Although such definitions of master therapist represent one potentially valid approach to defining such a concept, it can be argue that patient outcome data might provide the primary basis for defining the concept of master therapist and the basis on which a referral might be best made.

My colleagues and I see monitoring outcomes of individual therapists as an important research activity, one that may eventually enable the identification of the "empirically validated psychotherapist" and ultimately lead to

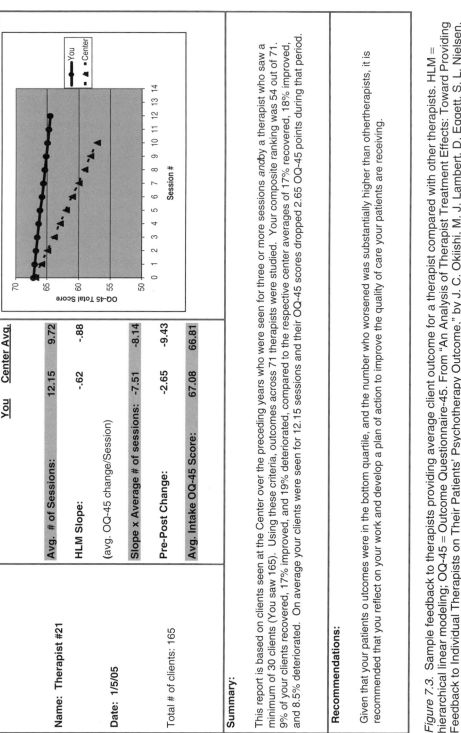

	You	Center Avg.
Name: **Therapist #21**		
Avg. # of Sessions:	12.15	9.72
HLM Slope:	-.62	-.88
(avg. OQ-45 change/Session)		
Date: 1/5/05		
Slope x Average # of sessions:	-7.51	-8.14
Pre-Post Change:	-2.65	-9.43
Total # of clients: 165		
Avg. Intake OQ-45 Score:	67.08	66.81

Summary:

This report is based on clients seen at the Center over the preceding years who were seen for three or more sessions *and* by a therapist who saw a minimum of 30 clients (You saw 165). Using these criteria, outcomes across 71 therapists were studied. Your composite ranking was 54 out of 71. 9% of your clients recovered, 17% improved, and 19% deteriorated, compared to the respective center averages of 17% recovered, 18% improved, and 8.5% deteriorated. On average your clients were seen for 12.15 sessions and their OQ-45 scores dropped 2.65 OQ-45 points during that period.

Recommendations:

Given that your patients o outcomes were in the bottom quartile, and the number who worsened was substantially higher than othertherapists, it is recommended that you reflect on your work and develop a plan of action to improve the quality of care your patients are receiving.

Figure 7.3. Sample feedback to therapists providing average client outcome for a therapist compared with other therapists. HLM = hierarchical linear modeling; OQ-45 = Outcome Questionnaire-45. From "An Analysis of Therapist Treatment Effects: Toward Providing Feedback to Individual Therapists on Their Patients' Psychotherapy Outcome," by J. C. Okiishi, M. J. Lambert, D. Eggett, S. L. Nielsen, D. D. Dayton, and D. A. Vermeersch, 2006, *Journal of Clinical Psychology, 62,* p. 1169. Copyright 2006 by Wiley. Reprinted with permission.

improved outcomes for patients seeking treatment if they have reliable information about therapist effects. In fact, given the amount of variability among therapist outcomes in the Okiishi et al. (2003, 2006) and Anderson studies and the increasing consistency of such a finding in other investigations (Crits-Christoph & Mintz, 1991; Luborsky et al., 1985; Orlinsky & Howard, 1980; Ricks, 1974; Strupp, 1980), it is arguable that the identification and study of the empirically validated psychotherapist may be one of the most effective ways of improving the effects of treatment.

Research on the individual therapist's contribution to outcome can eventually be used not only to impact the quality of clinical practice but also the theories that guide clinical interventions. Certainly some managed health care companies in the United States are moving in the direction of profiling therapists on the basis of their client outcomes, an activity that seems fraught with problems but also with potential benefit to clients. It would be nice to know more about what will happen to patients if they see one or another provider.

In our first attempt to examine the outcome of a master therapist, a therapist with a strong regional reputation for having unusually positive outcomes volunteered to collect outcome data on consecutive cases he saw in psychotherapy (Lambert, Okiishi, Finch, & Johnson, 1998). The therapist, Lynn Johnson, practiced solution-focused psychotherapy and had written a book on the approach. In this type of psychotherapy the emphasis is on current adjustment and on finding solutions to current problems under the assumption that clients may need to return in the future rather than that the therapy will inoculate the patient from future difficulties. Obviously, we could not separate the therapist from the techniques associated with his practices. His clients' outcomes were contrasted with those produced by clinical psychology graduate students in their first to fourth year of training who applied a variety of approaches but not solution-focused treatment. It was hoped that their clients' outcomes would provide a benchmark for routine care with which to compare Dr. Johnson. Figure 7.4 presents the results of this contrast in the form of a survival curve—modeling time (sessions) to recovery.

As can be seen, the recovery estimates were dramatically different; Dr. Johnson's patients had rapid recovery, whereas patients seen by trainees ultimately had the same outcome but took much longer to achieve it. After an average of 2 sessions 36% of clients meeting with Dr. Johnson met criteria for recovery, and only 2% of those seeing students had done so. Dr. Johnson had 46% of patients reach criteria after 7 sessions, a recovery rate that took 26 sessions if patients saw a trainee. Patients can expect to have a different experience seeing Dr. Johnson versus the student therapists and with respect to the amount of suffering while in treatment. Follow-up adjustment was not studied in either group of patients and remains an important consideration. In a separate 1-year follow-up study of rapid treatment responders,

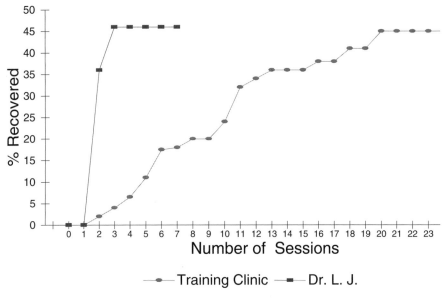

Figure 7.4. Contrasting an experienced therapist with trainee therapists' outcome. From "Outcome Assessment: From Conceptualization to Implementation," by M. J. Lambert, J. C. Okiishi, A. E. Finch, and L. Johnson, 1998, *Professional Psychology: Practice and Research, 29,* p. 68. Copyright 1998 by the American Psychological Association.

we found these patients maintained their treatment gains (6 to 24 months later), with early treatment response being a key variable in long-term adjustment rather than number of psychotherapy sessions (Haas, Hill, Lambert, & Morrell, 2002).

Clearly the idea of studying client outcomes in relation to who provides treatment has certain advantages for improving services to clients. It allows clinicians to contrast the outcomes they achieve in their practice with those of other clinicians, information that has heretofore been unavailable. Using such data to improve client care is complicated, but greater transparency in treatment effects will surely provide the opportunity to enhance outcomes and possibly affect theories of change.

In addition to focusing on the therapist's contribution to patient outcome as a means of maximizing outcomes within specific clinical settings, researchers have conducted a variety of other studies. In Chapter 8, examples of published studies are provided. These studies generally had two purposes. The first was to contribute findings to the science of psychotherapy, that is, the accumulating empirical foundations of effective practice (practice-based evidence). The second was for clinical decision making within a particular clinical setting for the purpose of changing practices within that setting—so called outcomes management.

8

USING OUTCOME DATA TO IMPROVE THE EFFECTS OF PSYCHOTHERAPY: SOME ILLUSTRATIONS

Many unpublished reports of outcome and program evaluation exist and guide routine care on a local level. These kinds of studies can reflect the degree of success of many evidence-based treatments reviewed by the National Registry of Evidence-Based Practice (http://www.samsha.gov) and other reviewing bodies such as National Institute for Clinical Excellence and the Cochrane treatment guidelines. From the point of view of clinical administrators, policy makers, and program evaluators, there is a great advantage to having such data when making informed decisions. This kind of information is the primary product of outcomes management and accountability research paradigms, that is, practice-based evidence. In addition to these kinds of studies and quarterly or annual reports comparing different treatment programs across large community or hospital treatment centers, a host of other studies are conducted to answer questions of importance. For example, in Chapter 7 explorations of the therapist's contribution to psychotherapy outcome were provided. Studying outcome on the basis of the individual therapist was incidental to the collection of session-by-session data on client's treatment response and the use of the data for the purpose of directly influencing patient outcome as treatment unfolded.

In this chapter several other findings are highlighted as illustrations of how practical practice problems encountered in a setting of care can be addressed once outcome data have been collected. Data collected through tracking treatment response and deposited in an archive can be used for solving the kinds of questions raised by clinicians and management once problems that need to be addressed are identified. The data analysis is intended to contribute to decisions to change ongoing services or make new policy decisions. Each of the studies reviewed here grew out of the interest of specific clinicians or administrators as the service setting developed a research culture in which the art of psychotherapy was integrated with the science of practice. The first study summarized focused on the issue of the necessity of intake interviews for enhancing patient outcomes (Is intake necessary?). The second study dealt with outcomes for ethnic minorities who sought treatment at the clinic (Are minority clients well served?). The third study investigated the outcome of clients treated as couples (Do individuals fare as well when treated as couples?). A fourth area of investigation involved several studies aimed at estimating how many sessions of psychotherapy are needed to bring about positive change, early dramatic positive treatment response, and what changes when in psychotherapy. Finally data are presented that explored the relationship between satisfaction ratings and outcome ratings in a treatment follow-up investigation. In each instance, research from other studies is provided to put issues of local importance in the context of clinical practice in general.

DOES PROVIDING AN INTAKE INTERVIEW IMPROVE
THE EFFECTS OF PSYCHOTHERAPY?

A common procedure in clinical practice is to begin therapy with an initial evaluation that can guide treatment or referral decisions. No systematic reviews of how frequently mental health workers conduct intake interviews was found in the literature. It seems likely that most psychotherapists conduct intakes at some point in a career. In some settings this practice does not occur, whereas in others it is considered crucial to offering professional services, although just how systematically and consistently it is executed is an open question. Certainly there are no generally agreed upon procedures and methods. In group practices in which many clinicians are available, such a procedure may be used because it presumably maximizes patient outcomes through appropriate matching of therapist expertise with client need. In general, the information obtained through intake is used to determine the best course of treatment and the appropriate therapist to provide it. There is little consensus on the specific form such interviews should take nor specific information about how to refer or assign clients from intake to treating psychotherapists (e.g., Miller, 1999; Robinson, 2000).

Although it is generally assumed that intake interviews increase the likelihood of matching clients with appropriate therapists or treatments, little empirical data has been generated to test this assumption (Beutler et al., 2004). A closely related research question has been examined in medicine under the rubric of continuity of care in which it is generally assumed that continuity in care is a good thing for patients (e.g., Haggerty et al., 2003) In mental health care the same assumption is made, but research has focused almost exclusively on care after release from inpatient psychiatric treatment and continuity during prolonged treatment for chronic mental illness (e.g., Adair et al., 2003) rather than on continuity from intake to treating clinician.

A few studies of this latter kind of discontinuity of care phenomenon (when the care of clients is divided between the person doing intake and the person actually delivering day-to-day services), however, can be found in the literature. Gottheil, Sterling, Weinstein, and Kurtz (1994), for example, studied premature termination (defined as not returning for a third session) with 634 cocaine-dependent individuals who either saw the intake counselor or another therapist for the second session. They reported that there was no reliable difference between the percentage of clients returning for third sessions after meeting with the intake therapist for a second session (86.4%) and clients returning for third sessions after meeting with a therapist different from the intake therapist for a second session (86.6%). The authors had expected significantly higher return rates among clients treated by their intake therapists. Their findings suggest that intake by a person different from the therapist did not appear to be a problem with regard to losing patients.

Wise and Rinn (1983) reported an opposite finding after searching records at their community mental health center. They found that 13 of 100 clients assigned to treatment with their intake therapists terminated prematurely compared with 33 of 100 clients assigned to treating therapists different from their intake therapists. These percentages yield a reliable odds ratio of 3.3, indicating that clients treated by therapists different from their intake therapists were 3.3 times more likely to terminate prematurely than clients treated by intake therapists. Premature termination was defined as leaving therapy before a fourth session. The authors did not report when and how clients were assigned to treating therapists, when and how follow-up appointments were made, or when and how clients learned the identity of their treating therapists.

If the use of intake appointments is to be based on empirical grounds, the policy maker has little empirical evidence on which to base a decision. These two studies that examined intake therapist discontinuity used different premature termination criteria; reported contradictory relationships between intake therapist discontinuity and premature termination; and did not look for relationships between intake therapist discontinuity, outcome, and appointment use. In the context of the clinic where much of the outcome research reported in this book was conducted, the importance of intake to patient outcome was questioned, and in the absence of a clear general answer, an answer based on typical intake procedures that had been used was sought. Nielsen et al. (2009) examined archival data by comparing records at the university counseling center for premature termination, outcome, and appointment use among clients referred by their intake therapists to different treating therapists versus clients retained in therapy by their intake therapists. The Nielsen study went beyond the prior two studies by examining not only premature termination but also amount of change clients reported (outcome) as well as the efficiency of resource use.

Intake therapist discontinuity, premature termination, outcome, and appointment use were examined among 16,377 clients who received 167,165 psychotherapy sessions ($M = 10.2$ sessions; $SD = 15.3$) between June 1996 and December 2005. The Counseling and Career Center (CCC), located in the university's student center, offers free psychotherapy without session limits to the university's full time students. Over the period studied, 50 licensed, professional psychotherapists, including 48 psychologists, 1 marriage and family therapist, and 1 licensed clinical social worker provided treatment, joined by 219 trainees, including 32 psychology residents, 42 predoctoral psychology interns, and 145 doctoral-level psychology students. Participating therapists described preference, training, and certification in many orientations, a majority endorsing a mixture of approaches. A sample of 210,218 records was drawn from the CCC's computerized appointment and record-keeping system: 207,908 (98.9%) of these records were psychotherapy appointments; 167,165 (80.4%) of these were records of appointments kept (i.e., sessions) by the 16,377 clients. Psychotherapy appointment types with results (i.e., kept, cancelled) are presented in Table 8.1. Intake therapist discontinuity can be studied only when it is clear that clients and therapists intended that psychotherapeutic treatment should continue after intake. The scheduling of appointments after intake provides prima facie evidence of intent to continue treatment and 14,360 clients met this criterion by scheduling appointments after intake and were included in the analyses that follow.

The Outcome Questionnaire-45 (OQ-45) was completed by 16,154 clients prior to 100,828 (60.8%) of 167,165 sessions attended. The OQ-45 was completed before intake sessions by 13,299 (92.6%) of the 14,360 clients who scheduled or attended appointments after intake. That is, the OQ-45 was completed by 92.6% of the clients who could have experienced intake therapist discontinuity. An intake and final OQ-45 were completed by 11,114

TABLE 8.1.
Appointment Consumption by Intake Therapist Continuity or Discontinuity

| Type of appointment consumption | Intake therapist continuity versus discontinuity | | | | | | Cohen's d |
| | Kept and treated by intake therapist (N = 6,366) | | Referred by intake therapist (N = 8,027) | | | | |
	M	SD	M	SD	t	p	d
Appointment kept—session	9.87	14.98	11.78	17.99	6.78	.001	.13
Appointment missed— no show	1.01	1.78	1.17	2.08	5.03	.001	.09
Appointment cancelled	.45	.98	.50	1.01	3.16	.002	.05
Appointment rescheduled by client	.68	1.38	.81	1.49	5.56	.001	.09
Appointment rescheduled by therapist	.41	.95	.44	.99	2.52	.012	.03

Note. Multivariate F (5, 14,387) = 12.01, $p < .00001$. Adapted from "Termination, Appointment Use, and Outcome Patterns Associated With Intake Therapist Discontinuity," by S. Nielsen et al., 2009, *Professional Psychology: Research and Practice, 40,* p. 275. Copyright 2009 by the American Psychological Association.

(77.4%) of these 14,360 clients. Students seeking services scheduled intake appointments or received walk-in intake sessions by contacting counseling center reception staff. Clients were asked to complete the OQ-45 prior to intake as well as forms confirming eligibility, providing contact information, affirming consent for treatment and use of data in center research, and describing reasons for seeking treatment. Appointments were made available on the basis of demand, caseload, and case management practices set by staff therapists. Goals for intake set by staff therapists included evaluating symptom seriousness to allow for case triage, determining eligibility for services, matching clients with therapists, and matching client problems with trainee skills, training needs, and interests.

Intake interviews were conducted by professional therapists and by trainees judged qualified by supervisors to conduct intake sessions and make intake disposition decisions. Intake therapists could end contact with intake clients, retain and treat intake clients in psychotherapy, refer intake clients for therapy with other facility therapists, refer intake clients to other center services, assign intake clients to extended assessment, or arrange for treatment elsewhere. Clients who continued in therapy after intake sessions learned the identity of treating therapists by the end of the intake session. Clients and therapists scheduled follow-up appointments after intake sessions; clients scheduled follow-up appointments after regular therapy sessions.

The analyses presented sought to examine associations between intake therapist discontinuity and premature termination as a sign of disrupted therapy. Six analytic steps were followed: (a) An operational definition of intake therapist discontinuity was developed; (b) intake therapist discontinuity was tested against four criteria for premature termination, which provided an index of disruption in early therapeutic process; (c) intake therapist discontinuity was tested against outcome, defined as change in OQ-45 scores, which provided an index of benefit; (d) intake therapist discontinuity was tested against appointment use as an index of cost; (e) the association between appointment use and outcome—that is, the association between costs and benefits—was tested; and (f) contradictory premature termination criteria were reexamined in light of costs and benefits.

Of 16,377 clients completing intake sessions, 2,017 (12.3%) scheduled no further appointments or received services other than therapy. Of the remaining 14,360 clients, 8,025 (55.9%) were referred to and scheduled one or more appointments after intake with therapists other than their intake therapists. Each such referred case was defined as an instance of intake therapist discontinuity. The remaining 6,335 clients (44.1%) scheduled one or more appointments after their intake sessions with their intake therapists. Each such case retained in therapy by an intake therapist was defined as an instance of intake therapist continuity.

Premature Termination

Premature termination research is complicated by an absence of agreed upon criteria (Hatchett & Park, 2003; Wierzbicki & Pekarik, 1993). The two studies that have examined intake therapist discontinuity (Gottheil et al., 1994; Wise & Rinn, 1983) exemplify this problem, setting premature termination criteria of nonreturn after intake (i.e., for a second session), nonreturn before a third session, and nonreturn before a fourth session. On the basis of meta-analysis of 125 studies, Wierzbicki and Pekarik suggested that therapist judgment provides the most valid indicator of premature termination, but therapists at the counseling center do not routinely record judgments about timeliness of terminations, and the size and retrospective nature of the sample made obtaining therapist judgments impossible. Hatchett and Park (2003) followed clients at a university counseling center and found that termination by nonreturn for a scheduled appointment agreed closely with therapist judgments about premature termination, whereas nonreturn after intake and nonreturn for a fourth session (median case length at their counseling center) agreed only modestly with therapist judgments.

Termination by nonreturn for a scheduled appointment was selected as the preferred criterion for premature termination on the basis of these findings. Terminations before a third and before a fourth session were also examined because these criteria were used in the two studies that previously examined intake therapist discontinuity (Gottheil et al., 1994; Wise & Rinn, 1983, respectively). Termination by nonreturn for the appointment scheduled after intake was also evaluated on the basis Garfield's (1994) suggestion that nonreturn after intake reveals a failure to begin therapy. These four criteria were reliably correlated with one another in this sample, yielding positive coefficients ranging from .15 to .75 ($ps < .001$).

Significant effects were present for all four criteria, but though the four criteria were positively correlated with one another, they yield contradictory views of premature termination. Clients referred from intake therapists to different treating therapists were 13% more likely than clients retained by intake therapists to terminate by missing a scheduled appointment. Referred clients were, however, 15.4% less likely than retained clients to terminate by missing the appointment scheduled after intake, 45% less likely than retained clients to terminate prior to a third session, and 41% less likely than retained clients to terminate prior to a fourth session.

To further investigate the apparent contradictions, terminations at Appointments 2 to 6 were examined, that is, terminations at Appointments 1 to 5 after intake. Compared with retained clients, referred clients were more than twice as likely to terminate by missing the appointment scheduled after intake and 25% more likely to terminate by missing Appointment 3 (odds ratio = 1.25). Missed-appointment termination was equally likely for referred and retained clients at Appointments 4, 5, and 6.

Outcome

Intake therapist discontinuity was unrelated to intake and final OQ-45 scores. Retained and referred clients did not differ for reliable change. Referred clients' scores were reliably higher (more disturbance) than retained clients' scores at Sessions 2, 3, and 4 but were statistically indistinguishable from retained clients' scores at Sessions 5 and 6. Percentages of retained and referred clients experiencing reliable change also differed at Sessions 2, 3, and 4. By the beginning of Session 2, 19.5% of referred clients had improved reliably, compared with 24.0% of retained clients. This difference in percentages was significant indicating that referred clients were 23.2% less likely than retained clients to have improved reliably by the beginning of Session 2 and were 16.6% less likely by Session 3 given referral from intake. By Session 4, reliable improvement was 13.1% less likely for referred clients.

Appointment Use

Therapy cost was examined as five nonoverlapping categories of appointment use: (a) appointments kept (i.e., sessions), (b) appointments missed without at least 1 day's prior notice (i.e., no shows), (c) appointments cancelled with proper notice, (d) appointments rescheduled by clients with proper notice, and (e) appointments rescheduled or missed by therapists. Compared with retained clients, referred clients attended more sessions and missed more appointments by no-showing, canceling, and rescheduling. Therapists also rescheduled or missed more appointments with clients who had been referred to them from intake than with clients whom they had retained from the intake sessions they had conducted. Referred clients consumed, on average, 15.08 ($SD = 21.06$) appointments of all kinds compared with 12.79 ($SD = 17.94$) appointments consumed by retained clients, representing 17.9% greater treatment cost for referred than for retained clients. Referring clients from intake to different treating therapists was associated with using more appointments and therefore with greater treatment cost. Treatment cost is important primarily in relation to benefits gained in therapeutic improvement. Clients who report more problems and distress on the OQ-45 at the beginning of therapy used more appointments during therapy. Clients who were still reporting more problems and distress on the OQ-45 at the end of therapy had used more appointments during treatment. The cost incurred in attending more sessions was not, however, correlated with more benefit measured as change in OQ-45 score. From these correlations it appears that discontinuity results in more costs but less benefit.

Summary and Implications

The findings of this archival study have clear implications for practice within the clinic where the study was conducted and in similar clinics that use similar procedures. Clients referred by intake therapists to different treating therapists were more likely than clients retained in treatment by their intake therapists to terminate by missing the two appointments after intake. Referred clients were also less likely to improve by the beginning of the first, second, and third sessions after intake. Referred clients used 17.9% more appointments (sessions and missed appointments) than retained clients. Therapists were also more likely to miss appointments with referred clients than with clients they had retained from the intake sessions they had conducted. Attending extra sessions was not correlated with more improvement, and missing appointments was negatively correlated with improvement.

Haggerty and colleagues (2003) suggested that continuity of care "implies a sense of affiliation between patients and their practitioners . . . often expressed in terms of an implicit contract of loyalty to the patient and clinical responsibility by the provider" (p. 1219). They described three elements of continuity: (a) Informational continuity exists when past events are available to guide current care; (b) management continuity exists when treatment is consistent over time; and (c) relational continuity exists when care givers are consistent over time. Entering psychotherapy through different intake and treating therapists seems a prima facie example of relational discontinuity. Safran, Muran, Samstag, and Stevens (2002) averred, "One of the most consistent findings emerging from psychotherapy research is that the quality of the therapeutic alliance is one of the better predictors of outcome across the range of different treatment modalities" (p. 235). If an alliance begins to form between client and intake therapist, the alliance will certainly be broken by referral or assignment to a different treating therapist. It seems not unlikely that rupture of inchoate alliances formed during intake interviews could impede, delay, or even prevent, through premature terminations, subsequent therapeutic process.

Based on these assumptions it is reasonable to argue that intake therapist discontinuity disrupted early therapeutic process, increasing the likelihood of premature termination, interfering with psychotherapeutic improvement, and leading to longer treatment as clients recovered from the disruption. Following this investigation several options were considered by the clinical staff and researchers. Some argued that therapists may have tended to accurately detect and refer more difficult cases from intake and that referral of more difficult cases would lead to greater premature termination rates, lower early improvement rates, and greater appointment use. However, there was no evidence that referred clients in this clinic were more disturbed than clients who continued treatment with their intake therapist.

Another suggestion was that intake procedures be modified and made more effective. Such a change would necessitate establishing consensus guidelines for intake and referral as well as some means of ensuring guidelines would be uniformly applied. The absence of consensus about best intake practices and the amount of time and expense involved in moving forward with this option did not make it an attractive one in this setting of care because of the large year-to-year turnover in student therapists. It seemed prudent therefore to discontinue intake and referral to other therapists except in rare and well-justified circumstances. This study is an excellent example of using practice-based evidence for enhancing clinical practices; the improved cost–benefit ratio resulted in making treatment at the CCC more efficient and effective for clients and the center.

DOES TREATMENT OUTCOME VARY AS A FUNCTION OF ETHNIC GROUP MEMBERSHIP?

Evidence suggests that ethnic minorities face greater stressors because of lower socioeconomic status, homelessness, unemployment, pressures for acculturation, and encounters with prejudice and discrimination (Hall, Bansal & Lopez, 1999; Smart & Smart, 1995a, 1995b;). The stress experienced by ethnic minorities begs the question of whether current mental health practices are meeting the demands of this population. The U.S. Surgeon General's (2001) *Mental Health: Culture, Race, and Ethnicity—A Supplement to Mental Health: A Report of the Surgeon General* suggests the answer is no, reporting that the mental health care provided to ethnic minority groups is inadequate. The immense diversity of ethnic groups in America is also a problem, with many factors involved such as language, religion, migratory status, internal sense of distinctiveness, and estimates of more than 100 distinct ethnic groups (Thernstrom, Orlov, & Handlin, 1980). Obviously the diversity of ethnic group clients who seek services will surpass the ability of treatment centers to provide therapists who make an appropriate match based on shared ethnicity.

Such practical constraints are among the factors that have given rise to the need for all therapists to be able to provide culturally sensitive services. Professional organizations have responded to changing demographics and heightened awareness of minority's needs by adopting documents such as the American Psychological Association's *Guidelines on Multicultural Education, Training, Research, Practice, and Organizational Change for Psychologists* (American Psychological Association, 2003). But little is known about the effects of such guidelines with regard to treatment outcomes. Within the CCC little was known about minority client outcomes, and it was not clear that minority clients were being well served.

One Clinic's Answer to This Question

Lambert et al. (2006) used existing archival data for the purpose of deciding if expending additional time and resources on training therapists in multicultural sensitivity to improve ethnic minority's treatment outcome would be of value. This was an especially important question for the CCC because of the paucity of minority patients and staff. The simple question asked in the study was, Do ethnic clients seen in the CCC have treatment outcomes that are distinguishable from Caucasian clients? Participants were 952 clients who received treatment for personal concerns at the CCC at Brigham Young University in Provo, Utah. Clients at the CCC present with a wide range of problems from simple homesickness to personality disorders.

The most common diagnoses in the final dataset were mood disorders (36.14%), anxiety disorders (22.11%), and adjustment disorders (16.83%).

Within this database there were 47 African Americans, 197 Asians or Pacific Islanders, 390 Hispanics, and 73 Native Americans. After we excluded those clients who did not have a posttreatment test outcome measure, the groups' compositions were 29, 118, 279, and 50. After ethnic group composition was completed, clients who had indicated they were Caucasian were matched as closely as possible on the basis of intake score, gender, marital status, and age. This resulted in matched groups of different sizes for comparison to Caucasian groups of the same size as their matched ethnic group. Each ethnic group was compared with a different Caucasian group, which was randomly selected except for the matching variables. This procedure maximized the likelihood that any differences in treatment outcome between an ethnic and comparison group would not be due to differences in pretreatment level of disturbance.

If those who had only an intake score are considered dropouts, the dropout rates were as follows: African American (38%), Asian or Pacific Islander (40%), Hispanic (28%), and Native American (32%). In comparison, the dropout rate across the entire Caucasian sample was 37%. Dropout rate differences were tested using chi-square analysis, with the only statistically significant difference being the lower dropout rate for the Hispanic group.

Table 8.2 presents the means and standard deviations of clients at intake and posttreatment testing along with the mean change score, t, p, and d values. As can be seen, the intake scores for matched groups were practically identical (as were other demographic variables). These results reflect the fact that there were a large number of Caucasian clients (approximately 11,000) from which to find a match with the ethnic group member.

As can be noted by examining the t values in Table 8.2, no statistically significant differences were found between any ethnic group and their matched Caucasian control. The effect sizes of the between-groups comparisons were very small, ranging from a high of −.19 (favoring Native Americans over matched controls) to a low of .003 (in the contrast between Hispanics and controls). For the most part, these effect sizes are close to zero and in two comparisons slightly favored Caucasian clients, whereas in two others effect sizes slightly favored minority clients.

Summary and Implications

These results suggested to the researchers that it is unlikely that ethnic group outcomes, at least as they were measured, could be improved by the implementation of multicultural sensitivity training. Minority clients did not appear to be disadvantaged by the treatment they were receiving. If multicultural

TABLE 8.2.
Pretreatment, Posttreatment, and Change Scores for Four Ethnic Groups Compared to Matched Caucasian Controls

Group	Pretreatment OQ-45		Posttreatment OQ-45		OQ-45 change		Significance of difference		
	M	SD	M	SD	M	SD	t	p	d
African American[a]	69.44	22.98	59.86	25.37	−9.58	23.09	.39	0.77	−.06
Caucasian control[a]	69.45	22.93	61.28	24.84	−8.17	22.61			
Asian or Pacific Islander[b]	75.82	23.53	65.85	24.36	−9.96	21.75	.84	0.46	+.08
Caucasian control[b]	75.82	23.21	63.97	23.87	−11.85	24.72			
Hispanic[c]	69.75	24.00	61.66	25.13	−8.09	71.78	.13	0.97	+.003
Caucasian control[c]	69.74	23.85	61.59	23.26	−8.15	21.22			
Native American[d]	76.08	24.26	60.02	28.39	−16.06	26.81	1.28	0.22	−.19
Caucasian control[d]	76.08	23.56	65.04	24.14	−11.04	23.33			

Note. OQ-45 = Outcome Questionnaire-45. In effect size for between-groups comparison, negative number indicates advantage for ethnic group. From "Psychotherapy Outcome, as Measured by the OQ-45, in African American, Asian/Pacific Islander, Latino/a, and Native American Clients, Compared to Matched Caucasian Clients," by M. J. Lambert, D. W. Smart, M. P. Campbell, E. J. Hawkins, C. Harmon, and K. L. Slade, 2006, *Journal of College Student Psychotherapy, 20(4),* p. 24. Copyright 2006 by Haworth Press. Reprinted with permission.
[a]$n = 29$. [b]$n = 118$. [c]$n = 279$. [d]$n = 50$.

sensitivity training were to be undertaken, the archival data would not provide a logical baseline for measuring the effects of such an intervention on ethnic minority clients seen by CCC staff, unless one assumes that such clients (seen by Caucasians) would be likely to have better outcomes than Caucasians being seen by Caucasians. It was concluded that such training might be valuable for a variety of reasons and have measurable benefits on staff knowledge and attitudes but would not appear to hold promise for improving ethnic client outcomes.

A surprising finding in the current study was the generally positive counseling outcomes and average attrition rates for the 50 Native American clients who were seen for multiple sessions. Given the dearth of psychotherapy outcome studies with this ethnic population, coupled with research suggesting that of all the ethnic groups that have been studied in America, Native Americans pose the greatest challenges to traditional treatments (Zane, Hall, Sue, Young, & Nunez, 2004). It was also surprising to see that these clients did relatively well in treatment. In fact, these clients showed the greatest relative benefit of all studied groups, including Caucasians. Unfortunately, because of the archival nature of the database, it was not possible to provide a better description of these clients. Such information would have been helpful because Native Americans are an incredibly diverse group with some 200 different languages used by different tribes and their members. These Native Americans came from a variety of settings, including living on reservations when they were not attending school, but had found their way into a private university with competitive admission standards.

It is obvious from this study that the collection of data and an accessible archive of such data allowed the clinical staff to evaluate the effects of their interventions with an important minority of their clientele. An unresolved question was the degree to which minority clients entered treatment at the same rate as nonminorities. The data did suggest that if they came to the center and attended an intake they were just as likely to continue with treatment as majority clients. Beyond the implications of these findings for the treatment setting in which they were collected are the implications they have for outcomes across settings. At least within university student populations the results are similar to past findings—ethnic clients who do not drop out of therapy respond to treatments as well as other clients. Some similarities between the findings reported here and those reported by Ozgur, Rude, & Baron (2003) who also studied university student clients (but who saw either ethnically similar or dissimilar therapists), suggest the results may generalize to other university counseling centers and beyond the cultural bounds of a private religious university.

Several limitations to these findings should be mentioned. First, the data were archival, and the study was not prospective. This resulted in our inability to look in-depth at important topics. We were not able to fully describe the background of therapists or measure their degree of sensitivity or training experiences related to ethnic minorities. We had no way of categorizing degree of acculturation in clients and could not analyze outcome on the basis of this important variable. We also did not have any socioeconomic data, precluding study and description of participants in a way that would help us understand more about the populations to which the results could be generalized. This study provides a good example of evidence-based practice that aims at testing the boundaries of effective treatment within a particular treatment setting. Had ethnic minority clients fared worse than their majority counterparts, steps could have been taken to address this problem.

DO INDIVIDUALS HAVE BETTER OUTCOMES WHEN SEEN AS A COUPLE OR AS INDIVIDUALS?

In the following study, another clinical issue is examined that was raised by the clinical staff following discussions of referring clients for couple treatment or for individual treatment. The center had therapists who preferred treating individuals with their partners and those who did not. The debate that ensued was based on theoretical orientation and therapist personal preferences with no real knowledge of the way such choices maximized treatment outcome for the individual patient. An analysis of archival data provided a first step in informing decision making on the basis of the consequences of past decisions and provided some surprising findings.

Sexton, Alexander, and Mease (2004) in their large-scale review of the effects of couple therapy on psychological disorders noted that much more research is needed in this area because most published research on couple therapy has examined marital adjustment rather than changes in psychological disorders. Despite the need for more research on the effects of couple therapy on psychological disorders, studies comparing individual versus couple therapy routinely fail to find superior outcomes for either treatment (e.g., Emanuels-Zuurveen & Emmelkamp, 1996). Such research commonly focuses on a single disorder (e.g., depression) and is performed as a clinical trial searching for the main effect of a type of treatment rather than examining interactions between client variables and treatments.

Research that attempts to examine the role of moderators and mediators on couple therapy outcome is even rarer, despite the fact that identification of such variables could have important implications for practice (Sexton et al., 2004). Existing research in this area has generally focused on client variables such as level of marital distress (Snyder, Mangrum, & Wills, 1993), or partner communication variables (Halford, Sanders, & Behrens, 1993). The examination of moderator variables in studies examining outcome of couple interventions on treatments of psychological disorders has seldom examined level of patient's psychological distress and linked such data to assignment of patients to couple or individual therapy.

The results of such research could be readily applied in routine care and have positive consequences on patient outcomes. Referral to a treatment modality is often made early in the treatment process and is likely to be based on clinician theoretical orientation rather than treatment outcome data. In addition, degree of patient disturbance has been shown to be a strong predictor of both the amount of change clients experience while in treatment and the number of sessions required for returning to a normal state of functioning (Anderson & Lambert, 2001). Further, degree of disturbance is easy to assess and apply in routine practice prior to decision making about treatments that are most likely to be successful.

Isakson et al. (2006) conducted a retrospective case control study to compare the effect of individual versus couple therapy on clients being seen in the CCC in which the majority of clients were seen in individual psychotherapy, but a minority were referred to or offered couple therapy. This allowed for a comparison of outcomes between married individuals who were seen in either of these treatment modalities. More importantly, an attempt was made to see if post hoc evidence could be found for matching clients on the basis of their initial level of disturbance with the best intervention modality: individual or couple therapy.

Participants were 235 married clients, 190 of whom (95 couples) were seen conjointly and 45 of whom were seen individually at the CCC. The procedure for inclusion of clients from the archival data was based on selecting all clients over a 6-year period who could be identified as having undergone therapy with their partner and who had at least an intake score on the outcome measure and a second score before they left treatment.

The 95 couples who were seen conjointly were subdivided into groups on the basis of their initial scores on the OQ-45. The Jacobson and Truax (1991) cutoffs for being either functional (nonclinical) or dysfunctional (clinical) were applied to each individual's intake score and resulted in four distinct groups: both partners in the clinical range ($n = 25$); both partners in the nonclinical range ($n = 25$); man in the clinical range, woman in the nonclinical range (n 24); woman in the clinical range, man in the nonclinical range ($n = 21$). The outcome of therapy for these latter two groups was contrasted with the outcome of 24 married male students who were clinically disturbed and 21 clinically disturbed female married students who were seen in individual psychotherapy. Clients in these latter groups began treatment in the dysfunctional range and were matched to the appropriate contrast group on the basis of their degree of initial disturbance. The selection of these clients allowed us to examine the degree to which clients whose initial level of disturbance was in the clinical range had similar outcomes when seen in individual therapy versus couple therapy.

An additional sample of 1,445 clients (benchmark group) seen in individual psychotherapy was also drawn from the archival database and used as a benchmark for the effects of individual psychotherapy at the clinic. This allowed for a rough comparison of couple therapy with that found in individual therapy across a broad sample of clients. The most common diagnoses were similar to those presented in the earlier studies undertaken at the CCC as were demographic variables related to the clients and therapists. The therapists provided therapy to both couples and individual therapy recipients. Over the years data were collected, approximately 10 therapists espoused a preference for seeing couples when possible, but no records were kept indicating which therapists had seen couples.

Therapists made judgments at intake to refer for couple therapy on the basis of information suggesting the marital relationship was an important aspect of the presenting problem. No records of clinical decision making leading to a referral to couple therapy were kept, and no systematic procedures to guide referrals were used as a matter of policy.

The archival data available for the Isakson et al. (2006) study allowed us to address the following questions: (a) Do clients treated conjointly as a couple have outcomes that are equivalent to clients (benchmark group) not seen in couple therapy? (b) Do clients who were categorized into one of the four groups on the basis of their level of disturbance at intake have different treatment outcomes (i.e., is there an interaction between initial level of disturbance within couples and treatment outcome?)? (c) Do married clients who begin treatment in the clinical range but who are seen in individual therapy have treatment outcomes that are equivalent to individuals seen in couple treatment? The lack of random assignment to treatment modality undermined our ability to make causal conclusions from the analysis.

The average pretreatment to posttreatment change score for the 1,445 clients in the benchmark group was −12.06, which is a statistically significant improvement ($d = 1.22$). The average change for clients who entered treatment in the nonclinical range (i.e., OQ-45, 63 or less) was −5.18 ($d = .21$). The average change for clients who entered treatment in the clinical range was −15.77 ($d = 1.54$). These results suggest that although clients are, on average, significantly improved at the time they leave treatment, a substantial amount of this gain is found within those clients who begin treatment with clinical levels of disturbance. In short, if a client does not report clinical levels of disturbance prior to therapy, there is a diminished likelihood of reporting significant improvement by the time he or she leaves treatment.

This general finding appears very similar for patients who underwent couple therapy. The average change for all clients included in the couples analysis ($n = 190$) was −7.15 ($d = .29$). The average change for clients who entered treatment in the nonclinical range was −1.80 ($d = .10$). The average change for clients who entered therapy in the clinical range was −12.50 ($d = .70$). None of the differences between benchmark clients receiving individual therapy versus all clients undergoing couple therapy reached statistical significance, suggesting that the observed differences in this comparison were not reliable and do not support differential effectiveness of the modalities.

Outcome

The results indicated that when both partners were in the clinical range, both showed statistically significant improvement from pretreatment to posttreatment testing (men, $d = 0.54$; women, $d = 0.66$). When neither partner was in the clinical range, women showed statistically significant improvement ($d = 0.50$), whereas men did not ($d = 0.01$). In addition, when the man was in the clinical range and the woman was not, then the man showed statistically significant improvement that was quite dramatic ($d = 1.09$). The opposite did not appear to be true; when the female client started treatment in the clinical range and the male client did not, the female client did not show statistically significant improvement ($d = 0.49$). It was also apparent that women improved about the same amount regardless of their state at the beginning of treatment unless they were in treatment with a partner who was not clinically disturbed. Men fared best when their female partner was not clinically disturbed.

Because of the differential findings for gender, initial severity, and outcome outlined previously, a comparison of married individuals receiving couples therapy and married individuals receiving individual therapy was conducted. In this separate analysis the 24 men who underwent couple therapy and who began treatment in the clinical range were compared with 24 randomly selected men undergoing individual therapy who were married and had initial OQ-45 scores in the clinical range. The 21 women who had received couple therapy were matched with 21 married women who had undergone individual therapy based on the same selection criterion. Partner OQ-45 scores for these matched clients were unknown because they never entered treatment.

Results indicated that there was not a statistically significant outcome difference between distressed married men in couple therapy and the distressed married men in individual therapy ($d = 0.30$). The couples' sample OQ-45 scores decreased (i.e., improved) by 20 OQ-45 points, and the matched male individual sample decreased by an average of −15 OQ-45 points. For distressed women, however, results indicated significantly greater improvement for married women who underwent individual therapy as compared with married women who underwent couple therapy. Although distressed women in couple therapy improved somewhat (i.e., decreased by −8.33 points), similarly distressed women in individual therapy improved by −22.39 points. This difference reached statistical significance ($d = 0.65$). The general outcome findings for couples' treatment outcome are illustrated in Figure 8.1.

Session Data

The amount of therapy received by clients was examined to see if differences in outcome might be related to the number of sessions clients were in treatment. Results indicated that when both partners entered couple therapy in the clinical range, they receive an average of 7.2 sessions, whereas an average of 3.3 sessions was attended by couple therapy clients when both partners entered treatment in the nonclinical range. This finding is consistent with expectations because more distressed individuals typically attend more sessions than less distressed individuals. When the man entered treatment in the clinical range and the woman did not, the couple received an average of 6.9 sessions. When the woman entered treatment in the clinical range and the man did not, an average of 4.3 sessions was completed.

In contrast with the matched sample of distressed men in individual therapy, distressed men in couple therapy achieved 5 points more change (on

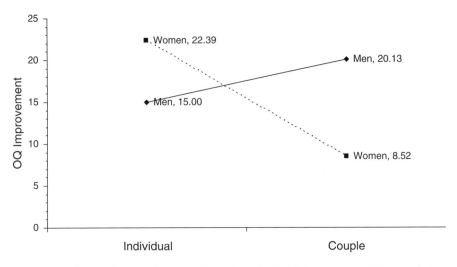

Comparison of OQ Improvement for Married Men and Women
Treated in Individual and Couple Therapy

Figure 8.1. Comparison of Outcome Questionnaire (OQ) improvement for married men and women treated in couple and individual psychotherapy. From "Assessing Couple Therapy as a Treatment for Individual Distress: When Is Referral Contraindicated?" by R. L. Isakson, E. J. Hawkins, J. S. Martinez, C. Harmon, K. Slade, and M. J. Lambert, 2006, *Contemporary Family Therapy, 28,* p. 318. Copyright 2006 by Springer. Reprinted with permission.

average) in approximately two fewer sessions. The converse was true for distressed women in couple therapy as compared with their matched sample counterparts in individual therapy. Women in individual therapy achieved approximately 14 OQ-45 points more change (i.e., improvement) but received an additional two sessions in relation to their matched counterparts. These results suggest that couple therapy provided the most effective and efficient method for eliciting change in distressed men who were married to nondistressed partners, whereas individual therapy appeared to be most beneficial for distressed women whose partners' distress level was unknown.

Summary and Implications

Results indicated that, on average, those entering couple therapy were less distressed than the benchmark sample, but once these differences were adjusted for, both therapy modalities were equally effective for reducing symptomatic distress, including symptoms of anxiety and depression. This finding is consistent with published literature on the topic (Sexton et al., 2004). In an attempt to examine the hypothesis that matching treatment modality on the basis of initial levels of psychological distress could help in determining when a referral to couple therapy would be indicated, an unexpected interaction was discovered. The interaction effect suggested that when clinically disturbed men are seen in couple therapy, the degree of disturbance experienced by their wives had little relationship to the gains they made in treatment. Male patients seemed to benefit in couple and individual therapy, albeit more rapidly when seen with their partner. In contrast, when a woman entered couple therapy in the clinical range and her male partner did not, she had a poor outcome relative to married women seen in individual therapy and women seen in couple treatment when both partners were equally disturbed.

It is unclear why such an interaction might occur (such that a non-disturbed woman may be more helpful to her disturbed partner than a non-disturbed man is to his clinically disturbed partner). Such an interaction may make sense in light of research documenting differences in the way men and women enter treatment. Women show some tendency to identify relationship problems, seek couple therapy, and then encourage men to attend at a greater frequency than the reverse (Doss, Atkins, & Christensen, 2003). It has also been suggested that women are socialized to feel more attuned to relationship issues and to feel more obligation to make a relationship work than men (Acitelli, 1992; Wamboldt & Reiss, 1989).

The findings on number of sessions attended may prove to be important in explaining the interaction effects found in the outcome data. It appears that the relatively poor outcome for clinically disturbed women (whose partners are not clinically disturbed) may be due to undergoing less treatment than would be expected (4.3 sessions vs. 6.9 for males and 7.2 when both are clinically disturbed), given their initial level of clinical disturbance. However, it should be noted that female clients in this circumstance average improvement per session was also relatively poor. In couple therapy, clinically disturbed female clients were seen for only 4.3 sessions and improved an average of 2 OQ-45 points per session, whereas in individual therapy, they were seen for 6.5 sessions and improved at a rate of 3.5 points per session. In contrast, clinically disturbed men were seen for an average of 6.9 sessions in couple therapy (changing at an average rate of about 3 points per session), whereas in individual therapy they were seen for 9.2 sessions and changed at a rate of only 1.63 points per session. These latter data argue for the greater efficiency of couple therapy for clinically disturbed male clients. Were these findings replicated in a prospective study in which the level of functioning of both members of a couple was assessed before initiating treatment, it would make sense to refer women to individual therapy if their partners are not also scoring within clinical levels of disturbance and to refer male patients to couple treatment if they have partners.

Before confidence can be shown in the results, they need to be replicated across settings, theoretical orientations, and with a research design that calls for random assignment of clients into individual or couple therapy on the basis of the four pretherapy disturbance classifications. Such research would also need to assess the level of disturbance in nontreated spouses at all assessment points, a practical problem that may be possible in formal research but impossible in routine care. The failure to know what levels of clinical disturbance were being experienced by partners of clients who received individual therapy in the current study makes interpretation of the results problematic. Obviously conducting a prospective study with so many patient groups and two treatment modalities would be a major undertaking. But such research would go a long way toward understanding the current findings. In the absence of such prospective research, the CCC was reluctant to change criteria for referring clients to couple versus individual therapy but agreed to monitor outcomes and treatment length using partner level of disturbance indicators and to revisit the issue of maximizing treatment effects on the basis of discrepancies between partner intake scores on the OQ-45 and matching clients with the ideal treatment modality.

Another important policy decision that was under review in the CCC was the issue of setting session limits. Rather than "arbitrarily" setting session limits, a review of empirical findings on this topic was undertaken to establish the consequences on patient outcome of setting different limits. Considerable research exists on this topic from a variety of routine treatment settings that monitor patient treatment response. The following section considers information from a number of studies, with some data coming from the CCC.

TREATMENT LENGTH AND TREATMENT OUTCOME

The amount of psychotherapy necessary to bring about positive outcomes has been a concern for decades and remains a topic of serious debate (Lambert, Bergin, & Garfield, 2004). Early concerns about excessively long, mainly psychodynamic therapy resulted in rejections of this form of care in the community mental health movement that emerged in the 1950s and 1960s because long treatment lengths were associated with unacceptably long waiting lists (Lambert, Bergin, & Garfield, 2004). This was more of a concern than the actual efficacy of treatment—long-term therapy was not viewed as practical. This is not to say that the serious challenges to the efficacy of psychodynamic and psychoanalytic therapy did not have an impact but that concerns about efficacy took a back seat to the need to make treatments available to the masses following World War II.

In response to such concerns, traditional long-term psychodynamic treatments were shortened, with numerous planned short-term therapies (25 or fewer sessions) being developed and advocated in the 1960s. More recent concern about treatment length has been associated with managing skyrocketing medical costs and is based on the assumption that positive outcomes can be achieved with few sessions (and even a single session). The usual method of cutting costs in the United States was to limit treatment to 4 to 8 sessions, providing standard limits for all patients. Such session limits have been and are advocated by managed behavioral health organizations in an effort to sell their "insurance product" to the various corporations that share the costs of employee and dependent mental health services. But even outside of insurance company policies, agencies and government entities have tended to ration services, typically in the absence of sound empirical findings. For example, data from the directors of counseling centers at 73 U.S. colleges and universities show that more than one half of such centers have a self-imposed session limit of 10 sessions (Stone & McMichael, 1996).

As is be shown here, limiting psychotherapy to this number of sessions is likely to be appropriate for fewer than one half of the clients who seek treatment, even when the least rigorous criterion, reliable improvement, is used to define a positive treatment response. It is also clear that reimbursement policies that limit psychotherapy to 4, 8, 10, or even more sessions is particularly disadvantageous to the most disturbed clients whose time to recovery is slower and who are most at risk for personal failures, self-harm, and hospitalization. It makes little sense to underserve individuals whose "burden of illness" is the greatest while appropriately caring for individuals who carry much less pain. The analogy for such inhumane decisions would be to triage people with minor injuries to get immediate care while leaving those who are near to death in the waiting room. It can also be noted here that many organizations that claim to be delivering evidence-based services ignore the fact that most outcome studies that have supplied the evidence (clinical trials) are based on treatment lengths that hover around 14 sessions (Hansen, Lambert, & Forman, 2003), not 4, 8, or 10 sessions.

Even a casual observation of the diversity of policies and practices concerning treatment length across the world immediately suggests that session limits are so varied that they cannot be based on empirical findings. The failure to use empirical data on patient treatment response to shape important policy decisions concerning treatment length appears irrational. Although it undoubtedly makes most sense to terminate treatments when the client has recovered rather than basing such decisions on theoretical or cost considerations, treatment response has rarely played a significant role in policy and practice within institutions that provide services.

Much can be learned from examining client treatment response over time. An empirical answer to the important question—How much therapy is enough?—can be approximated from such data.

Unfortunately, older empirical data have not been particularly clear on this issue. For example, of the 156 findings published from 1950 to 1992 on this topic, 100 indicated a positive relationship between therapy duration and outcome, and 6 indicated a negative relationship (Orlinsky, Grawe, & Parks, 1994). This correlational evidence is often used to support the general clinical belief and common sense view that longer term therapies (over 1 year) provide more benefit than short-term therapies. Unfortunately, the actual size of the overwhelming number of positive correlations between treatment dosage and outcome is quite small ($r < .15$), albeit statistically significant. Correlations of this size support a conclusion that treatment length is relatively unimportant to positive patient outcome just as easily as more therapy is better than less. Furthermore, correlating the number of sessions patients receive with eventual treatment outcome does not prove to be very informative for establishing policies for setting session limits.

Going beyond mere correlations, Howard, Kopta, Krause, Merton, and Orlinsky (1986) made an early attempt to address the question, How many sessions are required to produce meaningful change? and suggested that 50% of patients derive such a benefit by the 9th session and that the dose effect of psychotherapy could best be characterized as "negatively accelerating," a finding that is usually interpreted as indicating that each successive session of therapy has less impact on a patient's well-being because the slope of improvement over sessions of treatment is steep early on but flattens over time. Following the lead of these researchers in our research program, we addressed the issue of *dosage* in an attempt to shed further light on the relationship between number of sessions received and patient benefit, with the advantage that we used a standard definition of positive outcome and session-by-session data rather than statistical modeling based on pretreatment–posttreatment data, as Howard et al. (1986) did.

Survival Analysis

Using data ($N > 6,000$ patients) from a variety of clinical samples from across the United States that received routine clinical care (ranging from employee assistance programs to community mental health centers), we have at the time of this writing published five studies that estimate the dose–effect relationship (Anderson & Lambert, 2001; Hansen & Lambert, 2003; Kadera, Lambert, & Andrews, 1996; Snell, Mallinckrodt, & Lambert, 2001; Wolgast, Lambert, & Puschner, 2003). In each of these studies patients rated their functioning at each session of treatment on the OQ-45. Our standard definitions of reliable and clinically significant change were used as dependent variables (the binomial event of interest required for survival statistics), and the Kaplan–Meier survival analysis statistic (or related techniques) was used to provide a population estimate of the distribution model of sessions needed to reach the event of interest (normal functioning and reliable improvement) from the samples of treated individuals. In the largest study, Hansen and Lambert (2003) estimated the number of sessions needed for clinically significant change across treatment settings and levels of initial disturbance. The estimated speed of recovery is dependent on both setting of care and degree of disturbance. For example, in the employee assistance program 13 to 18 sessions of treatment were needed for 50% of clients to reach recovery (with 95% confidence), whereas 17 to 20 sessions were needed within community mental health centers. Survival curves for setting of care are illustrated in Figure 8.2. The number of sessions needed for 50% of patients to reach criteria was about 15 to 19 sessions.

These data provide one important source of information for policy decisions that limit the amount of psychotherapy a patient may receive and allow government agencies, insurance companies, employers, clinics, and consumers to understand the possible consequences of such policies. The findings suggest that limiting treatment to four sessions (a common practice) will result in insufficient treatment for the vast majority of patients. Even policy decisions that permit more than twice this number of treatments cannot be justified as a proper dosage on the basis of empirical findings.

It is also worth noting that the estimated time to recovery for patients in routine care produces recovery estimates that are similar to actual clinically significant outcomes for patients treated in randomized clinical trials (50% in 14 sessions; Hansen et al., 2003); but the actual clinically significant outcome (rather than modeled outcome) of patients in routine care is closer to 30% with an average dosage around 4 sessions (see Table 1.1). These data suggest the need for providers and service managers to give high priority to keeping patients in treatment longer, rather than setting session limits. In college counseling centers around 90% of patients have terminated treatment by the 15th session (Nielsen & Lambert, 2006; Wolgast et al., 2003) with the remaining 10% of clients using 30% to 40% of the total sessions delivered. Survival curves also show the same tendency to flatten as the number of sessions goes up, with few patients meeting criteria for reliable change and clinically significant change at subsequent sessions following the 25th session, 6 months of weekly treatment. We interpret such data as indicating that if a general session limit is set it would be more reasonable to think in terms of 20 to 25 sessions for most patients to have a measured benefit, depending on initial severity or treatment setting (which typically reflects patient severity as well).

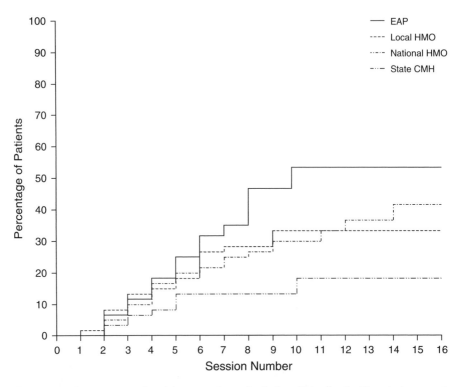

Figure 8.2. Percentage of patients meeting criteria for clinically significant change at four distinct treatment sites. EAP = employee assistance program; local HMO = local health maintenance organization; national HMO = national health maintenance organization; and state CMH = state community mental health center. From "An Evaluation of the Dose–Response Relationship in Naturalistic Treatment Settings Using Survival Analysis," by N. B. Hansen and M. J. Lambert, 2003, *Mental Health Services Research, 5,* p. 9. Copyright 2003 by Springer. Reprinted with permission.

Although setting general session limits has great advantages for managing costs and managing the delivery of services, it is not to the advantage of most patients (if limits are set at 20 or fewer) and diminishes the overall value of services (that are appropriately funded), especially for the most disturbed patients. Our data suggest that the highest quality of care will be provided by monitoring each client's treatment response and making treatment length a function of treatment response and mental health status, rather than arbitrary or theory-driven limits. Limiting treatment in accordance with treatment response requires frequent assessment of patient well-being, with termination instigated only when it becomes clear that no further progress can be expected if a patient continues to receive the same treatment, a difficult clinical decision and one that cannot be appropriately made in the absence of patient input. Many would regard termination of treatment for those who continue to suffer high degrees of distress to reflect a degree of inhumanity that should not be a part of mental health services.

What Changes, When?

It is possible that different aspects of individuals change at different rates and that fine tuning our examination of change over time may reveal order and predictability in the process. Original work in this area has been referred to as the "phase model of psychotherapy" first reported by Howard, Lueger, Maling, and Martinovich (1993). The phase model of *what* changes *when* posits that the client goes through three stages of treatment response during the course of therapy, with each stage occurring in a set sequence. The theory proposes that progressive movement occurs through the stages of (a) improvement in subjectively experienced well-being (remoralization), (b) reduction in symptomatology (remediation), and (c) enhancement in life functioning (rehabilitation). These latter two types of change can be seen as reflecting changes that traditionally fall in the domain of personality functioning, in contrast to remoralization, which is associated with a feeling state—renewed hope.

Presumably patients enter treatment in a state of demoralization in which they are conscious of having failed to meet their own expectations or those of others or of being unable to cope with some pressing problem. They feel powerless to change the situation by themselves and cannot extricate themselves from their predicament (Frank & Frank, 1993). The general characteristic of this phase seems to be the client's feelings of subjective discomfort, such as hopelessness or powerlessness. The therapist's ability to provide the client with hope that he or she can be helped seems particularly important at this stage.

Following the remoralization phase (immediate stress lessens), the client moves into the remediation phase. This term corresponds to the *middle* phase of a psychotherapy that lasts about a year (according to the phase model), with many patients never entering this phase. The phase model posits that this stage of therapy is focused on assisting the client in resolving his or her psychopathological symptoms, life problems, or both. Treatment at this stage would likely consist of facilitating mobilization of a patient's coping skills and/or helping the client to change personality-based (i.e., automatic, habitual) but ineffective coping skills. The theory suggests that some clients will come to the conclusion that the problems they have been experiencing have been encountered repetitively in their lives. Examples might include instability in jobs and problematic relationships. At this point the person may continue in therapy, thereby entering the rehabilitation phase of therapy in which he or she strives to unlearn longstanding maladaptive habits and beliefs and to replace these with a reorganized life view.

The focus in this phase seems to be on restructuring personality to enhance general life functioning. Clients who enter this phase will likely be different from one another in the amount of time required to achieve these rehabilitative goals. This is attributable to differential levels in variables such as the extent, intensity, and duration of the problems each client deals with. The amount of therapy expected to lead to gains for the client in each of the domains was not specified by Howard and colleagues (1993), but it appears that they imagined a therapy that goes on beyond 6 months, a rarity in today's world.

A number of studies have been reported providing some support for the phase model (e.g., Barkham, et al., 1996; Hilsenroth, Ackerman, & Blagys, 2001; Kopta, Howard, Lowry, & Beutler, 1994). Howard et al. (1993) described a study that tested the hypothesis that improvement in one phase temporally precedes improvement in another phase. Findings indicated that if a client had not experienced improvement in the area of demoralization, he or she was unlikely to have experienced remediation. Likewise, if improvement in remediation was minimal, the client was unlikely to have experienced improvement in life functioning. These analyses vaguely confirmed the authors' hypothesis; however, many clients in the Howard et al. study did not follow this pattern.

In our own investigation of this phenomenon (Catanni-Thompson, Lambert, & Boroto, 1996), we examined treatment as usual in an employee assistance program that offered one to eight sessions of psychotherapy. The outcome assessment was based on the OQ-45. The data collected included 1,757 clients who received therapy through a national employee assistance program under the direction of a national managed care organization. The managed care organization serves a wide range of companies, from smaller regional companies to Fortune 500 companies. All levels of employment, from blue-collar to executive workers were represented. Thus, the sample included workers or their dependants from all over the United States and from all levels of employment. The clients were typically seen at their place of employment. Of the original 1,757 clients, 1,603 met the criteria of having a minimum of three treatment sessions. An additional 874 clients were eliminated from the analysis because their initial score was below the cutoff demarcating the point at which a score is likely to reflect dysfunction (i.e., they were functioning at a level more typical of nonpatients than patients). Therefore, 729 clients who began therapy in the dysfunctional range were included in the study. One half the clients had an adjustment disorder, and about one third had mood or anxiety disorders. The typical therapists in this setting were master's level licensed mental health professionals, though in some states bachelor-level counselors were permitted to do certain types of counseling (e.g., chemical dependency treatment). Therapists provided services at the client's work site. The patients were tracked over a maximum of eight sessions, with termination occurring at the discretion of the client (or occasionally the therapist). The mean number of OQ-45s administered to each client was 4.2.

Clinically meaningful change in the domain of symptom distress (SD; mainly symptoms of anxiety, depression, and somatic anxiety) indicated 43% of the sample were improved by Session 8; approximately 18% met improvement criteria in the interpersonal relations domain (IR); and 26% of the clients showed improvement in the domain of social role functioning (SR). With regard to the temporal sequence of change, clinically significant change in SD was related to clinically significant change in IR as well as to clinically significant change in SR at Sessions 2, 5, and 8. Although these data are not sufficient to conclude that a causal relationship exists between change in SD and the domains of IR and SR, visual inspection of the data showed that improvement in the areas of *functioning* (IR or SR) is unlikely unless improvement in SD has been achieved. This pattern appeared to become more pronounced over time, with Session 8 showing the fewest individuals improved on IR or SR while unimproved on SD. The items of the OQ-45 measure different aspects of client functioning and change at different rates—some areas are more easily affected than others. But there is a low probability that change in psychotherapy is as empirically predictable and smooth as a phase model implies.

Nevertheless, our investigations of differential change in aspects of client functioning suggested that with relatively short doses of therapy intrapsychic pain yields most quickly followed by changes in work-related performance, followed by changes in interpersonal functioning, which seem to require more sessions of psychotherapy (see Figure 8.3). An important implication for practice is that people are multifaceted, and the change process is complex but has an underlying orderly progression of improvement in some patients. Patterns of improvement can be assessed to see the degree to which they conform to the usual and, more importantly, the degree to which they do not conform. If interpersonal relations are a significant aspect of the presenting concern of the patient, mental health treatment centers can expect to expend more sessions to significantly affect functioning in this area.

The Related Topic of Early Dramatic Treatment Response

Some investigations related to patterns of change over sessions of psychotherapy have been undertaken independently of survival analysis and the phase model, and these investigations have additional relevance for the practice of psychotherapy. Much of this research, like that on the phase model of treatment and survival curves, is borrowed from drug metaphors. In pharmacological research, a drug is deemed therapeutic when it induces an effect that differs from a placebo. In this regard, what often distinguishes an active drug

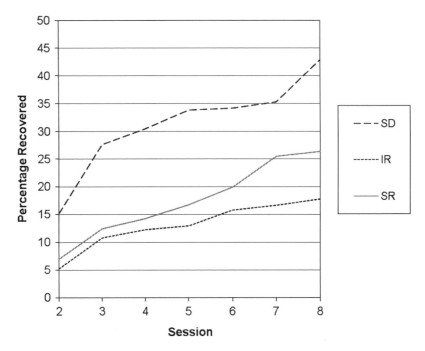

Figure 8.3. Dose–effect relations for symptom domains: Percentage of clients recovered at each session. Note: SD = symptom distress; IR = interpersonal relations; SR = social role performance. From *An Overview of Longitudinal Data Analysis Methodologies Applied to the Dose Response Relationships in Psychotherapy Outcome Research,* 1999, p. 343, by N. B. Hansen. Copyright 2000 by Nathan Hansen. Reprinted with permission of the author.

agent from a placebo effect is timing of response. Thus both the short-term effects as well as the course of drug action are important indicators of efficacy. An early response can mean a premature change in symptomatology due to the act of taking a drug being prescribed by a doctor (e.g., client expectancy) rather than the action of the drug on the patient's biology. This "placebo" response has been linked to poorer long-term outcomes, particularly relapse during follow-up of patients treated with antidepressant medications. Several studies have investigated this possibility and support the contention that a "premature" drug response (one that occurs before a therapeutic dose has been administered) foretells poor long-term therapeutic outcomes (e.g., Quitkin, McGrath, Stewart, Taylor, & Klein, 1996).

Few studies have investigated the timing of response in psychotherapy outside the domain of the phase model. Among those studies that have addressed this issue, the apparent finding is that early dramatic (as opposed to delayed or worsening) response to psychotherapy is positively related to better intermediate and long-term outcomes. These findings are the opposite of what has been reported for a drug response. As an example, Fennel and Teasdale (1987) examined patients participating in a trial of cognitive–behavioral therapy for depression. Among those receiving cognitive–behavioral therapy, there was considerable variability with respect to the amount of treatment received, their initial response, and final treatment outcome. Early responders appeared to engage in therapy in a different manner than later responders and had better long-term outcomes following therapy. For example, early responders appeared to proceed from one problem to the next in therapy (a sequential pattern), whereas delayed responders continued to revisit the same therapy topic across sessions. This suggested to the authors that early response to therapy, rather than a transitory placebo effect, may be associated with better negotiation and completion of important therapeutic tasks that are prerequisite to therapy-induced change. This also suggests that early response may be best predicted by client traits rather than the therapist or therapy itself.

Such findings are not unique. For example, Renaud et al. (1998) examined rapid response in adolescents treated for major depressive disorder and found that early responders compared with initial nonresponders showed better outcomes at the end of treatment and after 1-year and 2-year follow-ups. Ilardi and Craighead (1994) examined several studies of cognitive–behavioral treatment for depression. They argued that temporal changes (early rapid response) observed after the first 4 weeks of therapy support the notion that most changes occur before specific techniques have been administered in any relevant dose. The findings in this area are not limited to depression, with similar findings found in addictive disorders, panic, and bulimia nervosa. For example, numerous authors have suggested that early reductions in bingeing and purging are excellent predictors of final treatment response, with early response occurring within the first 4 weeks (five to six sessions) of treatment (e.g., Agras et al., 2000).

Two significant problems in the study of early response to treatment are apparent in the literature. First, there is a lack of agreement regarding how to define early treatment response. Among the various definitions of early response, Fennel and Teasdale (1987) used a median split to determine response rate, whereas others have used a single item from a questionnaire, the extent to which change occurred in clinician's ratings of improvement from one week to the next, determining if the clinician rated the client as having minimal or no psychopathology by the 1st or 2nd week of treatment, improvement of greater than 50% over a prespecified number of sessions, and the like.

An equally important problem is that few studies have actually measured response on a weekly basis, and therefore most studies have been unable to accurately identify the point in time at which a client responded to treatment. Typically studies have relied on reassessment conducted at midtreatment points in clinical trials. Such studies suggest that because the response was measured at the sixth session it occurred at the sixth session, although, in fact, it may have occurred after a single session.

Haas, Hill, Lambert, and Morrell (2002) used a unique method of quantifying early treatment response by using session-by-session self-report ratings of symptomology in relation to expected recovery curves on the basis of the average change of other clients who began treatment at the same level of disturbance (as described in Chapter 4, this volume). This strategy allowed for the creation of a standardized method for determining the timing (session) of treatment response and its size in relation to a typical response at a specific session of care, thereby providing a data-based standard rather than a sample-relative standard of early dramatic response. Data analytic techniques allowed for examination of early dramatic response as both a continuous and a discrete variable aimed at evaluating the clinical significance of change.

Participants were 147 clients who took the OQ-45 at intake prior to each psychotherapy session at the CCC and at a follow-up 6 to 24 months after termination of services. The method of identifying patients who had an early positive response to treatment was based on calculating a difference score between the "expected" and "actual" change for each participant, that is, each individual patient's response to treatment was judged against patients who showed similar levels of initial disturbance (had the same initial score on the OQ-45). Higher average difference scores indicate an early positive response, and negative scores indicate that a given participant responded to treatment more slowly than was expected. Clients in this study were classified into outcome categories at termination and follow-up on the basis of clinical significance criteria (Jacobson & Truax, 1991).

Hierarchical regression procedures controlling for initial severity were used to address the question of whether response rate was predictive of long-term outcomes. The dependent variable in each instance was termination OQ-45 scores. Because it has been shown that the severity of a disorder is related to final outcome as well as rate of response (Taylor & McLean, 1993), the client's intake OQ-45 score was entered first, and as expected, initial OQ-45 scores were highly predictive of termination OQ-45 scores. Results also indicated a significant negative effect for rate of response as measured by difference scores that followed after entry of the intake OQ-45. Thus, clients with faster rates of response to psychotherapy reported lower end-of-treatment OQ-45 scores. In the second hierarchical regression, which used the same format but used OQ-45 scores at follow-up as the dependent variable, an effect for early response and follow-up scores was also found. Clients with faster rates of response reported lower OQ-45 scores at follow-up an average of 1 year post therapy.

An examination of response rate and the clinical outcome categories showed that early dramatic responders were more likely to benefit to a clinically significant degree at both termination and follow-up. These results suggest that participants in the improved and recovered groups evidenced a more rapid response to treatment than participants in the casualty, deteriorated, and no change groups. There were no rapid responders who (at the end of treatment) were categorized as a casualty or deteriorated. In fact, only 16% of the rapid responders made no reliable change by the end of treatment. The remaining 84% were either categorized as improved or recovered. In an analysis of the tendency to maintain gains from termination to follow-up, participants who showed an early dramatic response to psychotherapy maintained their treatment gains following the termination of treatment.

The findings on early dramatic response to psychotherapy shed some light on the failure to find high correlations between number of treatment sessions and outcome; patients seem to depart from routine care close to the time they experience improvement rather than in relation to planned endings. Early departure from psychotherapy is often an indication of a positive response to therapy, whereas staying in treatment for many sessions suggests a failure to respond. To the degree that patients are socialized to need and value long courses of treatment, psychologists can expect the treatment length to reflect preferences on the part of therapists rather than treatment response. Nowhere is this clearer than in longer term therapies that are required of trainees. For example, many clients in psychoanalytic psychotherapy are trainees who do not have significant psychopathology at the beginning or end of the "intervention." In such situations any changes that may be experienced during treatment are not likely to be quantifiable by the methods that are widely used today for measuring psychotherapy outcome. Such practices may make psychotherapy look less effective than it is and certainly less efficient.

At present, the active mechanism linking early response to long-term outcomes is unknown. Whatever the active ingredients are, they appear to work quickly in many cases. The timing of improvements during psychotherapy has theoretical implications beyond placebo explanations for change. If response to therapy precedes introduction of theoretically important techniques, then it is difficult to attribute central importance to these techniques in the healing process. Early responders to psychotherapy may be more resilient, better prepared, more motivated, and thus more receptive to therapeutic influences of any kind. Early response may also indicate a better "fit" between client and therapist and reflect the positive effects of the working alliance, which is stable by the third session of treatment. For example, Krupnick et al. (2000) found that the early relationship ratings made by the client regarding his or her therapist were most predictive of outcome. This finding is notable because the authors encountered this result across treatment modalities, including two distinct psychotherapies as well as antidepressant medication and placebo conditions.

Whatever the mechanism of change, the emerging findings suggest that early dramatic treatment response is relatively common and foretells recovery and maintenance of gains. It is not just a "hello–goodbye" effect (i.e., patients excusing themselves from treatment by intentionally indicating that they are recovered when they are not). It suggests that many of these patients, were their progress monitored, could be discharged from treatment after just a few treatment sessions or, at the very least, that a discussion about the need for further treatment could be initiated. If clinics instigated outcome monitoring and action on the basis of this information, psychotherapy dosage could be optimized and become most cost effective.

Summary

Studying patterns of patient change over time has important implications for understanding the effects of psychotherapy. It is obvious that there is no one-to-one relationship between number of treatment sessions and eventual outcome. Substantial subsets of patients improve dramatically and early to treatment, and these clients tend to maintain their treatment gains long after therapy has ended. In fact, what is measured will have an effect on the dose–response relationship, with some patient problems showing a much slower response than others. Longer treatments do not necessarily produce better results than shorter treatments, but the amount of treatment needed for each patient can be predicted, albeit somewhat inaccurately, and depends mainly on initial level of disturbance. Standards and policies about how much therapy is enough can be based on actual treatment response, and best practices for patient benefit can use data that come from measuring and monitoring treatment response on a case-by-case basis. Impending failure of treatment is not accurately forecast by clinicians but can be forecast by actuarial methods. Systems of care that have an interest in best serving clients can easily make this predictive information available to practitioners.

THE RELATIONSHIP BETWEEN SATISFACTION WITH TREATMENT AND CHANGES IN PATIENT FUNCTIONING

The final topic and study considered in this chapter deal with the relationship between client satisfaction and treatment outcome. This is an important topic because satisfaction ratings are often obtained in treatment settings on a quarterly or yearly basis and serve as a method of evaluating services. Satisfaction ratings seemingly require much less effort to obtain (as they are collected once following treatment) and may be regarded by some as providing information comparable to measuring actual patient improvement. Are these two distinct forms of evidence equivalent and can one be substituted for the other?

Arguably the best know satisfaction survey of psychotherapy was conducted by *Consumer Reports* (CR). In their 1994 annual survey, the publishers and editors of CR magazine asked readers to describe their experiences with seeking help for mental health problems. They concisely summarized their findings.

> The results of a candid, in-depth survey of *Consumer Reports* subscribers—the largest survey ever to query people on mental-health care—provide convincing evidence that therapy can make an important difference. Four thousand of our readers who responded had sought help from a mental-health provider or a family doctor for psychological problems, or had joined a self-help group. The majority were highly satisfied with the care they received. Most had made strides toward resolving the problems that led to treatment, and almost all said life had become more manageable. (CR, 1995, p. 734)

CR's article and Seligman's (1995) elaborated report of CR's findings in the *American Psychologist* generated considerable interest, being cited hundreds of times and generating dozens of written responses both laudatory and critical (e.g., Bloom, 1997).

Nielsen et al. (2004), as noted in Chapter 2, conducted a study in the CCC to provide some empirical information on issues raised by those criticizing the survey and those who conducted the survey. Many of the assertions made were not based on empirical data but were speculative and could be clarified with data from our database. A major question about the study was the accuracy of retrospective views of improvement compared with measured improvement. Are patients' memories of change and actual change concordant? In addition, the degree of relationship between satisfaction and change could be examined.

CR (1995) and Seligman (1995) based the majority of their conclusions, including the paragraph just quoted, on an effectiveness score computed from responses to four items: (a) a 6-point satisfaction rating, (b) a 6-point rating of how much treatment had helped with the main presenting problem, (c) a 5-point retrospective rating of overall emotional state at the beginning of treatment, and (d) a 5-point rating of overall emotional state at the time of the survey. The two 5-point emotion ratings were combined, yielding a 9-point perceived emotional change score. The perceived emotional change score, problem resolution rating, and satisfaction rating were then combined, yielding a total effectiveness score. This 4-item CR effectiveness score (CRES4) was the focus of the Nielsen et al. (2004) study.

Defenders of CR's survey and conclusions (e.g., Howard, Krause, Caburnay, Noel, & Saunders, 2001) focused primarily on the importance of CR's goal of determining the effectiveness of mental health treatment as practiced and delivered in day-to-day treatment settings in contrast to carefully controlled clinical trials. Others who had a positive response were especially keen on the finding that longer length of treatment was associated with greater satisfaction and improvement. Critics noted several flaws that threatened the validity of CR's conclusions: Clearly the CR research design did not allow for causal explanations or generalization to typical treatment populations. Several flaws were germane to the research reported by Nielsen et al. (2004): The CR's survey instrument and therefore CR's conclusions about effectiveness lumped together and likely confused problem resolution, client satisfaction, and symptom change. In addition, CR's use of an unstandardized survey instrument possibly interfered with generalizing from CR's findings to effectiveness research conducted with validated instruments commonly used in treatment research. Another problem was CR's reliance on retrospective ratings, making the results vulnerable to recall biases. These three criticisms are directly relevant to the CRES4.

In the Nielsen et al. (2004) study several issues were examined. Did the CRES4 satisfaction and effectiveness measure correlate with a standardized measure of treatment outcome (the OQ-45)? Do retrospective ratings of initial levels of disturbance provide the same view of disturbance as ratings collected at the beginning of treatment and at follow-up? Because we had archival data for clients when they entered and terminated treatment, we were able to simply collect follow-up data by mailing out the CRES4 and the OQ-45. The follow-up materials sent to participants began with a letter reiterating the purpose of the follow-up survey as explained by telephone when participants were invited to participate. Clients were assured of confidentiality, including the promise that therapists would not be able to identify participants from their responses. The CRES4 and OQ-45 were printed on separate scannable sheets; the CRES4 retrospective ratings were presented first in the packet, then the OQ-45.

Method

Data were gathered from a randomly selected sample of 500 former clients, 3 from 433 who had received psychotherapy at the CCC. Nielsen et al. (2004) were able to contact 376 of these 500 and invite them to complete a follow-up survey; 365 consented and received by mail questionnaires, a preaddressed, stamped return envelope, and a $4.00 cash incentive; 302 completed and returned the surveys. It had been, on average, 29.6 weeks ($SD = 31.1$) since these former clients' final sessions and 55.8 weeks since their intake sessions

$(SD = 27.9)$. They had attended 3,212 sessions ($M = 10.6$ sessions; $SD = 13.6$), with treatment lasting, on average, 40.4 weeks ($SD = 42.1$).

The CRES4 asked the following questions: *Problem solution:* How much did treatment help with the specific problem that led you to come to treatment? *Satisfaction:* Overall, how satisfied were you with your therapist's treatment of your problem? *Pretreatment emotional status:* What was your overall emotional state when you started treatment? *Follow-up emotional status:* What is your overall emotional state at this time? Response options were very poor, I barely manage to deal with things, keyed 0; fairly poor, life is usually pretty tough for me, keyed 1; so-so, I have my ups and downs, keyed 2; quite good, I have no serious complaints, keyed 3; very good, life is pretty much the way I like it, keyed 4.

Results

The average CRES4 score among the former clients was 211.70 ($SD = 36.85$), which was lower than the average CRES4 reported among CR respondents treated by psychologists ($M = 220$, SD not reported; Seligman, 1995). Table 8.3 presents distributions of Nielsen et al.'s (2004) former clients cross-tabulated by CRES4 recall of pretreatment emotional state and CRES4 rating of emotional state at follow-up. Significantly more former clients reported improved emotional states at follow-up (224 of 302, 74.2%) than reported no change (65 of 302, 21.5%) or a more negative emotional state (13 of 302, 4.3%) at follow-up. Proportionally more former clients from the Nielsen

TABLE 8.3
Former Clients Distributed by Their Ratings of Overall Emotional
State at Follow-Up and by Their Recall of Their Overall Pretreatment
Emotional State

What was your overall emotional state when you started counseling?	What was your overall emotional state at this time?					
	0	1	2	3	4	Total
0 (very poor)	5	8	18	24	8	63
1 (fairly poor)	1	10	43	28	24	106
2 (so-so)	3	6	31	36	28	104
3 (quite good)	0	1	2	14	7	24
4 (very good)	0	0	0	0	5	5
Total	9	25	94	102	72	302

Note. From "The *Consumer Reports* Effectiveness Score: What *Did* Consumers Report?" by S. L. Nielsen, D. W. Smart, R. Isakson, V. Worthen, A. T. Gregersen, and M. J. Lambert, 2004, *Journal of Counseling Psychology, 51*, p. 29. Copyright 2004 by the American Psychological Association.

et al. sample recalled feeling emotional distress when they began treatment than did CR respondents: 169 of 302 (55.96%) former clients in the sample reported initial overall emotional states of very poor or fairly poor compared with 1,213 of the 2,900 CR respondents (41.8%) treated by mental health professionals (Seligman, 1995, p. 968).

Proportions of respondents who reported improvement from these distressed emotional states to a rating of so-so or better at follow-up were not reliably different in Nielsen et al.'s sample (86%) and the CR sample (90%). The difference between average recall of overall emotional state at intake and average rating of overall emotional state at follow-up was statistically significant among former clients in the Nielsen et al. sample, rising from an average recall rating of 1.34 at intake ($SD = 0.95$) to an average rating of 2.67 ($SD = 1.02$), an effect size of 2.21.

Because fairly poor was keyed 1, so-so was keyed 2, and quite good was keyed 3 for both recall of overall pretreatment emotional state and rating of overall emotional state at follow-up, former clients in this sample can be said to have remembered, on average, having felt fairly poor when they started treatment, then reported feeling quite good, on average, at follow-up. Emotional states and perceived change were reported with insufficient detail in the CR sample to allow comparisons. OQ-45 scores among former clients in Nielsen et al.'s (2004) sample dropped significantly from an average value of 67.64 ($SD = 23.35$) at intake to an average value of 53.65 ($SD = 24.00$) at follow-up; yielding a within-subjects effect size (d) of 1.14.

On the basis of criteria for clinically significant change outlined in Chapter 3, OQ-45 scores dropped 14 or more points among 144 of the 302 former clients (47.68%) in this sample, who can be said to have improved reliably. OQ-45 scores changed 13 or fewer points among 126 (41.72%) former clients who cannot be said to have changed reliably. Scores increased 14 or more points among 32 (10.6%) former clients who can be said to have deteriorated. Indices of clinical significance for the CRES4 perceived change scores and CRES4 item scores are unknown and will remain so without evaluation of raw CRES4 data from multiple normative samples.

Certainly the data just presented demonstrate that if the satisfaction and problem resolution criterion is used, almost all patients improve. In contrast, different conclusions can be drawn about psychotherapy outcome depending on the measure that is used and the method of data collection. On the basis of clinical significance criteria and ratings of functioning on a weekly basis, it appears that less than one half the treated clients had a significant treatment response, and many deteriorated. These different ways of reflecting the impact of psychotherapy and estimating treatment response were nonetheless correlated. First, OQ-45 scores and OQ-45 change scores are strongly correlated with CRES4 recalled emotion, rated emotion, and perceived emotional change (absolute values of $r = .52$). The CRES4 perceived change score component of the total CRES4 score appears to provide an index of change in distress, which is distinct from the problem resolution and satisfaction elements of the CRES4.

Given that the treatment length as reported by CR was longer than that delivered to the Nielsen et al. (2004) sample, a question of interest was the relationship between treatment duration and intensity of treatment. This is also an important consideration for treatment settings that schedule less than weekly psychotherapy. Total CRES4 score, which is a composite of perceived change, problem resolution, and satisfaction, was not reliably correlated with treatment length or intensity, though the correlation between number of sessions attended and total CRES4 score approached conventional standards for statistical significance: $r\,(300) = .11, .05 < p < .06$.

It was evident that distributions of OQ-45 scores and CRES4 emotion ratings are skewed relative to one another. CRES4 recollections of overall emotional state at intake were reliably shifted toward more negative representations of emotional state than OQ-45 scores actually gathered at intake. CRES4 ratings of overall emotional state gathered at follow-up were reliably shifted toward more positive representations of emotional state than OQ-45 scores gathered at follow-up. Change scores derived by subtracting OQ-45s gathered at follow-up from OQ45s gathered at intake suggested CRES4 perceived change scores were reliably shifted toward showing more improvement than was evident in OQ-45 change scores. Given significant exaggeration in both directions, CRES4 perceived change score overestimated improvement to a considerable degree compared with the OQ-45, yielding a within-client effect size nearly double the repeated-measures effect size evident from prospectively measured OQ-45 scores. The enthusiasm CR and Seligman expressed in 1995 for the degree of relief from symptoms reported by CR respondents should be tempered based on finding that CRES4 perceived change score exaggerated improvement apparent in prospectively measured OQ-45scores.

Comparison with the OQ-45 reveals relative strengths and weaknesses in the CRES4. The CRES4 overall emotional state ratings and the CRES4 perceived emotional change score derived from these two items were moderately correlated with OQ-45 scores and with the OQ-45 change score; absolute values of r were equal to or greater than .52. Correlations of such magnitude are within the range of validity indices found in psychotherapy outcome research. They fall short, however, of correlations between self-report measures such as the Symptom Checklist-90 and the OQ-45, which are typically around an $r = .80$ (Lambert, Morton, et al., 2004). The correlation between intake OQ-45 scores and the CRES4's retrospective rating of emotion at the beginning of treatment ($r = -.57$) was of the same magnitude, a surprising finding given an average recall interval of more than a year for the CRES4. The magnitude of this correlation was apparently unaffected by variations in recall interval.

Mintz, Drake, and Crits-Christoph's (1996) concern that CR's method may have confused change and satisfaction is supported by the results of the Nielsen et al. (2004) study. The three features of response to treatment addressed by the CRES4—perceived change in distress, problem change, and satisfaction—appear to be psychometrically distinct. The disparate CRES4 elements were dissimilar enough in the degree to which they were correlated with length of treatment as to call into question one of the main conclusions reported by CR (1995) and Seligman (1995), who concluded that longer treatment was more effective treatment. They reported finding a significant relationship between lengths of treatment and total CRES4 scores but did not report correlation coefficients or coefficients of determination by which the magnitude of the relationship between total CRES4 score might be evaluated, nor did they report any attempt to evaluate relationships between length of treatment and the constituent components of the total CRES4 scores. Based on these results, the CRES4 satisfaction rating, but not the CRES4 perceived change in emotional state score, would have been the likely source of the correlation between length of treatment and total CRES4 effectiveness score.

General or gross ratings of treatment effectiveness (and satisfaction) such as those used by the CR survey produce very large effect sizes compared with more fine-tuned symptom measures such as the OQ-45, as suggested by past psychotherapy research as summarized in Chapter 3. A different picture of outcome emerged depending on what was measured, with general satisfaction ratings and problem resolution relatively poorly correlated with outcome measures of symptomatic functioning. Retrospective ratings of outcome collected a year after treatment overstated the effects of treatment in comparison to more timely measurement. The relationship between length of therapy and client outcome is not strong, and length correlates mainly with satisfaction with treatment rather than amount of change experienced by clients. Treatment settings need to be sure to examine treatment effects as measured by degree of client disturbance separately from satisfaction with treatment; these are by no means interchangeable concepts.

SUMMARY

The five plus topics presented in this chapter provide the reader with some of the many possible and diverse ways in which the initiation of outcome monitoring on a week-by-week basis for the purpose of providing feedback on progress to therapists and clients can also assist in improving clinical practice in other important ways. Of course, archival data do not allow for experimental controls and prospective research designs that would make the interpretation of the findings more clear-cut. Nevertheless, archival data allowed the clinic in which the investigations were undertaken to use data from their clientele to play a role in decision making—practice-based evidence at work. Over time the clinic culture changed toward valuing and using empirical evidence as an important consideration in patient care.

The usual practice of using intake interviews to improve treatment outcomes was abandoned in favor of keeping continuity of care within a provider because the intake procedure being used slowed recovery on average. The change reduced costs of providing care while speeding up recovery. Of course, other decisions could have been made, such as modifying intake procedures, and constant data collection would reveal over time the possible consequences of innovative practices.

In the study of ethnic minority outcomes, which tested the boundary of effectiveness of ongoing treatment for such clients, it was found that outcomes and attrition from treatment were comparable across groups of Caucasian and ethnic clients, reassuring the center administration that inequities in quality of care were not a systemic problem that required greater expenditure of training resources. The study of couple treatment outcome was another boundary study that had the potential of matching treatment modality (individual vs. couple therapy) with couple presentation on the basis of degree of initial disturbance to maximize patient outcome. The surprising finding that more distressed women might be better served by referring them to individual therapy than couple therapy (if their male partner did not report psychological distress) provoked an important discussion about the possible causes and also a decision to reevaluate this finding in a future study as well as a decision to assess the level of functioning of partners when it was possible. Couple therapists found the differences in number of sessions women attended when their partners were not experiencing pain a phenomenon worth further investigation. Such an investigation is very difficult for individual therapists to accomplish on their own and requires systematic tracking of session and outcome data.

Investigations of length of treatment and outcome provided reliable information about the average number of sessions required to produce reliable change and return to normal functioning. This information questioned the wisdom of setting arbitrary session limits as a routine practice and reinforced the notion that monitoring treatment response provided a much better way to judge when therapy was successful or when it was not resulting in further client gains. The extent to which some clients had a rapid dramatic treatment response raised considerable discussion about the nature of change (for many clients it came as a sudden gain rather than a relatively slow incremental change) and preceded rather than followed many of the specific procedures that therapists thought necessary for improvement to occur. It was comforting to see that many clients maintained the positive level of adjustment an average of 1 year later.

In the final study summarized here, the relationship between satisfaction and outcome was examined, and the results shed light on the CR satisfaction survey, suggesting that there is indeed a methodological problem with retrospective ratings of outcome in that length of treatment was related to satisfaction with treatment not treatment gains. The study also showed a high level of satisfaction with treatment at the CCC well after treatment was completed. Exploration of archival data has helped answer other questions of interest that we have not published, such as outcomes in clients with same-sex attraction, outcomes of group psychotherapy, trainee versus professional staff outcome, and the like. All the studies reviewed here contributed important findings to the field and also affected practice in the setting where the studies were collected.

9

SUMMARY, IMPLICATIONS, AND FUTURE DIRECTIONS

In this chapter, an attempt is made to highlight what has been learned from over a decade of programmatic research aimed at measuring, tracking, and alerting therapists to patient treatment response that foretells a poor outcome. What is the take-home message with regard to clinical practice and outcomes management? What are the future directions for research in this area?

MEASURING, MONITORING, AND FEEDBACK PROVIDE ADVANTAGES FOR CLIENTS

As pointed out previously, the power of psychological treatments to assist patients overcome serious, sometimes incapacitating psychological suffering is well documented and commendable. In the face of this remarkable success there is also the fact that as many as two thirds of treated patients derive little or no benefit from treatments delivered in routine care, with 5% to 10 % of treated adults and 15% to 25% of children deteriorating while in treatment. These are problems that need solutions. In response to the need for more effective treatment, professional and government bodies as well as managed health care organizations have invested in the notion that providing evidence-based treatments will go a long way toward maximizing better patient outcome. The assumption seems to be that providing a "best practice" will be enough. Thus, considerable energy is expended, and even mandates for certain practices are being used to ensure that clinicians provide the right treatments. However, no clients are in need of an empirically supported treatment that does not help them (even under ideal circumstance as many as 40% of clients do not respond to evidence-based practices).

In contrast to this solution (and in addition to providing evidence-based treatments) is the notion that measuring psychological functioning on a regular basis during treatment under specific conditions will allow therapists to identify nonresponding and negatively responding clients before they leave their care, thereby allowing for corrective actions on the part of the therapist or treatment team. In pursuit of the goal of reducing treatment failure, it was deemed necessary to create brief measures of psychological functioning that could provide a "mental health vital sign" on a repeated basis. In the case of adults, the measure attempted to assess patients' symptoms, interpersonal functioning, and functioning in daily activities. The measure asked the patient (or caregiver in the case of a child) to look back over the last week and report difficulties and positive functioning.

A significant and specific impediment to solving the problem of poor outcomes is the failure of clinicians to recognize which clients are on the road to treatment failure. Evidence from a variety of methods and settings suggests that therapists do not recognize such cases in their case notes and cannot seem to identify them even when asked to do so. Therapists, like other professionals, maintain very positive views of themselves as being unusually effective and of their clients as seldom deteriorating. There is room for empirical methods to assist therapists in the important task of tracking progress and providing alarms when patients fall "off track."

This led to research aimed at accurately predicting treatment failures. Research presented in this book shows that accurate prediction of treatment failure can be accomplished through a variety of methods, with accurate identification of deteriorators approaching 90% to 100% for adults and 75% to 85% for children (vs. near 0% for clinicians). These methods provide a ratio of false alarms to correct hits of about 2 to 1. Fortunately the consequences of providing false alarms are not negative or nil; outcomes actually improve in such cases. It proved expensive but effective to place measures and algorithms for alerting therapist to impending treatment failure into software created for this purpose. Obviously, the sooner a clinician can be notified that a client's positive outcome is in doubt, the sooner preventive actions can be attempted. This is easily accomplished through the use of handheld computers for office or home use (or a computer terminal in the office or hospital). This typically means that patients come 5 or 10 min early to their appointment and complete the test; a clinician's report is sent to the provider within seconds, thereby allowing immediate feedback about current and past level of functioning as well as the implications of treatment response for end of treatment functioning.

Controlled studies of the consequence of such feedback in routine care suggested that it consistently helped those clients identified as at-risk for failure but did not help clients who were on track for a positive outcome. The size of the effect on these negatively responding clients was consistent across four studies, typically producing an effects size of .40 compared with treatment as usual offered by the same therapists. Deterioration among the experimental groups hovered around 13%, in contrast to the baseline rate of 21% for treatment as usual. The progress feedback and alarm warning also resulted in keeping these patients in treatment longer and shortening treatment for those who were on track for a positive outcome. These latter two findings proved to be inconsistent, suggesting that the effects for feedback about poorly progressing cases can be obtained without lengthening treatment and that shortened treatment in on-track cases is not inevitable. One half of the studies' research designs permitted sharing written and graphic progress feedback directly with clients, and one half made provisions for therapists to decide if, when, and how to give feedback to clients.

Because about 13% of clients who were predicted to deteriorate still deteriorated even when therapists were alerted, a series of three studies examined the extent to which problem-solving tools improved outcomes for these cases. The average effect size for these studies was .70 (compared with treatment as usual), with deterioration reduced to 8% (compared with the baseline of 21%) and reliable improvement and recovery rates reaching 50% (compared with the baseline of 20%). In the final study in this series (Slade, Lambert, Harmon, Smart, & Bailey, 2008) the deterioration rate for alarm-signal cases was reduced to less than 5%, a figure that seemed to approach the limits of what can be expected for this intervention because a certain portion of off-track clients are expected to deteriorate regardless of the power of psychotherapy.

Problem-solving tools were based on the identification of constructs that are known to be related to psychotherapy outcome. The content of the problem-solving tools evolved over time, and a new measure emerged to quantify the constructs of interest. This measure was titled the Assessment for Signal Clients, a brief 40-item self-report scale aimed at providing therapists with information about the therapeutic alliance, motivation, social supports, and life events. In many ways the nature of this scale and the way it is used typifies the difference between traditional psychotherapy research methods and those more appropriate for patient-focused research. Traditional research relies on estimating the degree of relationship between two variables such as the alliance and outcome, providing evidence of theoretical interest. Eventually the findings of such research find their way into training and practice. In contrast, within-patient-focused research measurement is used immediately in practice to directly enhance outcome. For example, the Assessment for Signal Clients does not provide a total score based on adding up subscale scores. Even the subscale scores may not be the most important aspect of the test. It may be helpful for a therapist to know that the alliance is relatively poor but more helpful to know there is a problem with the bond. However, therapists are most able to take action on the basis of the way clients respond to specific items like "My therapist seemed glad to see me." Item cutoff scores are used to inform therapists that the patient has answered an item in a below average manner.

The Clinical Support Tool intervention organizes therapist problem solving through the use of a decision tree that directs attention to the relationship, then motivation, followed by social support, life events, and diagnostic considerations, with the possible need for medication referral. Depending on which areas of functioning might be implicated in the negative treatment response, the therapist is reminded of therapeutic interventions that have proved successful in repairing alliance ruptures, changing motivation, and social supports. Intervention suggestions are not prescriptive and so rely on therapists' creative efforts and available resources such as group psychotherapy or the willingness of family members to join the patient in psychotherapy. The use of the Assessment for Signal Clients, decision tree, and intervention suggestions relies on therapists' ability to reflect on problem areas, seek supervision, and possibly make radical changes in their approach to the client. The research conducted to date has not attempted to identify the active ingredients of the Clinical Support Tool intervention. We do not know if it is necessary to have a decision tree or if providing only a decision tree would be sufficient to help therapists effectively problem solve with their off-track clients.

An aspect of the problem-solving strategy used is the importance of measuring constructs or factors that lead to changes in therapist behavior. There are many important variables that can be measured and used to provide feedback to therapists, but if no known effective actions are linked to the feedback, it seems less likely that therapists will be helpful to the client. There are certainly long-term advantages to being able to describe and explain treatment failure (the goal of traditional research), but problem solving with the individual client requires more than explaining negative change; it needs to provide alternative ways of helping in real time. Apparently the therapists who have been studied are able to use the material provided to the advantage of clients before they leave treatment.

ACCUMULATED DATA HAVE PROVIDED RESULTS THAT CAN BE USED BY SYSTEMS OF CARE AND THE PROFESSION

Once measures suitable for monitoring patient treatment response were developed and used for improving treatment at the point of contact, the available data provided ample opportunity to examine outcomes that are relevant for improving outcomes in systems of care. Importantly, such data provided information on levels of disturbance when patients enter treatment and leave treatment as well as over the entire course of treatment. In addition, because the lengths of treatments are typically indeterminate at inception, posttreatment data are available for nearly all clients who enter treatment and attend at least one more session, providing a more complete picture of outcome than is usually available. Because patient-focused research relies on classification of individuals' treatment response, outcome management can easily examine meaningful change and not merely statistically significant change. Researchers can also consider patterns of change as well as the final status of patients. Examining patterns of change allows those responsible for systems of care to more closely consider the costs and cost–benefit of change and allocate resources accordingly.

Before summarizing important findings from the resulting collected data, I offer a few comments about methodological advancements that prove important in outcomes management.

Methodological Issues

The first advancement of note related to the preceding considerations is the use of repeated measures data for selecting items to include in outcomes measures. Typically outcome measures are developed with the usual focus on traditional psychometric considerations. Of paramount importance in past research were reliability and validity, with little or no attention directed to the most important aspect of an outcome measure—will it reflect change that has occurred in patients? The work of Vermeersch and colleagues (2000, 2004) examined the items of the Outcome Questionnaire-45 (OQ-45) in large groups of individuals who either received or did not receive treatment. This enabled us to see on an item-by-item and week-by-week basis if and to what degree items changed over time. A valid item was one that showed a downward slope in patients undergoing treatment and a flat slope in those who did not. The OQ-45 is rich with such items. Those charged with selecting measures for the purpose of measuring patient outcome would be well served to choose one that can provide this kind of evidence.

The data collected from untreated cases also allowed us to examine the effects of repeatedly administering the measure—can the same test be taken on numerous occasions without interfering with its validity? Problems in this area have arisen in epidemiology studies and have been termed the retest artifact, the tendency for scores to reflect healthier functioning with repeated testing. It appears that the second time the OQ-45 is administered slightly less pathology is admitted to, but this effect is rather small and not additive. The effect does not increase with more administrations.

Another important statistical development was the use of estimates of clinically significant change. Through calculation of reliable improvement and the normal functioning cutoff, a uniform standard (rather than study by study) for judging meaningful change could be applied across settings of care and patient populations. This also resulted in validity studies of both mathematical formulas and comparisons with other outcome measures. The collected evidence suggested the Jacobson and Truax (1991) formulas provide trustworthy estimates of meaningful change that correspond to what would be obtained with other methods and measures. Systems of care now have a standard of mental health functioning and reliable change that can serve as benchmarks for judging the impact of interventions.

Collecting repeated measures over the course of treatment led to the use of survival analysis statistics for estimating time (sessions) to the events of interest, either reliable change or recovery. The use of this statistic had not been applied in psychotherapy but was a natural fit with clinically significant change statistics because they turn continuous data derived from our outcome measures into the binomial data required for use of survival statistics. Survival analysis and related statistics allow system administrators and others who examine the outcomes of treatment programs to rethink the amount of psychotherapy necessary to bring about change and also estimate the number of people who are not likely to show a benefit and consider what to do about this unfortunate fact.

Repeated measurement of client mental health status also led to the use of statistical methods uncommon in psychotherapy research. So-called multilevel or hierarchical linear modeling provided a handy statistical tool for looking at change-sensitive items as well as what changes when and questions related to efficiency and therefore cost of treatment. These issues are of paramount importance to administrators and those who pay the treatment bill. Most important for patient-focused research is the ability of these statistics to model change over time because the information can be used to visualize typical responses to treatment and set expectations for positive and negative courses of treatment. Most of these methods were borrowed from areas of study that have a history of examining longitudinal data such as education, developmental psychology, medicine, and even avalanche forecasting.

Amount of Psychotherapy and Cost–Benefit Considerations

Although the scientific emphasis in patient-focused research has been on improving ongoing treatment outcome, with the final development of a commercial product that facilitates widespread use, considerable research has followed a more traditional line by producing findings important to the setting in which the research was conducted and the profession at large.

Among the more important of these was the analysis of the amount of treatment necessary for a positive treatment response. Our research suggested that the more disturbed a patient is the more treatment it will take for recovery to occur, but the more likely it will be for a patient to show reliable change. Using a measure of psychological functioning such as the OQ-45 and Youth-OQ can assist in estimating needed treatment length and assignment to levels of care such as residential treatment. With only 50% of patients recovering after 18 to 20 sessions of individual psychotherapy, it makes little sense to have session limits of 4 or 8 sessions. Insisting on or funding such short treatment durations ensures only that the majority of patients will need to be wealthy enough to continue on their own. But too little treatment can have enormous costs for society. These begin with the heavy and painful burden that psychological disorders can exercise on individuals' daily lives—a greater burden than most physical disorders that are more fully financed in medical practice. But another layer of cost is born by family members who suffer a variety of consequences to their physical health and psychological well-being, including the degree to which children are put at a serious disadvantage in school and misbehave in their communities.

A very important consideration in justifying financial support for larger doses of psychotherapy is the extent to which psychological illness diminishes individuals' ability to work productively. Not only is absenteeism a problem, but coming to work and not doing the job—so-called presenteeism—is also a problem. We have estimated the amount of increased work productivity that can be achieved as a result of each session of psychotherapy attended by a patient. The dose–response data and work productivity data combine to make a strong argument for extending session limits placed on patients by insurance companies, employers, clinics, and government dictates. Psychological treatments are highly cost effective when viewed from an overall perspective. Because psychological functioning is highly related to work performance and the effects of treatment, adequate sessions of care are likely to make a large return on the costs of providing care by restoring work performance and life roles like homemaking. Medical cost offsets can also be achieved in high health care users under some circumstances. Much more research is needed to verify these results and to make more precise estimates of financial benefits to society and the workplace that ensue as a result of effective treatments.

Of course tracking patients' treatment response might make estimating the amount of psychotherapy needed for recovery less necessary because treatment can be terminated when a treatment response is obtained. We know from our research data that for a minority of patients (perhaps as many as one third) the road to recovery can be extremely rapid and lasting. This will depend a great deal on the nature of the sample, including the degree to which it is composed of patients who have a long history of psychological illness. It appears that the subset of early dramatic responders improves before they have participated in many of the specific activities that make up evidence-based treatments. This rapid treatment response is largely due to patient rather than therapy or therapist variables or the interaction between changes induced by the common factors of therapy and entry into treatment by resilient people.

Certainly findings on the dose–response relationship and early dramatic treatment response should be exploited by policy makers to make psychological treatments appropriate for the individual client. No doubt such information could be used to step up and step down treatments, saving considerable amounts of money by discontinuing treatments that are not necessary or not resulting in a benefit for the client.

The Therapists Contribution and What to Do About It

Two general ways of looking at therapists' outcomes produce overlapping but also discrepant findings and marked differences in who is rated as a top or bottom therapist. The first method, using pretreatment to posttreatment change of clients, is important because it answers the question of which therapists facilitate the greatest amount of change in clients. The second index answers the question of which therapists' clients change the fastest and is uniquely important from the point of view of length of suffering and cost of care. There are some therapists whose clients make very rapid recovery and other therapists whose clients make greater overall improvement. Systems of care that want to use outcome data based on individual therapist's outcome will want to examine the two indices separately as well as in combination.

Using either of these indexes of patient outcome within therapists, we have been unable to show that outcome is related to a number of therapist demographic or treatment variables such as therapist gender, age, type of training, or theoretical orientation. These findings are consistent with much of the past research on these variables. Were such variables significantly associated with client outcomes, systems of care could improve outcomes by showing a hiring preference for individuals who have specific credentials, genders, ages, or preference for specific theoretical orientations. Such is not the case.

Considerable variability in client outcome was found when examining client outcomes associated with specific therapists. Across the outcomes of thousands of clients and thousands of therapists, it must be said that client outcomes are normally distributed across therapists. Most therapists' patient outcomes cannot be distinguished from the outcomes of patients seen by other therapists. Even so, there is a subgroup of therapists who have exceptionally positive effects on their clients and a subgroup whose clients' outcomes are very poor. Differences in outcome between therapists are consistent with findings coming from other occupational groups and settings, from carpenters and police officers to medical doctors, clinics, and hospitals. Therapists are not as interchangeable as one might wish, but the costs and benefits of seeing one or another provider at the extreme end of the continuum can be documented.

To date little has been done to improve the quality of care or treatment outcomes on the basis of the variability of treatment response as it relates to individual psychotherapists. Several possibilities for taking action exist and can be used by administrators. Once outlier therapists are reliably identified (by virtue of large within-therapist sample sizes or repeated poor performance over time) and confidence in the results is verified, several actions can be taken. These can take the form of added training, changes in referral patterns, performance incentives, change in job roles, additional research, or combinations of the these interventions depending on the nature of the treatment setting.

In the supershrink studies by Okiishi and colleagues (2003, 2006), therapists were guaranteed anonymity when they gave permission for their outcomes to be studied. This made many of the options just noted impossible to implement. We did provide each therapist individualized feedback about his or her patients' outcomes, including deterioration rates and recovery rates of patients relative to the treatment center as a whole. Therapists were also provided with their rank ordering in efficiency and effectiveness. They obtained this feedback through use of identification numbers provided by a research consultant. We do not know how this affected therapists or clients. We do know that some therapists were a bit shaken by the findings (recall that virtually all therapists think that they are above average in their work as therapists) and made personal decisions to take action once they had discussed and absorbed the information.

The clinic administrator did not have access to the information and so could not use it to help therapists and clients, or to increase or decrease referrals to specific individuals. Even if the therapists were identified, little to no evidence supports the assumption that training activities based on evidence-based treatments undertaken by therapists (who are already licensed mental health professionals) would create uniformly positive and comparable patient outcomes. Given the cost of training and its uncertain outcomes, it makes little economic sense or logical sense to choose this as a primary solution for the problem of the therapist who is at the bottom of the continuum in facilitating positive client treatment response. In a clinic in which therapists have multiple job roles (and if the information were available for decision making), it might be possible to shift job roles relieving the higher end clinicians from administrative responsibilities and shifting lower end therapists away from seeing an abundance of clients and to more administrative work. Another possibility is to have high end therapists routinely supervise low end therapists. Certainly more could be done if the information on patient outcome by therapist were more "public."

It would also benefit clients and clinics if we knew more about those psychotherapists whose clients had unusually positive outcomes. Being able to describe treatment activities of exceptional therapists in written form or through videotapes and to pass that information on to other therapists within a clinic provides an unusual opportunity to get at effective treatment. We are in the process of exploring the in-session behavior of these individuals and their counterparts (ineffective therapists), but we are not in a position to provide others with the implications for selection and training. It is unfortunate that more is not being done to classify and study those individuals who routinely outshine their peers with regard to the facilitation of change. The general idea here is that practice-based evidence can be used to identify and understand individual therapists.

In follow-up research on CCC therapists we found a strong relationship between therapists' handling of difficult client interactions (e.g., hostile, dependant) and outcome with the clients they had seen in the past. This study suggested that improving some therapists' handling of such interactions could improve their clients' outcome but did not study if providing feedback to therapists on their performance changed the way they behaved in such situations or affected client outcome in general. In managed care, data on outlier therapists and clinics (top performers) were used as the basis for recognizing, publishing, and giving cash rewards for superior outcomes. Such data have also been used to alter referral patterns, thereby directing more patients to therapists with positive outcomes, making a solid contribution to patient well-being.

More can and should be done for clients who are in line to see an outlier therapist whose patients have well below average outcomes. However, this is an area fraught with difficulties. Because patients are not randomly assigned to therapists, outcome is limited to a single self-report measure, and experimental control is not exercised over the treatment process, the actions taken to improve client treatment response must be carefully considered. If the measured outcomes of clients within therapists is to impact practice it will be important to move cautiously and also study the consequences of the actions that are taken.

Additional Findings

Many other examples of practice-based evidence were provided in this book. Collecting session-by-session data and studying archival data suggested that ethnic minorities fared as well in treatment as matched Caucasian controls. Intake interviews slowed treatment response instead of enhancing outcomes as assumed. Satisfaction ratings such as those used by the *Consumer Reports* study overestimated actual improvement and the advantage of long-term treatment. Couple therapy appeared effective but with evidence that women who have partners who do not complain of personal problems are at a relative disadvantage in couple versus individual treatment. These findings barely touch the surface of the kinds of questions that can be asked and answered by virtue of routinely collecting outcome data. They merely illustrate some possibilities and examples. For the clinic and health system that wants to move toward managing services on the basis of patient outcome in addition to processes and best practices, these examples highlight the advantage of making treatment outcome primary. There are some notable difficulties and limitations.

Some Notable Difficulties and Limitations

Outcome research will not help patients unless it is collected routinely and often as treatment unfolds for the client. Even then, progress information needs to be fed back to clinicians before their clients leave treatment as lab test data with indicators of a problematic treatment response or positive responding. In addition, providing clinicians with problem-solving help for poorly responding individuals will maximize patient treatment response. Getting systems of care to implement procedures in the way they have proven to be effective and in the context of all the other concerns they have about delivering services, presents a serious challenge. There is always the temptation to go "part way" and thereby compromise the evidence-based practices advocated in this book. Certain compromises are made whenever evidence-based practices are transported into routine care environments, and outcome monitoring, despite being easy to transport, is no exception. It is too early to tell which compromises seriously undermine the usefulness of the procedures that have been recommended.

Another general limitation is the degree of predictive accuracy. The statistical and empirical algorithms used to predict treatment failure were based on large samples of treated patients who, in general, were seen in weekly psychotherapy. The received treatment was highly diverse, and the patients heterogeneous in diagnosis. We can estimate that about 20% of these cases were also on psychoactive medications. At this time prediction is based on sessions of received treatment (dosage). This method does not take into account the intentional use of infrequent sessions of treatment, such as once monthly appointments, group therapy that may be weekly for 2 or 3 hours per session instead of the usual 50 minutes, inpatient or residential care that is highly intensive, team-based treatments that involve a variety of providers and services, infrequent monitoring of treatment response based on clinic policies, and the like. We found some evidence that meeting every two weeks with a therapist instead of weekly slowed recovery and perhaps the current recovery curves would need to be modified for such a different fixed dosage. Perhaps inpatient care with multiple hours of treatment per week would produce somewhat different expected recovery curves and markers for being off track. We also know that infrequent (less than weekly) monitoring reduces predictive accuracy.

The variations in dosage (and possibly treatment methods) that would have to be considered to properly capture expected treatment response are endless. Consider, for example, monitoring treatment response and estimating expected recovery and deterioration when psychoactive drugs are the sole treatment or when they are combined with other medications and psychological interventions. Despite all the limitations for accurate prediction inherent in diverse practices and data collection procedures, the predictions are based on a general principle that will hold up across practices—patients are expected to improve, and getting worse is a good indicator that treatment is not going well. Although we can undoubtedly become more specific in our attempts to predict treatment failure, the algorithms identified a very high proportion of failures across studies (80%–100%) and even misidentified cases benefited from alarms sent to therapists. The practicing clinician may keep in mind that the central predictor of a negative outcome is an early negative response, and this may hold true regardless of the many variables that can affect expected treatment response. It is important to continue to improve predictive accuracy if the variables discovered can, in fact, be applied in routine practice to help patients. Little is gained when prediction accuracy is improved, but the variables cannot be easily and quickly collected.

Another general limitation of the proposed methods is the problem of low intake scores. A major problem arises when we track treatment response in individuals who do not complain of symptomatic distress, interpersonal difficulties, or life-functioning problems at the initiation of treatment. These patients are either not disturbed or have a very limited problem that does not cause much psychological pain. Some patients are so impaired that they cannot respond to the questions asked, cannot read at the fifth-grade level, will not cooperate with the testing, respond randomly or carelessly, or simply choose not to reveal themselves on self-report questionnaires. Because measured gains in treatment are unlikely for such cases, and the algorithms provide invalid predictions of alarm status, the clinician will need another means for tracking treatment response. We included the Brief Psychiatric Rating Scale in the OQ-Analyst (2009) to make clinician ratings an option for rating adult patients who have not provided a valid self-report. This is less of a problem with adolescents because tracking typically is based on both the patient report and that of their parents.

In some cases reassuring clients about the purpose for collecting self-ratings can solve the problem (e.g., ratings are used to understand the person's function for the purpose of making treatment more helpful). Nevertheless clinicians will need to give special thought to patients who provide exceptionally low scores at intake. Although most clinicians regard themselves as treating more difficult patients than their peers, the most difficult patients with regard to showing a measured benefit to psychotherapy are initially those who report little disturbance. Of course in clinical trial research such patients are not even considered for inclusion because they will be excluded from a study before receiving treatment.

Another limitation of proposed methods is the reliance on a single index for gauging outcome (with the exception of child outcomes for which data are routinely collected from either or both parents and from adolescents and their parents). As clinicians and researchers know and as discussed earlier in this book, there are significant limitations to relying on a simple self-report system as a proxy for the complex phenomenon of psychological functioning and well-being. A single source of outcome does not agree with outcome assessed from other points of view. Despite this limitation it is best to move forward with self-report assessment (which only approaches the complexity that the phenomena of growth and change deserves) because other practical outcome measures can be added when it is practical to do so. This is an instance of not letting the standard of perfection stand in the way of the good enough. Certainly more can be measured once success has been achieved with the simple. At this time, thousands of clients are able to report their discomfort and pain on a questionnaire in addition to focusing on specific issues within their therapy. They have little problem doing so, provided they see it as actually being used to further their treatment goals.

Our work with child outcomes is advancing, but research is much more difficult to conduct than adult research. For many children a self-report is not possible. Prediction of negative outcomes is less successful even though the rates of negative outcome are higher. The same informant is not always available for rating the child's behavior over time, and this magnifies the amount of missing data and makes it more difficult to interpret change over time. Parents have greater difficulty rating their child's inner distress levels than their day-to-day behavior. Formal studies on feedback to child therapists are just in the beginning stages and have not yet been published. It is not clear if the effects are greater or lesser than those found with adults. Child therapists and researchers are encouraged to undertake such studies to fill this gap in knowledge.

Unfortunately many administrators are stuck with the notion that "accountability" is present if a best practice is in place and if outcomes are measured at all. Thus, the potential of progress feedback and adjusting treatments on the basis of formal measurement of treatment response is not a widely shared vision. The way most systems of care are operating, it is highly unlikely that collected outcome data will have their intended consequence, except perhaps in the very long term. It is obvious that much more can be done with such data than is currently being done. This does not mean we cannot provide evidence-based treatments or account for our services, but these should be secondary to tracking, not the primary activity aimed at improving the consequences of clinical services.

FINAL THOUGHTS

This book summarizes and illustrates a method of improving treatment outcomes in patients undergoing professional care. Using treatment response to maximize treatment outcome starts with the use of a brief measure(s) that is created to reflect important dimensions of client functioning and improvement and deterioration if they occur (sensitive to change). Typical treatment response for an individual is understood and referenced against normal psychological functioning to identify an atypical or problematic response on the way toward this goal. A method of providing timely feedback to therapists (and possibly clients) on progress failures is a necessity. The addition of problem-solving tools for persons who are predicted to have a negative outcome provides an added benefit. The preceding procedures rely on contemporary electronic tools for collecting and delivering information to those involved in treatment (including the client). All of this is currently within the grasp of practicing clinicians and places them in a position to know their outcomes and address problems in meeting goals, rather than putting the control of such activities in the hands of administrators. Outcome measurement can be much more than it is (or is proposed to be) in the current climate of accountability.

The program of research has gradually moved from creating measures, predicting treatment failure, and testing the effects of progress feedback on clients to developing and testing problem-solving tools. Future research in this area needs to examine the extent to which other researchers are able to replicate this work and improve on it. We do not yet have a clear picture of where and with whom it fails to be helpful. Currently we are testing it with hospitalized patients with eating disorders, patients with substance abuse problems, and a variety of child samples. Undoubtedly the Clinical Support Tools can be improved and become more specific and tailored better for certain patients and treatment settings.

It has been a great privilege and pleasure to work with individuals in their struggle to improve their lives as well as to investigate methods of improving treatment response through empirical methods. I hope that others will extend and modify these practices so that when clients turn to mental health professions in their time of need and even desperation, they will be met with a system of care that is more likely to benefit them.

REFERENCES

Acitelli, L. K. (1992). Gender differences in relationship awareness and marital satisfaction among young married couples. *Personality and Social Psychology Bulletin*, *18*, 102–110.

Achenbach, T. M. (1991). *Manual for the Child Behavior Checklist/4-18 and 1991 profile*. Burlington: University of Vermont.

Adair, C. E., McDougall, G. M., Beckie, A., Joyce, A., Mitton, C., Wild, C. T., . . . Costigan, N. (2003). History and measurement of continuity of care in mental health services and evidence of its role in outcomes. *Psychiatric Services*, *54*, 1351–1356.

Agras, W. S., Crow, S. J., Halami, K. A., Mitchell, J. E., Wilson, G. T., & Kraemer, H. C. (2000). Outcome predictors for the cognitive behavior treatment of bulimia nervosa: Data from a multisite study. *American Journal of Psychiatry*, *157*, 1302–1308.

Ahn, H., & Wampold, B. (2001). Where oh where are the specific ingredients? A meta-analysis of component studies in counseling and psychotherapy. *Journal of Consulting and Clinical Psychology*, *48*, 251–257.

American Psychological Association. (2003). Guidelines on multicultural education, training, research, practice, and organizational change for psychologists. *American Psychologist*, *58*, 377–402.

American Psychological Association. (2005). *Policy statement on evidence-based practice in psychology*. Washington, DC: Author.

American Psychological Association, Presidential Task Force on Evidence-Based Practice. (2006). Evidence-based practice in psychology. *American Psychologist*, *61*, 271–285.

American Psychological Association, Task Force on Promotion and Dissemination of Psychological Procedures. (1995). Training in and dissemination of empirically validated psychologist treatments: Report and recommendations. *Clinical Psychologist*, *48*, 3–23.

American Psychiatric Association. (2000). *Diagnostic and statistical manual of mental disorders* (4th ed., text. rev.). Washington, DC: Author.

Anderson, B. (2007). Collaborative care and motivational interviewing: Improving depression outcomes through patient empowerment interventions. *American Journal of Managed Care*, *13*, 103–106.

Anderson, E. M., & Lambert, M. J. (2001). A survival analysis of clinically significant change in outpatient psychotherapy. *Journal of Clinical Psychology*, *57*, 875–888.

Anderson, T., Crowley, M. E., & Carson, K. L. (2001, August). *Therapist interpersonal skills (but not training) influence outcome and alliance*. Paper presented at the meeting of the American Psychological Association, San Francisco, CA.

Anderson, T., Ogles, B. M., Patterson, C. L., Lambert, M. J., & Vermeersch, D. A. (2009). Therapist effects: Facilitative interpersonal skills as a predictor of therapist success. *Journal of Clinical Psychology, 65,* 755–768.

Anderson, T., Ogles, B. M., & Weis, A. (1999). Creative use of interpersonal skills in building a therapeutic alliance. *Journal of Constructivist Psychology, 12,* 313–330.

Anderson, T., Patterson, C. L., & Weis, A. C. (2007). *Facilitative interpersonal skills performance analysis rating method.* Unpublished coding manual, Ohio University, Athens.

Andrews, G. (2000). A focus on empirically supported outcomes: A commentary on the search for empirically supported treatments. *Clinical Psychology: Science and Practice, 7,* 264–268.

Baer, R. A., & Nietzel, M. T. (1991). Cognitive and behavioral treatment of impulsivity in children: A meta-analytic review of the outcome literature. *Journal of Clinical Child Psychology, 20,* 400–412.

Bandura, A. (1997). Social cognitive theory of self-regulation. *Organizational Behavior and Human Decision Processes, 50,* 248–287.

Bankoff, E., & Howard, K. (1992). The social network of the psychotherapy patient and effective psychotherapeutic process. *Journal of Psychotherapy Integration, 2,* 273–294.

Barkham, M., & Margison, F. (2007). Practice-based evidence as a complement to evidence-based practice: From dichotomy to chiasmus. In C. Freeman & M. Power (Eds.), *Handbook of evidence-based psychotherapies: A guide for research and practice* (pp. 443–476). Chichester, England: Wiley.

Barkham, M., Margison, F., Leach, C., Lucock, M., Mellor-Clark, J., Evans, C., . . . McGrath, G. (2001). Service profiling and outcomes benchmarking using the Core-OM: Toward practice-based evidence in the psychological therapies. *Journal of Consulting and Clinical Psychology, 69,* 184–196.

Barkham, M., Rees, A., Stiles, W. B., Shapiro, D. A., Hardy, G. E., & Reynolds, S. (1996). Dose–effect relations in time-limited psychotherapy for depression. *Journal of Consulting and Clinical Psychology, 64,* 927–935.

Barkham, M., Stiles, W. B., Connell, J., Twigg, E., Leach, C., Lucock, M., . . . Angus, L. (2008). Effects of psychological therapies in randomized trials and practice-based studies. *British Journal of Clinical Psychology, 47,* 397–415.

Bauer, S., Lambert, M. J., & Nielsen, S. L. (2004). Clinical significance methods: A comparison of statistical techniques. *Journal of Personality Assessment, 82,* 60–70.

Beck, A. T., Ward, C. H., Medelson, M., Mock, J., & Erbaugh, J. (1961). An inventory for measuring depression. *Archives of General Psychiatry, 4,* 561–571.

Beckstead, D. J., Hatch, A. L., Lambert, M. J., Eggett, D. L., Goates, M. K., & Vermeersch, D. A. (2003). Clinical significance of the Outcome Questionnaire (OQ-45.2). *The Behavior Analyst Today, 4,* 79–90.

Bergin, A. (1997). Neglect of the therapist and the human dimensions of change: A commentary. *Clinical Psychology: Science and Practice, 4,* 83–89.

Berrett, K. M. S. (1999). Youth Outcome Questionnaire: Item sensitivity to change (Doctoral dissertation, Brigham Young University, 1999/2000). *Dissertation Abstracts International, 60,* 4876.

Beutler, L. E. (2000). David and Goliath: When empirical and clinical standards of practice meet. *American Psychologist, 55,* 997–1007.

Beutler, L. E., Malik, M., Alimohamed, S., Harwook, T. M., Talebi, H., Noble, S., & Wong, E. (2004). Therapist variables. In M. J. Lambert (Ed.), *Bergin and Garfield's handbook of psychotherapy and behavior change* (5th ed., pp. 227–306). New York, NY: Wiley.

Bishop, M., Bybee, T. Lambert, M. J., Burlingame, G. M., Wells, G. M. & Poppleton, L. (2005). Accuracy of a rationally derived method for identifying treatment failure in children and adolescents. *Journal of Child and Family Studies, 14,* 207–222.

Blanchard, E. B., & Schwartz, S. P. (1988). Clinically significant changes in behavioral medicine. *Behavioral Assessment, 10,* 171–188.

Blatt, S. (1995). The destructiveness of perfectionism: Implications for the treatment of depression. *American Psychologist, 50,* 1003–1020.

Blatt, S. J., & Zuroff, D. C. (2002). Perfectionism in the therapeutic process. In G. L. Flett & P. L. Hewitt (Eds.), *Perfectionism: Theory research and treatment* (pp. 393–406). Washington, DC: American Psychological Association.

Bloom, B. (1997). Brief therapy research commentaries: An evaluative commentary. *Crisis Intervention and Time-Limited Treatment, 3,* 245–249.

Bohart, A. C., Elliott, R., Greenberg, L. S., & Watson, J. C. (2002). Empathy. In J. C. Norcross (Ed.), *Psychotherapy relationships that work* (pp. 89–108). Oxford, England: Oxford University Press.

Brabec, B., & Meister, R. (2001). A nearest-neighbor model for regional avalanche forecasting. *Annals of Glaciology, 32,* 130–134.

Brown, G. S., Jones, E., Lambert, M. J., & Minami, T. (2005). Evaluating the effectiveness of psychotherapists in a managed care environment. *American Journal of Managed Care. 2,* 513–520.

Brown, J., Dreis, S., & Nace, D. (1999). What really makes a difference in psychotherapy outcome? Why does managed care want to know? In M. A. Hubble, B. L. Duncan, & S. D. Miller (Eds.), *The heart and soul of change* (pp. 389–406). Washington, DC: American Psychological Association.

Bryk, A. S., & Raudenbush, S. W. (1992). *Hierarchical linear models: Applications and data analysis methods.* Thousand Oaks, CA: Sage.

Burlingame, G. M., Earnshaw, D., Ridge, N. W., Matsumo, J., Bulkley, C., Lee, J., & Hwang, A. D. (2007). Psycho-educational group treatment for the severely and persistently mentally ill: How much leader training is necessary? *International Journal of Group Psychotherapy, 57,* 187–218.

Burlingame, G. M., Lambert, M. J., Reisinger, C. W., Neff, W. L., & Mosier, J. I. (1995). Pragmatics of tracking mental health outcomes in a managed care setting. *Journal of Mental Health Administration, 22,* 226–236.

Burlingame, G. M., Mosier, J. I., Wells, M. G., Atkin, Q. G., Lambert, M. J., Whoolery, M., & Latowsky, M. (2001). Tracking the influence of mental health treatment: The development of the Youth Outcome Questionnaire. *Clinical Psychology & Psychotherapy, 8,* 315–334.

Burlingame, G. M., Wells, M. G., Cox, J. C., Lambert, M. J., & Latowski, M. (2005). The Youth Outcome Questionnaire. Salt Lake City, UT: OQ Measures.

Burlingame, G. M., Wells, M. G., Lambert, M. J., & Cox, J. C. (2004). Youth Outcome Questionnaire (Y-OQ). In M. E. Maruish (Ed.), *The use of psychological testing for treatment planning and outcome assessment* (3rd ed., Vol. 2, pp. 235–274). Mahwah, NJ: Erlbaum.

Burns, B., & Hoagwood, K. E. (Eds.). (2005). Evidence-based practice: Part I. Effecting change [Special issue]. *Child and Adolescent Psychiatric Clinics of North America, 14*(2).

Butcher, J. N., Dahlstrom, W. G., Graham, J. R., Tellegen, A., & Kaemmer, B. (1989). *Minnesota Multiphasic Personality Inventory (MMPI–2). Manual for administration and scoring.* Minneapolis: University of Minnesota Press.

Bybee, T. S., Lambert, M. J., & Eggett, D. (2007). Curves of expected recovery and their predictive validity for identifying treatment failure. *Tijdschrift voor Psychotherapie [The Dutch Journal of Psychotherapy], 33,* 419–434.

Cannon, J., Warren, J., Nelson, P., & Burlingame, G. M. (in press). Change trajectories for the Youth Outcome Questionnaire Self-Report: Identifying youth at risk for treatment failure, *Journal of Clinical Child and Adolescent Psychology.*

Carey, J. (2000). *Psychometrics of the Severe Outcome Questionnaire.* Unpublished doctoral dissertation, Brigham Young University, Provo, UT.

Cartwright, D. S., Kirtner, W. L., & Fiske, D. W. (1963). Method factors in changes associated with psychotherapy. *Journal of Abnormal and Social Psychology, 66,* 164–175.

Catanni-Thompson, K., Lambert, M. J., & Boroto, D. (1996). Symptomatic versus personality change in brief psychotherapy: The phase model of psychotherapy. Unpublished manuscript, Brigham Young University, Provo, UT.

Chambless, D. L. (1996). In defense of dissemination of empirically supported psychological interventions. *Clinical Psychology: Science and Practice, 3,* 230–235.

Chambless, D. L., Baker, M. J., Baucom, D. H., Beutler, L. E., Calhoun, K. S., Crits-Christoph, P., . . . Woody, S. R. (1998). Update on empirically validated therapies, II. *The Clinical Psychologist, 51,* 3–16.

Chambless, D. L., & Hollon, S. D. (1998). Defining empirically supported psychological interventions. *Journal of Consulting and Clinical Psychology, 66,* 7–18.

Chambless, D. L., Sanderson, W. C., Shoham, V., Bennett Johnson, S., Pope, K. S., Crits-Christoph, P., . . . McCurry, S. (1996). An update on empirically validated therapies. *The Clinical Psychologist, 49,* 5–18.

Clement, P. W. (1996). Evaluation in private practice. *Clinical Psychology: Science and Practice, 3,* 146–159.

Cohen, J. (1988). *Statistical power analysis for the behavioral sciences* (2nd ed.). Hillsdale, NJ: Erlbaum.

Consumer Reports. (1995, November). Mental health: Does therapy help? pp. 734–739.

Crits-Christoph, P., Baranackie, K., Kurcias , J.,S., Beck, A. T., Carroll, K., Perry, K., . . . Zitrin, C. (1991). Meta-analysis of therapist effects in psychotherapy outcome studies. *Psychotherapy Research, 59,* 81–91.

Crits-Christoph, P., & Gallop, R. (2006). Therapist effects in the TDCRP and other psychotherapy studies. *Psychotherapy Research, 16,* 178–181.

Crits-Christoph, P., & Mintz, J. (1991). Implications of therapist effects for the design and analysis of comparative studies of psychotherapies. *Journal of Consulting and Clinical Psychology, 59,* 20–26.

de Jong, K., Nugter, M. A., Polak, M. G., Wagenborg, J. E. A., Spinhoven, P., & Heiser, W. J. (2007). The Outcome Questionnaire (OQ-45) in a Dutch population: A cross-cultural validation. *Clinical Psychology & Psychotherapy, 14,* 288–301.

Derogatis, L. R. (1983). The SCL-90: Administration, scoring, and procedures for the SCL-90. Baltimore, MD: Clinical Psychometric Research.

Doss, B. D., Atkins, D. C., & Christensen, A. (2003). Who's dragging their feet? Husbands and wives seeking marital therapy. *Journal of Marital and Family Therapy, 29,* 165–177.

Drum, D. J., & Baron, G. (1998, November). Highlights of the research consortium outcomes project. Paper presented at the meeting of the Association of University and College Counseling Center Directors, Santa Fe, NM.

Duncan, B. L., & Miller, S. D. (2005). Treatment manuals do not improve outcome. In J. C. Norcross, L. E. Beutler, & R. F. Levant (Eds.), *Evidence-based practices in mental health* (pp. 140–148). Washington, DC: American Psychological Association.

Duncan, B. L., & Miller, S. D. (2008). *The Outcome and Session Rating Scales: The revised administration and scoring manual, including the Child Outcome Rating Scale.* Chicago, IL: Institute for the Study of Therapeutic Change.

Duncan, B. L., Sparks, J., Miller, S., Bohanske, R., & Claud, D. (2006). Giving youth a voice: A preliminary study of the reliability and validity of a brief outcome measure for children. *Journal of Brief Therapy, 5*(2), 66–82.

Dunlap, W. P., Cortina, J. M., Vaslow, J. B., & Burke, M. J. (1996). Meta-analysis of experiments with matched groups or repeated measures designs. *Psychological Methods, 1,* 170–177.

Dunn, T. (2004). *The Youth Outcome Questionnaire-30.1 (Y-OQ-30.1): A study of reliability and discriminant validity.* Unpublished doctoral dissertation, Brigham Young University, Provo, UT.

Dunning, D., Heath, C., & Suls, J. M. (2004). Flawed self-assessment: Implications for health, education, and the workplace. *Psychological Science in the Public Interest, 5,* 69–106.

Eells, T., Kendjelic, E. M., & Lucas, C. P. (1998). What is in a case formulation?: Development and use of a content coding manual. *Journal of Psychotherapy Practice and Research, 7*, 144–153.

Ehrlinger, J., & Dunning, D. (2003). How chronic self-views influence (and potentially mislead) estimates of performance. *Journal of Personality and Social Psychology, 84*, 5–17.

Elkin, I. (1999). A major dilemma in psychotherapy outcome research: Disentangling therapists from therapies. *Clinical Psychology: Science and Practice, 6*, 10–32.

Elkin, I., Falconnier, L., & Martinovich, Z. (2007). Misrepresentations in Wampold and Bolt's critique of Elkin, Falconnier, Martinovich, and Mahoney's study of therapist effects. *Psychotherapy Research, 17*, 253–256.

Elkin, I., Falconnier, L., Martinovich, Z., & Mahoney, C. (2006). Therapist effects in the National Institute of Mental Health Treatment of Depression Collaborative Research Program. *Psychotherapy Research, 16*, 144–160.

Ellsworth, J. R., Lambert, M. J., & Johnson, J. (2006). A comparison of the Outcome Questionnaire-45 and Outcome Questionnaire-30 in classification and prediction of treatment outcome. *Clinical Psychology & Psychotherapy, 13*, 380–391.

Emanuels-Zuurveen, L,. & Emmelkamp, P. M. G. (1996). Individual behavioural therapy v. marital therapy for depression in martially distressed couples. *British Journal of Psychiatry, 169*, 181–188.

Evans, C., Connell, J., Barkham, M., Marshall, C., & Mellor-Clark, J. (2003). Practice-based evidence: Benchmarking NHS primary care counselling services at national and local levels. *Clinical Psychology & Psychotherapy, 10*, 374–388

Farnsworth, J., Hess, J., & Lambert, M. J. (April, 2001). *A review of outcome measurement practices in the* Journal of Consulting and Clinical Psychology. Paper presented at the meeting of the Rocky Mountain Psychological Association, Reno, NV.

Fennel, M. J. V., & Teasdale, J. D. (1987). Cognitive therapy for depression: Individual differences and the process of change. *Cognitive Therapy and Research, 11*, 253–271.

Finch, A. E., Lambert, M. J., & Schaalje, B. G. (2001). Psychotherapy quality control: The statistical generation of expected recovery curves for integration into an early warning system. *Clinical Psychology & Psychotherapy, 8*, 231–242.

Flowers, J. V. (1979). The differential outcome effects of simple advice, alternatives and instructions in group psychotherapy. *International Journal of Group Psychotherapy, 29*, 305–316.

Forsyth, R. P., & Fairweather, G. W. (1961). Psychotherapeutic and other hospital treatment criteria: The dilemma. *Journal of Abnormal and Social Psychology, 62*, 598–604.

Frank, J. D. (1961). *Persuasion and healing.* New York, NY: Oxford University Press.

Frank, J. D., & Frank, J. B. (1993). *Persuasion and healing* (3rd ed.). Baltimore, MD: Johns Hopkins University Press.

Freedheim, D. K. (1992). *History of psychotherapy: A century of change.* Washington, DC: American Psychological Association.

Froyd, J. E., Lambert, M. J., & Froyd, J. D. (1996). A review of practices of psychotherapy outcome measurement. *Journal of Mental Health, 5,* 11–15.

Garb, H. N. (1998). *Studying the clinician.* Washington, DC: American Psychological Association.

Garb, H. N. (2005). Clinical judgment and decision making. *Annual Review of Clinical Psychology, 55,* 13–23.

Garfield, S. L. (1982). Eclecticism and integration in psychotherapy. *Behavior Therapy, 13,* 174–183.

Garfield, S. L. (1994). Research on client variables in psychotherapy. In S. L. Garfield & A. E. Bergin (Eds.), *Handbook of psychotherapy and behavior change* (4th ed., pp. 72–113). New York, NY: Wiley.

Garfield, S. L. (1996). Some problems associated with 'validated' forms of psychotherapy. *Clinical Psychology: Science and Practice, 3,* 218–229.

Garfield, S. L., & Kurtz, R. (1977). A study of eclectic views. *Journal of Consulting and Clinical Psychology, 45,* 78–83.

Garland, A. F., Hurlburt, M. S., & Hawley, K. M. (2006). Examining psychotherapy processes in a services research context. *Clinical Psychology: Science and Practice, 13,* 30–46.

Gawande, A. (2007). *Better: A Surgeon's Notes on Performance.* New York, NY: Metropolitan Books.

Gibson, R. L., Snyder, W. U., & Ray, W. S. (1955). A factors analysis of measures of change following client-centered psychotherapy. *Journal of Counseling Psychology, 2,* 83–90.

Gladis, M. M., Gosch, E. A., Dishuk, N. M., & Crits-Christoph, P. (1999). Quality of life: Expanding the scope of clinical significance. *Journal of Consulting and Clinical Psychology, 67,* 320–331.

Glaister, B. (1982). Muscle relaxation training for fear reduction in patients with psychological problems. *Behaviour Research & Therapy, 20,* 493–504.

Goodheart, C. D., Kazdin, A. E., & Sternberg, R. J. (Eds.). (2006). *Evidence-based psychotherapy: Where practice and research meet.* Washington, DC: American Psychological Association.

Gottheil, E., Sterling, R. C., Weinstein, S. P., & Kurtz, J. W. (1994). Therapist/patient matching and early treatment dropout. *Journal of Addictive Diseases, 13,* 169–176.

Grawe, K. (2007). *Neuropsychotherapy: How the neurosciences inform effective psychotherapy.* Mahwah, NJ: Erlbaum.

Gray, D., Konkel, K., Achilles, J., Burlingame, G. M., Haggard, L., Norman, J., & McMahon, W. (2000). *Juvenile offenders: Suicide risk and psychiatric symptoms.* Poster session presented at the meeting of the American Academy of Child & Adolescent Psychiatry, New York, NY.

Grove, W. M., Zald, D. H., Lebow, B. S., Snitz, B. E., & Nelson, C. (2004). Clinical versus mechanical prediction: A meta-analysis. *Psychological Assessment, 12,* 19–30.

Haaga, D. A. F., & Stiles, W. B. (2000). Randomized clinical trials in psychotherapy research: Methodology, design, and evaluation. In C. R. Snyder & R. E. Ingram (Eds.), *Handbook of psychological change: Psychotherapy processes and practices for the 21st century* (pp. 14–39). New York, NY: Wiley.

Haas, E., Hill R., Lambert, M. J., & Morrell, B. (2002). Do early responders to psychotherapy maintain treatment gains? *Journal of Clinical Psychology, 58,* 1157–1172.

Haggerty, J. L., Reid, R. J., Freeman, G. K., Starfield, B. H., Adair, C. E., & McKendry, R. (2003). Continuity of care: A multidisciplinary review. *British Medical Journal, 327,* 1219–1221.

Halford, K., Sanders, M., & Behrens, B. (1993). A comparison of the generalization of behavioral marital therapy and enhanced behavioral marital therapy. *Journal of Consulting and Clinical Psychology, 61,* 51–60.

Hall, G. C. N., Bansal, A., & Lopez, I. R. (1999). Ethnicity and psychopathology: A meta-analytic review of 31 years of comparative MMPI/MMPI–2 research. *Psychological Assessment, 11,* 186–197.

Hannan, C., Lambert, M. J., Harmon, C., Nielsen, S. L., Smart, D. W., Shimokawa, K., & Sutton, S. W. (2005). A lab test and algorithms for identifying clients at risk for treatment failure. *Journal of Clinical Psychology: In Session, 61,* 155–63.

Hansen, N. B. (1999). *An overview of longitudinal data analysis methodologies applied to the dose–response relationships in psychotherapy outcome research.* Unpublished manuscript.

Hansen, N. B., & Lambert, M. J. (2003). An evaluation of the dose–response relationship in naturalistic treatment settings using survival analysis. *Mental Health Services Research, 5*(1), 1–12.

Hansen, N. B., Lambert, M. J., & Forman, E. M. (2002). The psychotherapy dose–response effect and its implications for treatment delivery services. *Clinical Psychology: Science and Practice, 9,* 329–343.

Hansen, N. B., Lambert, M. J., & Forman, E. M. (2003). The psychotherapy dose–effect in naturalistic settings revisited: Response to Gray [Letter to the editor]. *Clinical Psychology: Science and Practice, 10,* 507–508.

Harmon, S. C., Lambert, M. J., Smart, D. M., Hawkins, E., Nielsen, S. L., Slade, K., & Lutz, W. (2007). Enhancing outcome for potential treatment failures: Therapist–client feedback and clinical support tools. *Psychotherapy Research, 17,* 379–392.

Hatchett, G. T., & Park, H. L. (2003). Comparison of four operational definitions of premature termination. *Psychotherapy: Theory, Research, Practice, Training, 40,* 226–231.

Hatfield, D. R., McCullough, L., Plucinski, A., & Krieger, K. (2009). Do we know when our clients get worse? An investigation of therapists' ability to detect negative client change. *Clinical Psychology & Psychotherapy,* Advance online publication. doi:10.1002/cpp.656

Hatfield, D. R., & Ogles, B. M. (2004). The current climate of outcome measures use in clinical practice. *Professional Psychology: Research and Practice, 35*, 485–491.

Hawkins, E. J., Lambert, M. J., Vermeersch, D. A., Slade, K., & Tuttle, K. (2004). The effects of providing patient progress information to therapists and patients. *Psychotherapy Research, 14*, 308–327.

Hendryx, M., Dyck, D., & Srebnik, D. (1999). Risk-adjusted outcome models for public mental health outpatient programs. *Health Services Research, 34*, 171–195.

Henry, W. P., Schacht, T. E., & Strupp, H. H. (1990). Patient and therapist introject, interpersonal process, and differential psychotherapy outcome. *Journal of Consulting and Clinical Psychology, 58*, 768–774.

Herink, R. (Ed.). (1980). *The psychotherapy handbook: The A to Z guide to more than 250 different therapies in use today.* New York, NY: New American Library.

Herz, G. (2009). Measuring progress and outcomes. *Independent Practitioner, 29*, 179.

Hill, C. E., & Lambert, M. J. (2004). Methodological issues in studying psychotherapy processes and outcomes. In M. J. Lambert (Ed.), *Bergin and Garfield's handbook of psychotherapy and behavior change* (5th ed., pp. 84–135). New York, NY: Wiley.

Hill, R. W., Huelsman, T. J., Furr, M. R., Kibler, J., Vicente, B. B., & Kennedy, C. (2004). A new measure of perfectionism: The Perfectionism Inventory. *Journal of Personality Assessment, 82*, 80–91.

Hilsenroth, M. J., Ackerman, S. J., & Blagys, M. D. (2001). Evaluating the phase model of change during short-term psychodynamic psychotherapy. *Psychotherapy Research, 11*, 29–47.

Hollon, S. D (1996). The efficacy and effectiveness of psychotherapy relative to medications. *American Psychologist, 51*, 1025–1030.

Horowitz, L. M., Rosenberg, S. E., Baer, B. A., Ureno, G., & Villasenor, V. S. (1988). Inventory of interpersonal problems: Psychometric properties and clinical applications. *Journal of Consulting and Clinical Psychology, 56*, 885–892.

Horowitz, L. M., Strupp, H. H., Lambert, M. J., & Elkin, I. (1997). Overview and summary of the core battery conference. In H. H. Strupp, L. M. Horowitz, & M. J. Lambert (Eds.), *Measuring patient changes in mood, anxiety, and personality disorders: Toward a core battery* (pp. 11–54). Washington DC: American Psychological Association.

Howard, K. I., Kopta, S. M., Krause, M. S., Merton, S., & Orlinsky, D. E. (1986). The dose–effect relationship in psychotherapy. *American Psychologist, 41*, 159–164.

Howard, K .I., Krause, M. S., Caburnay, C. A., Noel, S. B., & Saunders, S.M. (2001). Syzygy, science, and psychotherapy: The *Consumer Reports* study. *Journal of Clinical Psychology, 57*, 865–874.

Howard, K. I., Lueger, R. J., Maling, M. S., & Martinovich, Z. (1993). A phase model of psychotherapy outcome: Causal mediation of change. *Journal of Consulting and Clinical Psychology, 61*, 678–685.

Howard, K. I., Moras, K., Brill, P. L., Martinovich, Z., & Lutz, W. (1996). Evaluation of psychotherapy: Efficacy, effectiveness, and patient progress. *American Psychologist, 51*, 1059–1064.

Hunsley, J. (2007). Addressing key challenges in evidence-based practice in psychology. *Professional Psychology: Research and Practice, 38*, 113–121.

Huppert, J. D., Bufka, L. F., Barlow, D. H., Gorman, J. M., Shear, M. K., & Woods, S. W. (2001).Therapist variables, and cognitive–behavioral therapy outcome in a multicenter trial for panic disorder. *Journal of Consulting and Clinical Psychology, 69*, 747–755.

Ilardi, S. S., & Craighead, W. E. (1994). The role of nonspecific factors in cognitive behavior therapy for depression. *Clinical Psychology: Science and Practice, 1*, 138–156.

Institute of Medicine. (2001). *Crossing the quality chasm: A new health system for the 21st century*. Washington, DC: National Academy Press.

Isakson, R. L., Hawkins, E. J. Martinez, J. S., Harmon, C., Slade, K., & Lambert, M. J. (2006). Assessing couple therapy as a treatment for individual distress: When is referral contraindicated? *Contemporary Family Therapy, 28*, 313–322.

Jacobson, N. S., & Christensen, A. (1996). Studying the effectiveness of psychotherapy: How well can clinical trials do the job? *American Psychologist, 51*, 1031–1039.

Jacobson, N. S., Dobson, K. S., Truax, P. A., Addis, M. E., Koerner, K., Gollan, J. K., . . . Prince, S. E. (1996). A component analysis of cognitive–behavioral treatment for depression. *Journal of Consulting and Clinical Psychology, 64*, 295–304.

Jacobson, N. S., Follette, W. C., & Revenstorf, D. (1984). Psychotherapy outcome research: Methods for reporting variability and evaluating clinical significance. *Behavior Therapy, 15*, 336–352.

Jacobson, N. S., Roberts, L. J., Berns, S. B., & McGlinchey, J. B. (1999). Method for defining and determining the clinical significance of treatment effects: Description, application, and alternatives. *Journal of Consulting and Clinical Psychology, 67*, 300–307.

Jacobson, N. S., & Truax, P. (1991). Clinical significance: A statistical approach to defining meaningful change in psychotherapy research. *Journal of Consulting and Clinical Psychology, 59*, 12–19.

Jennings, L., & Skovholt, T. (1999). The cognitive, emotional, and relational characteristics of master therapists. *Journal of Counseling Psychology, 46*, 3–11.

Jensen, J. P., Bergin, A. E., & Greaves, D. W. (1990). The meaning of eclecticism: New survey and analysis of components. *Professional Psychology: Research and Practice, 21*, 124–130.

John, O., & Robins, R. (1994). Accuracy and bias in self-perception: Individual differences in self-enhancement and the role of narcissism. *Journal of Personality and Social Psychology, 66*, 206–219.

Johnson, D. P., & Slaney, R. B. (1996). Perfectionism: Scale development and a study of perfectionistic clients in counseling. *Journal of College Student Development, 37,* 29–41.

Kadera, S.W., Lambert, M.J., & Andrews, A. A. (1996). How much therapy is really enough? A session-by-session analyses of the psychotherapy dose–effect relationship. *Journal of Psychotherapy Practice and Research, 5,* 132–151.

Kazdin, A. E. (1977). Assessing the clinical or applied importance of behavior change through social validation. *Behavior Modification, 1,* 427–452.

Kazdin, A. E. (1986). Comparative outcome studies of psychotherapy: Methodological issues and strategies. *Journal of Consulting and Clinical Psychology, 54,* 95–105.

Kazdin, A. E. (1998). *Research design in clinical psychology* (3rd ed.). Boston, MA: Allyn & Bacon.

Kazdin, A. E. (2008). Evidence-based treatment and practice—New opportunities to bridge clinical research and practice, enhance the knowledge base, and improve patient care. *American Psychologist, 63,* 146–159.

Kendall, P. C. (1999). Clinical significance. *Journal of Consulting and Clinical Psychology, 67,* 283–285.

Kendall, P. C., & Grove, W. M. (1988). Normative comparisons in therapy outcome. *Behavioral Assessment, 10,* 147–158.

Kendall, P. C., Holmbeck, G., & Verduin, T. (2004). Methodology, design, and evaluation in psychotherapy research. In M. J. Lambert (Ed.), *Methodology, design, and evaluation in psychotherapy research* (5th ed., pp. 16–43). New York, NY: Wiley.

Kendall, P. C., Marrs-Garcia, A., Nath, S. R., & Sheldrick, R. C. (1999). Normative comparisons for the evaluation of clinical significance. *Journal of Consulting and Clinical Psychology, 67,* 285–299.

Kendall, P. C., & Norton-Ford, J. D. (1982). Therapy outcome research methods. In E. C. Kendall & J. N. Butcher (Eds.), *Handbook of research methods in clinical psychology* (pp. 429–460). New York, NY: Wiley.

Kivlighan, D. M. (1985). Feedback in group psychotherapy: Review and implications. *Small Group Behavior, 16,* 373–385.

Kluger, A. N., & DeNisi, A. (1996). The effects of feedback interventions on performance: A historical review, a meta-analysis, and a preliminary feedback intervention theory. *Psychological Bulletin, 119,* 254–284.

Kopta, S. M., Howard, K. I., Lowry, J. L., & Beutler, L. E. (1994). Patterns of symptomatic recovery in psychotherapy. *Journal of Consulting and Clinical Psychology, 62,* 1009–1016.

Kramer, T. L., Evans, R. B., Reid, L., Mancino, M., Booth, B. M., & Smith, G. R. (2001). Comparing outcomes of routine care for depression: The dilemma of case mix. *Journal of Behavioral Health Services & Research, 28,* 287–300.

Kraus, D. R., & Horan, F. P. (1999). Outcomes roadblocks: Problems and solutions. *Behavioral Health Management, 17,* 22–26.

Krupnick, J. L., Stotsky, S. M., Simmens, S., Moyer, J., Watkins, J., Elkin, I., & Pilkonis, P. A. (2000). The role of the therapeutic alliance in psychotherapy and pharmacotherapy outcome: Findings in the National Institute of Mental Health Treatment of Depression Collaborative Research Program. *Journal of Consulting and Clinical Psychology, 64,* 532–539.

Lambert, M. J. (1983). Introduction to assessment of psychotherapy outcome: Historical perspective and current issues. In M. J. Lambert, E. R. Christensen, & S. S. DeJulio (Eds.), *The assessment of psychotherapy outcome* (pp. 3–32). New York, NY: Wiley.

Lambert, M. J. (1992). Psychotherapy outcome research: Implications for integrative and eclectic therapists. In J. C. Norcross & M. R. Goldfield (Eds.), *Handbook of psychotherapy integration* (pp. 94–129). New York, NY: Basic Books.

Lambert, M. J. (2001). Psychotherapy outcome and quality improvement: Patient-focused research. *Journal of Consulting and Clinical Psychology, 69,* 147–149.

Lambert, M. J. (2009). Advantages and disadvantages of using practice-based evidence in marketing psychological services. *Independent Practitioner, 29,* 180–181.

Lambert, M. J., Bergin, A. E., & Collins, J. L. (1977). Therapist induced deterioration in psychotherapy patients. In A. S. Gurman, & A. M. Razin (Eds.), *Effective psychotherapy: A handbook of research* (pp. 452–481). New York, NY: Pergamon Press.

Lambert, M. J., Bergin, A. E., & Garfield, S. L. (2004). Introduction and overview. In M. J. Lambert (Ed.), *Bergin and Garfield's handbook of psychotherapy and behavior change* (5th ed., pp. 3–15). New York, NY: Wiley.

Lambert, M. J., Christensen, E. R., & DeJulio, S. S. (1983). *The assessment of psychotherapy outcome.* New York, NY: Wiley.

Lambert, M. J., Gregersen, A. T., & Burlingame, G. M. (2004). The Outcome Questionnaire. In M. Maruish (Ed.), *The use of psychological tests for treatment planning and outcome assessment* (3rd ed., Vol. 3, pp. 191–234). Mahwah, NJ: Erlbaum.

Lambert, M. J., Hatch, D. R., Kingston, M. D., & Edwards, B. C. (1986). Zung, Beck, and Hamilton rating scales as measures of treatment outcome: A meta-analytic comparison. *Journal of Consulting and Clinical Psychology, 54,* 54–59.

Lambert, M. J., & McRoberts, C. (1993, April). *Survey of outcome measures used in JCCP: 1986–1991.* Poster session presented at the annual meeting of the Western Psychological Association, Phoenix, AZ.

Lambert, M. J., Morton, J. J., Hatfield, D., Harmon, C., Hamilton, S., Reid, R. C., . . . Burlingame, G. M. (2004). *Administration and scoring manual for the Outcome Questionnaire-45.* Salt Lake City, UT: OQMeasures.

Lambert, M. J., & Ogles, B. M. (2004). The efficacy and effectiveness of psychotherapy. In M. J. Lambert (Ed.), *Bergin and Garfield's handbook of psychotherapy and behavior change* (5th ed., pp. 139–193). New York, NY: Wiley.

Lambert, M. J., & Okiishi, J. (1997). The effects of the individual psychotherapist and implications for future research. *Clinical Psychology: Science and Practice, 4,* 66–75.

Lambert, M. J., Okiishi, J. C., Finch, A. E., & Johnson, L. (1998). Outcome assessment: From conceptualization to implementation. *Professional Psychology: Practice and Research, 29*, 63–70.

Lambert, M. J., Smart, D. W., Campbell, M. P., Hawkins, E. J., Harmon, C., & Slade, K. L. (2006). Psychotherapy outcome, as measured by the OQ-45, in African American, Asian/Pacific Islander, Latino/a, and Native American clients compared to matched Caucasian clients. *Journal of College Student Psychotherapy, 20*(4), 17–29.

Lambert, M. J., Vermeersch, D. A., Brown, G. S., & Burlingame, G. M. (2004). *Administration and scoring manual for the Outcome Questionnaire-30.2.* Salt Lake City, UT: OQ Measures.

Lambert, M. J., Whipple, J. L., Bishop, M. J., Vermeersch, D. A., Gray, G.V., & Finch, A. E. (2002). Comparison of empirically derived and rationally derived methods for identifying patients at risk for treatment failure. *Clinical Psychology & Psychotherapy, 9*, 149–164.

Lambert, M. J., Whipple, J. L., Harmon, C., Shimokawa, K., Slade, K., & Christopherson, C. (2004). *Clinical support tools manual.* Provo, UT: Brigham Young University.

Lambert, M. J., Whipple, J. L., Smart, D. W., Vermeersch, D. A., Nielsen, S. L., & Hawkins, E. J. (2001). The effects of providing therapists with feedback on patient progress during psychotherapy: Are outcomes enhanced? *Psychotherapy Research, 11*, 49–68.

Lambert, M. J., Whipple, J. L., Vermeersch, D. A., Smart, D. W., Hawkins, E. J., Nielsen, S. L., & Goates, M. K. (2002). Enhancing psychotherapy outcomes via providing feedback on client progress: A replication. *Clinical Psychology & Psychotherapy, 9*, 91–103.

Lipsey, M. W. (1990). *Design sensitivity.* Newbury Park, CA: Sage.

Locke, H. J., & Wallace, K. M. (1959). Short marital adjustment and prediction test: Their reliability and validity. *Marriage and Family Living, 21*, 251–255.

Lord, R. G., & Hanges, P. J. (1987). A control system model of organizational motivation: Theoretical development and applied implications. *Behavioral Science, 32*, 161–178.

Luborsky, L. (1971). Perennial mystery of poor agreement among criteria for psychotherapy outcome. *Journal of Consulting and Clinical Psychology, 37*, 316–319.

Luborsky, L., Barber, J. P., Siqueland, L., & Johnson, S. (1996). The revised helping alliance questionnaire (HAq-II): Psychometric properties. *Journal of Psychotherapy Practice and Research, 5*, 260–271.

Luborsky, L., McClellan, T., Woody, G., O'Brien, C., & Auerbach, A. (1985). Therapist success and its determinants. *Archives of General Psychiatry, 42*, 602–611.

Lueck, W. (2004). *The relationship between diagnostic classification and scores on the Outcome Questionnaire-45.* Unpublished doctoral dissertation, Brigham Young University, Provo, UT.

Lueger, R. J., Howard, K. I., Martinovich, Z., Lutz, W., Anderson, E. E., & Grissom, G. (2001). Assessing treatment progress of individual clients using expected treatment response models. *Journal of Consulting and Clinical Psychology, 69,* 150–158.

Lunnen, K. M., & Ogles, B. M. (1998). A multiperspective, multivariable evaluation of reliable change. *Journal of Consulting and Clinical Psychology, 66,* 400–410.

Lutz, W., Lambert, M. J., Harmon, S. C., Tschitsaz, A., Schurch, E., & Stulz, N. (2006). The probability of treatment success, failure and duration—What can be learned from empirical data to support decision making in clinical practice? *Clinical Psychology & Psychotherapy, 13,* 223–232.

Lutz, W., Leach, C., Barkham, M., Lucock, M., Stiles, W. B., Evans, C., . . . Iveson, S. (2005). Predicting rate and shape of change for individual clients receiving psychological therapy: Using growth curve modeling and nearest neighbor technologies. *Journal of Consulting and Clinical Psychology, 73,* 904–913.

Markland, D., Ryan, R., Tobin, V., & Rollnick, S. (2005). Motivational interviewing and self-determination theory. *Journal of Social & Clinical Psychology, 24,* 811–831.

Marks, I. M., & Mathews, A. M. (1979). Brief standard self-rating for phobic patients. *Behaviour Research & Therapy, 17,* 263–267.

McConnaughy, E. A., Prochaska, J. O., & Velicer, W. F. (1983). Stages of change in psychotherapy: Measurement and sample profiles. *Psychotherapy: Theory, Research, and Practice, 20,* 368–375.

McGlynn, E. A. (1996). Domains of study and methodological challenges. In L. I. Sederer & B. Dickey (Eds.), *Outcomes assessment in clinical practice.* Baltimore, MD: Williams & Wilkins.

McKenzie, K. R. (2005). *Effective use of group psychotherapy in managed care.* Arlington, VA: American Psychiatric Publishing.

Melson, S. J. (1995). Brief day treatment for nonpsychotic patients. In K. R. Mckenzie (Ed.), *Effective use of group therapy in managed care* (pp. 113–128). Washington, DC: American Psychiatric Press.

Merrill K., Tolbert, V., & Wade, W. (2003). Effectiveness of cognitive therapy for depression in a community mental health center: A benchmarking study. *Journal of Consulting and Clinical Psychology, 71,* 404–409.

Meuller, R. M., Lambert, M. J., & Burlingame, G. M. (1998). Construct validity of the Outcome Questionnaire: A confirmatory factor analysis. *Journal of Personality Assessment 70,* 248–262.

Millenson, M. L. (1997). *Demanding medical excellence: Doctors and Accountability in the Information Age.* Chicago, IL: University of Chicago Press.

Miller, R. (1999). The first session with a new client: Five stages. In R. Bor & M. Watts (Eds.), *The trainee handbook: A guide for counseling and psychotherapy trainees* (pp. 146–167). Thousand Oaks, CA: Sage.

Miller, S. D., Duncan, B. L., Sorrell, R., & Brown, G. S. (2005). The Partners for Change Outcome System. *Journal of Clinical Psychology: In Session, 61,* 199–208.

Minami, T., Wampold, B. E., Serlin, R. C., Kircher, J. C., & Brown, G. S. (2007). Benchmarks for psychotherapy efficacy in adult major depression, *Journal of Consulting and Clinical Psychology, 75*, 232–243.

Mintz, J., Drake, R. E., & Crits-Christoph, P. (1996). Efficacy and effectiveness of psychotherapy: Two paradigms, one science. *American Psychologist, 51*, 1084–1085.

Monroe, S., Imhoff, D., Wise, B., & Harris, J. (1983). Prediction of psychological symptoms under high-risk psychosocial circumstances: Life events, social support, and symptom specificity. *Journal of Abnormal Psychology, 92*, 338–350.

Morrow-Bradley, C., & Elliott, R. (1986). Utilization of psychotherapy research by practicing psychotherapists. *American Psychologist, 41*, 188–197.

Mumma, G. H. (2004). Validation of idiosyncratic cognitive schema in cognitive case formulations: An intraindividual idiographic approach. *Psychological Assessment, 16*, 211–230.

Mylar, J. L., & Clement, P. W. (1972). Prediction and comparison of outcome in systematic desensitization and implosion. *Behaviour Research & Therapy, 10*, 235–246.

Nathan, P. E. (1998). Practice guidelines: Not yet ideal. *American Psychologist, 53*, 290–299.

Nathan, P. E., Gorman, J. M., & Salkind, N. J. (2002). *Treating mental disorders: A guide to what works* (2nd ed.). New York, NY: Oxford University Press.

National Institute of Mental Health, National Advisory Mental Health Council. (1999). *Bridging science and service: A report by the National Advisory Mental Health Council's Clinical Treatment and Services Research Workshop* (NIH Publication No. 99-4353). Washington, DC: Author.

National Institute of Mental Health, National Advisory Mental Health Council. (2001). *Blueprint for change: Research on child and adolescent mental health. A report by the National Advisory Mental Health Council's Workgroup on Child and Adolescent Mental Health Intervention Development and Deployment.* Bethesda, MD: Author.

National Institute of Mental Health, Research Task Force. (1975). *Research in the service of mental health* (DHEW Publication No. ADM 75-236). Rockville, MD: Author.

Newman, M. G. (2000). Recommendations for a cost-offset model of psychotherapy allocation using generalized anxiety disorder as an example. *Journal of Consulting and Clinical Psychology, 68*, 549–555.

Nielsen, S. L., & Lambert, M. J. (2006). *Psychotherapeutic treatment as usual at a large university counseling center: Dose effect or goldilocks response?* Unpublished manuscript, Brigham Young University, Provo, UT.

Nielsen, S., Okiishi, J., Nielsen, D., Hawkins, E., Harmon, S. C., Pedersen, T., . . . Jackson, A. (in press). Termination, appointment use, and outcome patterns associated with intake therapist discontinuity. *Professional Psychology: Research & Practice, 40*, 272–278.

Nielsen, S. L., Smart, D. W., Isakson, R., Worthen, V., Gregersen, A. T., & Lambert, M. J. (2004). The *Consumer Reports* effectiveness score: What *did* consumers report? *Journal of Counseling Psychology, 51,* 25–37.

Nietzel, M. T., Russell, R. L., Hemmings, K. A., & Gretter, M. L. (1987). Clinical significance of psychotherapy for unipolar depression: A meta-analytic approach to social comparison. *Journal of Consulting and Clinical Psychology, 55,* 156–161.

Norcross, J. C. (Ed.). (2002). *Psychotherapy relationships that work: Therapist contributions and responsiveness to patient needs.* New York, NY: Oxford University Press.

Norcross, J. C., Hedges, M., & Castle, P. (2002). Psychologists conducting psychotherapy in 2001: A study of the Division 29 membership. *Psychotherapy: Theory, Research, Practice, Training, 39,* 97–102.

Norcross, J. C., Karg, R. S., & Proshaska, J. O. (1997). Clinical psychologists in the 90s: Part 1. *The Clinical Psychologist, 50,* 4–9.

Ogles, B. M., Lambert, M. J., & Fields, S. A. (2002). *Essentials of outcome assessment.* Hoboken, NJ: Wiley.

Ogles, B. M., Lambert, M. J., & Masters, K. S. (1996). *Assessing outcome in clinical practice.* New York, NY: Allyn & Bacon.

Ogles, B. M., Lambert, M. J., Weight, D. G., & Payne, I. R. (1990). Agoraphobia outcome measurement: A review and meta-analysis. *Psychological Assessment: A Journal of Consulting and Clinical Psychology, 2,* 317–325.

Ogles, B. M., Lunnen, K. M., & Bonesteel, K. (2001). Clinical significance: History, application, and current practice. *Clinical Psychology Review, 21,* 421–446.

Okiishi, J. C., Lambert, M. J., Eggett, D., Nielsen, S. L., Dayton, D. D., & Vermeersch, D. A. (2006). An analysis of therapist treatment effects: Toward providing feedback to individual therapists on their patients' psychotherapy outcome. *Journal of Clinical Psychology, 62,* 1157–1172.

Okiishi J. C., Lambert, M. J., Nielsen, S. L., & Ogles, B. M. (2003). In search of supershrink: Using patient outcome to identify effective and ineffective therapists. *Clinical Psychology & Psychotherapy, 10,* 361–373.

OQ-Analyst. (2004). *Users guide.* (Available from OQ Measures, P.O. Box 521047, Salt Lake City, UT 84152-1047)

Orlinsky, D. E., Grawe, K., & Parks, B. K. (1994). Process and outcome in psychotherapy—Noch Einmal. In A. E. Bergin & S. L. Garfield (Eds.), *Handbook of psychotherapy and behavior change* (4th ed.). New York, NY: Wiley.

Orlinsky, D. E., & Howard, K. I. (1980). *Varieties of psychotherapeutic experience: Multivariate analysis of patients' and therapists' reports.* New York, NY: Teachers College Press.

Otto, M. W., Pollack, M. H., & Maki, K. M. (2000). Empirically supported treatments for panic disorder: Costs, benefits, and stepped care. *Journal of Consulting and Clinical Psychology, 68,* 556–563.

Ozgur, E., Rude, S., & Baron, A. (2003). Symptom improvement and length of treatment in ethnically similar and dissimilar client–therapist pairings. *Journal of Counseling Psychology, 50*, 52–58.

Parloff, M. B. (1982). Psychotherapy research evidence and reimbursement decisions: Bambi meets Godzilla. *American Journal of Psychiatry, 139*, 718–727.

Pautler, T. (1991). A cost effective mind–body approach to psychosomatic disorders. In K. N. Anchor (Ed.), *The handbook of medical psychotherapy: Cost effective strategies in mental health* (pp. 231–248). Ashland, OH: Hogrefe & Huber.

Pelletier, L. G., Tuson, K. M., & Haddad, N. K. (1997). Client motivation for therapy scale: A measure of intrinsic motivation, extrinsic motivation, and amotivation for therapy. *Journal of Personality Assessment, 68*, 414–435.

Pilkonis, P. A., Imber, S. D., Lewis, P., & Rubinsky, P. (1984). A comparative outcome study of individual, group, and conjoint psychotherapy. *Archives of General Psychiatry, 41*, 431–437.

Prochaska, J. O., DiClemente, C., & Norcross, J. C. (1992). In search of how people change: Applications to addictive behaviors. *American Psychologist, 47*, 1102–1114.

Prochaska, J. O., & Prochaska, J. M. (1999). Why don't continents move? Why don't people change? *Journal of Psychotherapy Integration, 9*, 83–102.

Quality Assurance Project. (1982). A treatment outline for agoraphobia. *Australian and New Zealand Journal of Psychiatry, 16*, 25–33.

Quality Assurance Project. (1983). A treatment outline for depressive disorders. *Australian and New Zealand Journal of Psychiatry, 17*, 129–146.

Quality Assurance Project. (1984). Treatment outlines for the management of schizophrenia. *Australian and New Zealand Journal of Psychiatry, 18*, 19–38.

Quality Assurance Project. (1985a). Treatment outlines for the management of anxiety states. *Australian and New Zealand Journal of Psychiatry, 19*, 138–151.

Quality Assurance Project. (1985b). Treatment outlines for the management of obsessive compulsive disorders. *Australian and New Zealand Journal of Psychiatry, 19*, 240-253.

Quitkin, F. M., McGrath, P. J., Stewart, J. W., Taylor, B. P., & Klein, D. F. (1996). Can the effects of antidepressants be observed in the first two weeks of treatment? *Neuropsychopharmacology, 15*, 390–394.

Renaud, J., Brent, D. A., Baugher, M., Birmaher, B., Kolko, D. J., & Bridge, J. (1998). Rapid response to psychosocial treatment for adolescent depression: A two-year follow-up. *Journal of the American Academy of Child and Adolescent Psychiatry, 37*, 1184–1191.

Ricks, D. R. (1974). Supershrink: Methods of a therapist judged successful on the basis of adult outcomes of adolescent patients. In D. Ricks, M. Roff, & A. Thomas (Eds.), *Life history research in psychopathology* (pp. 275–297). Minneapolis: University of Minnesota Press.

Riemer, M., & Bickman, L. (2004). The contextualized feedback intervention theory: A theory of guided behavior change. Unpublished manuscript.

Riemer, M., Rosof-Williams, J., & Bickman, L. (2005). Theories related to changing clinician practice. *Child Adolescent Psychiatric Clinics of North America, 14,* 241–254.

Riggio, R. E. (1986). Assessment of basic social skills. *Journal of Personality and Social Psychology, 51,* 649–660.

Ringel, J. S., & Sturm, R. (2001). National estimates of mental health utilization and expenditures for children in 1998. *Journal of Behavioral Health Services & Research, 28,* 319–333.

Robinson, D. J. (2000). *Three spheres: A psychiatric interviewing primer.* Port Huron, MI: Rapid Psychler Press.

Rosenblatt, A., & Attkisson, C. C. (1993). Assessing outcome for sufferers of severe mental disorders: Conceptual framework and review. *Evaluation & Program Planning, 16,* 347–362.

Ross, S. M., & Proctor, S. (1973). Frequency and duration of hierarchy item exposure in a systematic desensitization analogue. *Behaviour Research & Therapy, 11,* 303–312.

Roth, A., & Fonagy, P. (2005). *What works for whom? A critical review of psychotherapy research* (2nd ed.). New York, NY: Guilford Press.

Russell, R. L., Greenwald, S., & Shirk, S. R. (1991). Language change in child psychotherapy: A meta-analytic review. *Journal of Consulting and Clinical Psychology, 59,* 916–919.

Sabalis, R. F. (1983). Assessing outcome in patients with sexual dysfunctions and sexual deviations. In M .J. Lambert, E. R. Christensen, & S. S. DeJulio (Eds.). *The assessment of psychotherapy outcome* (pp. 205–262). New York, NY: Wiley.

Safran, J. D., & Muran, J. C. (2000). *Negotiating the therapeutic alliance: A relational treatment guide.* New York, NY: Guilford Press.

Safran, J. D., Muran, J. C., Samstag, L. W., & Stevens, C. (2002). Repairing alliance ruptures. In J. C. Norcross (Ed.), *Psychotherapy relationships that work* (pp 235–254). New York, NY: Oxford University Press.

Sapyta, J., Riemer, M., & Bickman, L. (2005). Feedback to clinicians: Theory, research, and practice. *Journal of Clinical Psychology, 62,* 145–153.

Seggar, L. B., Lambert, M. J., & Hansen, N. B. (2002). Assessing clinical significance: Application to the Beck Depression Inventory. *Behavior Therapy, 33,* 253–269.

Seligman, M. E. P. (1995). The effectiveness of psychotherapy: The *Consumer Reports* study. *American Psychologist, 50,* 965–974.

Sexton, T. L., Alexander, J. F., & Mease, A. L. (2004). Levels of evidence for the models and mechanisms of therapeutic change in family and couple therapy. In M. J. Lambert (Ed.), *Bergin and Garfield's handbook of psychotherapy & behavior change* (5th ed., pp. 590–646). New York, NY: Wiley.

Shirk, S. R., & Russell, R. L. (1992). A reevaluation of estimates of child therapy effectiveness. *Journal of the American Academy of Child & Adolescent Psychiatry, 31,* 703–709.

Shore, M. F., Massimo, J. L., & Ricks, D. F. (1965). A factor analytic study of psychotherapeutic change in delinquent boys. *Journal of Clinical Psychology, 21,* 208–212.

Singer, J. D. (1998). Using SAS PROC MIXED to fit multilevel models, hierarchical models, and individual growth models. *Journal of Education and Behavioral Statistics, 23,* 323–355.

Slade, K., Lambert, M. J., Harmon, S. C., Smart, D. W., & Bailey, R. (2006). *Clinical support tool manual.* Unpublished manuscript, Brigham Young University, Provo, UT.

Slade, K., Lambert, M. J., Harmon, S. C., Smart, D. W., & Bailey, R. (2008). Improving psychotherapy outcome: The use of immediate electronic feedback and revised clinical support tools. *Clinical Psychology & Psychotherapy, 15,* 287–303.

Slife, B. (2004). Taking practice seriously: Toward a relational ontology. *Journal of Theoretical and Philosophical Psychology, 24,* 157–178.

Smart, J. F., & Smart, D. W. (1995a). Acculturative stress of Hispanics: Loss and challenge. *Journal of Counseling and Development, 73,* 390–396.

Smart, J. F., & Smart, D. W. (1995b). Acculturative stress: The experience of Hispanic immigrants. *The Counseling Psychologist, 23,* 25–42.

Smith, M. L., & Glass, G. V. (1977). Meta-analysis of psychotherapy outcome studies. *American Psychologist, 32,* 752–760.

Smith, M. L., Glass, G. V., & Miller, T. L. (1980). *The benefits of psychotherapy.* Baltimore, MD: Johns Hopkins University Press.

Snell, M. N., Mallinckrodt, B., Hill, R. D., & Lambert, M. J. (2001). Predicting counseling center client's response to counseling: A 1-year follow-up. *Journal of Counseling Psychology, 48,* 463–473.

Snyder, D. K., Mangrum, L. F., & Wills, R. M. (1993). Predicting couples' response to marital therapy: A comparison of short- and long-term predictors. *Journal of Consulting and Clinical Psychology, 61,* 61–69.

Spielberger, C. D. (1983). *Manual for the State–Trait Anxiety Inventory (STAI Form Y).* Palo Alto, CA: Consulting Psychologists Press.

Spielberger, C. D., Sydeman, S. J., Owen, A. E., & Marsh, B. J. (1999). Measuring anxiety and anger with the State–Trait Anxiety Inventory and the State–Trait Anger Expression Inventory. In M. Maruish (Ed.), *The use of psychological tests for treatment planning and outcome assessment* (3rd ed., pp. 994–1021). Mahwah, NJ: Erlbaum.

Spielmans, G. I., Masters, K. S., & Lambert, M. J. (2006). A comparison of rational versus empirical methods in prediction of negative psychotherapy outcome. *Clinical Psychology & Psychotherapy, 13,* 202–214.

Stein, D. M., & Lambert, M. J. (1995). Graduate training in psychotherapy: Are therapy outcomes enhanced? *Journal of Consulting and Clinical Psychology, 63,* 182–196.

Steiner, D. L. (2003). Diagnostic tests: Using and misusing diagnostic and screening tests. *Journal of Personality Assessment, 81*, 209–219.

Stiles, W. B. (2005). Dialogue: Convergence and contention. In J. C. Norcross, L. E. Beutler, & R. F. Levant (Eds.), *Evidence-based practices in mental health: Debate and dialogue on the fundamental questions* (pp. 105–107). Washington, DC: American Psychological Association.

Stiles, W. B., Honos-Webb, L., & Surko, M. (1998). Responsiveness in psychotherapy. *Clinical Psychology: Science and Practice, 5*, 439–58.

Stiles, W. B., & Shapiro, D. A. (1994). Disabuse of the drug metaphor—Psychotherapy process outcome correlations. *Journal of Consulting and Clinical Psychology, 62*, 942–948.

Stone, G. L., & McMichael, J. (1996). Thinking about mental health policy in university and college counseling centers. *Journal of College Student Psychotherapy, 10*, 3–27.

Strupp, H. H. (1980). Humanism and psychotherapy: A personal statement of the therapist's essential values. *Psychotherapy: Theory, Research and Practice, 17*, 396–400.

Strupp, H. H. (1993). The Vanderbilt Psychotherapy studies: Synopsis. *Journal of Consulting and Clinical Psychology, 61*, 431–433.

Strupp, H. H., & Anderson, T. (1997). On the limitations of therapy manuals. *Clinical Psychology: Science and Practice, 4*, 76–82.

Strupp, H. H., & Hadley, S. W. (1977). A tripartite model of mental health and therapeutic outcomes: With special reference to negative effects in psychotherapy. *American Psychologist, 32*, 187–196.

Tanenbaum, S. J. (2005). Evidence-based practice as mental health policy: Three controversies and a caveat. *Health Affairs, 24*, 163–173.

Taylor, S., & McLean, P. (1993). Outcome profiles in the treatment of unipolar depression. *Behaviour Research and Therapy, 31*, 325–330.

Texidor, M. S., & Taylor, C. L. (1991). Chronic pain management: The interdisciplinary approach and cost effectiveness. In K. N. Anchor (Ed.), *The handbook of medical psychotherapy: Cost effective strategies in mental health* (pp. 89–99). Ashland, OH: Hogrefe & Huber.

Thernstrom, S., Orlov, A., & Handlin, O. (Eds.). (1980). *Harvard encyclopedia of American ethnic groups*. Cambridge, MA: Harvard University Press.

Thoits, P. (1986). Social support as coping assistance. *Journal of Consulting and Clinical Psychology, 54*, 416–423.

Thompson, K. C. (2004). The development of recovery curves for the *life status questionnaire* as a means of identifying patients at risk for psychotherapy treatment failure. *Dissertation Abstracts International, 64*, 5238.

Tingey, R., Lambert, M. J., Burlingame, G. M., & Hansen, N. B. (1996). Assessing clinical significance: Proposed extensions to the method. *Psychotherapy Research, 6*, 109–123.

Tomarken, A. J. (1995). A psychometric perspective on psychophysiological measures. *Psychological Assessment, 7*, 387–395.

Trivedi, M., & Kleiber, B. (2001). Using treatment algorithms for the effective management of treatment-resistant depression. *Journal of Clinical Psychiatry, 62*, 25–29.

Trotter, V. K., Lambert, M. J., Burlingame, G. M., Rees, F., Carpenter, B., Staffan, P. R., . . . & Eggett, D. (2009). Measuring work productivity with a mental health self-report measure. *Journal of Occupational and Environmental Medicine, 51*, 739–746.

Trull, T. J., Nietzel, M. T., & Main, A. (1988). The use of meta-analysis to assess the clinical significance of behavior therapy for agoraphobia. *Behavior Therapy, 19*, 527–538.

Trusler, K., Doherty, C., Mullin, T., Grant, S., & McBride, J. (2006). Waiting times for primary care psychological therapy and counselling services. *Counselling and Psychotherapy Research, 6*, 23–32.

U.S. Surgeon General. (2001). *Mental health: Culture, race, and ethnicity—A supplement to mental health: A report of the Surgeon General.* Rockville, MD: U.S. Department of Health and Human Services

Vermeersch, D. A., Lambert, M. J., & Burlingame, G. M. (2000). Outcome Questionnaire: Item sensitivity to change. *Journal of Personality Assessment, 74*, 242–261.

Vermeersch, D. A., Whipple, J. L., Lambert, M. J., Hawkins, E. J., Burchfield, C. M., & Okiishi, J. C. (2004). Outcome Questionnaire: Is it sensitive to changes in counseling center clients? *Journal of Counseling Psychology, 51*, 38–49.

Walfish, S., McAlister, B., O'Donnell, P., & Lambert, M. J. (2009). *Are all therapists from Lake Wobegon?: An investigation of self-assessment bias in mental health providers.* Manuscript submitted for publication.

Wamboldt, F. S., & Reiss, D. (1989). Defining a family heritage and a new relationship identity: Two central tasks in the making of a marriage. *Family Process, 28*, 317–335.

Wampold, B. E. (2001). The great psychotherapy debate: Models, methods, and findings. Mahwah, NJ: Erlbaum.

Wampold, B. E., Ahn, H., & Coleman, H. L. K. (2001). Medical model as metaphor: Old habits die hard. *Journal of Counseling Psychology, 48*, 268–273.

Wampold, B. E., & Bolt, D. M. (2006). Therapist effects: Clever ways to make them (and everything else) disappear. *Psychotherapy Research, 16*, 184–187.

Wampold, B. E., & Bolt, D. M. (2007). Appropriate estimation of therapist effects: One more time. *Psychotherapy Research, 17*, 256–257

Wampold, B. E., & Brown, G. (2005). Estimating therapist variability in outcomes attributable to therapists: A naturalistic study of outcomes in managed care. *Journal of Consulting and Clinical Psychology, 73*, 914–923.

Wampold, B. E., Minami, T., Baskin, T. W., & Tierney, S. C. (2002). A meta-(re)analysis of the effects of cognitive therapy versus "other therapies" for depression. *Journal of Affective Disorders, 68,* 159–165.

Wampold, B. E., Mondin, G. W., Moody, M., Stich, F., Benson, K., & Ahn, H.-n. (1997). A meta-analysis of outcome studies comparing bona fide psychotherapies: Empirically, "all must have prizes." *Psychological Bulletin, 122,* 203–215.

Warren, J. S., Nelson, P. L., Baldwin, S. A., Mondragon, S. A., & Burlingame, G. M. (2009). *Predicting negative outcomes in youth psychotherapy: Community mental health vs. managed care settings.* Manuscript in preparation.

Warren, J. S., Nelson, P. L., Mondragon, S. A., Baldwin, S. A. & Burlingame, G. M. (in press). Youth psychotherapy change trajectories and outcomes in usual care: Community mental health versus managed care settings. *Journal of Consulting and Clinical Psychology.*

Waskow, I., & Parloff, M. (1975). *Psychotherapy change measures.* Rockville, MD: National Institute of Mental Health.

Weiss, B., Catron, T., Harris, V., & Phung, T. M. (1999). The effectiveness of traditional child psychotherapy. *Journal of Consulting and Clinical Psychology, 67,* 82–94.

Weisz, J. R. (2004). *Psychotherapy for children and adolescents: Evidence-based treatments and case examples.* New York, NY: Cambridge University Press.

Weisz, J. R., Donenberg, G. R., Han, S. S., & Weiss, B. (1995). Bridging the gap between laboratory and clinic in child and adolescent psychotherapy. *Journal of Consulting and Clinical Psychology, 63,* 688–701.

Weisz, J. R., Hawley, K. M., Pilkonis, P. A., Woody, S. R., & Follette, W. C. (2000). Stressing the (other) three rs in the search for empirically supported treatments: Review procedures, research quality, relevance to practice and the public interest. *Clinical Psychology: Science and Practice, 7,* 243–258.

Weisz, J. R., Weiss, B., Alicke, M. D., & Klotz, M. L. (1987). Effectiveness of psychotherapy with children and adolescents: A meta-analysis for clinicians. *Journal of Consulting and Clinical Psychology, 55,* 542–549.

Wells, E. A., Hawkins, J. D., & Catalano, R. F. (1988). Choosing drug use measures for treatment outcome studies: 1. The influence of measurement approach on treatment results. *International Journal of Addictions, 23,* 851–873.

Wells, K. B., Sturm, R., Sherbourne, C. D., & Meredith, L. S. (1996). *Caring for depression.* Cambridge, MA: Harvard University Press.

Westen, D., & Morrison, K. (2001). A multi-dimensional meta-analysis of treatments for depression, panic, and generalized anxiety disorder: An empirical examination of the status of empirically supported treatments. *Journal of Consulting and Clinical Psychology, 69,* 875–889.

Westen, D., Novotny, C. M., & Thompson-Brenne, H. (2004). The empirical status of empirically supported psychotherapies: Assumptions, findings, and reporting in controlled clinical trials. *Psychological Bulletin, 130,* 631–663.

Whipple, J. L., Lambert, M. J., Vermeersch, D. A., Smart, D. W., Nielsen, S. L., & Hawkins, E. J. (2003). Improving the effects of psychotherapy: The use of early identification of treatment failure and problem-solving strategies in routine practice. *Journal of Counseling Psychology, 58*, 59–68.

Wierzbicki, M., & Pekarik, G. (1993). A meta-analysis of psychotherapy dropout. *Professional Psychology: Research and Practice, 24*, 190–195.

Wilson, G. T., & Thomas, M. G. (1973). Self versus drug-produced relaxation and the effects of instructional set in standardized systematic desensitization. *Behavior Research and Therapy, 11*, 279–288.

Wise, M. J., & Rinn, R. C. (1983). Premature client termination from psychotherapy as a function of continuity of care. *Journal of Psychiatric Treatment and Evaluation, 5*, 63–65.

Wolf, M. M. (1978). Social validity: The case for subjective measurement or how applied behavior analysis is finding its heart. *Journal of Applied Behavior Analysis, 11*, 203–214.

Wolgast, B. M., Lambert, M. J., & Puschner, B. (2003). The dose–response relationship in a college counseling center: Implications for setting session limits. *Journal of College Student Psychotherapy, 8*, 15–29.

Woody, S. R., & Sanderson, W. C. (1998). Manuals for empirically supported treatments: 1998 update. *Clinical Psychology Review, 51*, 17–21.

Worchel, P., & Byne, D. (Eds.). (1964). *Personality change.* New York, NY: Wiley.

Zane, N. W., Hall, G. C. N., Sue, S., Young, K., & Nunez, J. (2004). Research on psychotherapy with culturally diverse populations. In M. J. Lambert (Ed.), *Bergin and Garfield's handbook of psychotherapy and behavior change* (5th ed., pp. 767–804). New York, NY: Wiley.

Zimet, G. D., Dahlem, N. W., Zimet, S .G. & Farley, G .K. (1988). The Multidimensional Scale of Perceived Social Support. *Journal of Personality Assessment, 52*, 30–41.

Ziskin, J. (1995). *Coping with psychological and psychiatric testimony.* (5th ed., Vol. 2). Los Angeles, CA: Law and Psychological Press.

Zuroff, D., Blatt, S., Sotsky, S., Krupnick, J., Martin, D., Sanislow, C., & Simmens, S. (2000). Relation of therapeutic alliance and perfectionism to outcome in brief outpatient treatment of depression. *Journal of Consulting and Clinical Psychology, 68*, 114–124.

INDEX

ABOUT THE AUTHOR

Michael J. Lambert, PhD, is a professor of psychology at Brigham Young University and holds the Susa Young Gates University Professorship. He also holds an honorary professorship in the School of Psychology at the University of Queensland, Brisbane, Australia. He has been in private practice throughout his career. His research spans 38 years, emphasizing psychotherapy outcome and the measurement of change. He has edited, authored, or coauthored nine academic research-based books and 40 book chapters and has published more than 150 scientific articles on treatment outcome.

Dr. Lambert received Brigham Young University's highest honor for faculty research, the Maeser Award, in recognition of his cumulative research accomplishments and the Distinguished Psychologist Award from Division 29 (Psychotherapy) of the American Psychological Association. In 2003, he was the recipient of the Distinguished Career Research Award from the Society for Psychotherapy Research for his lifetime contributions to research on professional practice. In 2004, he edited *Bergin and Garfield's Handbook of Psychotherapy and Behavior Change,* the most authoritative summary of the effects of psychological treatments. His current research focuses on reducing treatment failure and nonresponse through the use of advanced statistical methods and computer applications.